The Destruction
of the
Soviet Economic
System

Of Related Interest

Cold War Capitalism
The View from Moscow, 1945–1975
Richard B. Day

The Great Market Debate in Soviet Economics
An Anthology
Edited by Anthony Jones and William Moskoff

Controversies in Soviet Social Thought
Democratization, Social Justice, and the Erosion of Official Ideology
Murray Yanowitch

Hard Times: Impoverishment and Protest in the Perestroika Years
The Soviet Union 1985–1991
William Moskoff

Property to the People
The Struggle for Radical Economic Reform in Russia
Lynn D. Nelson and Irina Y. Kuzes

Radical Reform in Yeltsin's Russia
Political, Economic, and Social Dimensions
Lynn D. Nelson and Irina Y. Kuzes

New Rich, New Poor, New Russia
Winners and Losers on the Russian Road to Capitalism
Bertram Silverman and Murray Yanowitch

THE
DESTRUCTION
OF THE
SOVIET
ECONOMIC
SYSTEM

AN INSIDERS' HISTORY

EDITED BY
MICHAEL ELLMAN AND
VLADIMIR KONTOROVICH

M.E. Sharpe
Armonk, New York
London, England

Copyright © 1998 by M. E. Sharpe, Inc.

All rights reserved. No part of this book may be reproduced in any form
without written permission from the publisher, M. E. Sharpe, Inc.,
80 Business Park Drive, Armonk, New York 10504.

Library of Congress Cataloging-in-Publication Data

The destruction of the Soviet economic system : an insiders' history /
edited by Michael Ellman and Vladimir Kontorovich.
p.   cm.
Includes bibliographical references and index.
ISBN 0-7656-0263-6 (cloth : alk. paper)
ISBN 0-7656-0264-4 (pbk : alk. paper)
1. Soviet Union—Economic policy—1986–1991. 2. Perestroĭka.
I. Ellman, Michael. II. Kontorovich, Vladimir.
HC336.26.D48   1998
338.947′009′048   dc21
97–52682
CIP

Printed in the United States of America

The paper used in this publication meets the minimum requirements of
American National Standard for Information Sciences—
Permanence of Paper for Printed Library Materials,
ANSI Z 39.48-1984.

BM (c)   10   9   8   7   6   5   4   3   2   1
BM (p)   10   9   8   7   6   5   4   3   2   1

Contents

Preface and Acknowledgments

For most of the twentieth century, there existed two rival ways of organizing modern society and economy: Western capitalism and Soviet socialism. The sudden disappearance of the latter transformed the world as much as the Bolshevik Revolution did earlier in the century. This book is concerned with the economic history of the collapse of the Soviet civilization, with its centrally planned economy, one-party government, and official ideology, that occurred between 1985 and 1991. (The collapse of income and product following the breakup of the system is not addressed here.) Other aspects of that immense event—ideology, political changes, international affairs, public beliefs and attitudes—are addressed only to the extent that they interacted with the economy. This does not mean that we consider the economy the main cause of collapse. Indeed the opposite is the case. It merely reflects our interests and professional baggage.

The end of the Soviet system is described here by eyewitnesses who were then directly involved in running its key institutions. Their unique testimony constitutes the bulk of this book. The motivation for such an approach and the description of the methods used for collecting the evidence are discussed in Chapter 1. Chapter 2 presents our account of the collapse based on our reading of the evidence in this book.

Haverford College and the University of Amsterdam provided financial support for this work. Vladimir Drebentsov and Lev Freinkman gave generously of their time and effort. This book would have never appeared but for their dedication. Igor Prostiakov, Vitaly Rasnitsyn, Yelena Starostenkova, and Aleksei Melentiev helped in locating the contributors. The editors are grateful to Philip Hanson, Holland Hunter, Frederick Pryor, and Vladimir Shlapentokh for their helpful suggestions on Chapter 2. Its various drafts benefited from the discussions at the Serious Soviet Scholars Seminar at the University of Pennsylvania, the Fifth World Congress of ICCEES (the International Council for Central and East European Studies) in Warsaw, and the AAASS (the American Association for the Advancement of Slavic Studies) convention in Washington, DC. Alexander Katsenelinboigen translated most of the Russian texts. Catharine Cooke, Maxim and Nadezhda Dolgikh, Victor Frank, Sara Kirschhoff, E.V. Kontorovich, and Leonid Kontorovich translated the rest. Patricia Ellman helped with the editing.

Chapter 7.2 was written when the author, Alexander Tsipko, was a Fellow of the Kennan Institute in Washington, DC. Philip Hanson is indebted to Michael Ellman, Vladimir Kontorovich, and Elizabeth Teague for comments on an earlier draft of Chapter 8.5.

Glossary

AN   *Akademiia nauk,* Academy of Sciences of the USSR

AUCCTU   All-Union Central Council of Trade Unions

CC   Central Committee of the CPSU

CM   Council of Ministers of the USSR

CMEA   Council for Mutual Economic Assistance (often referred to in the West as Comecon)

collegium   Governing body of a ministry or a commission/committee, composed of the top boss, his deputies, and the heads of main structural divisions

CPSU   Communist Party of the Soviet Union

GDR   German Democratic Republic (i.e., East Germany)

GKNT   State Committee on Science and Technology of the CM

Gosbank   State Bank of the USSR

Goskomstat State Committee for Statistics at the CM

Goskomtsen State Committee for Prices of the CM

Gosplan   State Planning Commission of the CM

Gossnab   State Supply Committee of the CM

Gosstroi   State Committee for Construction of the CM

GRU   Chief Intelligence Administration of the General Staff (i.e., military intelligence)

GVK   State Foreign Economic Commission (sometimes abbreviated to GVEK)

KGB   Committee for State Security

khozraschet Economic accounting *or* business-like management

Komsomol   All-Union Communist Union of Youth (organization for fourteen to twenty-eight-year-olds)

MIC	Military-industrial complex
MVD	Ministry of Internal Affairs, responsible for police
MVES	Ministry of Foreign Economic Relations
MVT	Ministry of Foreign Trade
NEP	New Economic Policy: Soviet economic regime in the 1920s allowing for small-scale private initiative and market-type relations in the state sector
NMP	Net Material Product, Soviet concept of national income excluding most services
OS	Open Sector
PSO	Design and Construction Association
RAPO	Regional Agro-Industrial Association
samogon	Illicitly produced vodka (i.e., moonshine)
START	Strategic Arms Reduction Treaty
TsEMI	Central Economic-Mathematical Institute of the AN
TsSU	Central Statistical Administration (from 1987—Goskomstat)
VNIKI	Research Institute of the Ministry of Foreign Trade
VPK	Military Industrial Commission of the CM

Chronology of Collapse

Date	Political events	Economic reforms and policies	Performance
1982			Third year of the weakest postwar GDP growth, perhaps even a decline
Nov.	Brezhnev dies, Andropov becomes General Secretary		
1983	War hysteria in the Soviet media	Discipline tightening campaign begins	Industry and railroads visibly improve
March	Reagan proposes SDI		
July		CC and CM decree initiating 'large-scale experiment'	
1984			
Feb.	Andropov dies, Chernenko becomes General Secretary		
April		Politburo approves Concept for improving the management of the economy	
August		Politburo decides to extend the 'large-scale experiment'	
Nov.	CC decree on certification of workplaces		

Date	Political events	Economic reforms and policies	Performance
1985			
March	Chernenko dies, Gorbachev becomes General Secretary		
April	Gorbachev's 'inaugural' CC Plenum speech		
May	Anti-alcohol campaign announced		
June			Rapid growth of *samogon* sector begins
July		Meeting at CC on technological progress	
Aug.		CC and CM decree on acceleration of technological progress	
Sept.	Ryzhkov replaces Tikhonov as Chairman of the CM		
Oct.		Comprehensive program for development of consumer sector toward the year 2000 adopted	
Nov.	Gorbachev-Reagan summit meeting in Geneva	Agroprom formed; soon followed by energy, machine-building, and foreign economic relations super ministries	
1986			Budget deficit rises to 6.2% of GDP from 2.4% in 1985; fall of world petroleum prices and of dollar leads to 40% deterioration of Soviet terms of trade with West; USSR has $4 billion trade deficit with West after reducing volume of imports from West by 14%

Date	Political events	Economic reforms and policies	Performance
Jan.		Remuneration rules for scientists and engineers liberalized	
Feb.	27th Congress of CPSU	Main directions of the Twelfth Five-Year Plan adopted with its strategy of 'acceleration'	
April	Chernobyl disaster		
May	Antibureaucracy campaign in the media	CC and CM decrees on intensifying the fight against unearned incomes	
June		Twelfth Five-Year Plan formally adopted by Supreme Soviet	
Sept.	Afghan mujahedin bring down first Soviet helicopter using U.S. made Stinger missile	Construction sector reform Foreign trade reform relaxes state monopoly	
Oct.	Gorbachev-Reagan summit in Reykjavik		
Nov.		Law on individual labor activity; pay of medical staff raised	
Dec.	Sakharov returns to Moscow; demonstration in Alma Ata		
1987		General introduction of 'large-scale experiment'	Widespread shortages of sugar; imports from West fall a further 2%
Jan.	CC Plenum on political change (personnel policy and democratization)	Decree allowing joint ventures with foreigners 'State acceptance' quality control in industry introduced	Dip in industrial production

Date	Political events	Economic reforms and policies	Performance
Feb.		CC, CM, and AUCCTU decree on spread of multi-shift work	
June	CC Plenum on economic reform	'Radical reform' announced	
Aug.	Demonstrations in the Baltic republics on anniversary of Molotov-Ribbentrop pact		
Oct.	Demonstration in Yerevan for transfer to Armenia of Nagorno-Karabakh and Nakhichevan		
Nov.	18 November—the anniversary of the declaration of Latvian independence in 1918—celebrated as national holiday in Latvia; Yeltsin dismissed as Moscow Party secretary		
1988	Stalin's repression massively publicized		Annual emission of cash reaches 15%
Jan.		'Radical reform' introduced; Vneshekonombank issues bonds for 100 million Swiss francs	
Feb.	Mass demonstration in Yerevan in support of unification with Nagorno-Karabakh; bloody anti-Armenian riots in Sumgait, Azerbaidjan; demonstration in Lithuania on seventieth anniversary of independence		
March	Nina Andreeva's letter published	Law on cooperatives	
April	Agreements signed in Geneva providing for withdrawal of Soviet troops from Afghanistan and ending the war there		

Date	Political events	Economic reforms and policies	Performance
June	Nineteenth Party Conference approves political reform; officially sanctioned meetings in the Baltics commemorating deportations of 1941; People's Front organized in Estonia	Sugar rationing introduced in Leningrad	
Sept.	Politburo abolishes sectoral departments of the Party at all levels; massive personnel changes at the top		
Nov.	Estonian Supreme Soviet declares Estonia sovereign		
Dec.	Adoption of the new election law for the People's Congress; Armenia devastated by an earthquake		Stagnating railroad traffic indicates slow-down in the economy
	Gorbachev addresses UN, announces unilateral reduction in armed forces by half a million		
1989			Output declines in many sectors; annual emission of cash reaches 21%; rapid growth of cooperatives
Feb.	Last Soviet troops leave Afghanistan		
Mar.	Elections to People's Congress; regional Party officials lose many races	Decision to abolish Agroprom announced	
Apr.	Massacre of civilians in Tbilisi	Leasing of enterprises by their workers permitted	
May	First Congress of People's Deputies meets; proceedings televised		

Date	Political events	Economic reforms and policies	Performance
July	Miners' strike	State Commission on Economic Reform chaired by Abalkin created	
Aug.	Non-Communist government formed in Poland following Solidarity victory in partially free elections;		Official talk of a near-crisis situation
Oct.	Collapse of regime in Hungary	Tax on excessive growth of wages introduced; State Commission on Economic Reform publishes radical report stressing market	
Nov.	Fall of Berlin Wall; 'Velvet Revolution' in Czechoslovakia (Nov.–Dec.)	Conference on economic reform in Moscow; ruble devalued tenfold for non—commercial transactions	
Dec.	Gorbachev-Bush summit in Malta; Lithuanian Communist Party secedes from CPSU; overthrow of regime in Romania, shooting of Ceausescu	'Revitalization program' delaying market transition adopted by Congress of People's Deputies	
1990			GNP declines by 5.1%[1]: unprecedented fall in intra-CMEA trade[2]; Western banks reduce their exposure to the USSR by $11 billion
Jan.	Bloody riot in Baku put down by the army; at forty-fifth session of CMEA in Sofia, Ryzhkov proposes that from January 1991 trade within CMEA should be at world market prices and settled in hard currency		
Feb.	Mass demonstrations in Moscow and other Soviet cities for democratic reforms		

Date	Political events	Economic reforms and policies	Performance
Mar.	Gorbachev elected President; Presidential Council and Federation Council formed; Article 6 of Soviet constitution rewritten to abolish power monopoly of CPSU; Lithuania proclaims independence		Dramatic worsening of shortages in retail trade
May	Yeltsin elected Chairman of the Russian Supreme Soviet	Government reform strategy announced; intention to raise retail prices announced New Law on Enterprise reverses election of managers by workers for Union-owned enterprises	
June	Russian Supreme Soviet declares Russia sovereign; 'war of laws' begins		
July	Twenty-Eighth Party Congress; Party's ruling organs restructured along federal lines; Yeltsin leaves CPSU; first congress of state enterprise managers	Presidential decree announces transition in USSR trade with CMEA partners to convertible currency and world market prices from 1 January 1991; Russian government invites Union enterprises to switch to its jurisdiction	
Sept.	USSR Supreme Soviet endorses Gorbachev's proposal to form a committee to prepare a new Union Treaty; mass demonstrations in Ukraine reject idea of new Union Treaty	Russia adopts '500 days' reform package; presidential decree obliges producers to continue selling to established customers	

Date	Political events	Economic reforms and policies	Performance
Oct.	Ukrainian Supreme Soviet decides not to sign Union Treaty till after adoption of new Ukrainian constitution; Gorbachev awarded Nobel Peace Prize	USSR Supreme Soviet adopts 'Main Directions for Economic Stabilization' Armenia extends food rationing; Uzbekistan publishes a program for transition to a market economy; Russia adopts law transferring control of most assets in Russia from USSR to Russia	
Nov.	Draft Union Treaty published; meeting on conversion between Russian leadership and almost 300 top defense industry officials ends in stalemate; Yavlinsky resigns as Russian Deputy Prime Minister; anti-Gorbachev demonstrators in Red Square during official October Revolution demonstration	Russian Supreme Soviet creates Russian central bank; Cheliabinsk extends food rationing and restricts it to locals only; Sobchak appeals to West for emergency food aid for Leningrad	
Dec.	Shevardnadze resigns and warns of coming dictatorship; Ryzhkov resigns; Presidential Council and CM replaced by Security Council and Cabinet	Leningrad extends food rationing; Uzbekistan abolishes its Gosplan	Black market value of the ruble falls from about fifteen to the U.S.$ in January to about twenty-four
1991			Budget deficit reaches 26% of GDP; NMP falls 8.5%[3]; acute liquidity crisis causes 19%[4] cut in volume of imports from West; large-scale capital flight
Jan.	Decree on combating 'economic sabotage' Military crackdown in Vilnius	Republics start intercepting the revenues of the Union budget Exchange of large-denomination bills, savings accounts frozen	Attempt within CMEA to trade at world market prices and settle in convertible currencies formally begins

Date	Political events	Economic reforms and policies	Performance
Feb.	Miners' strike demanding Gorbachev's resignation; Yeltsin calls for Gorbachev's resignation in television interview		
Mar.	Continuation of USSR wins in a referendum; Warsaw Pact dissolved; large pro-Yeltsin demonstration in Moscow		
Apr.	Georgia declares independence	Consumer prices rise 64%	Retail shortages reduced (April–May)
May		Gosplan replaced by Ministry of Economics and Forecasting	
June	Prime minister asks the Congress of People's Deputies for special powers	CMEA dissolved	
	Yeltsin elected president of Russia by popular vote		
July	Gorbachev meets G7 in London and requests economic assistance; START I signed		
Aug.	Failed coup; Gorbachev resigns as general secretary of the CPSU and recommends CC to dissolve itself; CC offices seized by anti-Communists		
Oct.	Yeltsin announces forthcoming Russian economic reform in speech to Russian Congress of People's Deputies	G7 and republics negotiate over responsibility for Soviet debts (Oct.–Dec.)	

Date	Political events	Economic reforms and policies	Performance
Nov.	Russian Congress of People's Deputies grants Yeltsin special powers to implement economic reform; Government of young radicals appointed in Russia, Gaidar becomes Minister of Finance and Economics and Deputy Prime Minister; Communist Party banned in Russia		Vneshekonombank unable to meet its commitments; retail trade shortages worsen—bread shortages in Moscow
Dec.	Overwhelming majority in Ukrainian referendum for Ukrainian independence; Russia, Ukraine, and Belarus renounce 1922 Union Treaty; USSR dissolved		Black market value of the ruble falls to about 140 to the U.S.$; annual increase in Russian consumer prices reaches 160%[5]

Notes

1. According to official statistics.
2. Volume of Soviet exports to CMEA partners falls by c. 13–15%, volume of Soviet imports from CMEA partners falls by 8–10%.
3. Preliminary estimate for the CIS by the Statistical Committee of the CIS. According to the revised official Russian statistics, in 1991 Russian GDP fell by 5%.
4. January–September.
5. December on December.

The Destruction
of the
Soviet Economic
System

1

About the Study

Michael Ellman and Vladimir Kontorovich

1.1 What Is Known About the Collapse

The collapse of the USSR was a major historical event with far-reaching consequences, analogous to the collapse of the Roman Empire. Identification of its cause or causes will generate numerous hypotheses and be long debated. At the moment we are at the stage in which the most varied explanations are being offered but little is being done to test them. Perhaps the most popular view blames the collapse on the workings of impersonal economic forces. According to one of its versions, the Soviet system never worked, so its demise requires no more explanation than the disappearance of a mirage.[1] Alternatively, the Soviet economy's early vitality had been sapped in its last three decades by the exhaustion of natural resources, adverse demographic developments, the advent of computers, or some other equally unavoidable occurrence.[2]

Other explanations focus on the decisions of political leaders rather than inexorable trends. A popular economics explanation derives from public choice theory (van Winden and de Wit 1993; Boettke 1993). It tends to suggest that the Soviet ruling class destroyed the system in order to openly appropriate the pieces of the state-owned economy.[3] The weaknesses of this argument are twofold. First, there is a tendency, derived from elementary demand theory, to identify the results of actions with the intentions of the actors. This ignores the possibility that a result may be the unintended consequence of actions aimed at something else. Second, there is a tendency to substitute theory for data.

In the sociological literature, Lane (1996c, chapter 8) has put forward an explanation combining structural and conjunctural elements. This has the merit of drawing attention to a number of important factors, such as the long-run decline in economic growth rates, the role of the West, the role of the intelligentsia, the destabilizing effects of the abandonment of Marxism-

Leninism, and the crucial importance of the policies implemented by the Gorbachev leadership. However, this explanation too is data-poor. For example, Lane (1996c, p. 125) asserts that the Gorbachev leadership realized that its policies would lead to the end of Communism in Eastern Europe and deliberately undertook these policies in order to end the Cold War. Yet Dobrynin (1995, p. 632), the former Soviet ambassador in the United States, explicitly denies that Gorbachev anticipated the consequences of his policies in Eastern Europe. Similarly, the importance of the "expectations gap"/"public dissatisfaction with the standard of living" (Lane 1996c, pp. 155, 183) in explaining the origins of perestroika is doubtful (see Chapters 2 and 3.1 below).

Our own work points to the unintended consequences of government actions and the centrality of noneconomic factors. In an attempt to spur a sluggish but viable economy the rulers damaged political and ideological pillars that brought the whole social system, including the economy, down (Ellman and Kontorovich 1992a; Kontorovich 1993; Ellman 1993, pp. 55–58).

There are also many hard-to-classify one-liner explanations in the literature. They point to the demonstration effect of the West, or to the crushing burden of military expenditures, or to the exhaustion of petroleum reserves, or to the deterioration in the terms of trade, or to the very low rate of scrapping and long service lives of Soviet fixed capital (Harmstone and Patackas 1997), as the cause of the collapse. This survey is not complete, and it does not do justice to all the arguments. Its purpose is to show that we are still at a very early stage in understanding the collapse.

1.2 Why Learn from the Insiders?

To make progress in understanding the end of the Soviet system, it is necessary to combine theory with data. The mechanism through which the alleged causes worked has to be specified in detail. Hypotheses that have been supplied with a causal structure can then be subjected to tests of logic, economic theory, and empirical evidence. One would hope that in the process, some competing explanations will be weeded out, while others will be merged and refined.

Within this research program, the main objective of our study is to introduce new evidence. The source of this evidence are the participants of the events themselves. We turned to them because insider information is inherently important, is largely untapped, and has special relevance to our hypothesis of collapse.

Much valuable knowledge about the workings of any organization is never committed to paper, but exists in the minds of its members.[4] In the past, such inside information about the Soviet system was practically un-available to Western researchers, because the actors could not speak. These constraints have now been relaxed, and students of transformation are conducting massive field research in the post-Communist economies. This approach has taken time to spread to the study of the old regime, while fading memory and mortality erase invaluable information. Nevertheless, some field work on the collapse has already been undertaken by journalists (Pryce-Jones 1995), political scientists and sociologists (White et al. 1996; Lane 1996a), and economists (Kotz with Weir 1997).

Our hypothesis of the collapse also steered us toward collecting the testimony of participants. In order to argue about the 'unintended consequences,' one needs to establish intentions. This, as well as the perceptions of policy makers, rejected options, and reasons for not taking the seemingly obvious steps, can only be supplied by the insiders.[5] The rest of this chapter explains how we went about collecting the insiders' accounts. The latter constitute Chapters 3–10. In Chapter 2, we pick out and discuss what we consider to be the main findings which emerge from the accounts of the insiders.[6]

1.3 The Focus of the Study

In studying major historical events, such as the English or French Revolutions, or the collapse of the USSR, it is necessary to take account of both structure and conjuncture (Stone 1972, chapter 3). This means that one must look at both the structures within which events unfold, and the conjunctural circumstances within which individuals make decisions. We concentrate on the latter, because in this book we are not concerned with the Soviet system's long-run viability. Our goal is to explain why it collapsed in 1991 rather than in, say, 2001. Our objective is similar to that of a historian who wants to explain why the Austro-Hungarian Empire collapsed in 1918. The structural factor—the inviability of a multinational empire in a world of nations—cannot explain why the Austro-Hungarian Empire collapsed in 1918, since it was equally valid in 1908 and in the absence of war would have been equally valid in 1928. What explains the collapse in 1918 is a conjunctural event—defeat in war—which took place in a state that was structurally weak.

One's explanation of the collapse is to a large degree predetermined by the model of Soviet society one considers valid. In our view, the Soviet system was a highly centralized structure subsuming practically all organized social activity. This does not mean that the top leaders made all the decisions, or that their decisions were always carried out. As in all large organizations, power had to be delegated to the lower rungs of the hierarchy, and at all levels commands were disobeyed when there was the opportunity or a good excuse. The power of the leadership was also limited by the internal and external situation. Furthermore, routine decisions were much influenced by the data and proposals flowing from a wide variety of local and central bodies. However, on all the issues for which the leaders cared, they were able to take initiatives, sometimes very radical ones, and dismiss those officials lacking at any rate verbal enthusiasm for the latest policy.

In this, we are in agreement with the monohierarchical (Ellman 1989), monoorganizational (Rigby 1990), or monoarchical (Brus 1993) model of the Soviet system. This was a minority position in Western social science in the 1970s and 1980s. The view of the USSR as a pluralistic society driven by the interplay of various interest groups was predominant (e.g., Hough 1983). Some of our contributors, when theorizing about the workings of the Soviet system, echo this kind of Western thinking. They stress the *diktat* of the ministries and see the central Party-state apparatus as splintered into a collection of sectoral lobbies (as emphasized by Belanovsky in Chapter 10.5). If this is how it was, then a study of collapse should focus on the objectives, perceptions, and relative power of the various interest groups rather than those of the rulers.[7]

If we turn from the contributors' theorizing to the experiences they recount, however, there is much that supports the monoorganizational model. Prostiakov (Chapter 4.4.2) demonstrates the extent of the power wielded by even the weakest, both politically (allegedly) and physically, general secretaries. Chernenko's incapacity blocked all but the most routine policy decisions. Brezhnev, also gravely ill, fired one of the top officials in the country, Kosygin, by calling him over the telephone.[8] By contrast, the heads of the largest sectors and regions appear as mere executors of the ruler's will. A deputy chairman of the VPK (reputedly the most powerful sectoral interest) first heard about the coming conversion of military industry when his boss came back from a meeting with the general secretary (Chapter 9.1). Regional Party secretaries loathed the elections of enterprise managers, an innovation imposed on them by "a person or a group of persons," yet dutifully participated in the campaign (Chapter 7.4). Yun's description of Gorbachev's personnel policy is compatible with the monoorganizational model (Chapter 5.2.1). When analyzed in depth, sectoral pressure on the central authorities turns out to be just pleading and begging.[9]

Quite apart from these particular instances, the general picture drawn by actors on different rungs of the hierarchy is one of highly centralized decision making with little heed given to feedback from the lower rungs. In fact, this is suggested as one of the reasons for the failures of Gorbachev (see the contributions by Prostiakov and Yun' in Chapter 5). Gorbachev's rule actually made the monoorganizational nature of the system more visible than before. An activist ruler with a radical agenda rolled over every established interest, and only after six years of extremely radical change and acute economic and political crisis was there any serious opposition on their part. This led even some of the erstwhile champions of the pluralist model to recall that the Soviet Union was, after all, a totalitarian system (Hough 1987, p. 21).

The canonical Soviet model was in effect up till 1989, when the rules of the game were greatly modified by the changes in political structure and society. Even then, the inertia of obedience led the top Party brass to vote dutifully for proposals they hated (see Medvedev in Chapter 7.1.1). Accordingly, our study of collapse focuses on the rulers: their intentions, their perception of the state of the world, their sources of information and advice, and even their personal characteristics.

1.4 How the Study Was Done

There are a number of different methods for gathering and analyzing information from insiders. Oral history, applied to the study of collapse by Pryce-Jones (1995), produces firsthand accounts by important actors in the historical process, but does not go deeply into anything. It is colorful but superficial. The method of questionnaires, used by Lane (1996a), imposes on the respondents a structure devised by the researcher. It is unreliable in a situation like the present one, when the very questions to be asked are subject to dispute.

This study is based on papers commissioned from the specially selected insiders. From December 1993 through February 1995 we contacted potentially knowledgeable individuals from a variety of institutions of the old regime. The nature of the project was explained to them in personal meetings, and papers about the developments at their workplaces during the collapse were commissioned. The initial topic of each paper was formulated broadly, so as to find the author's area of competence. Each paper went through a number of drafts, with authors being asked to expand or elaborate on the issues that were of interest to us. The authors were not limited to reporting what they had seen. However, we tried to discourage broad theorizing.

Our contributors include individuals from almost all the main Union institutions: the Politburo; the Economic Department of the CC; the CM; planning, supply, statistics, and economic reform committees; CMEA; Ministry of Foreign Trade; General Staff, military industry; and regional Party committees. The full list can be found at the end of this chapter. Major omissions (due to resource constraints) include sectoral ministries and sectoral departments of Gosplan, Union republics, finance and banking, and enterprises.

Several considerations besides the institutional background determined the composition of our contributors. Because of the study's open format, we sought reflective people able to recount their experience. For this reason, on several occasions we turned to former advisors, rather than to the decision makers themselves. Five of our contributors held positions in research institutes of Gosplan, Gossnab, TsSU, and MVT. These institutes conducted little academic research, but rather served as in-house consultants and policy planners for the official bodies to which they were attached.

Many former officials whom we approached refused to participate in the study. The primary reason, stated or implied, was fear of dealing with foreigners. Another important reason was that the officials of the old regime occupy important positions in the new one or in the private sector, and are too busy to take on additional obligations. The small honorarium we offered did nothing to change their minds. Unwillingness to write about people who are still active and influential, and hatred of the West, were cited as reasons for refusal in a few cases. Despite all this, we did not end up with pro-Western retirees as our only authors. The contributors include people doing very well under the new regime, and span the contemporary Russian political spectrum. We do not see any systematic bias in our selection process. There is enough of an overlap in the subjects covered by the contributors to allow us to check them against each other.

We anticipated difficulty in getting former officials from the military-industrial complex and provincial Party officials to participate in this study. The information-gathering procedure was modified for these two groups. Russian academics specializing in economic sociology conducted extensive interviews with selected individuals. Their papers summarizing the interviews form Chapters 3.2 and 7.4. Another modification was required to deal with the most numerous group of insiders, the Soviet people. Our data-gathering method clearly is not suited to the study of mass processes. Instead, contributions on the public perception of the economic situation in the mid-1980s and the grassroots reaction to Gorbachev's reforms are based on survey data. The former is a reinterpretation of published results by a leading expert on Soviet public opinion (Chapter 3.1). The latter presents survey results obtained by Russia's leading economic sociologist (Chapter 9.3).

The design of the study was inevitably informed by our understanding of the collapse. Its central questions are why the Soviet leaders started the potentially dangerous changes, and why they did not turn back once the danger became real. To answer these we look at the leaders' motives and decisions, and trace their consequences for the economic institutions and processes. The open format of the study ensured that the contributors were not forced into supporting our interpretation, but rather gave us their own readings of the events. In some cases the papers (edited to fit into a book) are included as a unit, in other cases they have been split into two or more parts since they throw light on two or more periods or issues. The paragraph headings were supplied by the editors.[10] Copies of the original papers may be obtained from the editors.

1.5 The Contributors

In this list, contributors are normally identified by the institutions at which they worked in 1984–1991. However, no attempt is made here to present a full job history for each contributor for the period in question.

Sergei Belanovskii, head of the Sociology Laboratory at the Institute for National Economic Forecasting, AN, Moscow.

Yurii Belik was deputy head of the Economic Department of the CC.

Moisei Eydelman was long-time head of the division in charge of the national economic balance at TsSU and a major figure in the introduction of input-output into Soviet statistics. He was director of TsSU/Goskomstat Research Institute, 1979–1989; senior research fellow of the institute, 1989–1993.

Lev Freinkman was a researcher at Gossnab Research Institute.

Philip Hanson was a member of George Soros's team of advisors to Soviet government in 1988–1989. He was also professor of economics at the University of Birmingham, UK.

Gregory Khanin was an economist at the Tuva Interdisciplinary Department of the Siberian Division of the AN in Kyzyl. He is also co-author of a sensational article, published in a Soviet literary journal in 1987, attacking the reliability of Soviet statistics.

Vadim Kirichenko was director of Gosplan Research Institute, 1975–1987.

Viktor Kurierov was a researcher at Research Institute of the Ministry of Foreign Trade (VNIKI).

Yurii Kuznetsov researcher at the Sociology Laboratory of the Institute for National Economic Forecasting, AN, Moscow.

Boris Ladygin worked in the CC from 1970–1990 as a consultant on CMEA and related economic issues.

Vadim Medvedev was a key figure in Gorbachev's team, a CC secretary, a member of the Politburo, and a member of the Presidential Council.

Vladimir Mozhin was first deputy head of the Economic department of the CC.

Nikolai Nesterovich was deputy director of the Gossnab Research Institute.

Igor Prostiakov was a department head at the Council of Ministers, 1982–1984 and 1985–1988. He was also a senior official of the Politburo Commission on Improvement of Economic Management, 1984–1985.

Rozalina Ryvkina was head of the Economic Sociology Laboratory, Institute for Socio-Economic Studies of the Population, AN, Moscow.

Vladimir Shlapentokh was one of the founders of sociology in the USSR. He is now a professor of sociology, Michigan State University, East Lansing, Michigan.

Alexander Tsipko was a Soviet philosopher; in 1986–1990 he was a CC official. He is the author of a famous article, published in four parts in 1988–1989, denouncing Marxism-Leninism.

Yevgenii Yasin headed a department at the State Commission on economic reform (Abalkin commission) in 1988–1990.

Oleg Yun' was with the Department of New Methods of Management of Gosplan and was an Economic Council member.

Gennadii Zoteev worked at Gosplan's Department of Long-Range Economic and Social Development from November 1982 till April 1988, first as head of the section on the balance of the national economy and subsequently as deputy chief of the Department.

Notes

1. This view, due to von Mises 1922, can now be heard even from those who share nothing else with the Austrian school. Arthur Schlesinger Jr. 1992 speaks of "Communism's inherent unworkability and the valiant resistance it engendered among its victims."

2. Loginov 1992, p. 4; Holzman 1992; Treml 1993, pp. 53–55; Fukuyama 1993, p. 16.

3. This argument, too, takes a variety of forms, such as Gaidar 1994 and van Winden and de Wit 1993. For an earlier argument on these lines, see Trotsky 1937. For an eclectic variant that combines a 'regulation school' approach to the origins of perestroika, with an 'unintended consequences' interpretation of Gorbachev's own actions, and a public choice interpretation of the transition to capitalism, see Kotz with Weir 1997.

4. This concerns basic operating procedures, and not just inherently secret matters. See, on this, Nelson and Winter 1982, Chapter 5.

5. For this reason a former advisor to Chernenko pours scorn on the idea that archival research can reveal 'the truth' about the USSR (Pechenev 1996, pp. 3–22).

6. This is not to deny the value of published material, notably the rich memoir literature. We have analyzed it in Ellman and Kontorovich 1997 and in Ellman 1998. Another study that uses it is Hough 1997.

7. Fukuyama 1993 blames Sovietologists' failure to predict the collapse on their alleged excessive attention to the rulers and neglect of civil society, induced by their acceptance of the totalitarian model.

8. This information is in the full text of the paper by Prostiakov, edited extracts from which are presented in Chapters 4.4.2, 5.1, and 5.2.2.

9. This is apparent, for example, in the contribution by the former deputy chairman of Gosplan, N. Lebedinsky, which is not included in the present book.

10. The editors have also added some editorial footnotes. These are indicated in the notes to the chapters by "[Ed.]." Any notes not so indicated are by the author of the corresponding text.

2

What We Learn from the Insiders

Michael Ellman and Vladimir Kontorovich

> . . . *often in history concrete results do not merely fall short of the objectives of political actors, but are actually their diametrical opposites.*

> L. Stone
> *The Causes of the English Revolution 1529–1642*, p. 128.

2.1 Soviet Society in the Mid-1980s

Domestic Politics and Economics

Our contributors did not give us any indication of political instability on the eve of Gorbachev's accession.[1] Close reading of the public opinion polls conducted by Soviet sociologists shows that Soviet people were reasonably satisfied with their economic situation and supported the system's main values (Shlapentokh, Chapter 3.1). Shlapentokh attributes this complacency to the "adaptive nature of human beings, particularly while under the pressure of ideology and fear of the totalitarian machine." Popular opposition to the regime, clearly demonstrated at the ballot box, in the media, and on the streets in the late 1980s, was a *result,* not the cause of its disintegration. Hence, the causes of the collapse have to be sought in elite actions and not in the discontent of the masses.[2]

On the eve of Gorbachev's becoming general secretary, even anti-Communist intellectuals would have been happy with quite modest reforms, such as the emergence of a Soviet Kadar or Deng. For them at that time, the rapid reintroduction of capitalism or destruction of the USSR were unimaginable and unwanted (Tsipko, Chapter 7.2).

The Soviet leaders were afraid of spontaneous popular disturbances ignited by economic hardship since the Novocherkassk riots of 1962 (Pavlov

1995). Andropov, in the words of one of his aides, kept in mind the possibility of Polish-style trouble (oral communication), and Gorbachev cited this as a motive as well (Mozhin, Chapter 5.3.2).[3]

We now know that the country went through the shock of a huge price increase and a sharp drop in living standards in 1992. Yet these caused no street disturbances, even though the repressive apparatus was immobilized, fear of the authorities had largely disappeared, and the elite was torn by acute policy conflicts. The absence of riots has been cited as proof of his policies' correctness by the architect of the 1992 price liberalization Yegor Gaidar (1992). The illusory fear of possible economically motivated riots led to policies (postponing price increases) that worsened the economic situation and thus strengthened political forces (the various national independence movements) which played a major role in the collapse of the Soviet system.

All our authors, both in writing and in conversations, admitted that changes in the economy were needed, even if they objected to what was actually done. Officials involved in formulating various steps of economic reform (Medvedev, Chapter 4.4.1; Prostiakov, Chapter 4.4.2; Yun', Chapter 5.2.1; Mozhin in an unpublished portion of his contribution) supplied long lists of the system's shortcomings that, in the view of the rulers, needed mending in the mid-1980s. All these flaws had been plaguing the Soviet system for as long as it existed, had been repeatedly described by Soviet economists and concerned inefficiency and the inability to measure up to the world's leading countries rather than the inviability of the economy.[4]

The elite, while clearly seeing the flaws of the system, was rather content with it, perhaps due to the chronic nature of the economic problems. In Zoteev's words (Chapter 4.3): "Gosplan was characterized by calm and inertia, and worked in low key without any great ambitions. . . . Similar attitudes prevailed in the Economic Department of the CC. . . . My thesis, shared by many of my colleagues in Gosplan was that the Soviet system was inefficient but stable."

"Calm and inertia" prevailed even though the long-term forecast developed by Gosplan in 1984 envisaged average annual growth rates of utilized national income in the range of 2.8–3.2% through the end of the century. These rates, which were to be incorporated in the new Party program, amounted to about a 1.5% p.a. growth rate of GNP, at the low end of the range of Western forecasts.[5]

Eydelman (Chapter 4.1) states that the leadership relied on the official statistics, which exaggerated the rate of growth. This naturally influenced their perception of what was going on: "official statistics gave the leadership a relatively favorable picture of socioeconomic development. The conclusion the leadership drew from these reports was that the Soviet economy was developing (albeit with shortcomings), and in certain branches it was even developing well."

Amid the complacency of the late 1970s and early 1980s, some social scientists and leading government officials were sending the rulers confidential reports detailing the economy's problems and suggesting ways to fix them (see Khanin, Chapter 4.2; Zoteev, Chapter 4.3). The leadership, however, ignored these reports. Prostiakov (Chapter 4.4.2) explains the position of the conservative majority of the Politburo under Chernenko by their personal outlooks. He also seems to assign Chernenko's immobilism entirely to his physical incapacity. Against this background, Gorbachev's hyperactivism emerges as just one of several possible strategies, determined by his personality as much as by external circumstances.

In the Brezhnev-Chernenko period (Khanin, Chapter 4.2), "the proponents of reform felt insecure and afraid to voice their views for fear of being accused of heresy and being expelled from the ruling elite. This group was waiting for Brezhnev's death and the coming crisis, hoping to gain power and implement the reforms afterward." According to Medvedev (Chapter 4.4.1), this faction "proceeded from the assumption that in the beginning of the 1980s the growth of industrial production had stopped, and the real income of the population had actually declined, even though this was not confirmed by the data of the TsSU."[6]

The first independent step of this group in the field of economic policy prior to coming to power seems to have been the organization of the high-level discussions of economic policy in 1982–1984 arranged by Gorbachev (Kirichenko, Chapter 5.3.1). Their most radical element seems to have been the discussion (on 6 July 1984) of price policy and subsidies. This was recognized as a very sensitive issue, and organizing such a high-level discussion of it, with representatives of quite different policy positions, was a radical move by the standards of the time. Gorbachev's own contribution to the discussion was marked by "persistent ambiguity and vacillations," an ominous indicator of his inability even to outline, let alone implement, a coherent and logical price policy if he should attain supreme power.

Foreign Policy and Defense

On the surface of the Soviet civilization, the defense industry was a nonsector, as practically nothing was published about it in the open press. It turns out that the same veil of secrecy kept even most of the regime's top officials ignorant of the military-economic issues. Early in Gorbachev's rule even CC secretaries could not discuss the topic of the military burden and had no information about it (Medvedev, Chapter 4.4.1).[7] Military-economic information was collected separately and channeled directly to the top leadership, bypassing regular statistical channels (Eydelman, Chapter 4.1). Gosplan's long-range projections department did not even mention the issue of the military burden in its internal deliberations, though the defense department was the largest one in Gosplan (Zoteev, Chapter 4.3).

This means that research into the military aspects of collapse today encounters two barriers. One is the reluctance to speak about Soviet secrets that in many cases are also the secrets of the new Russian state. Another is that most highly placed insiders have little direct knowledge of the matter. Witness Mozhin (Chapter 5.3.2) citing the military burden number from Prime Minister Pavlov's book, which in turn does not give any source for it.[8] Keeping in mind the segregation between the military sector and the rest of the economy, we solicited the accounts of those whose job it was to deal with the military economy and related issues—General Staff officers and officials of the Military-Industrial Commission and its subordinate units. Their contributions are set out in Chapters 3.2, 9.1, and 10.5.

Both the liberal Westernizer Shlykov and the more conservative Danilevich and Gareev argue that Soviet foreign policy, as determined by the CC, was driven by Marxist-Leninist ideology, which postulated a conflict with 'imperialist' countries and support for assorted anti-Western movements.[9] Such a policy dictated a military doctrine of preparing to fight practically the whole world (Chapter 3.2).

Just as the Soviet leadership was misled about domestic economic developments because of poor statistics, it was also misled about the external threat by highly exaggerated data supplied by military intelligence (the GRU), according to the former GRU colonel Shlykov (Chapter 3.2). Although the CIA also made mistakes in assessing the enemy, "the order of magnitude of their mistakes was much less than ours." Shlykov blames these errors on the absence of independent experts on military and international affairs in the USSR. He goes so far as to credit Western think tanks with winning the Cold War, a sentiment frequently expressed by the Russian Communists and nationalists, if with a different accent.

A doctrine regarding almost the whole world as potential enemies and exaggerated assessment of the enemies' capabilities would have been enough to impose an extremely heavy burden on the economy. This burden was made even heavier by the ambition of mirroring Western weapons systems, institutional bias in favor of the proliferation of systems and their modification, and technological backwardness (Chapter 3.2).

All the respondents agree that the burden of defense was onerous indeed, yet there is a clear difference in prospective. Danilevich in Chapter 3.2

complains that the "spare no expense for defense" slogan did not protect General Staff requests from being regularly pared down by Gosplan. Konovalov in the same chapter focuses on the heavy toll the policy based on this slogan exacted on the civilian sector. Since our military respondents were no more aware of the defense sector's burden on the overall economy than Mozhin or Medvedev, it is not surprising that they also disagree about its role in the demise of the USSR. While some view it as fatal, others argue that, heavy as it was, it was bearable (Lobov and Gerasev, Chapter 3.2), yet still others maintain that it could have been reduced without any harm to the country's security, thus saving the system (Gareev, Shlykov, and Larionov, Chapter 3.2).

2.2 Inspiration for the First Steps

In April 1984 the Politburo adopted the Concept of improving the management of the economy, intended to form the basis of a new reform (see Prostiakov, Chapter 5.1). Formulated on the instructions of a Politburo Commission of nine in which the Gorbachev team had three members, the document was "marked by compromises and the reconciliation of various points of view." It tells us about the stock of ideas and proposals for economic reform at the highest political level inherited by Gorbachev in March 1985.

The Concept aimed to introduce "elements of the market that would have been regarded during the period of the 1965 reform as inherently capitalistic." This included gradual lifting of the state monopoly of foreign trade and permitting cooperatives and individual economic activity. Hence, Prostiakov's contribution shows that some of the most radical reform measures of 1986–88 had actually been approved in principle by the Politburo under Chernenko.

Early in his tenure as general secretary, Gorbachev made several speeches exhorting his subjects to achieve world supremacy in one or another area of the economy (see Belik, Chapter 5.4.2). These were not just isolated oratorical excesses. Catching up with the United States in terms of productivity was made an objective of the Twelfth Five-Year Plan and the projections toward the year 2000 (Zoteev, Chapter 4.3). That was a pet idea of N.S. Khrushchev, the last general/first secretary who had been a great optimist regarding the Soviet system. In the words of a leading intellectual supporter, Gorbachev overestimated the strength of the system (Tsipko 1995).

The new ruler, while announcing ambitious goals, did not quite know how to reach them. Prostiakov, describing the work of the Politburo's Economic Management Commission in 1984 writes that: "One got the impression that the leaders did not know what should be done and how" (Chapter

4.4.2). According to Medvedev (Chapter 5.3.3), in 1985–1986 "the country's leadership, the government and economic structures, as well as society at large, were not yet ready for profound changes in the economic mechanism."

Still, there was a certain consistency about the first crop of Gorbachev's policy initiatives: they were all command in nature, as opposed to the ones that would emerge in only a few years. Encouraging the market, nonstate property, and doing away with central planning did not play any significant role in economic policy through 1987 (see Chapter 5). True to the decades-old pattern, the Twelfth Five-Year Plan called for increases in the share of investment and military expenditures in the national income (see Kirichenko, Chapter 5.4.4). Many of the noneconomic policies were equally orthodox.[10]

Against this background, the statement that "From the very beginning Gorbachev and his associates considered deep, serious economic reform unavoidable" (Medvedev, Chapter 5.3.3) implies that Gorbachev was ready to adopt policies promising the achievement of his objectives even if they would previously have been unacceptable by the standards of the Brezhnev-Andropov-Chernenko period. Although Gorbachev regarded economic reform as necessary, in 1985 he did not regard it as urgent (Ellman and Kontorovich 1997, p. 270).

2.3 The Internal Dynamics of Perestroika

Navigating Without a Compass

The leading Soviet economists were put to work devising strategies for attaining the new ruler's ambitious objectives (Yasin, Chapter 6.2.3). The proposals of academic advisors were much bolder than those generated inside the government/Party apparatus. Leading personalities in Gosplan and the CC Economic Department opposed the acceleration campaign (Zoteev, Chapter 4.3; Belik, Chapter 5.4.2). As the ruler's preference for swift and dramatic action was made clear, both organizations fell into line. Still, the source of ideas was elsewhere.[11]

The proposals of the academics listened to by the leadership were at best ineffective, and often destructive. Conservative former Gosplan hands in conversations with the editors blamed the disastrous results of the reforms on the influence academic economists wielded on Gorbachev. Academics and Westernizers such as Zoteev (Chapter 6.2.2) and Yasin (Chapter 6.2.3) concur.[12]

Yasin points out (Chapter 6.2.3) that the 1987 reform was influenced by the "two main schools of progressive Soviet economists: the traditional

Marxist political economists who thought that 'market socialism' was feasible, and the adherents of the theory of the optimally functioning economy." The former had no idea how to design a viable and efficient reformed economic system, and the latter in their theoretical work and policy proposals largely ignored such key issues as money, the state, and property rights.

By 1989, Gorbachev openly expressed dissatisfaction with academic advice on reforms, and there was an angry exchange on the subject in *Pravda.*[13] The only result was switching to a different set of establishment advisors. As Khanin (Chapter 4.2) observes, "Government and Party officials, as well as the chieftains of academic economics, judged a scholar on the basis of his official status and the extent of his loyalty." Hanson argues in Chapter 8.5 that: "Those economists who were, in the late Soviet context, liberal reformers (Ivanov and Abalkin, for example) did not see the social order being fundamentally altered, or at least not quickly. Those who were rather more radical (Petrakov for instance) were not really trusted by the powers that be. Those who were really radical (Gaidar, Yavlinksy, Yasin, Boris Fedorov, Seliunin) were either too young, too discreet (Yasin), or too indiscreet (Seliunin) to be given a chance, at that time, to make policy."

While there was a variety of positions within the Party-state apparatus with respect to particular official policies, the critics and whistle blowers had to appeal to the very top of the hierarchy, where decision-making power resided. If their views were not accepted there, they missed the only chance to be heard (Yun', Chapter 6.2.1; Prostiakov, Chapter 5.2.2; Shlykov and Gareev, Chapter 3.2). It was the architecture of the system, rather than uniformity of outlook or lack of feedback that was responsible for the persistence of harmful policies. No permanent political base existed for continued promotion of views diverging from the official line until 1989.

The Twelfth Five-Year Plan and the 1987 reform introduced only marginal changes in a system that the advisors should have understood well. Yet ignorance did play its role, too. Though the agenda at Gorbachev's meetings with economists and officials in 1982–1984 was wide-ranging, Kirichenko points out in Chapter 5.3.1 that "The budget deficit and its financing, credit, . . . emission, and inflation, were never discussed . . . all information regarding these problems was classified. . . . the prevailing mindset . . . considered output in physical units, capital goods, production capacities, and labor resources to be the main factors in the Soviet economy." Mozhin provides analogous information about the discussions at Politburo meetings (Chapter 5.4.3). This lack of understanding played a crucial role in explaining how the leadership in 1985–1986 embarked on its deficit-increasing course.

The sheer ignorance of the leading economists played an even greater role in the failure of post-1989 policies aimed at the transition to the market (Mozhin, Chapter 8.2; Zoteev, Chapter 6.2.2).[14] Since the 1960s, Soviet economists had accumulated a stock of ideas (however unworkable) for decentralization within the framework of the Soviet system. This stock carried them through 1988. When they were called upon to advise on the transition to the market, they were absolutely unprepared, because such a contingency (the system's self-liquidation) had previously seemed impossible (see Mozhin, Chapter 8.2). The attempts to learn about the market by sending CC missions abroad (see Belik, Chapter 8.4), reminiscent of the Soviet ritual of 'studying the progressive experience,' were not a substitute for real knowledge.

At the time, neither advisors nor advisees appeared to realize how little they knew. Later, some of the advisors were surprised at the results of the transition they themselves had preached, and became advocates of the 'administrative methods' they used to malign.[15] (Economists were not the only ones surprised by the course of events. Tsipko writes in Chapter 7.2: "If we had known the high price that the average Soviet citizen would have to pay for our vehement denunciations of the official ideology, we would probably have been more cautious in our assault on the Soviet past.")

As usual, the most damaging element of the economic ignorance was not what the experts did not know, but what they thought they knew that was not so. The rulers, their advisors, and the educated public shared an unspoken assumption about the economy (and society) that shaped the policy proposals of that period: that anything is possible in social reforming. With the right policies, the Soviet economy can be made as dynamic as the best capitalist economies (acceleration strategy). Command policies can be followed by decentralizing ones and vice versa, without subtracting from the effectiveness of either kind (sequencing of policies in 1985–1987). Plan and market can be mixed in various proportions, and the mix will possess the desirable properties of both systems, as in various reform projects in 1984–1990 (see Yun', Chapter 5.2.1; Prostiakov, Chapter 5.2.2; Mozhin, Chapter 6.1.2; and Yasin, Chapters 6.2.3 and 8.3). A feature of the market economy, transplanted into the command one, will work there just as well as it did in the market economy. Kurierov (Chapter 9.4) described the foreign trade reform as being "inspired not so much by the immediate economic needs of that system, as by abstract ideas, based on the experience of a fundamentally different economic system, of how foreign economic relations should be organized in a contemporary 'civilized' state." The failure to consider possible negative consequences of policies (Yasin, Chapter 8.3) followed directly from the chief assumption.

This assumption of infinite malleability of the economy can be gleaned from the unspoken objective of the 1987 'radical reform,' as formulated by Yasin in Chapter 6.2.3: "The main idea of the reform was 'socialism with a human face,' . . . a third way, neither capitalism (i.e., a normal market economy), nor 'barracks socialism' of the type previously epitomized by the USSR. In other words, something beautiful, humane, and more efficient."

The assumption of infinite malleability is not specifically Soviet/Marxist, but rather is shared by much of modern social science, as Kornai (1980, pp. 156–157) long ago observed.

The ignorance of the rulers and their economists led to a situation in which, as Mozhin (Chapter 8.2) notes: "In spite of all the efforts, Gorbachev was unable to introduce any major economic reforms. . . . He . . . decided to utilize models that had proved effective in Western countries, but without renouncing the Soviet version of socialism. It turned out that such a symbiosis was impossible."

Economic Reform and the Loss of Control

Policies introduced with great fanfare would be supplanted by others well before they could have a chance to bear fruit. The strategy of acceleration, based on investment in producer goods sectors and adopted in 1986, could not have been expected to bring results for a few years. Yet it was judged inadequate by January 1987 (Medvedev, Chapter 6.1.1). The 'large-scale experiment' was spread to all branches of industry starting in 1987, only to give way to the 'radical reform' a year later "without really analyzing the results of the experiment or giving enterprises a chance to adjust to the new conditions" (Yun´, Chapter 5.2.1; see also Freinkman, Chapter 8.1). Yun´ attributes the high frequency of policy changes to "the leadership's desire to see the results of their economic policy as soon as possible," that is, the conflict between the ambitions of the rulers and the short-run ineffectiveness of their policies.

Though in some cases the policy switches were undoing past mistakes (repudiation of Agroprom and of the election of enterprise managers by workers), they were costly and destabilizing. Still, in themselves they did not threaten the survival of the system. The 'radical reform' of 1987 could have easily turned out to be just one more step on the 'treadmill of reform,'[16] rather than a prelude to real change.

The main reason this did not happen was the truly radical changes in politics and ideology in 1987–1989. Only then did radical economic changes follow. Conversion of military industry, announced in 1988, and cuts in military expenditures after 1989, reversed the trend planned for 1986–1990 and the whole post-1962 military buildup, denying the primacy of military industry built into the Soviet system since the prewar years. The switchover from the investment drive in the Twelfth Five-Year Plan to a consumer orientation from 1988 onward went against the producer goods bias which had characterized the USSR since the mid-1920s. Official acceptance of a market economy as an objective at the end of 1989 was a revolutionary break with the entire history of the USSR and of Lenin's party. The renunciation of the official ideology made it possible for the advisors to offer market reform ideas (Yasin, Chapter 8.3), and at the same time made proposals that favored a Party- and government-run economy suspect with the public (Yasin, Chapter 7.1.4). And the public mattered since Gorbachev semi-enfranchised it, seeking an ally in his struggle with the 'bureaucrats' discussed in the next section.

Economic reforms caused the government to loosen control over the flow of funds in the enterprise sector, thereby unleashing inflation (Yasin, Chapter 6.2.3; Freinkman, Chapter 8.1).[17] This in turn undermined even the traditional Soviet markets, such as the one for consumer goods, and made the avowed purpose of expanding market relations unattainable. This would not have mattered so much if the command methods of resource allocation were still functioning. Indeed, the architects of the 1987 reform intended to retain administrative control over part of the economy. Yet their design turned out to be unworkable. While it was possible to construct and enforce a comprehensive production and distribution plan for the economy, a partial plan could not be compiled and executed (Yasin, Chapter 6.2.3; Freinkman, Chapter 8.1). The circulation of goods and services in the economy was disrupted by the worsening quality of the plans and accelerating inflation.

More generally, the central administrative organs started losing their leverage over the enterprises even in the spheres where they intended to keep it. Other than pure coercion (Freinkman, Chapter 7.3), it was the center's command over resources that made enterprises do its bidding. To the degree that the center renounced rationing of inputs, it lost its ability to order outputs, or anything else for that matter (Freinkman, Chapter 8.1).

Besides the various illusions discussed in the previous section, the reform procedure itself was a source of the reforms' shortcomings. Working out a reform plan for the whole economy all at once was too unwieldy a task, and had to be partitioned by sector. Yet the result was a reform of the supply sector that did not mesh with the financial sector (Nesterovich, Chapter 9.2), a reform of foreign trade that took no account of the domestic economy (Kurierov, Chapter 9.4), and so on.

Political Reform and Loss of Control

If one believes that the Soviet economy can be reformed by political decree, how does one account for the failure of past reforms? These reforms must have been scuttled by their political opponents in the ministries or in the Party apparatus. The rhetoric about the resistance to perestroika was an important element of politics from 1986 onward. Gorbachev still maintains that the sectoral ministries "could have swallowed up anyone, including the chairman of the government and even the general secretary" (*Istoricheskie* . . . 1995, p. 123). A serious reformer, therefore, had to make political changes aimed at neutralizing the antireform forces.

Yet our authors provide no evidence of resistance to reforms. In Chapter 9.4 Kurierov shows that, far from "swallowing up anyone," the officials of the Ministry of Foreign Trade had a negligible influence on the radical reforms in their sector. Their Ministry was attacked, weakened, and then abolished, and the institutional structure of foreign trade was dramatically changed, without their being able to do anything about it. Other contributors describe Gosplan, Gossnab, and VPK as following, sometimes unwillingly, whatever reform decree had been thrust upon them. The analysis by Yasin and Yun´ in Chapter 6.4 of the internal contradictions of the 'radical' reform makes the notion of political opposition as the cause of its ineffectiveness redundant. The emphasis by the Gorbachev team on sabotage by the antiperestroika forces is a time-honored maneuver on the part of Soviet leaders, going back at least to the so-called wreckers of the Stalin era (see Kurierov, Chapter 9.4).

Such demagoguery was not the only reason for the political reforms of 1988–1990. Medvedev argues (Chapter 7.1.1) that "The genealogy of political reform dates back to the efforts to reform Soviet society during the Khrushchev thaw." In other words, perestroika must be seen not as a narrowly economic project, but as an attempt to resume the radical de-Stalinization of Soviet life initiated by Khrushchev.

According to Yasin (Chapter 7.1.4), the economic reform of 1987 was an attempt to implement the Chinese model, which was torpedoed by the later political changes. "The Party [in the traditional system] would try to fix all the leaks sprung by the economic system. When its influence began to wane, the impact on the economy was immediate, no matter what the effect of other reforms was. After this, any kind of Chinese-style gradual reforms became impossible."

The removal of the Party from economic management appears to our contributors to be the single most important blow to the economy. Freinkman in Chapter 7.3 discusses the role of Party coercion in ensuring the enterprise managers' compliance with orders, and the consequences of renouncing coercion on the economy's governability. Kuznetsov (Chapter 7.4), on the basis of a detailed study of the functions of local Party committees, tells us that "The Party's withdrawal from the economy . . . caused an institutional vacuum which resulted in serious disorganization of the economy." He is seconded by Belik (Chapter 7.1.3), Mozhin (Chapter 7.1.2), and others.[18] It is important to note that Kuznetsov and Yasin are not people nostalgic for the system Gorbachev destroyed. Kuznetsov writes from a libertarian position, and Yasin is a radical reformer who in the mid-1990s became Minister for the Economy in the post-Soviet Russian government.

Tsipko in Chapter 7.2 tells us that the ideologists of perestroika already in 1986 had intellectually abandoned Soviet post-NEP institutions and were aiming at a Leninist alternative to Stalinism. The ideological liberalization that proceeded apace with de-Stalinization played a crucial role in the political changes. This is somewhat unexpected, in the light of the evolution of Western scholarship with regard to this subject in the decades preceding the collapse.[19]

There were not a large number of adherents to many of the views of Marx and Lenin in the upper echelons, where great power and nationalist views predominated (Tsipko, Chapter 7.2). Still, the official ideology was extremely important—enough so for Tsipko, for instance, to devote his whole life to subverting it. Ideology reinforced consumer contentment (Shlapentokh, Chapter 3.1), dictated foreign and military policy and the priority of various sectors of the economy (Danilevich, Gareev, and Konovalov, Chapter 3.2), and determined which reforms were and were not up for discussion (Yasin, Chapter 6.2.3). The dismantling of the received ideology permitted a beginning to be made on cutting military expenditures, but also uncorked consumer dissatisfaction (Shlapentokh, Chapter 3.1), oppositional political activity, and escalating demands for systemic change.

Political and ideological changes wrought by 1990 made it impossible to turn back when the harsher consequences of reforms started to surface.

The crucial role of political and ideological changes in undermining the economic system, demonstrated in this book on the basis of detailed empirical studies, is what one would expect on the basis of Kornai's (1992, Chapter 15) argument about the priority of political factors in creating and maintaining the traditional socialist economic model.

2.4 Why They Did Not Turn Back

Our contributors agree that Gorbachev and his team did not initially intend to destroy the Soviet system. If so, why did they not reverse course when it became clear that the system was falling apart?

The economic changes of 1987 were designed with the old political structure in mind. That structure would have allowed the rulers to keep under control the ill effects of such risky features as the election of managers. After all, the 1983 law on labor collectives contained quite radical provisions for workers' self-government, which remained on paper.[20] Yet the political reform that followed soon after the economic one made such damage control impossible. After that, "events unfolded spontaneously, no longer under the control of the government or Party" (Yasin, Chapter 7.1.4).

The government economic program of December 1989 has been described by Yasin (Chapter 8.3) as an attempt at a rollback. It failed because of the impossibility to enforce the commands from the center in the political climate of the time: "commands did not reach those who were supposed to execute them, and if they did, were not followed. Ministers convened in the Kremlin, orders were issued, quotas for material and financial resources were allocated, but none of it worked anymore." Significantly, this describes the early months of 1990, before the republics' rush to claim sovereignty which is now generally recognized as an irreparable blow to both the political and economic systems.

In January–February 1990, the top economic leadership explicitly considered, and rejected, turning back as a way of overcoming the crisis (see Ellman and Kontorovich 1997, pp. 273–274). Yasin's observation in Chapter 10.1 about the lack of attempts to roll back the reforms prior to August 1991 coup is certainly true on the level of broad government programs.

However, at the level of particular policies and institutions there were numerous reversals. The supply system was reintroduced already at the end of 1988 (Freinkman, Chapter 8.1), and the number of goods that could be freely exported was reduced (Kurierov, Chapter 9.4). A series of presidential edicts made factories' supply relations of 1990 obligatory for 1991 ('O neotlozhnykh merakh . . .' 1990) and announced a war on 'economic sabotage' ('O merakh po obespecheniiu . . .' 1991). These may have been just pragmatic attempts to fix particular elements that were not working, as Yasin (note 1, Chapter 10) characterized the repeal of enterprise director elections. Still, taken together, these minirollbacks negated much of the 1987 reform. The slipping political authority of the government meant that some of these measures remained on paper.

An important reason they did not turn back was the political importance of people who wished to do away with the command economy. Gorbachev himself, from 1986 onward, rejected the entire history of post-NEP 'socialist construction' (Tsipko, Chapter 7.2). Hence he was unlikely to do much to try to save the command economy. His main efforts went into trying to save the Union, which he continued to believe in. The radical economists who worked out the '500 Days' program in 1990 did not seriously think that "a market economy could be built in 500 days" (Yasin, Chapter 8.3). They realized, however, that (ibid.) "the old genotype could be destroyed and replaced by a new one," and this they endeavored to do by advocating their program.

The question in the title of this section is interesting only for the period when 'they' were in control, and were in a position to choose whether to go further or turn back. With the republics becoming actors, this was clearly no longer the case. The republics' drive for sovereignty and the personal rivalry between Yeltsin and Gorbachev became the main forces buffeting the economy in mid-1990 (Freinkman, Chapter 8.1; Yasin, Chapter 10.1; Kurierov, Chapter 10.2). Yet again politics undermined the Soviet economy.

The weakening structure of the Union finally caused a pause in economic reform and a tentative political retreat. It started in October 1990, as Gorbachev withdrew his support from the '500 Days' economic program (see Yasin, Chapter 8.3). The rejection of the program is ascribed by Gorbachev's aides to the fact that it envisioned too loose a federation (*Istoricheskie* . . . 1995, pp. 68, 76). However, while experimenting with emergency powers, Gorbachev was simultaneously negotiating with the republics on a new Union treaty.[21]

The prospect of the disintegration of the Union finally spurred Gorbachev's conservative opponents into action in August 1991. Party officials had been visibly opposed to perestroika since 1987, but did little to change the course of the country due to lack of courage, customary obedience, and lack of political alternatives to Gorbachev (Medvedev, Chapter 7.1.1; Mozhin, Chapter 7.1.2; and Yasin, Chapter 10.1). The August 1991 coup was the answer to their prayers (Belik, Chapter 10.3), but not for long.

Just as in the earlier stages of Gorbachev rule (see 'Navigating Without a Compass,' above), the myths proffered by the learned advisors made going ahead with radical economic changes seem more attractive than it should have been to a sober observer. One such myth was the belief that reforms would make things better also in the short run. It was only in April 1990 that an official reform program recognized that reform would lead to an initial fall in living standards, the emergence of unemployment, and increased inequality (Yasin, Chapter 8.3). The program was rejected by the Presidential Council precisely because of these ominous forecasts (which turned out to be underestimates) of the immediate effects of reform on living standards. Both Gorbachev and Yeltsin in April–May 1990 indignantly rejected the idea of implementing a reform which would reduce living standards.

Another myth entertained at the time was the reincarnation of the infinite malleability idea (see pages 19–20). It held that one can pick at will the most desirable institutions of other countries and transplant them on one's own soil (see Belik, Chapter 8.4).

Yet another myth concerned the role of the state in a market economy. In early 1990 a radical variant of reform appeared increasingly more attractive because it seemed not to need a strong state (Yasin, Chapter 8.3). That is, the radical reformers thought one does not need a strong state for a well-functioning market, thus ignoring a well-established relationship between the two (see, e.g., Crouch 1986, p. 180).

2.5 Conclusion

The insider testimony assembled in this book suggests that the USSR was killed, against the wishes of its ruler, by politics, not economics. The immediate cause of death, the dissolution of the Union, was the result of the chain of events set in motion by Gorbachev starting in 1985. The new ruler was not under pressure of popular dissatisfaction to introduce the changes. Unlike much of the Soviet elite, he was ambitious and optimistic about the system's capabilities.

The ruler had very little idea about concrete ways of reaching his objectives. This created unique opportunities for the social scientists who rushed to offer their pet solutions, from the state-strengthening acceleration policy of 1985–86 to a variant of market socialism in 1987–1988. The proposed policies, when adopted, did not bring results as fast as the ruler desired, and so the next set of advisors was summoned from the top of the academic bureaucracy to offer something new and better. The substance of the economic innovations, and their rapid succession, harmed the economy and sorely disappointed the high hopes engendered in the public mind by the 'new broom' ruler.

Our contributors attribute the resounding failure of the advisors to the special circumstances of Soviet social science: isolation from the West, ideological shackles, and inhibitions on debate and criticism. While true, this explanation appears incomplete. Soviet Academicians concocting fantastic reform plans were acting on assumptions quite common in modern social science and public policy thinking. When called to give advice on such a monumental scale, Western economists commit blunders of the same kind, if perhaps on a smaller scale.

While disappointing and harmful, the economic changes on their own did not threaten the country's survival. It was the political innovations, introduced in order to hasten the pace of economic change, overcome imaginary bureaucratic resistance to reforms, and cleanse the bloodstains of Stalinism, that proved decisive. Lifting ideological restraints on speech and thought allowed the discussion of previously unthinkable social changes, and fanned popular discontent. Withdrawal of the Party from economic management made the economy ungovernable in the old ways. A new foreign policy made it impossible to justify the garrison state established since the early days of Soviet power. Finally, the chain broke in its weakest, imperial link, as the metropolitan power and its acquired territories went their separate ways.

Military and foreign policy considerations must have played an important role in forcing many of the decisions leading to the collapse. The burden imposed on the economy by the ideologically motivated confrontation with the rest of the world appeared unsustainable even to many in the military establishment. Extreme secrecy, compartmentalism, and centralization of military policy decisions mean that few people can possess conclusive knowledge of the subject. While we believe that this book makes progress in elucidating the role of military concerns in the collapse, the issue will remain unclear until the relevant archives are opened. It took seventy years and the opening of the archives to see clearly the important role played by the 1927 war scare in subsequent Soviet policy (Simonov 1996b). Well-founded conclusions on the role of the war scare of the early 1980s in the genesis of perestroika cannot currently be reached because of the inaccessibility of analogous documentary material.

The things that we did not find in our study are also worth mentioning. Dissecting corpses has been invaluable in the study of anatomy. Our inquest found no traces of civil society, the power of organized interests, or citizen political participation, until the system started to fray in 1989. Particular sectors, such as military industry and agriculture, possessed special status due to their protectors in the CC apparatus and their importance for achieving the goals of the Party. Gosplan was lobbied by sectoral and regional interests, but these were easily overridden by the general secretary on matters of importance to him.

We found no evidence to support the fashionable theory that the Soviet system was toppled by the Party and state officials in order to turn their power into private wealth. Just as these officials, though loathing Gorbachev, were incapable of collective action to defend the system, they were equally incapable of consciously hastening its demise. If they landed on their feet after the system had crashed, it was due to their individual survival skills, rather than some grand design.

Notes

1. They are echoed by the memoirists: "Political instability was not an issue in the early and mid-1980s" (Pavlov 1994).

2. This lends empirical support to the approach taken by Shtromas 1981; Lane 1996a; Kotz with Weir 1997; and Hough 1997.

3. Gorbachev was personally involved in formulating the Soviet response to the Polish crisis as the chairman of the Politburo's Polish committee after the death of Suslov. See Pechenev 1991, p. 96; Shakhnazarov 1993, p. 124; and Gorbachev 1995b, pp. 338–339.

4. Pavlov (1995, p. 35) ridicules the thesis (propagated by Gorbachev's team) about the 'near-crisis' state of the economy in 1985. Even Gorbachev's keen supporter and former close aide A.S. Cherniaev (1997, p. 331) in retrospect argues that although the USSR did suffer from major structural problems in 1985, "these were not of an acute character: both Soviet society in its stagnation form and the 'Cold War' could have held out for another ten to fifteen years."

5. The CIA predicted annual Soviet GNP growth of 1–2%"for the foreseeable future" (Rowen 1982, p. 2), while Bond and Levine (1983, p. 18) forecast a 2.3–3.3% p.a. growth rate for 1980–2000.

6. The CIA saw continuous positive growth of both GNP originating in industry and consumption in that period (CIA 1985, pp. 64–65).

7. This was no different from the late Brezhnev period, when the level and rate of growth of military expenditures were exclusively the preserve of the general secretary (Gorbachev 1995b, p. 198).

8. We discussed with Pavlov his possible participation in this project, but nothing came of it.

9. The contributors' political stance is deduced from the full texts of their interviews.

10. "Gorbachev doggedly pushed for . . . a struggle with religion. In 1985–88 the CC adopted several decrees on 'intensifying the struggle with church ideology.' In 1988 the CC ordered a number of party and state organs to prepare a 'Long range program for educating the Soviet population in the spirit of scientific atheism' " (Alekseev, 1995).

11. Similarly, the General Staff and the Ministry of Foreign Affairs were bypassed in the crucial negotiations with the West (Kornienko 1994).

12. Yegor Gaidar in Bekker (1994) on the top economists: "[I]t must have taken a lot of effort to destroy the consumer market and the financial system completely in just six years, and to fully deplete the currency reserves and stocks of grain by the end of 1991." Yasin (1994, p. 145) writes that in 1987, "everything the Academy members and professors were suggesting was immediately incorporated into the decrees and directives of the CC and the CM. Later it turned out that our economists were just plain ignorant. . . . As the result, their suggestions ruined the Soviet economy."

13. Gorbachev 1989; Chekalin 1989; Shatalin 1989.

14. See also Yasin 1994, p. 145.

15. As in the 1994 program of 'the Academicians' ("Eshchë raz . . ." 1994).

16. A term coined by Gertrude Schroeder for the reorganizations of the 1970s (Schroeder 1979).

17. Recall the advisors' ignorance of monetary matters mentioned in the previous section.

18. In particular, some of the respondents in Chapter 3.2, in the unpublished parts of the interviews.

19. The obligatory official ideology was considered one of the main characteristics of the Soviet system in the totalitarian model which dominated in the 1950s. In the 1970s the totalitarian model was supplanted by the idea that Soviet society was (or was becoming) normal, much like any Western society. Ideology was therefore given short shrift, and concepts devised for the analysis of democracies started to be applied to the USSR. One of the most authoritative books in political Sovietology, Hough and Fainsod

(1979), has no index entry for 'ideology,' and only four entries for 'Marx and Marxism' in the part dealing with the contemporary period, but scores of references for 'citizen participation.' Our contributors did not have much to say on the latter.

20. *'O trudovikh kollektivakh i povyshenii ikh roli v upravlenii predpriiatiiami, uchrezhdeniiami, organizatsiiami.'* (*Resheniia* 1985, pp. 101–115).

21. In the winter of 1990–1991 a decree was prepared, with support from the KGB, introducing presidential rule in Lithuania, but Gorbachev refused to sign it (Shironin 1996, p. 224). In this respect, Gorbachev's behavior in August 1991 with respect to the USSR was analogous to his behavior about nine months earlier with respect to Lithuania.

3

The USSR in the Mid-1980s:
Structural Factors

3.1 Standard of Living and Popular Discontent
Vladimir Shlapentokh

The "Objective" Standard of Living

The popular discontent caused by the low standard of living is often viewed as a major factor which persuaded the Soviet rulers to liberalize the system in hope of economic improvement. Thus, Aslund (1992, p. 4) pointed to, among other things, "a very low standard of living in the Communist system," contending that "in the end, only fanatics and ignoramuses could defend this system." Rush (1993, p. 19) spoke about "widespread dissatisfaction and disillusionment throughout Soviet society," while the CIA and DIA in 1991 stated that (Dallin and Lapidus 1995, p. 336) "Soviet consumers are reluctant to endure further hardships."[1] Other analysts painted an even gloomier picture.[2]

This contribution shows that the standard of living theory (SLT) has little empirical support. There were no manifestations of mass discontent in the late 1970s and early 1980s. Most Soviet people, while critical of many aspects of their society, considered their life 'normal' and were essentially satisfied with it.

On the eve of perestroika, the standard of living in the Soviet Union was much lower than in the West. Scholars differ only on the size of the gap, with estimates ranging from one-third to one-fifth of the contemporary American level.[3] A large number of publications describing shortages of various goods in the Soviet economy appeared in the West in the 1970s and 1980s.[4] Even Soviet propaganda during that period did not dispute the country's lag in personal consumption, suggesting that other advantages still made life in the Soviet society much better than in the West.[5]

However, personal consumption was increasing between 1975 and 1985. This fact tends to be obscured by all the attention which has been paid to the declining growth rate of the economy. Yet most major indicators of well-being grew in this period: real income per capita and per family, average salary, pensions, the volume of goods sold to the population, including major foodstuffs, the consumption of food per capita (with some decline in the consumption of sugar and potatoes), the stock of durable goods at the disposal of households, the number of houses built, and the number of people who improved their housing conditions.[6]

There were also 'objective' tendencies impairing the quality of life in the country, such as the deterioration of the quality of goods and the growth of the time spent by the population waiting in lines. Moreover, whatever the growth in the objective standard of living of the Soviet population, it could not have guaranteed their loyalty to the existing order. The French people's discontent with the monarchy before 1789 was growing just at the time when their lives began to improve (Tocqueville 1955).

How People Perceive Their Well-Being

Theories that see the discontent of Russians with their lives as a cause of perestroika confuse objective and subjective indicators of the standard of living.

The Quality of Life Concept

In the 1950s, sociologists came across a paradoxical phenomenon: While the standard of living in Western European countries surpassed prewar levels, the degree of satisfaction with life in general and its various aspects was much lower than in the past. The cause of this phenomenon lay in the new aspirations, which were much higher than before the war and which now determined people's assessments of their lives.

Another discovery of great importance was that human 'happiness' or 'well-being' depends not only on purely material factors like consumption or housing conditions, but also on the natural and social environment, social inequality, the level of education, human relations, and other similar factors. Assessing the impact of these, mostly 'qualitative,' factors on human life could be done only by asking individuals about their satisfaction with these conditions.[7]

This led sociologists to elaborate a new concept—the quality of life— which made a clear distinction between 'objective' and 'subjective,' as well as between 'quantitative' and 'qualitative,' indicators of the standard of living. The concept of quality of life lies at the intersection of cognitive psychology, phenomenological sociology, and symbolic interactionism. These three closely related schools study the images which individuals form in dealing with the external world. These images are not mirror reflections of reality, but complex cognitive structures shaped by numerous factors.[8] Such developments in the social sciences made it clear that people's perceptions of how they live are not identical to the 'objective' indicators by which economists describe the standard of living.[9]

Of course, 'real practice,' as measured by objective indicators, significantly affects human feelings and cognitive structures, particularly when people's lives suddenly change for the better or worse 'objectively.' But the human inclination to adapt to existing conditions of life and the choice of points of reference with which to compare one's life, also play important roles.

Psychological Adaptation to the Social Environment

The ability to positively accept existing conditions which are, at least for the time being, impossible to change, and particularly to adjust psychologically to adverse conditions of life, is one of the most important elements of the human soul. Psychologists call it a 'coping mechanism.' It manifests itself, for example, in the inclination to choose only realistic goals in one's life, such as the level of income or education aspired to (Lindzey and Aronson 1985, pp. 829–835, 958; McClelland 1961).

The first studies of quality of life discovered that, in stable societies, the intergroup variation in the rate of satisfaction with any single area of life is amazingly small. Americans and West Europeans, for instance, whatever their major social and demographic characteristics, were satisfied with very diverse elements of their lives in almost identical ways: about 60–80% of people were satisfied with their jobs, housing conditions, marital lives, places of residence and so on, while no more than 10–20% were dissatisfied with these factors. No more than 6–8% of the variation in satisfaction can be ascribed to the major social and demographic characteristics.

Social conformism is a part of the coping mechanism. The desire to be in sync with those who control power and ideology in a society is well described in sociology and in political science, particularly by the students of totalitarian societies (Shlapentokh 1984, 1986). Conformism is so important that the human mind has to divide its resources between two goals—to seek the 'objective facts' about the world, and to find a way, with the help of an ideology, to distort these 'facts' in order to secure a comfortable state of mind. Even more important is the need to conform so as not to come into conflict with the environment—the state, society, and particular groups.[10]

The pragmatic function deals mostly with concrete facts and is based on individual experience. The ideological function operates with generalizations and uses second-hand information from the media, educational institutions, literature, and art—the propagandistic apparatus of society (Shlapentokh 1985, 1986).

Along with the 'real life' and 'adaptation to the existing conditions,' people's perceptions of their lives are affected by information about the life of the 'other.'[11] Comparisons with the lives of other groups in the population serve as the basis for understanding the well-being of each social group. Theorizing about the Soviet people's discontent with their life assumes "their awareness of and impatience with" their low standard of living in comparison with that of the West (Houslohner 1995, p. 49).

The Official Ideology Was Still Effective in 1985

From the 1960s to the early 1980s, ideological and moral erosion continued unabated. It was particularly strong among intellectuals (Shlapentokh 1990). Increasing numbers of people abandoned some tenets of the official ideology, such as the leading role of the working class, social equality, or a Communist society as a 'real future.' A significant number of Soviet citizens, although not a clear majority, revealed their dissatisfaction with the official media (Shlapentokh 1986, pp. 66–68). Many observed various flaws in the life around them, particularly at their places of employment, in retail trade and services. Television images of the decrepit rulers fed widespread skepticism about their wisdom.

Yet the official ideology retained a great deal of its effectiveness. According to the available data, the majority of the Soviet people supported such official tenets as Soviet and Russian patriotism, the supremacy of socialism, and Soviet social and moral superiority over the West. They saw the Communist Party as the true leading force in society, trusted its leadership, and strongly supported almost all of its domestic and especially foreign policies. Most Soviet people backed the invasions of Czechoslovakia in 1968 and of Afghanistan in 1980, and the shooting down of the Korean Airlines jet in 1983.[12] As the prominent journalist Leonid Pochivalov wrote in 1987, most Russians were sure that the Soviet Union had gained the "universal love of ordinary people in all countries of the world," who "wanted to imitate the Soviet order without reservations."[13]

Russians essentially accepted the official image of Soviet life. This postulated: the way of life in the country is much better than that in the West; the limited superiority of the West in the consumption of goods is more than recompensed by the high degree of stability (e.g., good pensions and the absence of unemployment), free health care and education, low level of crime, social justice, and moderate social differentiation; the life of the Soviet people is at a much higher moral and cultural level than that of people in the West.[14]

Fear of the authorities was still an important factor that deterred the would-be critics. As further developments showed, fear of the KGB lingered on not only after 1989 when the country took an evident step toward democracy and when political harassment practically ceased, but also after the anti-Communist revolution in 1991 (Albats 1994). The harsh measures against dissidents in the 1970s, though much milder than the repressions prior to 1953, were authoritative signals that society was still being run by 'Big Brother,' and that the best individual policy for survival and success was to believe in his ideology. The number of people who were ready to sign open letters of protest rarely surpassed fifty. The number of participants on Human Rights Day, 10 December, in Moscow was no higher than 100–200 (Alexeieva 1984, p. 349). The slightest manifestation of hostility to the regime was enough for the KGB to initiate investigations and to inform the Kremlin about their vigilance.[15]

This fear prevented many Russians from discussing publicly, and often even privately, the quality of their lives in general. Lack of public information about life in the country and abroad forced many Russians to think that their own problems in everyday life were peculiar only to their city or region.[16] This also contributed to a popular perception of life in the country very different from that of the defenders of the SLT.

With a strong ideology still able to strike a chord in the souls of many Russians, and with considerable fear of the authorities, most Soviet citizens were loyal to and respected 'the system,' believed in its invincibility despite all its flaws, and adjusted their minds accordingly. They possessed a dual mentality, typical of people living in totalitarian societies. It combined a pragmatic and realistic approach to the issues of everyday life with most of the official dogmas. The Soviet people were almost ideal subjects for the Soviet leadership.[17] The depth of the 'loyalty' of the Soviet people to 'the system' was so great that, barring a major disaster, the Soviet leadership would have been able to tap it for many years to come.[18]

Sociological Data: Soviet People Liked Their Lives

The majority of Russians were satisfied with their professions, jobs, and salaries (50–80% among various groups), with their clothes (70–80%), with their leisure time (about 80%), as well as with their vacations (up to 80%).[19] Russians greatly enjoyed the feeling of job security and the slack labor discipline that allowed mass drinking during the workday.[20] A national survey conducted in 1976 found that on a 5–point scale, most Russians evaluated their lives with a grade of 4. The American way of life did not deserve more than a 2 or a 3, with the best life being in Czechoslovakia, which scored almost a 5.[21]

In the late 1970s, the American and Soviet people assessed the quality of their work life and its individual elements almost identically, according to research conducted in 1986. The residents of Jackson and Pskov, two cities chosen for a comparative study of time usage, for instance, almost evenly appreciated their jobs on the whole, giving them a score of 3.9 (on a scale where 1 meant 'completely dissatisfied,' and 5—'completely satisfied'). Forty-nine percent of Americans and 44% of Russians were satisfied with the amount of their free time. The number of Americans and Russians who gained more satisfaction from work than from leisure were 14% and 17%, while those who claimed more satisfaction from leisure were 29% and 22%, and 57% and 61% derived equal satisfaction from both (Robinson et al. 1989, pp. 106–131).

Of course, most Russians were dissatisfied with several aspects of their lives, such as shortages of goods (and in particular the lack of meat and fish, as well as fruits and vegetables),[22] the unending lines, as well as the low quality of consumer goods.[23] The respondents in various surveys from 1960 to the 1980s were not satisfied with the moral atmosphere in the country and were inclined to accuse 'others,' but not 'themselves,' of numerous sins, including heavy drinking, sloppy work, and theft.

Many Russians hated the local authorities and blamed them for several of the deficiencies in their lives. However, they rarely assessed the whole system based on concrete negative facts. The dual mentality mentioned above permitted the Soviet people (as it does in any society) to combine seemingly opposite views on 'reality.'[24]

One would expect the Soviet immigrants in the United States to give a negative evaluation of their life in the USSR. Yet in the survey conducted in the late 1970s, 59% claimed to have been satisfied ('very' or 'somewhat') with their 'standard of living,' while only 14% were 'very dissatisfied' (Millar 1987, p. 33).

Most Soviet memoirists acknowledge that 'the average Soviet individual' did not feel miserable or as though he did not have a decent life.[25] Some authors attributing the origin of perestroika to 'objective' factors agree (Latsis 1990, pp. 169–178). Only 11% of the letters to the editor published in major Soviet newspapers between 1985 and 1987 were devoted to quality of life issues, while more than a third were about morality and 12% were about the improvement of Party life (Shlapentokh and Shlapentokh 1990, p. 175).[26]

While the majority of Russians were satisfied with their lives, no fewer than one-third were not. Yet this was the least educated and least active part of the Russian population, which did not present any threat to the Soviet system (Starikov 1989, pp. 180–206).

Soviet people could not change their lives and so adjusted to existing conditions and, as a rule, found them quite tolerable.[27] In a Novosibirsk survey in the early 1980s, for instance, only 8% complained that they lacked money for a normal life (Borodkin 1990, p. 143). When asked about how much they would like their salary to be increased, Russians rarely gave a figure higher than 10% of their actual salary (Shlapentokh 1970, p. 132). Only 7% of villagers in the early 1980s had modern furniture; however, only 11% wanted to have it. While more than 50% of villagers did not have refrigerators, no more than one-third claimed to want one (Levykin 1987, p. 60).

Housing conditions in the USSR present another example of adjusting to 'what you have.' Objectively, they were quite bad, compared with the West (Morton 1987, pp. 95–115). However, as sociological data showed, about 80% of Russians by the middle of the 1980s considered these conditions "as good or average" (Borodkin 1990, pp. 86–87). The level of dissatisfaction with housing began to rise in the late 1950s when residential construction started to pick up—a paradoxical fact explained by the emerging anticipation that housing conditions could indeed be improved.[28]

Soviet society in the 1960s and 1970s was not isolated from the world as much it was before 1953. A growing number of people listened to foreign radio broadcasts, traveled abroad, and met foreign guests in the country. Still, the influence of official ideology and fear of the KGB deprived the Soviet people of most information about life abroad and even in their own country. For instance, data about the average income and the distribution of income was highly classified.

The coping mechanism isolates people from facts which can be unsettling to them. This is how most Russians continued to stick to the official images of life in the USSR despite the flow of information from the West. Only with glasnost and the decline of fear, when people could talk openly and publicly about life in the West did Russians begin to get more or less adequate information about the lives of 'others.'

The social differentiation in the country and the existence of a privileged class, the nomenklatura, had some impact on ordinary people's evaluations of their own lives. Most people knew that 'they,' the apparatchiks, lived much better than 'us,' as Gorbachev (1987, p. 100–101) recognized in the first years of perestroika. However, full information, more or less, on this subject could be obtained by Russians only after 1985. The members of the privileged class kept their lifestyles inconspicuous. As in any caste society, people do not envy those who belong to upper classes which they have no chance of joining. For these reasons, the life of the elite had no significant impact on the assessment by Russians of their lives.[29]

The real reference group for Russians (as for most people in the world, particularly in stable societies) comprised people from the same social and professional groups.[30] Russians did not 'operationally' compare their lives with Americans or with the nomenklatura, not even with their colleagues in different professional categories, but only with people in the same professional group. Social envy was extended only to members of one's own group, while envy of people belonging to other groups was minimal. This, combined with ideological pressure, fear, and the desire to see their lives as 'normal' accounted, to a great extent, for the Soviet people's positive evaluation of their lives.

Moderate Optimism About the Future, Aversion to Change

Official ideology was able to implant its optimism into a majority of the Soviet people. Almost until 1987, they believed that their lives were much better than before the Revolution, before the war, and in the aftermath of the war. This was true even in the 1930s, when the country suffered from hunger and mass terror. In that decade, millions of Soviet people, particularly the youth, believed Stalin's words that "life has become better, life has become merrier," and would be immensely better in the future. Since there were no sociological studies at the time, I will refer only to indirect data on the strong support of the regime by the urban population.[31]

While life was 'objectively' much better in the post-Stalin period, the level of satisfaction with it decreased. This can be attributed to the fact that the pressure of ideology and the fear of repression were significantly weaker, even if they were quite strong in comparison with what happened after 1987. Still, Soviet ideology, enforced by a gigantic propaganda machine employing millions of people, maintained its optimistic tenor.[32] Thus, it is not surprising that the majority of Russians continued to uphold the images of the future which Soviet ideology imposed on them.

With the gradual decline of fear and the erosion of ideology after Stalin's death, the official image of the future was no longer painted in such glowing colors. By the 1980s, the notion of a Communist paradise had almost disappeared from the media. It was replaced by so-called mature or developed socialism, which had already provided Soviet people with a style of life much better than in the West and which would be improving systematically.[33] However, the leadership was still very much concerned about maintaining the optimistic, or at least not alarming, view of the future by the Soviet people. Thus, purely theoretical debates about the eventual end of the earth or the universe were practically impossible even in scientific publications.[34]

Russian intellectuals, including dissidents, did not share the official optimism in the 1970s and 1980s. However, their mood was far from apocalyptic. They believed that the status quo, regardless of how bad it was in their opinion, would survive for decades without any cataclysm.[35]

An important indicator of the general satisfaction of Soviet people with their lives was their negative attitude toward any serious changes in the economic sphere along with their enthusiastic reception of the political changes introduced with glasnost. Despite their grousing about the lines they had to wait in, most Russians opposed radical changes in the economic order, unless an immediate improvement was guaranteed. Even in June 1990 when the shortage of goods in state stores had increased greatly in comparison with 1985, only 4% of the respondents in the Russian republic were for freeing prices on all foodstuffs, and 47% accepted the deregulation of prices for some goods, while 48% were against any change. Hostility toward freeing prices for nonfood products was even higher: 3%, 36%, and 60% respectively (Goskomstat 1991b, pp. 14, 15).

In 1989–1991, at the peak of antisocialist euphoria, no more than one-third of Russians supported serious changes in the economic system. In VTsIOM's survey in 1989, only 18% answered the question "What should be done for the improvement of life?" with "Encourage private entrepreneurship under state control," while 50% demanded 'firm order' (Levada 1990, pp. 70–71).

Radical Increase in Discontent After 1987

Psychological adjustment works for most people when society is stable and static, and when there are few alternatives for changing people's lives and statuses. When a society is in flux and new alternatives are emerging, dormant aspirations activate, and people radically change their assessments of their lives.

Those who view the discontent with the quality of life in Soviet society as the cause of the upheavals of the late 1980s confuse the data about popular attitudes of two radically different periods—before 1987 and after (Smith 1991, p. 16). With perestroika, people saw alternatives as possible in their lives, the impact of socialist ideology declined radically, and fear practically disappeared. It became possible for the Soviet people to publicly evaluate their standard of living. They were even encouraged by the Kremlin to do so, an important factor for those who had lived all their lives under a totalitarian regime. As they received much more information about life abroad as well as about the secret life of their elite, they radically reconsidered their previous estimates of their lives (Levada 1990, pp. 44–47).

At the same time, the sale of consumer goods in the period of perestroika grew much faster than in the previous five years. Between 1985 and 1990 sales increased 45%, while between 1980 and 1985 it grew only 20%.[36] Meanwhile, the number of people complaining about lack of money more than doubled, from 8–10% to 21%, while the number of people who claimed that they had "enough for everything they wanted" decreased from 8% to 1%. In 1990, 30% of Russians declared that their life in recent years had deteriorated and only 18% said that it had improved.[37]

A very important cause of the growing dissatisfaction with life since 1985 was the perception of increased social polarization. Contrary to the expectations of Russian liberals, the growing social differentiation angered most Soviet people (Levada 1990, pp. 51–54). This anger, a *result* of the reforms and a phenomenon of the early 1990s, was mistakenly projected backward into the late 1970s and 1980s by several authors.[38]

The Standard of Living in Soviet Politics

In early 1985 the Soviet Union was probably the most politically quiet place on the planet, with antigovernment activity reduced practically to zero. Fewer than one hundred people were arrested for political reasons in all the national republics in 1980–1981 (Alexeieva 1984). Most of the intellectuals who in the 1960s were publicly critical of the regime, in the 1970s retreated from even the appearance of oppositional activity and began to support the official ideology with a special focus on nationalism.

The dissident movement almost completely ignored the standard of living of the masses as a factor which could have widened their support in the country. This can be seen in *samizdat*'s indifference to the material life of the people.[39] Russian literature and movies in this period were sensitive to human issues, yet apathetic about the material life of Soviet citizens (Shlapentokh and Shlapentokh 1993). This confirms that the standard of living was not a politically explosive issue.

Of course, the standard of living was a factor in Soviet domestic and even international policy (witness the importance of grain imports in the USSR). Soviet political culture assumed that under no circumstances could workers be denied the timely payment of their wages, nor could they be fired from their jobs or evicted from their apartments. Apparatchiks who did not follow these norms would have been reprimanded or even fired as 'politically immature.'

The leaders in the post-Stalin period were concerned with the mood of the masses and even in some cases were afraid of worker riots. However, fear never ran very high and never directly influenced fundamental political decisions of the Kremlin. This apprehension could become a relatively significant factor for a short time in the period of the transition from one leader to another (e.g., between Stalin and Khrushchev and between Khrushchev and Brezhnev) or when some real events, such as the Novocherkassk events in 1962 or the revolt in Poland in 1970, produced temporary impressions on the leaders and caused cosmetic changes in economic policy.[40]

Most of the time Soviet leaders were well aware of the lack of any dangerous discontent of the masses (at least if there were no decline in mass consumption) and did not see the necessity of modifying the essence of the Soviet system just to raise the standard of living of the population. They never seriously contemplated significantly cutting military expenditures, nor permitting the small private businesses which, even in their opinion, could have enhanced economic efficiency in the country but also would have endangered the fundamentals of the regime.[41]

Like any new leader, Gorbachev wanted to improve the life of the people, but he was not doing it under the pressure of fear. His first economic program—acceleration—focused on machine-building, and not on consumer goods. The secret memo sent by A. Yakovlev to Gorbachev at the end of 1985, which elaborated the initial program of perestroika, did not even mention the low standard of living (Yakovlev 1994, pp. 205–212). Speaking about the causes of perestroika in 1987, Gorbachev (1987, pp. 11–31) noted "the slackening of the growth of standard of living, the difficulties with food, housing conditions, consumer goods and services" among several other nonessential factors, and focused much more, for instance, on the anger of the masses "about neglecting the great values born by the October Revolution and the heroic struggle for socialism."

The fact that the standard of living was lower than in the West was not a direct cause of perestroika. The adaptive nature of human beings, particularly while under the pressure of ideology and fear of the totalitarian machine, explains why most Soviet people, even the most active and educated of them, regarded life before 1985 as normal and were far from threatening the Kremlin with any mass actions.

3.2 The Arms Race and the Burden of Military Expenditures
Sergei Belanovsky

Foreign Policy and Military Doctrine

A.A. Danilevich (colonel-general, former deputy-chief of the General Staff):[42] "Soviet weapons development policy in the 1950s–1980s was grounded in an overt and uncompromising opposition to the United States, NATO, and in some years to China. This struggle fueled the highly competitive field of weapons development and military technology. The arms race drained our socioeconomic resources and exacted a political, environmental, and moral toll. At the same time, it promoted basic and applied science as well as the development and implementation of new technologies.

"Our involvement in the arms race was also spurred by the militant ideology espoused by the CPSU. The uncompromising ideological principles underlying our military and foreign policy played an important role. The command economic system was another factor contributing to this weapons research policy. Also don't forget the painful experience of our early defeats in 1941; these memories loomed large in the mind of the leadership and the nation.

"Another factor was the special interests of the Soviet military-industrial complex (MIC). MIC was quite powerful and had a big influence on the country's political leadership. It supported our push for the rapid development of new weapons systems and military technologies as well as for superiority in the military field.

"There is another factor which explains why we created such a huge quantity of weapons. We perceived our main opponent to be the United States, and the second one to be the European NATO countries, in particular Germany. As a result of our political mistakes we began also to be in conflict with China. This was a serious threat. If one considers Brezhnev and Grechko, then in the 1970s they were not so much afraid of the United States as of China. Our strongest conventional forces were stationed in the east. We considered that Western politicians and military leaders were more sober and rational than was the case in China. With China anything was possible.

"In the 1960s and 1970s, twenty-three countries were categorized as our potential enemies. Among our main allies, we counted the six countries of the Warsaw Pact and seven other countries. Forty countries were considered basically neutral, but their orientation, especially in case of war, was uncertain. It is often said that USSR squandered its resources by helping all these countries, including extending them military aid. However, just consider the global balance of power—we had to do something about this lopsided situation. If the forty countries regarded as neutral joined the enemy, we would have to face sixty-three rather than twenty-three countries. So we had to try to convince these countries, or at least some of them, to come on our side. Hence the policy of 'nurturing.'

"The Soviet leadership was not impartial in its assessment of external military threats, frequently overstating their gravity. Some threats were simply concocted by our short-sighted policy. These alleged threats were grounded in pure ideology, fueled by the simplistic logic of global confrontation, the quest for an 'iron shield' around our borders. . . . I recall a 1987 meeting of the Defense Council at which our military doctrine was discussed. Akhromeev spoke about the likely scenario in case of global military conflict. His attitude enraged Shevardnadze, who said: 'Is this the basis for our defense strategy? You want to fight practically the entire world!' We did not plan to fight the *entire* world, but the balance of power and our perception of the war was such that the potential confrontation would not be limited to, say, the United States and the Soviet Union. However, Shevardnadze was right that even this projection of twenty-three potential adversaries was a heavy burden for our country to carry."

V.V. Shlykov (department chief at the Main Intelligence Administration [GRU] of the General Staff, 1980–1988):

Q: "Who lobbied in favor of aid for Angola or Ethiopia?"
A: "It was championed by the International Department of the CC. Their guiding principle was to promote the cause of the revolution. This aid was based on purely ideological grounds; there was no economic gain and it really made no sense. It would be a mistake to seek an intelligent basis for this policy. In reality, a memo would arrive, it would be approved, and the whole thing would start living a life of its own.
"There were numerous proposals to stop aiding these countries. But all of them were blocked. People resisted my ideas because it would have been necessary to make major changes. You start with tanks and you end up revamping the entire economy and then the political system."

Q: "Was there any anxiety about a nuclear first strike?"
A: "Our politicians didn't fear anything like that. We had an inert hierarchical leadership concerned exclusively with preserving its own power. Aid to Angola and other countries, this ideological expansionism, allowed them to feign allegiance to Communism and to portray themselves as ideologically motivated individuals. The leadership never took the nuclear combat plans of the military seriously. At that time, the army was under the stringent control of the Party."

XXXX (deputy chairman of the VPK in June 1986–February 1992, head of the Defense Industry Department of Gosplan 1981–1986): "We judged everything by the standards of the Great Patriotic War [the Soviet-German War 1941–1945]. This was a great pity. Many of our generals oriented themselves to the experience of the Second World War."

The Assessment of Enemy Capabilities

V.V. Shlykov: "Among the responsibilities of our department was the assessment and forecasting of the military-economic potential of foreign countries. Certain figures were simply outrageous (now, this fact ought to be acknowledged). For instance, in 1973 and 1975 we forecast that if a war started, perhaps within three–six months following mobilization, the Americans would be able to produce 70,000 tanks within a single year. I discovered later while working in the intelligence department (so the data is very reliable) that the Americans could produce at most 600 tanks under the aforementioned circumstances. In other words, our plans were based on forecasts that were off by a factor of more than 100.

"Such errors were not unusual. We were off target by a multiple of ten in the estimated U.S. wartime output of aircraft. We published these figures in special circulars, the so-called Orange books, that were intended primarily for the top leadership—members of the Politburo, the general secretary—an extremely narrow circle of people. These books contained exhaustive data on the potential of the Western countries. Data on the United States took 350 pages; we had data for every major country, including Japan and China. I know for a fact that these figures were taken literally in planning our defense strategy and preparing the country for the arms race.

"We had ample opportunity to acquire accurate information. These overblown figures were unwarranted and, in effect, they were imposed upon the intelligence community. At that time, we had at our disposal space reconnaissance units and unlimited funding; the intelligence staff could obtain any information we might need. It was not long before we realized (by about 1980 when I took over as department chief) that all our data was distorted or simply false. What was most unnerving was that these data actually steered the country off course, even from the national security point of view.

"This is precisely the reason we accumulated 64,000 tanks. It wasn't because we wanted to lunge at Europe, as was believed across La Manche [the English Channel], but because we thought we needed this huge advantage in the number of tanks at the start of a war. Once the war began, according to our estimates, in one year the United States would be able to produce seventy thousand tanks and the USSR only thirty to thirty-five thousand. For the very same reason, we accumulated 45,000 nuclear warheads, which is a lot more than all the Western countries combined. This crazy story is still waiting to be told.

"I realized full well that the country was heading for a catastrophe because of the absurd data issued by the intelligence service. While still hold-

ing a high post, I acknowledged that all this preposterous information originated in our agency. I tried to introduce certain corrections. I made it clear
that we had failed to find real evidence suggesting that the West was gear-
ing up for a war.

"At that time there emerged highly classified [U.S. military] programs,
which, contrary to our perception of the openness of the West, were skillfully camouflaged. We naturally managed to uncover the truth about all
these secret programs. When I suggested that it was not tank battles that the
West was preparing for, everyone dismissed the notion. The top officials at
the Defense Ministry came from the old-guard school of tank division marshals and they simply refused to listen. When they were shown documents
containing specific and reliable information, they refused to recognize these
figures because they didn't want to assume the responsibility.

"I went to Gosplan and other agencies and even to Gorbachev himself,
but nobody wanted to change anything because it meant acknowledging the
huge mistakes we had made. One of the senior people at Gosplan told me:
'Do you realize that we invested billions of rubles into this!? Who is going
to be held responsible? No way. Your organization should write an official
memo, saying it made a mistake. Then we will talk.' However, our organization was very big. There was a hierarchy of people above me which led
all the way to the army generals who didn't want to change anything. I told
them that such and such a document which I had written contained false
information. The response was: 'Everything is fine. You were telling the
truth.' When I proposed sending these documents containing our figures for
expert evaluation (for instance, to Primakov's institute) I was told: 'We
cannot trust them with this information!'

"If we consider the long-term perspective, Gorbachev ignored the incred-
ibly high level of militarization of our economy. Actually, he was not alone.
Nobody seriously considered this facet of our economy. Apart from the
intelligence service, not a single organization, not a single academic institute addressed this issue. I had a good idea of the research potential of such
institutes as the Institute for World Economy and International Relations or
the Institute for USA and Canada. We did authorize such projects lasting
for the duration of several five-year plans. However, people were reluctant
to conduct a serious investigation into these problems. Kokoshin and
Arbatov stated straight out: 'We don't want to deal with any highly classified information or documents marked 'secret' because we wouldn't be
allowed to travel abroad.' They would be very blunt about this.

"The only organization willing to address these problems was
Blagovolin's department at the Institute for World Economy and International Relations. I think Blagovolin had not made one single trip abroad

prior to 1988 or 1990. In 1983, when Alexander Yakovlev was head of the Institute, the department was dissolved. For all intents and purposes, the work at all the institutes came to a halt. If I had to say who won the war and why, I wouldn't hesitate to say that it was the Americans. They beat us not because they had more tanks, but because they had more think tanks which addressed these issues. We didn't have a single think tank."

Q: "Which think tanks do you have in mind?"
A: "Those probing into strategic security and economic issues. Their experts came up with a more adequate assessment of our capabilities. More importantly, their self-assessment was more realistic. It was subject to self-criticism and adjustment. Debates raged between the CIA, military intelligence, etc. Later on I had a chance to meet with the actual players. The Americans also made serious errors, particularly in those areas where the USSR was weak. Still, the order of magnitude of their mistakes was much less than ours. Their estimates were not a hundred times too high, but perhaps 50–30% out, and primarily with regard to such macroindicators as defense appropriations as a share of the Soviet GNP."[43]

A.A. Danilevich: "I often hear it said: 'Why did we need 63,000 tanks?' We did a comparative analysis of the U.S./NATO and Soviet/Warsaw Pact recovery capacity. We anticipated that losses would be much greater than during World War II. Our study revealed that during the war the Americans would not only be able to make up for the losses suffered but actually increase their military capacity. By the end of the first year of the potential war, the United States might have twice as many tanks as they had at the beginning of the war. Our situation was very different. Given our estimated losses (calculated using computers with results corroborated at the testing grounds), our industrial capacity, and mobilization potential (if our industry were to switch to wartime status), our economy was incapable of maintaining the existing level of armaments, not to speak of any buildup. After one year of war, the ratio would be five to one in their favor.

"A quick war would have enabled us to achieve our goals before our army's collapse. But what about a prolonged war? Was there any way to resolve this dilemma? Yes, by accumulating large reserves of weapons sufficient to start and sustain an effective war effort for some length of time. Do you know how many tanks we had on the eve of the Great Patriotic War [the Soviet-German war of 1941–1945]? We had twenty-two thousand tanks, of which fifteen thousand were in the west. Germany had only five thousand tanks, of which three thousand were used to attack the USSR. And what happened after the first month of the war? Our losses equaled 100% of our tanks. It was necessary to take account of this experience."

Military Planning and Weapons Procurement

Some Institutional Actors

XXXX (deputy chairman of the VPK in June 1986–February 1992, head of the Defense Industry Department of Gosplan in 1981–1986): "The head office of the VPK which controlled (to some extent) the MIC was rather small. Including all the support staff (cleaners, secretaries, etc.) we had a little over 300 people."

Q: "Was this an academic council *[nauchnyi sovet]*?"
A: "We all made recommendations but what actually happened was something else. Was the head office an academic council? Well, we had chief design engineers, academicians, etc. One of the Deputy Chairmen of the VPK headed our . . .[44] council. They analyzed long-term issues and came up with recommendations on the proper course of action. This was how our council operated. The primary task of the VPK was to rate our domestic weapons development programs, to make sure our weapons [were] up to standard, to supervise the work of developmental pilot projects, and to oversee their implementation. But it was Gosplan, the Ministries, and other agencies which managed serial production. Actually, during the last year or year and a half, an attempt was made to force the VPK to handle problems it was not able to handle, such as to manage the actual production process. As an 'industry man' who had been on the receiving end of precise instructions from above, I can tell you that this whole idea was ridiculous.

"VPK as an administrative unit was set up at the beginning of the 1950s. Its main function was to keep an eye on foreign defense technologies using our research institutes, design bureaus, etc., and make sure that our domestic weapon systems are at least as advanced as theirs. In terms of quantity, we surpassed the West in some types of weapons and lagged behind in others."

Q: "What was the task of the CC's Defense Department?"
A: "They were our bosses. The Defense Department of the CC dealt with individual items. They would inquire why we don't have enough shells, cartridges, etc. They would supervise the actual implementation of the plan. For instance, they would inquire why the plan isn't being fulfilled. They acted like they were another CM. But they had more authority and none of the responsibilities. They were not the ones responsible for plan fulfillment; they didn't have to probe into why certain things were not done. They just inquired: why are plan targets not met?"

Q: "Did your relationship with the CC go sour?"

A: "Everybody had a difficult time with the CC. I was loyal to them—I did not make any noise, I didn't quarrel or quibble with them. For instance, when I came to work for Gosplan, I worked for half a year as deputy chairman of the department. The department chief never actually interacted with the CC. He told me: 'I don't want and will not work with them.' He wouldn't talk to them. The CC got involved in problems it was not competent to handle. They shouldn't have meddled in the production of individual items or in research. It was none of their business. But the system kept an eye on absolutely everything. And that is how it survived.

"The monopoly of the Party, that is, the CC, was really excessive. It was more than just an ideological organization. It acted more like a division within the CM endowed with tremendous authority. They would stick their head into every single issue. It was hard to deal with them. They would say: 'This must be so and so.' We told them this was wrong, but the CC would demand that things be done the way it said they should be done."

"Weapons Were Pushed on the Generals by Industry"

M.A. Gareev (army general, former deputy chief of the General Staff): "We were drawn into the arms race and exceeded a certain threshold. This was largely responsible for the eventual collapse of the Soviet Union and everything else that has befallen our country. Our military-industrial complex became a state within a state. MIC had its own people in the CC, the government, and every place else. They would impose a policy that was not necessarily beneficial to our armed forces, but one which ensured more appropriations, bonuses, promotions, and so on. This became especially apparent when the MIC got one of its own people—Ustinov—appointed as Defense Minister. During that period, our armed forces were essentially at the mercy of the MIC and as a result the arms race certainly drained the country's resources.

"We often produced weapons that were not essential. For instance, at one of the military exercises, Admiral Gorshkov said he needed aircraft carriers and other ships costing billions of rubles to prevent the Americans in time of war [from] taking oil from the Persian Gulf. He was told that faced with a war, it would suffice to add two more tank armies to the Transcaucasian or Turkestan Military District. In the event of war, these armies could advance toward the Persian Gulf, thus eliminating any need for naval involvement. In addition, the cost of the latter program would be much less. There were many other instances where we could have resolved the problems in ways other than the Americans. We lacked the resources of the United States.

"One big handicap of our defense system was that unlike other countries, we didn't have independent research units. All research organizations were state-run and were thus subordinated to specific departments. They could only support the policies of the leaders of the organizations they were subordinated to. In the West they had the Rand Corporation and other organizations."

Q: "In your proposals to your superiors were there any specific proposals regarding the production of arms?"
A: "We didn't need to increase the output of old-model tanks, which we continued to produce. The old tanks are always needed because the new tanks replace the old. No army would argue with that. However, industry was actually more zealous. Take the following example. The chief of the Armored Vehicles Administration suggested cutting down on the production of tanks at the Tagil, Kurgan, and Cheliabinsk factories. Ustinov's response was: 'What will the workers do?'

"In some cases, the navy was forced to take delivery of ships with no guns or navigation equipment. The reason was simple—if the ships were rejected the workers' wages wouldn't be paid. At first, Ustinov would say that ships would not be accepted until they were finished. He was then told that the workers were unhappy because they were not getting paid, to which Ustinov replied: 'The Politburo demands that the workers be paid.'"

V.V. Larionov (major-general in the reserve, member of the Academy of Military Sciences): ". . . till 1985 . . . our defense budget failed to conform to our security needs. The appropriations were reconciled neither with the General Staff nor with the Ministry of Defense; the latter were not consulted with regard to the amount of weapons that was needed. The weapons procurement budget was determined by the VPK, not the General Staff. I witnessed numerous meetings of the Research and Development Committee of the General Staff, and subsequently, when I worked in the General Staff, I attended meetings held by the Defense Ministry and the General Staff. I heard the Defense Minister and the chief of the General Staff voice their protest over, say, the number of tanks they were saddled with. They asked why we need all these tanks when so little is allocated for maintenance. The weapons procurement program just kept on expanding. Even Yazov lamented—"why are we given so many tanks when we have plenty of tanks already?" And take Ogarkov 'the wise.' It was he who had to sign Ustinov's requests and Ustinov's defense budget. He protested and was promptly fired from the post of the chief of the General Staff. It was not a form of protest; Ogarkov simply refused to sign certain provisions in the defense budget.

"We faced a dilemma with aircraft that couldn't fly: spare parts were in short supply and no money was allocated for servicing and repairing the aircraft. Money was not appropriated for these things, but plenty was given to the enterprises for producing more aircraft. The weapons procurement appropriations are part of a different budget item. The Air Force Command did not control the number of planes it was given. It did not contract for these planes, it was saddled with these planes. The situation was similar in the Navy Command. It had to accept everything that was allocated to it. This policy really highlights the gap between the weapons procurement budget and the appropriations for servicing, repairing, and maintaining the equipment."

Q: "A myth arose that it was the military that demanded more tanks, more aircraft, etc."
A: "The military was saddled with these weapons."

Q: "What would the military have asked for if the leadership had listened to them?"
A: "The military would have asked for money to maintain the weapons they already had, so the equipment could be repaired and made ready for combat. They would ask for less additional equipment and more resources to cover the operational expenses."

A.A. Danilevich: "When Grechko was the Defense Minister, he demanded from the MIC that our weapon systems be on par with world standards and U.S. weapons in particular. Ustinov would make similar demands, but pressured by enterprise directors and design bureaus he would approve projects that were only halfway finished and order the navy to accept unfinished ships. He used to argue and make a lot of noise, but in the end he would say, 'All right, we will take it.' Grechko would never have allowed this to happen."

XXXX: "I was deputy director of the Chief Planning Directorate of a defense industry ministry when I encountered the following situation. Gosplan had a planning indicator called welded metal structures. What this meant was that everything we welded—from railroad cars to tank hulls—was calculated in terms of weight and metal was allocated accordingly. We began to use a new thinner yet stronger metal for one of our metal structures. Naturally, the welded structures indicator dropped as our metal consumption was reduced by several thousand tons. When I went over to the Ministry to defend the plan I was told by one rather old man: 'I don't care about the new technology. Just do anything so that everything stays the same.'"

Table 3.1

Number of Types of Weapons Produced in the Mid-1980s

	USSR	US
Artillery and small arms	62	37
Armored vehicles including infantry, combat, and other vehicles	62	16
Anti-aircraft guns	26	4
Land-based missiles	4	3
Space reconnaissance systems	10	5
Main battle tank	3	1
Communications control systems	20	4
Fighter aircraft	8	5
Nuclear submarines	5	2
Large surface ships	9	4

Source: Compiled from the numbers cited by Danilevich.

"The Generals Got What They Asked For"

A.A. Danilevich: "A major drawback of our defense industry was the extensive duplication of materiel and weapon systems. Compared to the United States, the USSR produced three to four times as many types of the same kinds of weapons.

"Our policy was driven by our desire to be on top. We had no idea when a war might erupt, but we thought it might start at any moment. We were on edge. For instance, the introduction of a new tank design raised the following problem: outfitting the entire army with the new tank was impossible, since the country produced only 2,000 tanks a year, with 63,000 tanks in use by the armed forces. It would take 30 years to replace our tank fleet completely. Our only option was to continue to produce the old-type tanks and at the same time, begin to introduce the new one. Now, suppose we develop a new technology that is three–four times better in its combat performance features than the old system. We were forced to pursue the same 'mixed strategy,' and as a result, the old and the new weapons piled up simultaneously. This created serious problems in standardization, production, and maintenance. On one hand, we wanted to maintain a consistently high level of defense capability, but on the other hand, our weapons procurement policy gave rise to serious problems."

V.V. Shlykov: "Ours was an army of tanks complemented by a rather meager air force and navy. The 'tank people' couldn't care less about SDI or other complex weapon systems they couldn't comprehend. What was the army's line of reasoning? 'We have our finger on the button; the army has missiles; we can knock the enemy out anytime.' R&D institutes affiliated with the military-industrial complex wanted to secure additional appropriations (the army wasn't paying for any of this, so it didn't care whether we dealt with this problem or not), lobbied the government (which is nothing new) where MIC had its own people. The army and the MIC hierarchies were severed. The two didn't really intersect."

XXXX: "The calculations we made emulated the logic of our military doctrine. Suppose (just suppose) that our mission is to get from Moscow to La Manche [the English Channel] in two weeks. We begin to calculate and 'place' minefields in certain areas. Now we find out we don't have enough tanks. We say we need to produce more tanks. We actually played these kinds of war games. The last T-34 tanks were decommissioned about ten years ago. We have guns from the Second World War. We have shells manufactured in the 1940s. We produced the new and kept the old. As a result our industry was overloaded. Still the generals lived very well. All this was the whim of the military."

I.S. Belousov (1984–1988, USSR Minister of Shipbuilding; chairman of the VPK and deputy chairman of the CM from 1988): "Conflicts did arise between the army, industry, and the R&D sector. During my time, however, we managed to reconcile our differences with the Defense Ministry. The VPK's decisions on weapons development were mandatory both for industry and for the Ministry of Defense (this line of command was incorporated into the VPK's Charter, but it was not always adhered to). In other words, it was the experts and the scientists who, together with the military, had the final say in which weapons to produce."

Resource Allocation for Defense and the Civilian Economy

A.A. Danilevich: "The basic premise was: 'Spare no money for defense.' We were to be given as much money as we needed, but in reality things were different. I worked in the General Staff and I know firsthand that the annual and five-year plans for weapons procurement always provoked serious conflicts. Our proposals were based on specific strategic aims; so we knew which weapon systems and how many units we need to fulfill these objectives. However, in the twenty-five years that I served in the military, not once did the General Staff meet our requests. Not once did Gosplan endorse our estimated requirements. They were always reduced two- or three-fold. We could barely secure appropriations in a limited number of areas, which were still a lot less than what we needed. Naturally, Gosplan was concerned with the entire economy not just with the needs of defense. Nowadays, people say this wasn't the case, but what I have described is true. We were always subject to resource constraints."

I.S. Belousov:

Q: "Did the Afghan war require increased output of weapons?"
A: "No. In Afghanistan we used primarily the arms and munitions accumulated over the course of many years. The Afghan setting required certain types of weapons which we no longer manufactured, so their production was resumed. However, these weapons comprised a small share of what we employed in the Afghan war."

V.N. Lobov (army general, former chief of the General Staff):

Q: "Did you feel that the country might not be able to sustain such a furious arms race?"
A: "I did not foresee an impending crisis. The fact that the standard of living of our people was lower than that in the West was apparent. We lacked adequate housing, the quality of our products was poor, the availability of computers and telephones was inadequate. We really lagged far behind in these areas. However, we didn't collapse for economic reasons but because in 1985 we were placed under a weak political will. This led to amorphous decisions or the complete lack of decisions."

A.A. Konovalov (Institute of USA and Canada):

Q: "Were there any cases when we decided not to produce a certain weapons system, for example, a new kind of rocket, because we lacked the resources for this?"
A: "No. It was formulated differently. I suspect that our decision-making process was strongly influenced by foreign powers. They looked for ways to undermine or neutralize our tremendous military force. They could not afford to spend as much on defense. So, they provoked us into developing weapon systems which they themselves had never developed. For example, a lot of publicity was generated when they began to manufacture the supersonic long-range bomber "Convair" B-58. No sooner did they announce the development of the supersonic bomber than we started to develop an even faster supersonic interceptor. This is how the MIG-25 was born. It had a cruising speed of 2 Mach so it could intercept the American bomber.

"The Americans produced three B-58s. Two of them crashed during test flights and one was turned over to the Museum of Aeronautics. Then the project was killed. We, on the other hand, produced several hundred, if not thousands, of MIG-25s, for which at the time there was no real target. Subsequently, part of the fleet was turned over to the strategic reconnaissance units. Stories similar to the MIG-25 abound.

"On top of the ploys undertaken by other countries, there was also an internal push for new weapons. We have nobody but ourselves to blame for this because our system of reporting encouraged all these frequent modifications. The only way to make a career was to first submit a report describing the new weapon system with better features than the previous one; then state that it was successfully tested; and thirdly make sure it was adopted by the armed forces. The rest was simple—a Lenin Prize secretly awarded, promotion in rank, etc. So, everyone was interested in developing new modified versions of old weapons. As a result, some weapon systems were only finished half-way when they went into production."

Q: "At some point, the alarm sounded that the country can't continue to produce all these weapons."
A: "The first genuine warning was sounded during the 1991–1992 budget talks. This was at the time of the summer 1992 nonpayments crisis. This took place in Russia, not the USSR. While the Soviet Union endured, this sentiment was never voiced, never."[45]

XXXX:

Q: "Is it true that the administrative system proved adequate in the military sector but not so in the civilian sector?"
A: "I wouldn't say so. The administrative system couldn't care less if you manufacture tanks or mobile excavators. In both cases, you have a certain number of units, you have total weight, you have a plan. And the system must provide for both. There is no difference."

Q: "But the defense industry performed much better. Why was that?"
A: "Many of our civilian industries also performed well. Civilian production was efficiently maintained at many of our defense plants."

Q: "Why were things better organized in the military sector of the economy?"
A: "Probably because more was demanded of them. The defense plants had the military inspectors in addition to the quality control department. The institution of military inspectors represented one more level of control. This kind of culture trickled down to the civilian output manufactured at defense

plants. Military inspectors were sometimes asked to approve civilian goods made at defense plants in order to raise the overall level of management."

Q: "Some people contend that the MIC contained all the finest high-tech resources, thus condemning the civilian sector of the economy to technological stagnation. Would you comment?"
A: "When I was transferred to the VPK, I came across a statistical abstract of the inventory of industrial equipment for 1986 or 1987. The study was conducted by the TsSU. The parameter list included the age of the equipment, its origin (domestic versus foreign), etc. Judging by all these indicators, the military sector actually lagged behind the civilian sector. Perhaps in some areas defense industry did usurp resources. If we had to produce 100 electric locomotives and 100 tanks, but only had enough materials for 100 tanks and 90 locomotives or for 100 locomotives and 90 tanks, the tanks won out. These were our priorities, but to blame the defense industry for sucking all the life out of the economy is too extreme."

Q: "For instance, why did the hydraulic equipment employed in the military sector perform quite well, while its record in the civilian sector was so poor?"
A: "Because management, the factory, the quality control department, etc., didn't work the way they should have. About the hydraulic equipment. We purchased two or three plants from the Germans. One was turned over to defense industry and one to civilian industry. Both had exactly the same equipment, but there was a gap in productivity. In the defense sector, the plant performed very well. But not so in the civilian sector. It is all in the attitude toward one's work and the demands placed upon one's work. I would be hard pressed to pinpoint the exact cause for this variation in performance. Perhaps it was the result of the widespread irresponsibility.

"In the civilian sector, they would forget to test some component, or to weld a hole, whatever. Nothing like that could ever happen in the military sector. Their quality control was much more stringent. Everybody was scared—you wouldn't like it if you got caught (scared not so much of the quality control department but of the military inspector). The quality control department in the civilian sector was neglected. You just rubbed the right person the right way and that was it. That was the extent of quality control."

A.A. Konovalov: "I spent twelve years working in the defense industry. Among other things we manufactured optical equipment. We had huge R&D facilities. One time, the deputy minister or perhaps the minister himself of one of the defense industry ministries had major kidney problems. We were asked to develop an artificial kidney machine, supposedly for future medical use.

We looked at the specifications of the best Dutch and British artificial kidneys. And we developed something that at the time was on par with the best European equipment.

"When everything was finished we invited over the artificial kidney specialists from the Ministry of Medical Supplies Industry. Our machine looked like a console. They had a system the size of 'Buran,' perhaps a little smaller.[46] It was housed in a huge room with tram car wheels and trolley bus-type electrical components, blocking switch, etc. I was really shocked by their initial reaction. When they arrived they didn't ask about the basic design, nothing like that. They asked: 'What is this?' They had never seen the silicone tubing, transistors, or plastic that we used. They had never seen anything of the kind because of the very strict regulations governing the transfer of technologies: all components incorporated into a weapon system were precluded from being used for civilian production.

"These people from the VPK are not lying. They could have gone on with the arms race if someone had paid for the thousands of engineers, if someone had supplied them with everything from rare-earth metals to gold and fissionable materials. We could still have competed with our arms and brains, but the country could no longer afford all this stupidity."

Q: "Strangely enough, they don't see it that way."
A: "It is hard to generalize because they are all different. There are some who recognized the gravity of the situation. Those in the VPK didn't feel that way. They lived pretty well, so naturally they detest Gorbachev."

Q: "Perhaps, we could have held out for another 20 years?"
A: "We couldn't have stayed afloat for another 20 years. We were under a lot of pressure. At one point we purchased Swiss equipment and began to produce something for defense. But we still needed chemicals, polymers, composite materials. To keep all these machines running, we had to purchase the necessary materials. Which we did, especially the materials required for the most modern equipment. It would have been necessary to discover a new Tyumen.[47] Even this, however might not have been enough in view of the decline of world oil prices in the 1980s."

SDI

I.S. Belousov:

Q: "Was the SDI program 'the straw that broke the camel's back'?"
A: "There are two views on this subject. I don't have a firm position on this

issue and I am not sure which view is correct. The first approach, the one we really 'fell for' (and I did too) was that SDI represented a qualitative shift. Both sides would have had strategic nuclear capabilities as specified in the various agreements (such as SALT-2). However, in the long run quantitative parity could have resulted in a situation where one side (in case of a military conflict) would have had the capacity to deliver sufficient nuclear warheads to the other country, while the latter wouldn't be able to deliver enough warheads in spite of having quantitative parity in terms of the availability of nuclear warheads, missiles, etc. We actually accepted this approach. Naturally, the situation was unacceptable, and we embarked upon major countermeasures. I should actually qualify my statement. We had certain ideas for an alternative plan. But I am not in a position to speak about this because these ideas were developed by scientists who explored ways to ensure parity in this area.

"The other approach was that SDI was a pure bluff. This has its proponents, but I tend to think that the Americans wanted to take advantage of their scientific potential and really pursue this avenue of development. I am certain that SDI could have yielded major results, perhaps in fifteen years rather than in five. Of course, any such developments would have upset the previous military parity."

Q: "Could we really have competed with the United States in developing SDI or some alternative program?"
A: "We could have competed in terms of basic science and ideas. However, bringing these ideas to life was way beyond us. Therefore, alternative ways to respond to SDI had to be found."

M.A. Gareev:

Q: "What did you propose in response to SDI?"
A: "SDI was unfeasible even for the Americans. The Americans themselves did not expect to fully implement the goals of SDI. The United States had two real goals. First, to achieve a technological breakthrough. The fruits of this could also have been used in the civil sector. The second was to tempt the USSR into a new round of the arms race which would both be very expensive and also very difficult because of the Soviet technological lag.

"Some of our scientists argued that SDI was feasible. Others however, myself included, argued on both economic and technological grounds that it was not necessary to launch an analogous program. We developed our own program, 'The destruction of the enemy's cosmic systems.' In this way we undermined SDI."

V.V. Shlykov: "The notion that Gorbachev's perestroika was started as a result of Reagan's Star Wars program was concocted in the West and is completely absurd. In reality, nobody cared and nobody considered a practical response to the Star Wars program. Kokoshin argued that SDI is a bluff and that star wars were unfeasible. This was analogous to the leaders of the MIC arguing that the cruise missile program was a bluff, a hoax designed to draw us into the arms race."

Q: "Was SDI a bluff?"
A: "No. It was a splendid idea—to channel military expenditures into something so inspiring as shielding the country from any possible mishap. At the same time, SDI spurred the development of new technologies. It was a real shot in the arm for the economy. Thanks to SDI, the Americans were able to produce fewer tanks. The actual implementation of SDI would have consumed considerably more resources. The United States wanted to maintain its potential; the Americans were getting a head start.

"My own view was that if the United States decided to go ahead with SDI it would invest sufficient resources (up to one-half of its GNP) to solve the problem in the shortest possible time. In our country this approach is impossible. Everything we do we do as a last-ditch effort. If we don't succeed and we know that the Americans are spending much less than we are on some project, we treat this as a sign that they are bluffing, that they lack serious intentions. This is not always true, however.

"I was in contact with our senior military officers and the political leadership. They didn't care about SDI. Everything was driven by departmental and careerist concerns. Any serious issue was shunned. We raised this issue in the context of our potential vulnerability and provided highly reliable and valuable intelligence information which corroborated our findings. However, since this information didn't square with the personal ambitions of the politicians, including Gorbachev (not to speak of marshals and such) it was simply ignored. No one took national security seriously, nobody. Everyone thought that in case of real trouble we can use our nuclear weapons. . . .

"Ogarkov was elevated to the status of a cult figure; allegedly, he advocated high-precision weapon systems. The analysts dreamt this whole thing up. They failed to understand the real issue."

Q: "In the 1970s at Semipalatinsk the USSR successfully tested an X-ray laser. Some people thought, 'Now they will have to catch us up.'"
A: "Absolutely. The laser equipped with an X-ray booster is a Russian invention. In this field we surpassed the Americans in many areas. However, we spent tens of times more resources on all these programs than the

Americans. Moreover, our breakthroughs were sporadic and useless for defense systems. For the Americans this was the key issue. Perhaps politically for them nuclear boosters in space were unacceptable. We had no such constraints."

Q: "If my understanding is correct, those isolated breakthroughs we made could not be implemented because. . . ."
A: "Absolutely correct. It would have been a waste of money."

Q: "Was a comprehensive analysis of SDI ever conducted?"
A: "Who could have come up with such an analysis? You are looking for elements of intelligence, logic, or concern for the nation's welfare, but all these were lacking. There were people who were lobbying and there were scoundrels trying to secure money for themselves (for such weapons as particle beam weapons, lasers equipped with nuclear boosters, etc.). These projects were a waste of money. Once we recognized this, we said to ourselves, 'The Americans are simply trying to ruin us.' Gorbachev wasn't concerned about SDI. Nobody really dealt with SDI seriously and now they say it was a bluff and that this system couldn't be developed.
    "The Americans abandoned the SDI once they realized we were not getting sucked into a counterprogram. If we calculate the amount of money we spent on research along the lines of SDI, it would certainly add up to a lot more than what the Americans spent."

M.I. Gerasev (Institute for the USA and Canada):

Q: "Comment on Reagan's statement that the United States 'will finish the USSR off' with SDI."
A: "It is absolute rubbish. Our response to this program with greater defense appropriations had no bearing on the economic health of the country. Look at the figures. We budgeted only about 5–10 billion rubles for all these counterprograms."

Q: "Do you think this amount was sufficient to develop our own SDI?"
A: "It was evident that as it was formulated, the American program could not be implemented. So we came up with the idea of asymmetric response, which we touted for a long time to scare the Americans. Our program was very credible. It was not a bluff. We didn't have a detailed plan, but steps were taken in that direction. I think our general approach was correct (perhaps this is the reason I took part in this program).
    "We had plenty of zealots who greeted Reagan's SDI with open arms.

They came running with comprehensive projects expecting to be showered with funds. I am deeply convinced that neither the SDI nor the arms race in general contributed to the collapse of the Soviet Union. I don't think it was such a heavy burden."

V.N. Lobov:

Q: "Didn't we realize that they were bluffing?"
A: "I wish we did! Also, there is some truth to every bluff. In 1988 I said that SDI is a bluff. Subsequently the Americans themselves said so on several occasions. The whole idea of SDI was to boost America's own technological potential using the technologies developed by their allies. They said they can develop SDI using their own technologies but it would take dozens of years. If the United States could get Japan, Germany, Great Britain, and France to provide their technology, then the United States could develop SDI within ten years. If all the technologies were assembled under one roof, they could have achieved a technological breakthrough, perhaps in an area other than SDI. It is a good thing the U.S.'s allies refused to play along. In any event, as long as the possibility existed, we had to take some kind of countermeasures. Even if SDI was a bluff, we had to expose it! Who knows, perhaps it is not a bluff? However, to prove this you have to make investment, conduct experiments, etc."

YYYY (deputy director of an engineering research institute in the defense sector):

Q: "Could we have weathered Star Wars from the technological point of view?"
A: "Star Wars did create a climate in which certain leading individuals would push for projects and programs which we didn't need. The USSR never led in the weapons development department, always playing catch-up. The SDI program probably targeted this weakness. However, the resources allocated to develop countermeasures were a far cry from the figures subsequently stated by Rutskoi, Yeltsin, and many Soviet scholars, especially those working at the Institute for World Economy and International Relations and the Institute of the USA and Canada. All too often they would wallow in speculation using their own figures. They pounced on this subject: MIC bankrupted the country, the Cold War ruined us. We did go overboard and made mistakes, which could have been avoided because we had a real opportunity to mend our policy. But these mistakes were not fatal and they didn't spell our doom."

The Military Balance

XXXX: "We could hold our own in almost every area of weapons development. One area where we were behind by a few years was in infrared and night vision. In this area we lagged by several years. In electronics, we were five to six years behind the West.

"We maintained strategic parity in all vital areas. In other areas we were content (unlike the United States) to manufacture simple weapons. As far as long-range nuclear missiles are concerned, we chose to take a different route from the Americans. They expanded their submarine force while we invested in land-based missiles. But we did not lose with this arrangement."

M.I. Gerasev: "On average we lagged behind. But as far as defense is concerned, we could make up for these deficiencies with other things such as greater quantity and less advanced technologies. By that time, we were falling behind. I don't know how fast. The dynamics of R&D in the military sector reveal that our greatest weakness was information processing technology. For instance, U.S. satellites could remain in orbit for years while we had to bring our satellites down every three–four months. Our system was not efficient in the area of command and control of our armed forces. However, all these limitations were latent and would only surface in actual combat. In certain areas, such as space reconnaissance, we were forced to spend much more money and make one launch after another. We had literally tens of thousands of 'Kosmos' and 'Molniia' satellites."[48]

Q: "Do you mean to say that the element of bluff in our defense policy became more and more pronounced, but since no one planned to attack us we could live with the bluff?"
A: "Certainly! This whole arms race was really absurd. The only true test of one's military superiority is on the battlefield."

M.A. Gareev: "We had strategic parity. We could use our strategic nuclear arsenal to strike at them and neutralize any advantage they might have. In other words, anything they could do to us we could do to them, especially in view of our superiority in long-range nuclear missiles. We did have superiority in nuclear missiles. Our army was superior—we had more troops as well as the best artillery and tanks. We did lag behind in the artillery command and control systems. Still, we were more advanced in military theory, plus we had the experience of war, which nobody else had. All these factors gave us certain advantages over the Americans. For one thing, the Americans still lack advanced military science.

"In military strategy one always has to distinguish between direct and indirect actions. The most patent manifestation of hostile indirect activity was the extraordinary effort to undermine the Soviet Union. This included economic discrimination, and measures aimed at preventing the inflow of modern technologies; it also included drawing us into the arms race, taking counteractions against us on a global scale, attempting to cripple our allies like Cuba, North Korea, etc.; subversive activities inside the Soviet Union; training people who would carry out the West's plans by training them in ideological infiltration; patronizing people who were simply interested in undermining the USSR. Ultimately, with all these maneuvers the United States succeeded in accomplishing something that Hitler failed to achieve with a real war."

Ideas for Reforming the Military Economy

M.A. Gareev: "The arms race was, in some sense, justifiable—if we had failed to get involved in the arms race imposed upon us by the West, we would simply have gotten crushed. The problem was to participate in the arms race, but to do so in a sensible manner."

Q: "Which specific areas of the arms race do you consider unwarranted?"
A: "We should have done something about our policy of global confrontation. However, to do this we would also have had to change the underlying ideology. Our ideology dictated that once we had instituted a socialist state in our country we should spread it throughout the world. To reverse this premise, we would have had to remold our entire system of government, our political regime. This wasn't realistic. Many reforms aimed at restraining our defense expenditures (which I and Marshal Ogarkov tried to implement) were doomed because our proposals were detached from an overall restructuring of our society, our political system, and our economy at large. Many areas offered substantial savings. Just recall the huge amounts of money we wasted on Egypt, Ethiopia, Angola, Salvador. . . . Billions and billions. All this aid was ideologically motivated."

Q: "What specific proposals did you make in your memos?"
A: "The idea was not to fuel conflicts, but to negotiate and adhere to the spirit of the Helsinki Accords. I also proposed to steer clear of such ventures as Afghanistan. That war was very costly. We also advocated a more rational arms procurement policy focusing on specific weapon systems rather than all the weapons produced by the United States. We proposed not giving aid on ideological grounds, reducing the armed forces, etc.
    "If the arms race had been conducted in a more sensible manner, we

could have sustained it and still maintained strategic parity, we could have matched the Western powers and ensured global stability. We also had an opportunity to preserve the Soviet Union. During the last fifteen years, every time a new Minister or Chief of the General Staff was appointed, I would submit a report to the effect that our armed forces were not what they ought to be; that we could sidestep many pitfalls and avoid being drawn into the arms race, especially in those areas in which we should not be involved.

"Marshal Ogarkov proposed that we have three rather than five branches of the armed forces. To really shift gears, the country's political regime had to undergo major alterations, and no leader, no matter how progressive, was willing to go that far. This explains my statement that perestroika was vital to changing the country's economic policy and its political orientation."

Q: "Describe the reform plan devised by you and Marshal Ogarkov."
A: "Deep cuts in civil defense, which we considered frivolous and unwarranted. Halt the production of aircraft carriers. We recommended not tailgating the Americans by simply reacting to or mimicking SDI, but finding cheaper and more effective ways to counteract this initiative. The fourth proposal was to reexamine the overall organization of our armed forces and to reduce the number of branches of the military (including air-defense systems).

"We could have cut the size of our armed forces. It was obvious that our armies could not remain where they were forever. At that time, if we had acted swiftly and proposed to cut the size of our forces, say, in Germany, the Germans would have been more than willing to build apartments for the servicemen and to support the remaining units. The Germans were willing to do anything in return for our reduced military presence in Germany.

"Another theme of our proposal was to be more discriminating in extending foreign aid to countries where we had no vital national interest."

Q: "Did this represent your personal view or did Marshal Ogarkov agree with you?"
A: "We laid out the proposal for him. He basically supported our position, but not everything we proposed was given the go-ahead. Ultimately, the number one reason we failed to carry out the proposed measures was not that the heads of the military commands opposed us. The biggest stumbling block was our economic strategy and political orientation—without changes in the latter a true reform was impossible. And no one was about to go that far."

Q: "Who opposed you?"
A: "The main opposition came from the military-industrial complex. The heads of the military commands were also opposed to the proposed changes. The Central Directorate was also opposed because it had a vested

interest in these defense contracts. The CC was also adverse to our program, particularly the Department of Industry, because industry had its own people in the CC."

Q: "Why was our policy toward Ethiopia and other countries financed by the Soviet Union not changed?"
A: "The greatest opposition came from the KGB, particularly the foreign intelligence department, and from Gromyko personally. They buried any commonsense proposal, not just mine or Marshall Ogarkov's. We were not the only ones to put such proposals on the table. Other people came to the realization that major changes were needed."

Q: "Didn't your opponents recognize these facts and how do you explain their position?"
A: "There was the ideology of global confrontation and the urge to possess everything that was at the disposal of our adversary, that is, the imperialist countries. But the key reason is that the country lacked a leadership capable of independent thinking and making its own decisions. The leadership was paralyzed by the need for consensus: they needed to garner twenty–thirty signatures, which was practically impossible. We should have given up on a lot of things and concentrated our efforts in the key areas. But our leadership was feeble; it was not prepared to make tough willful decisions, to act decisively like Stalin. As a result, nothing definitive was ever done."

Q: "Could you identify the industries that lagged furthest behind?"
A: "We always lagged behind the West in electronics and computers because we lacked a strong microelectronic base. Our MIG-21 was loaded with huge boxes and a large number of vacuum tubes. We cannot even begin to compare the MIG-21 with the U.S. Phantom in which all these devices are much more compact. Our inferiority in this area was manifest in our military reconnaissance technologies, navigation equipment, target identification systems, electronic countermeasures, computers—all the equipment which uses electronics.

"We even came up with the following plan. At one time the USSR had thrown all its resources at developing nuclear weapons. Similarly, it was now necessary to develop a strong microelectronic base. We needed a big leap. We needed to merge our research facilities and set up new ones; to invest a lot of resources and put the best scientists to work in the area of microelectronics, just as we had done at one point with the nuclear weapons program. However, our leadership lacked the decisiveness to follow through with this program."

V.V. Shlykov:

Q: "If you had been able to communicate with the leadership in 1985, what would you have proposed?"
A: "The most important step would have been to embark upon a major demilitarization of our economy, that is, to get a clear picture of what Russia really needed to ensure its security and to stop producing all these nonessential weapons. It wasn't necessary to compete with the entire world in the output (quantity as well as quality) of all these weapons."

Q: "Was Ogarkov a true reformer of our military? What is the basis for his reputation?"
A: "Ogarkov was no reformer. His reputation as such is unwarranted. Actually, at one point a scandal erupted and he was relieved of his duties. This is probably the reason behind his reputation as an army reformer. He probably contradicted Ustinov over some operational matters, but he never actually addressed strategic issues."

V.V. Larionov:

Q: "Back in 1985, should the defense burden on the economy have been reduced?"
A: "Certainly, especially in view of the fact that a nuclear war could not be won. Any future war would be suicidal. Everyone understood this. Ogarkov lost his post because he refused to sign a number of weapons procurement orders. Ustinov's response was, 'We will sign it ourselves.' This was the fate of our MX project. Ogarkov was dead set against this idea concocted by Ustinov's son and his designers. They claimed the Americans had such a system, so why shouldn't we? MX is a mobile missile which is transported via underground passageways. Ogarkov was against this kind of missile system because it would take money away from other more vital areas, such as the development of new control systems. Ogarkov understood that this project represents impudent lobbying on the part of the MIC."

Could It Have Gone On?

M.I. Gerasev:

Q: "Was the USSR unable to sustain the arms race, and did this precipitate the crisis?"
A: "For many years USSR was able to sustain a much more fierce arms

race and the country could still have endured for years to come. The outcome which we observed would have taken place sooner or later, but only because the country couldn't afford to spend one-third, perhaps even more, of its GNP on defense. This would have been the real economic cause for the impending crisis. However, the crisis would have affected other countries, since no country can endure this kind of an arms race."

Q: "What is your perception of this crisis?"
A: "Militarism was a key element of the Soviet economic and political system, bearing particularly strong on our domestic policy. If we renounce the methods employed by Stalin (which were impossible anyway after his death), then we are left with a limited arsenal of tools to control society within a totalitarian framework. Militarism is one of the key components of such a control mechanism. Since 1917 our psychological outlook was that of people living in a besieged castle. In the early and mid-1960s this feeling began to erode. There was the Cuban Missile Crisis, but I did not grasp its full significance until much later. My generation basically grew up without this feeling of an imminent threat to our country. So, there emerged this disparity between the state's aspiration to keep our society militarized and the needs of the people who no longer felt the pressure of an external threat and wanted to improve their standard of living. The system itself had no mechanism to accommodate such a major shift

"The steps taken by Gorbachev struck at the very heart of the system, something that he himself certainly failed to realize. Gorbachev didn't wish to abandon the socialist system, just to give our system a civilized veneer and to eliminate certain elements of militarism."

Q: "Could the arms race have lasted any longer? What do you mean by saying that the arms race would have spelled trouble for everyone, not just the Soviet Union?"
A: "Imagine that Brezhnev is still alive. We would still be living with the old regime; nothing would have changed. Perhaps things would be a little worse, but the country would be under control. We would still have the same totalitarian system; we would be going to Party meetings and demonstrating with the same red flags. Despite the widespread recognition of the absurdity of the whole situation, we would have continued to live the way we lived."

Q: "Didn't our civilian sector deteriorate?"
A: "It didn't. It was growing and the standard of living was on the rise. It is true that at the end of the 1980s the economy stopped growing. The system

was nearing its limit, its point of saturation. The share of resources allocated to the civilian sector was not cut, but it could not support the same rate of growth as before. I don't think that our civilian sector was crumbling. In the mid-1980s (prior to perestroika) our lives were certainly much better than in the mid-1970s. Wages were higher."

A.A. Konovalov:

Q: "Is it true that the USSR collapsed because it lost the arms race with the United States?"

A: "I would like to divide my answer into two parts. First, the USSR collapsed because it was based on an absolutely false ideological dogma, which was contrary to human nature and normal economic laws. On such a basis no state could survive forever. Unfortunately, Russia and the USSR were fantastically rich countries, therefore this crazy experiment could last almost eight decades. No other country could have put up with it so long. This is the broad historical perspective.

"Secondly, on a more concrete level, in the 1970s and 1980s the USSR suffered total defeat in World War III. It was a peculiar war, but it was definitely a war, a world war. If we consider such indicators as the share of National Product, the actual amount of resources, and all the money allocated for defense, we would have to conclude that USSR fought much harder after 1945 than before 1945. Precise data is lacking, but I have trust in my sources.

"So, Gorbachev is not some monster who came and toppled our system. The country would have collapsed without Gorbachev. Perhaps, the agony could have been prolonged by a year or two, but the result would be the same. [Huge resources] were wasted on this idiotic military machine, on this notion that we are living in a besieged castle. There was one famous slogan known also from the time of Andropov and Ustinov: we shall not skimp on defense. We could tighten our belt in any area but defense."

Notes

1. See also Kort 1993, p. 295. Hedrick Smith (1991, p. 6) suggests that almost all strata of the Soviet population were "incensed about" their life.
2. By 1985 (Holman et al. 1991, pp. 82–83), "The level and quality of living conditions in the Soviet Union were rapidly and steadily declining, placing a larger and larger part of the Soviet population below the poverty threshold."
3. Estimates of Soviet per capita consumption as a percentage of that in the United States in the mid-1970s are "less than one third" (Birman 1989, pp. 2–3); 34% (Schroeder 1987, p. 15); 20–25% (Birman 1989, p. 160; also 1983, p. 378).

4. See for instance Teckenberg 1987, pp. 31–41; Matthews 1987, pp. 43–63; Field 1987, pp. 65–82.

5. The 'style of life' concept was advanced for that purpose. It included such non-material factors as the fear of unemployment, the level of morals and criminality, and the status of culture in society (Arnol'dov et al. 1984; Kapustin et al. 1982).

6. Goskomstat 1988, pp. 392, 399, 408, 421, 425, 426, 455, 468. [These are Soviet official statistics and exaggerate the improvements. Nevertheless, Khanin's 'alternative' estimates (1996, table 1) also show a growth in consumption in 1975–1985. Although these estimates indicate that the growth in per capita household consumption in 1981–1985 was less than 1% p.a., that is still an improvement and not a worsening. Ed.]

7. See Allard 1972; Greenfield 1973; Campbell, Converse, and Rogers 1976; Campbell 1971; OECD 1976; and Sen 1987.

8. Schutz 1976; Luckman and Berger 1966; Blumer 1969; and Goffman 1959.

9. The awareness of the difference between 'objective' and 'subjective' indicators of well-being predates these developments in social science, as the fable of the 'sour grapes' and the concept of the 'happy slave' attest. Tocqueville (1955, p. 317) spoke about "this disposition of [the] soul that makes men insensible to extreme misery," musing whether it should be treated "as a blessing of God, or as the last malediction of His anger."

10. About social conformism, see Kiesler and Kiesler 1969.

11. Runciman 1966; Ferge and Miller 1987; Townsend 1970, 1979. See also the theoretical concepts of comparison in Campbell, Converse, and Rogers 1976; Thibault and Kelly 1959; and Crosby 1982.

12. Firsov 1977; Grushin and Onikov 1980; Kochergin and Kogan 1980; Strelianyi 1992.

13. *Literaturnaia gazeta,* 26 August 1987.

14. Kim 1983; Vishnevskii 1989; and Glezerman, Rutkevich, and Vishnevskii, 1980.

15. A report to the Minister of Internal Affairs about the events during the celebration of the anniversary of the October Revolution in 1956 mentions nine flyers with "counter-revolutionary contents" found on the outskirts of Barnaul, five pictures of Soviet leaders with "anti-Soviet captions," which were thrown about during the demonstrations in Batumi, and a few inscriptions scribbled on the walls of an opera theater in Tallinn (*Izvestiia,* 6 November 1991).

16. Labeling negative occurrences as 'atypical' was an important tool of Soviet propaganda. At the same time, a 'typical' accusation leveled by the Party and the KGB against Soviet citizens was "making wrong generalizations."

17. More on the dual mentality of the Soviet people in Shlapentokh 1985 and 1986. See also a brilliant description in Yashin 1954.

18. This loyalty even outlived the Soviet system. In 1994–1995, about 40–50% of the former Soviet people (and a much higher share of the elderly who had a long experience in the Soviet Union) revealed their nostalgia for a socialist society. See the discussion of the Duma elections in *Izvestiia,* 21 December 1995; *Sovetskaia Rossiia,* 21 December 1995; *OMRI Daily Digest,* no. 246, part 1, 20 December 1995. The drastic deterioration of the material life of most Russians in 1992–1995 was a major cause of this development. However, it would have been impossible without the internalization of Soviet norms in the past.

19. No more than 8% of men and 5% of women were inclined to use additional free time, if they had it, for moonlighting to earn more money (Gordon and Klopov 1972).

20. According to various sources, the number of workers with low labor discipline during the 1970s and 1980s was about 30–40%. Few of them ran the risk of being fired

during those 'good times' (Shlapentokh 1989, pp. 52–53).

21. From the author's personal archive. I was the head of the methodology section of the survey.

22. In the 1980s, about half of the families complained about shortages of meat (Borodkin 1990, p. 75). In 1990, the number of families with the same grievance increased by nearly one-third in comparison to 1985, despite the growth in sales of this product (Goskomstat 1991a, p. 125; Goskomstat 1991b, p. 245).

23. In the 1960s and 1970s, only 3% of the population in Russia considered the produce at free market prices affordable (Grushin and Onikov 1980, p. 413; also Shlapentokh 1969, pp. 154–164).

24. For just this reason, the Soviet people were much more critical of the local authorities than of those in Moscow, as several studies found. For instance, of all letters sent to newspapers by the residents of Taganrog, only 9% raised issues related to society in general, and only 6% were concerned with the city and the region. The rest concerned developments in residential blocks, factories, and the family (Grushin and Onikov 1980, p. 413; Shlapentokh 1969, pp. 154–164).

25. Orlova 1983; Kopelev 1975, 1978.

26. Of course, editorial selection of letters to be published was biased against those letters critical of the standard of living.

27. This was also true of the prewar period, as reflected in the interviews of displaced persons in the 1950s (Harvard project). Despite their hostility to the Soviet regime, 77% of all professionals, 70% of semiprofessionals, and 62% of skilled workers reported being satisfied with their jobs. These figures are not very different from figures characterizing the same feelings in the 1940s in the United States (91%, 82%, and 84%) and in West Germany (75%, 65%, and 47%). Satisfaction with salary (compared to others with the same type of job) was also quite high: 84–86% for professionals and managers, 77% for white-collar employees, and 73% for skilled workers (Inkeles and Bauer 1968, pp. 104, 114).

28. See Gordon and Klopov 1972; Grushin and Onikov 1980, p. 250; Yadov 1967, 1977, 1979; Levykin 1984, p. 94; Shlapentokh 1969, 1970, 1975, 1976, pp. 62–63, 1986, 1989.

29. About the Soviet elite's life, see Arbatov 1992, p. 219.

30. Festinger (1954, pp. 117–140) empirically proved the rather trivial statement that the people with whom we compare ourselves are similar to us.

31. Even committed enemies of Stalin's regime attested in their memoirs, with evident reluctance, that "the crowd supports Stalin" (in the words of Vernadsky 1992). See also the books published by dissidents in the West before glasnost (Orlova 1983; Kopelev 1975, 1978; Grigorenko 1982; Ulanovskaia and Ulanovskaia 1982).

32. According to my computation, no fewer than 2 million full-time workers were engaged in ideological work in the Soviet Union before 1985 (Shlapentokh 1986, pp. 6–7).

33. See for instance Kim 1983; Vishnevskii 1989; and Glezerman, Rutkevich, and Vishnevskii 1980.

34. Fear of a new war did linger in the Soviet mind. It was, however, relatively weak, since the official ideology promoted the idea of detente rather than confrontation with foreign powers. During the Cuban missile crisis in October 1962, the Soviet people remained calm. In the late 1960s, when Soviet-Chinese relations became tense, the fear of war began to spread. It was, however, at a low intensity, since the Kremlin was trying to hush up the catastrophic vision of the 'yellow peril.'

35. See Shlapentokh 1990. Shpagin (1994) wrote that Russian intellectuals in the 1970s and 1980s, unlike their ancestors in the 'Silver age' (the pre–World War I decade)

did not experience fear, "the apocalyptic presentiment, an apprehensiveness which tore the personality into parts and broke the world around."

36. Goskomstat 1991a, p. 116. [These figures are in current prices and take no account of the increased inflation in the second period compared to the first. However, Khanin's 'alternative' estimates also show household consumption rising faster in 1986–1990 (14.2%) than in 1981–1985 (8.3%). See Khanin 1996, Table 1. [Ed.]

37. Goskomstat 1991b, pp. 285, 312; and Borodkin 1990, p. 143.

38. In 1989, 28% of Soviet people considered themselves as belonging to the three highest social groups in a ten-level hierarchy. In 1991, only 5% felt this way (Levada 1993, p. 19).

39. Timofeiev 1982 being a remarkable exception (see Shlapentokh 1990).

40. A strike and a protest march in Novocherkassk terrified the Kremlin so much that two members of the Politburo were dispatched to the city, the whole military district was put on alert, and troops were ordered to fire on the people, killing twenty-four. Seven strikers were later executed (Remnick 1993, pp. 414–419).

41. Under Chernenko the Politburo did approve a document which if implemented would have given the green light, if not to 'small private businesses' at any rate to cooperatives and individual economic activity. See Prostiakov's contribution in Chapter 5.1. [Ed.]

42. The whole of Chapter 3.2 is an edited (by the editors of this book) version of the transcripts of the interviews by Belanovsky. The headings have been added by the editors. For Belanovsky's own Russian edited version of five of the interviews, see Belanovsky (1996a, 1996b, 1996c). [Ed.]

43. The U.S. intelligence estimates of the number of Soviet bombers and missiles were also erroneous, tending to exaggerate them in the 1950s and to understate them in the 1960s. See Steury (1996). [Ed.]

44. The interviewer failed to catch this word. [Ed.]

45. According to Marshal Akhromeev, the General Staff proposed freezing military expenditures already in 1976 (Akhromeev and Kornienko 1992, pp. 22–23). [Ed.]

46. 'Buran' was a Soviet space shuttle. [Ed.]

47. This is a reference to the giant oil province in West Siberia that was so important to the USSR in the 1970s and 1980s. [Ed.]

48. Konovalov on the technological lag: "I don't even want to mention such things as the lack of water at Baikonur—we had to push the shit aside with our feet while we launched the most advanced satellites into space."

4

The USSR in the Mid-1980s: Rulers' Perceptions

4.1 Monopolized Statistics Under a Totalitarian Regime
Moisei Eydelman

The Status of TsSU/Goskomstat

The Central Statistical Administration of the USSR (TsSU) was the main source of economic information for the supreme authorities of the country.[1] This information covered the levels and rates of growth of the economy as a whole as well as its sectors and subsectors, except for the military industry.[2] TsSU was a monopolist, controlling all the statistical information in the country. [In 1957], when the branch ministries were disbanded and the regional economic councils created, all enterprises and organizations were obligated to present statistical reports only to the organs of TsSU.[3] The organizations and enterprises would send copies of these reports to their superiors. TsSU became the only agency in the country possessing data collected from all organizations and enterprises, processed and aggregated for the economy, as well as for districts and regions. This precluded external verification of the accuracy of the information.

When the branch ministries were restored [in 1965], they were once again allowed to receive reports from their enterprises and aggregate them for the ministry as a whole. Nonetheless, TsSU continued to be in charge of all statistical reports for the national economy, its sectors, and regions of the country.[4] All forms of primary accounting and reporting at enterprises and organizations, indicators to be reported, the deadlines for submitting the reports and the addresses to which they should be sent, as well as instructions as to how to fill them in, had to be confirmed by TsSU.

The statistical information of ministries and agencies was mainly used for their internal needs and for the evaluation of their performance. When it was necessary to obtain a detailed technical-economic description of the conditions of a sector and the perspectives of its development, extensive use would be made of the information of the corresponding ministries and agencies. TsSU ran systematic checks on the accuracy of the data and corrected any embellishments and distortions that were discovered. As a rule, when there was a discrepancy between the data of TsSU and that of another agency, TsSU's were preferred.

The ministries and agencies regularly submitted reports on the work of their enterprises to the corresponding departments of the CC and the CM. These reports contained data on the fulfillment of the production plans, labor productivity, costs, and financial indicators. The departments of the CC and the CM would frequently send these data to the TsSU for verification. If TsSU found a discrepancy with its data, it would correct the ministries' reports. After some sort of a formal verification, the CC and CM would, as a rule, accept TsSU's data.[5] The same procedure took place with regard to the economic information presented to the top leadership by research institutes.

The foreign sources of information about the economic situation in the USSR were usually viewed as anti-Soviet propaganda by bourgeois economists consciously directed against the successful economic development of the USSR.

Did the leadership trust the accuracy of the information it received from TsSU? This question does not have a simple answer.[6] In any case, the official statistics were used unreservedly in all the Party's documents, presentations, reports and speeches, books and publications. Based on them the leadership judged the economic situation in the country, the advantages and disadvantages of the existing economic system, and conducted economic policy.

Information for the Leadership

The top leadership received from the TsSU a variety of bulletins, topical information (*ekspress-informatsiia*), analytical notes, and reports with a frequency ranging from weekly to annual. Weekly and monthly information (especially topical information and weekly bulletins) was usually brief and addressed issues of current interest. Quarterly and especially annual information was more comprehensive, with elements of analysis of the country's socioeconomic development and criticism of inadequacies in plan fulfillment and the realization of economic reforms. These criticisms were generally directed against specific ministries and agencies, such as Gosplan, Gossnab, and Gosstroi. The policies of the Party and the Soviet government were not subject to criticism.

TsSU would also present information to the authorities on demand as well as on its own initiative on topics of special current importance, such as: time lost due to absenteeism and machine idle time; failure to meet plan targets for quantity and quality of output; inadequacies in the work of construction enterprises and its low quality; loss of agricultural products in harvesting, storage and transport; interruptions in the supply of bread and other basic products to individual towns; unsatisfactory work of retail trade, catering, and health care organizations.

As a rule, TsSU would present its information to the Soviet leadership with the classifications 'Top Secret' (TS) or 'Secret' (S). It contained data which could not appear in the open press under the laws of the time. For instance, data on production and stocks of strategic raw materials, performance of particular branches of nonferrous metallurgy, the chemical and petrochemical industries, and some branches of machine-building, could not be published. The information presented to the Soviet leadership contained data regarding serious breaches of production and labor discipline, leading to accidents and huge economic losses; grave violations of financial discipline; monetary problems; growing inflationary processes; and much other negative information, which it was forbidden to publish in the open press.

TsSU's bulletins and reports classified TS or S contained aggregate statistics and analysis of the current economic and social situation in the country, with criticisms of the negative processes. TsSU included statistical data and specific facts that indicated the disproportions and imbalances in the development of Soviet economy, which grew worse from year to year. Enterprises and departments were reported for systematically missing their production targets and for not complying with their supply contracts.

Statistical bulletins and reports devoted much space to the low technological level of enterprises and organizations, the slow implementation of new technologies, the decline in the efficiency of production and the quality of output. Also included were international comparisons. It was noted that, especially in the late 1980s, the lag between the level of economic development of the USSR and that of the most developed foreign countries had grown significantly. Part of the reports was reserved for social problems. Here, along with the usual data on the fulfillment of measures decreed by the Party and government, were also data and notes concerning significant problems in this area. In the last two–three years of the Soviet regime, data were also reported on the decline in the standard of living and the growth of social tension in the country.

The main criterion used to classify statistical information was whether it was possible to determine, based on the particular piece of data, the country's military potential and the volume of strategic resources, or to uncover negative processes and phenomena discrediting the socialist system. The draft classification of data into TS, S, and OUO ('for official use only') prepared by TsSU would be examined by the appropriate ministries, agencies, and the departments of the CC and the CM. A commission including representatives of the Ministry of Defense, MVD, KGB, Gosplan, and corresponding departments of the CC and the CM organized all this work, collected the comments, generalized them, and compiled the final version of the document. The final document would be confirmed at the top.

All the information concerning the distribution of these materials was recorded in a separate list: the type of material (with a list of indicators), its classification (TS/S/OUO), the recipient organization, when and how many copies should be sent. The information presented to the top leadership was released in strict accordance with the number of recipients. These were usually the general secretary of the CPSU, the chairman of the CM, and individual members of the Politburo dealing with particular issues.

Academic economists had to use the information published in the open press. When it was necessary for a project included in the plan of a research institute, the top officials of the ministry or agency to which the institute was subordinated had to request the release of information (OUO and occasionally S) from TsSU. With the information also came an obligation not to publicize it.

Statistics Under Perestroika

In the 1980s, TsSU was an official body of considerable political weight, although at times it was subject to harsh criticism from the leadership of the country. The Decree of the CC and CM 'On Measures for the Radical Improvement of Statistics,' of 17 July 1987, stated that "The existing statistical system does not fully provide the reliable, timely, profoundly analytical information needed by the authorities in charge of the economy at national, branch and regional levels."[7] The same Decree also pointed out the necessity to expand significantly the role of the organs of official statistics in implementing the objectives of economic and social development of the country.

By the end of the 1980s, requests for statistical material linked to the perestroika of management, planning, and the economic mechanism—for instance, the performance of enterprises that had changed completely over to full *khozraschet,* self-financing, and self-repayment—became more frequent.[8] Another change that occurred at the same time was the increased attention to negative processes. New terms, indicators, and economic categories, such as inflation, crisis phenomena in the economy, hidden price increases, the ruble's purchasing power, cost-of-living index, shadow economy, private farms, and many others, started to appear in the TsSU's statistical materials and analytical notes. Inflationary processes were described using the balance of money incomes and expenditures of the population, indexes of the ruble's purchasing power, and price indexes for goods and services.

However, all this information was delivered in a factual-detailed way. It did not indicate, and using it, it was impossible to realize and foresee, that the country was heading for an immense economic catastrophe. The negative processes in the economy and in social life were explained away as temporary difficulties brought about by perestroika and the ongoing economic reforms.

After the 1987 Decree on statistics, the volume of openly published information significantly increased. Many indicators were declassified or reclassified to lesser categories (e.g., from TS to S, or from S to OUO). The main indicators of the balance of the national economy and input-output tables, the balance of money incomes and expenditures of the households, a number of balances of labor and labor resources, and many sectoral indicators such as the gross output of machine-building and its individual branches, were declassified. However, the information having to do with military output or discrediting the foundations of the political system, continued to be classified and unavailable for the general academic community.

'Improving' Published Statistics

If certain statistics happened not to coincide with the leadership's interests or its image of the economic situation in the country, or caused doubt as to their accuracy, corrections would be made. And these were often quite significant.

Thus, when the notorious anti-alcohol campaign was being conducted in 1985, the TsSU's calculations initially showed a decline in the 1985 growth rate of the national income compared to the previous year. The Party leadership did not like this, so TsSU changed its estimates by excluding production of alcoholic beverages in both 1984 and 1985. As a result, the rates of growth of the national income were overstated. The national income data for 1986 and 1987 were similarly distorted.[9]

Especially significant corrections and modifications were made in the reports on the completion of annual and five-year plans. Examples of such corrections are numerous but difficult to list, since they were usually made by the TsSU on an oral directive from CC and CM officials. Here is a typical example of changes to the statistical information. TsSU drafted a report on the completion of the Eighth Five-Year Plan (1966–1970) showing that output targets for the main types of industrial products had not been met. When the draft was discussed at the CC, it was suggested to report that the plan both as a whole and for industrial production had been successfully fulfilled. For this purpose, the notorious index of gross industrial production in value terms was 'stretched' to meet the target. At the meeting of the CC's commission examining the draft report, the first deputy director of TsSU, L. Volodarsky, noted that it was erroneous to emphasize a successful fulfillment of the plan for industrial production in the light of the underfulfillment of the plan for the main industrial products in physical units. He was told that he did not understand the great political significance of the report. Similar changes were made to the TsSU reports on the results of the annual and five-year plans almost until the end of the 1980s.

All statistical yearbooks, collections of articles, and other statistical materials intended for the open press would be previously examined at the CC. There, significant corrections would be made both in the presentation and in the actual data, primarily to eliminate negative information and to embellish reality.

The Exaggeration of Rates of Growth

The government's awareness of the country's economic situation in the 1980s was mainly determined by the accuracy and quality of the information it received, rather than by its volume. The official estimates of the level and rates of development of the Soviet economy had long been harshly criticized by individual Soviet and foreign economists. Their calculations showed that national income, industrial production, and real income were greatly overstated.

In the 1980s researchers from the Institute of Economics and Organization of Industrial Production of the Siberian Division of the AN USSR recalculated the growth rates of industrial production. These topics were explored on a wider scale by individual researchers from other institutes. Articles and books describing the methodological problems and results of the recalculations were published by K. Val'tukh, Yu. Petrov, et al. I would like to note the originality of the methods used by G. Khanin to calculate growth rates for an extended period, based on alternative estimates and indirect calculations. However, the estimates of the individual researchers often were not sufficiently well founded, mainly due to lack of the necessary information.

A radical reevaluation of both levels and growth rates of the main macroeconomic indicators was undertaken under my direction at Goskomstat's Institute of Statistics. Estimates of gross social product, national income, the output of industry, construction, agriculture, transport, and other branches of material production were developed for the USSR and Russia for the period 1961–1990. I submitted the report urging such a project, together with the methodology and detailed proposal, to the leadership of Goskomstat at the end of 1989. The *collegium* of Goskomstat included the project in the research plan of the Institute of Statistics. The work started at the beginning of 1990 and was completed by the middle of 1993.

Unique statistical materials, stored in official archives and previously inaccessible for research, were used for the calculations. For the evaluation of Soviet industry, over 200 sectors, subsectors, and types of production covering 80% of the total volume of industrial output were considered. Data on about 2,500 specific products were used for the calculations concerning industry.

The reevaluation for 1961–1990 revealed the official overstatement of the growth rates of gross social product by over 1.7 times, national income by 2.1 times, and industrial production by more than 2 times, of which machine-building and metalworking were overstated by 3.2 times.[10] In our estimation, the annual average growth rate of the gross social product and national income, respectively, decreased from 4.4% and 3.4% during the period 1961–1975 to 1.6% and 1.1% during 1976–1990. By contrast, the TsSU estimate for gross social product in 1976–1990 was 3.1%, and for the national income it was more than double our estimate. Since the population increased by 13.9% in 1975–1990, the per capita growth rate in that period was under 1% p.a.

In the 1980s, the downward trend accelerated, with the growth rate of gross social product averaging about 1% and that of the national income even less. According to official statistics, they were 2.8% and 2.4%, respectively, or two and a half times higher than our estimates.[11]

By overstating the rates of economic growth, especially in the 1980s, official statistics gave the leadership a relatively favorable picture of socio-economic development. The conclusion the leadership drew from these reports was that the Soviet economy was developing (albeit with shortcomings), and in certain branches it was even developing well. No warnings of the imminent collapse of the Soviet economy ever made their way into the reports presented to the authorities.

4.2 An Uninvited Advisor
Gregory Khanin

I Recalculate Soviet Growth Rates

In 1972 I defended my Candidate of Sciences dissertation on the stock market in capitalist countries. At that time I was the only academic specialist in this field in the USSR, and a Doctor of Sciences degree for further work in this field would not have taken long to get. However, I was drawn to the issues of the domestic economy and the fate of Soviet society. Any publications or dissertation defense on the subject would be out of the question, at least in the foreseeable future. Even much less controversial research was repressed at that time. I did not rule out direct persecution by the authorities. Still, my youth, academic inquisitiveness, and sense of civic responsibility prevailed.

I started estimating the real rates of growth of the Soviet economy since 1955. My immediate superior at the Control Systems Research Institute of the Ministry of Instrument-Making, V. Obraz, and the institute's director, F. Solodovnikov, encouraged my efforts.

In a year I came out with the first significant results, which definitely showed a steady decline in the growth of the Soviet economy since the late 1950s. According to my calculations and contrary to the widespread view of Soviet and Western scholars, the Eighth Five-Year Plan (1966–1970) was no exception to the slowdown trend. Considering the exhaustion of the extensive sources of growth, I argued that the decline might well lead to total stagnation by about the mid-1980s. From reading Western economic literature kept in the restricted section of the library, I knew that American Sovietologists had arrived at more positive results. I analyzed the causes of discrepancies in our estimates and was confident that my approach was correct.[12] It was not just the numbers, which I knew were authentic since almost identical results were obtained using different techniques, but the all-encompassing precipitous decay of Soviet society which convinced me that truth was on my side.

My findings pointed to an impending crisis of the economy and the society as a whole. I thought that the sooner the coming crisis was acknowledged, the sooner the Soviet leaders would undertake an economic reform. There was no doubt in my mind that the reform should be market-oriented.[13] Like a number of other Soviet economists, I was then a keen supporter of the market economy and thought that the transition to a regulated market economy would not only spur economic development but also promote the democratic evolution of Soviet society.

The first opportunity to make my results public came in 1973 at the TsEMI annual summer conference in Zvenigorod.[14] My friend Victor Volkonsky, a respected member of the Institute, invited me to attend, with the approval of the Institute's officials. I approached the chairman of one of the sessions (I believe Petrakov) and offered to give a talk on the subject in question. He agreed.

Hidden price increases, exaggerated output statistics, and other negative economic trends were no revelation to the people attending the meeting. As I later found out, a similar project was undertaken by S. Shatalin and B. Mikhalevsky at TsEMI in the mid-1960s.[15] Alternative estimates for industry as a whole and for its individual subsectors had also been calculated at other research institutes. Perhaps what made the strongest impression on the audience was the scope of my calculations and the diversity of estimating methods, some of which had not been used by anyone before. (At that time I used three different methods to estimate the growth of industrial production and two methods for the national income.) The fact that all this work was done by a single person was impressive. Also, my results were more pessimistic than those of the other researchers. The conclusion about the coming end of economic growth was convincingly demonstrated. After the talk I was bombarded with questions regarding my methodology and the results. There were about forty people from TsEMI and other Moscow economic institutes at my talk. Given the networking among economists, my presentation certainly became widely known among Moscow economists soon after the conference.

The following event describes the political climate in the country at the time. When I gave a detailed account of my presentation to my friend V. Shlapentokh, he asked me quite seriously whether I had noticed anybody following me. More than ten years after our conversation, the journal *Ogonek* published a report about a Ukrainian economist who performed similar work and was imprisoned for seven years after a search of his apartment unearthed his calculations.[16]

Over the course of the next three years I came up with several novel methods for estimating the real growth of industrial output, national income, construction, the capital stock, and the material intensity of national income. I considered the last two indicators to be my greatest achievement. They were either not calculated in the West and in the USSR, or calculated in an extremely inadequate way. I wrote a 250–page manuscript presenting the original data and detailed results of my calculations. My friends, colleagues, and superiors who read the manuscript, or heard me present it, reacted favorably.

Attempts to Inform the Leaders

Meanwhile, the Soviet economy was going downhill. I decided the time was ripe for my work to have an impact in steering the country along a more constructive course. I kept a close watch on the Soviet press and realized (time proved me right) that there were still proreform forces inside or close to the leadership. The writings of F. Burlatsky, G. Shakhnazarov, and V. Zagladin; of Academicians Arbatov and Inozemtsev; and of the publicists A. Bovin and E. Henry differed in tone and content from the pigheaded dogmatism prevailing in Soviet scholarly literature. Obviously, these people were backed by some influential politicians. I did not know who they were and, as time has shown, overestimated their capacity for political action.

I decided to bring the results of my work to the attention of the Soviet leadership, hoping that my findings could help chart a new economic and political course. I also sought to legitimize my research by appealing to the leadership. The thought of turning my material over to *samizdat* did occur to me, but I did not wish to jeopardize my freedom by engaging in direct political confrontation with the authorities.

The letters I sent to the official bodies were two- to three-page-long descriptions of the basic results of my research. More detailed calculations were offered 'upon request.' The letters ended with the conclusion about the impending danger of economic stagnation and the need to prevent it by reforming the economy. The reform was to significantly increase enterprise autonomy and expand the scope of market relations.

I took the letter addressed to L. Brezhnev to the notorious side-street housing—the forwarding office for letters addressed to the CC. I was notified that my letter had been received and forwarded to the appropriate department of the CC. That was the end of our correspondence.[17] The letter addressed to N. Baibakov and sent to Gosplan ended up in the hands of the chief of the macroeconomic [*svodnyi*] department, V. Vorobiev.[18] He met with me and was rather polite but tense during our conversation, perhaps fearing the potential repercussions. Much later I learned that around that time, Vorobiev presented a report on the state of the Soviet economy with ideas similar to mine on price inflation, real growth, and the impending dangers.[19]

I started to seek less direct and public avenues of relaying my message to the leadership. There might be someone in the leadership who was hiding his real views and who might need my results to initiate the political struggle. Examining the biographies of the members of the Politburo trying to pinpoint the 'closet' revisionist, I found them all rather mediocre. The only person who seemed to be somewhat out of the ordinary was A. Shelepin (of course, I was gravely mistaken as far as his political views were concerned). At that time, Gorbachev was not a member of the Politburo, nor even a secretary of the CC.

I put together a list of the most gifted Soviet scholars and political writers who might somehow be connected with revisionists in the Soviet leadership. The list was not too long, for there weren't many people in the country with these rare qualities. I also modified my presentation, writing a twenty-page paper with a detailed explanation of my methodology, the results, and the forecast for the year 1990. Complete termination of economic growth in the mid-1980s was predicted. An old Moscow typist who typed the paper declared with pride that she worked at a government office and had typed many important and classified documents in her lifetime. As she handed over the typed paper, she said to me with sympathy, "This is a bombshell."

The first man to look at my manuscript was Alexander Bovin, author of brilliant antidogmatic articles in *Izvestiia* who had worked in the CC for a long time. Bovin saw me at his office at the newspaper. He said that although he was not an economist and it was hard for him to judge my methodology, he thought that I was basically right. However, he gave no indication of wanting to pursue the matter. Bovin expressed his bitterness about what was happening in the country in no uncertain terms, saying, "Once he dies we will have to start from scratch." This confirmed the presence of an opposition group within the Party, but I was struck by how helpless it was. Suppose he did not die for another ten years, would the country just continue to go downhill?

My second potential intermediary was Ernst Henry, whose books *Hitler Against Europe* and *Hitler Against the USSR* impressed me in my youth.[20] His writings on China and international relations were superior in originality and brilliance to anything appearing in the Soviet political literature. His work on China targeted not only Mao but also Stalin, who at that time was supposed to be portrayed in a positive light. In our conversation and in his publications Henry manifested himself as an ardent opponent of all forms of totalitarianism. He held a low opinion of Brezhnev's regime and foresaw its inevitable collapse. I never heard him express hostility toward the West. On the contrary, he favorably evaluated many aspects of life in England compared with that in the USSR.

E. Henry read my manuscript and gave it to his friend from the Comintern days, S. Dalin, who was one of the biggest names in Soviet economics. (He mentioned the name very reluctantly in our last conversation, fearing repercussions for Dalin in case I made our dealings public.) Dalin's positive assessment largely determined Henry's respect for me. When I told Henry about the impending stagnation of the Soviet economy, he added "followed by a decline in production." The thought did occur to me, since my calculations pointed to the possibility of decline, but at the time this seemed so impossible that I was afraid to commit my thoughts to paper. Following our conversation I examined the possibility of a drop in output and soon incorporated it into my forecasts.

Henry praised Andropov, who, he said, read Hegel. He also praised V. Zagladin and G. Shakhnazarov, prominent officials of the CC dealing with the international Communist movement who shared many of his political views. Our meetings took place over a period of about two years. After that he began to eschew me, probably because he learned about my reputation as a semidissident. At one point he promised to pass my paper to V. Zagladin (then the first deputy chief of the Foreign Department of the CC), but later he retracted this proposal.

The third potential intermediary was Vasilii Seliunin, a popular journalist at the CC's newspaper *Sotsialisticheskaia industriia*. Soon after I made his acquaintance I discovered that he did not have any connections at the 'top.' Nonetheless, we formed a friendship which lasted until his death. Our joint article in *Novyi mir* (Seliunin and Khanin 1987) to a large extent marked the beginning of glasnost.

The Institute of the USA and Canada and the Institute of the World Economy and International Relations were the academic institutions close to the ruling circles in which I had a degree of trust. At the end of the 1970s I sent a letter containing a brief account of my results to Academician A. Arbatov. A rather amicable reply signed by V. Kudrov recommended me (citing Arbatov) to submit my paper for publication in the proceedings of the Institute intended for internal use only. But when I did that, I found out from Kudrov that this idea had been abandoned.

Around that time I gave a talk at the same department of the Institute of the World Economy and International Relations where my Candidate of Sciences dissertation had been reviewed. It was headed by S. Nikitin, an expert on economic indices and a decent person. Nikitin later told me that at the end of the 1950s, at the request of Academician E. Varga, he had estimated real growth rates for the Soviet economy. The project was terminated due to the hostile attitude of the CC. Both he and Varga got into trouble because of the work they did. My lecture was attended by about thirty people. I presented a highly detailed account of my methods, and the forecast which did not rule out a decline in GNP starting in the mid-1980s. Nikitin shared my bleak forecast of the future of the Soviet economy. There was a general feeling of a gloomy future and of inability to change it.

The Struggle to Publish the Results

I decided to distill the more 'palatable' elements from my work (methodology illustrated with examples from the various sectors of the economy) and to incorporate them into a Doctor of Sciences dissertation. The first thing to do for the defense was to get my results published. V. Volkonsky introduced my article to the editorial board of *Izvestiia Akademii Nauk. Seriia ekonomicheskaia* and persuaded his friend and chief editor, A. Anchishkin, to try publishing it. I am grateful to Anchishkin for proceeding with the publication in spite of the risk involved. At the time Anchishkin was one of the most influential Soviet economists and his support was important.

The one crucial factor that made the first publication (Khanin 1981) and the subsequent ones possible was the choice of the title and the manner of presentation. I made it a point to omit absolute figures. Only ratios were cited to show the difference in the final results generated by different methods. The primary focus of my articles was the explanation of my methodology and qualitative evidence pointing to new trends in the economy uncovered by alternative estimates. Any competent economist could easily generate absolute figures using the described techniques and the ratios of results cited. However, to the best of my knowledge, nobody in the USSR ever did that. The article went largely unnoticed because it was published in a journal with a small circulation.

Thanks to Alec Nove, who squeezed every last drop of information from my article, it became known in the West as early as 1983 [Nove 1983— Ed.]. Another article appeared later in the same journal with the material presented in much the same manner (Khanin 1984).

My attempts to defend the Doctor of Science dissertation started at TsEMI. Although headed by such allegedly liberal-minded scholars as N. Fedorenko and N. Petrakov, the Institute was unwilling to undertake such a risky venture. The Gosplan Research Institute, with its more conservative leadership, considered my dissertation for a few months. Nothing came of it. Defending my dissertation at the Economics Institute of the Siberian branch of the AN, headed by A. Aganbegian, was out of the question. It was Aganbegian who had ordered my dismissal from Novosibirsk University in the early 1970s and a few years later demanded an inquiry into my 'dubious' proposal to use world market prices to evaluate the performance of production units.[21]

Since dissertation defense required an outside review, I decided to give a talk at the Institute for Systems Research of the AN and the GKNT. Deputy director S. Shatalin, a reputed liberal, embraced the idea of my lecture and scheduled it for the spring of 1986. By that time I had modified my method of estimating the growth of the fixed capital stock. The new method yielded a much steeper decline of the capital stock growth rates. This, together with other factors, meant a bigger future fall in the national income. According to my calculations, continuation of the existing trends would mean a 20% drop of the national income by 1990. Emboldened by the start of perestroika, I announced this gloomy projection in my lecture. The auditorium had standing room only. One of the first comments from the audience was: "I don't understand why we have to listen to all this anti-Soviet stuff." I calmly replied that there was nothing anti-Soviet about it, just the objective presentation of facts. To my surprise, there were few questions. Shatalin himself asked a few irrelevant and even strange questions, thanked me, declared the seminar closed, and retreated to his office. When I started to gather my charts, one of the staff said to me: "Did you notice how nervous he was during your lecture? He cut off the discussion when he realized just how dangerous the paper was." When I came back to Shatalin's office he was rushing out to some meeting. As we were saying our good-byes in the foyer, he said: "The only man who can help you is Gorbachev."

The only place left for dissertation defense was A. Anchishkin's Institute for Economic Forecasting. I dealt primarily with his deputy Yu. Yaremenko, an honest and competent economist. The Institute considered my dissertation for about two years. It was favorably discussed on several occasions. However, Yaremenko would not risk arranging the defense even as late as 1986, that is, after the start of perestroika, and finally turned it down.

Having earlier received firm assurances for the defense of my dissertation from the Institute for Economic Forecasting, I had resigned from my part-time teaching job at the Institute for Continuing Education of the Ministry of Construction Materials, which I had held for seven years. When the defense fell through and I returned to Novosibirsk in the summer of 1986, I could not find a job in my field and had to teach geography at a high school in a nearby town for half a year. In the late fall of 1986 I was invited to the newly formed Tuva Interdisciplinary Department of the Siberian branch of the AN USSR in Kyzyl. I returned to Novosibirsk at the end of 1989 after finding a job in an organization that dealt with computer programming.

Starting in 1987, I could publish my work with no restrictions. The national authorities still expressed very little interest in my research, although by that time it was widely known both in the USSR and abroad. Only in 1989, at V. Volkonsky's request, was I included in the Commission on Improving Price and Output Statistics. I attended one of its meetings, but received no further materials from the Commission. Government and Party officials, as well as the chieftains of academic economics, judged a scholar on the basis of his official status and the extent of his loyalty. Judged by either of these criteria I was unacceptable.

Soviet Economics and Soviet Power

In the 1970s and 1980s there was limited opportunity to conduct research even on such obviously sensitive topics as the reliability of statistics, and to share the results with the scientific community. Even prior to my first publication I spoke publicly about my research many times without being subjected to direct persecution. I believe my experience was more typical than that of the Ukrainian economist mentioned above. The Ukrainian KGB was notorious for its zeal in rooting out dissent. Not to be played down is the personal decency of my immediate superiors, although I have not heard of any of them being harassed for the kind of research I was doing.

Soviet economic officials and academics had long known about the distortions in the official economic data. There had been numerous discussions of the issue in the economics literature since the 1920s (see Khanin 1991). However, the debate centered around methodological issues. The publication of alternative estimates of economic growth was forbidden. Nevertheless, such estimates were made. I know of the estimates for the national economy by S. Nikitin, and by S. Shatalin and B. Mikhalevsky. The estimates for particular sectors were even more numerous. The academic community was extremely interested in these results. The state and Party organs were extremely wary of alternative estimates since they destroyed the myth of the planned economy's superiority. This was especially true after 1960, when the Soviet Union started lagging behind in the economic race with the capitalist countries.

While the government and Party organs were afraid of the alternative estimates, they also felt the need for objective information. During the mid- to late 1970s the official statistics were perceived as totally false by all informed persons. There was a general consensus regarding the sorry state of the economy and its inevitable decline. However, the higher the level of the hierarchy, the more hostile the officials were toward the disclosure of the true state of the Soviet economy, for it meant an indictment of their economic policy.

It seems that the KGB and some of its top officials were more eager to uncover the true state of the country's economy, for they were less involved in the development of economic policy. Also, being well-informed about the deteriorating situation, they feared for the future of the system. Even the KGB, however, was forced to proceed with its hands tied behind its back, since exercising too much independent initiative meant trouble. A strange incident in the summer of 1982 suggests that economists were not the only people interested in my work. I was standing on the street when a man approached me. He told me that he was a colonel in the KGB and produced his identity documents to prove this. We had an innocent conversation, and then he invited me out on Sunday for a boat trip. Since I was very hostile to the KGB and fearful of some dirty trick, I declined his invitation. No further attempts to contact me were undertaken. Later on, when I reflected on the significance of this approach, I came to the conclusion that the KGB was interested in my research and wanted to obtain additional and possibly reliable information about the true state of the Soviet economy. From Tatiana Koriagina, who then worked in Gosplan's research institute, I heard that at about the same time the KGB displayed great interest in the work of the planners. It interviewed many employees of the institute and of Gosplan itself, trying to pinpoint the reasons for the failure of the economy and the poor performance of the planning bodies.

Given the structure of the Party and the government, any unauthorized initiative, even by a high-ranking official, was quashed no matter how much it served the interests of the system. The officials were taught this lesson by the fate of the numerous 'anti-Party factions.' The system was driving itself into a corner. By that time, the upper layer of Soviet officials as a rule lacked the civil courage or the commitment to Communist ideology necessary to take an independent action, even though it entailed no risk of being killed or imprisoned. The dissenting sentiments inside the Party and government apparatus failed to materialize into any concrete action.

Even though the Soviet leadership knew about the fabrication of the official statistics and the deteriorating economic situation, the true magnitude of the impending crisis was underestimated. This was due, in part, to a lack of reliable alternative data on economic growth. Moreover, the Soviet leadership failed to recognize the general social crisis enveloping the country as a result of its previous course of development. The official academic world was unable to provide such information, while the unofficial one lacked access to the leadership.

The desirability of market-type reforms was widely recognized. However, the proponents of reform felt insecure and afraid to voice their views for fear of being accused of heresy and being expelled from the ruling elite. This group was waiting for Brezhnev's death and the coming crisis, hoping to gain power and implement the reforms afterward.

4.3 The View from Gosplan: Growth to the Year 2000
Gennadii Zoteev

Long-Term Planning at Gosplan

In 1973 Gosplan, jointly with the AN and the GKNT, was entrusted with long-range forecasting of technological, social, and economic trends. Highly detailed projections fifteen–twenty years into the future, broken down into five-year periods, were to be issued every five years. The very energetic president of the AN, M. Keldysh, devoted substantial attention to this project, picking Alexander Anchishkin as its chief organizer. Anchishkin, elected a corresponding member of the AN USSR in 1981, was the creator of the Comprehensive Program of technological progress and its socioeconomic ramifications.

Initially, the forecasts extended to the year 1990 and were selectively used by Gosplan in constructing the 1976–1980 Five-Year Plan. The next round of forecasts extended to the year 2000, with the 1981–1985 period elaborated in greater detail. By the time this project was finished around 1980, Anchishkin enjoyed a reputation as a great organizer of large-scale preplanning and forecasting projects. N. Baibakov [then chairman of Gosplan] invited him to form a department in Gosplan devoted exclusively to long-range planning. The department, composed of six subdivisions (fifty posts), was created in April 1982, and I was invited to head the subdivision on the balance of the national economy.

The CC, and in particular its Economic Department, kept a close eye on the department's first steps. One reason for this was their need for Gosplan's help in drafting the new version of the Program of the CPSU. The embarrassing experience of Khrushchev's Party Program with his promise to build Communism by the year 1980 and to catch up and overtake the United States in terms of productivity was still very much alive. The Party apparatchiks wanted to save the new Program from turning into a target of numerous jokes as was the case with Khrushchev's Program.

One of the main tasks assigned to Gosplan's newly formed Department of Long-Range Economic and Social Development was to compile the estimates of the country's economic growth until the year 2000. Subsequently, certain key economic indicators were to be incorporated into the new draft version of the Party Program, assuming the status of political directives.

Gosplan's Outlook in the Early 1980s

Despite the substantial decline in the rates of economic growth, the war in Afghanistan, the infirmity of many members of the Politburo, problems with the food supply, and numerous other challenges, Gosplan officials showed no signs of confusion or deep concern, or of anticipating an impending collapse. On the other hand, there were no signs of optimism either, as no one expected any major changes or held high expectations for the future.[22] Gosplan was characterized by calm and inertia, and worked in low key without any great ambitions. I was struck by this placidity and self-assurance. Similar attitudes prevailed in the Economic Department of the CC. Naturally, the bosses were not happy about plans not being fulfilled, about the shortages and poor quality of consumer goods, but this dissatisfaction was low-key and matter-of-fact.

My sources of information expanded considerably in the new job. A huge stream of current statistical information, provided primarily by TsSU, was mostly stamped 'For Official Use Only,' but sometimes 'Secret' and 'Top Secret.' Every employee had a safe and a system of special notepads in which to write classified data. Initially, I would spend hours at my desk copying the data into my notepads. At that time, photocopying was generally discouraged, and photocopying classified material was very dangerous, since the KGB had a formidable presence in Gosplan.

There was also an incessant stream of government correspondence (resolutions, decrees, memos, background briefs, requests from the ministries and departments). Professional contacts with my immediate superiors and colleagues from other departments; the *collegium* meetings; meetings of the vice-chairmen of Gosplan; and conferences at the CC CPSU, Ministry of Finance, Gossnab, and TsSU were perhaps the most valuable source of information. Analysis of this information yielded fascinating results.

Even before I started to work at Gosplan, I realized (thanks primarily to Western literature on the Soviet economy) that the planning system was highly inflexible, sluggish, and inefficient. However, I thought this system had no internal reason to rapidly self-destruct and was quite capable of just drifting in the current of economic history for at least another twenty–thirty years. My thesis, shared by many of my colleagues in Gosplan, was that the Soviet system was inefficient but stable. The first six months of work at Gosplan only served to reinforce my position. Indeed, witnessing the blatant incompetence of the upper echelon of management led me to reformulate my thesis: if the country is ruled by such dimwits and it has still not crumbled, then the system is strong. It can even operate on a kind of 'automatic pilot.'

The rank-and-file employees of Gosplan (particularly those in the branch departments) were highly competent and professional, while the vice-chairmen and heads of departments were often economically ignorant. However, obedience and Soviet coercive command-style ethics forced even the good economists to keep their mouths shut or, at the very least, to eschew major arguments with senior personnel even if the latter made patently incompetent decisions. For decades there existed in Gosplan an 'army mentality.' As a rule, if a superior called a specialist into his office, it was simply to dictate a decision that was made beforehand based on political, ideological, careerist, bureaucratic, or other noneconomic considerations. The specialist's task was to 'validate' the decision, no matter how flawed it was. "Orders are not discussed, they are carried out"—this was the motto of the command economy.

Thank God the system's inertia was so strong that many decisions (both good and bad) were simply never executed. Particularly harmful for the

Soviet economic system were the various political initiatives arising from the bowels of the CC apparatus and then passed on to Gosplan for further elaboration and implementation. Gosplan's staff was extremely adept at seeking out ways to let some new political-ideological venture initiated by the CC 'slide,' and did not hide its disregard for the political *apparatchiks.*

Gosplan Meets Gorbachev

Gosplan had considerable clout when A.N. Kosygin was chairman of the CM. Kosygin relied heavily on Gosplan and acted as a buffer between the Party and the government when contradictions arose. By standing up for Gosplan, Kosygin was protecting his own position. Gosplan's political weight declined when Kosygin ceased to be chairman of the CM. Gosplan's chairman, N.K. Baibakov, never challenged the limits on Gosplan's political role established by Stalin. The first person to engage in a major confrontation with Gosplan weakened by Kosygin's retirement was Gorbachev.

The May 1982 Plenum of the CC approved the Food Program, but did not establish the amount of money (primarily capital investment) Gosplan was to allocate to the agricultural sector. Gorbachev, who was a member of the Politburo, was in charge of devising and implementing the Food Program. He wanted to force as many concessions from Gosplan as he could, for it was Gosplan that determined, on the basis of the annual plans, the allocation of funds to the various branches and regions of the country.

The Eleventh Five-Year Plan (1981–1985) had already been compiled and adopted by the Party Congress. A significant increase in allocations to the agricultural sector would wreak havoc with the plan's priorities and proportions. The Food Program covered the period from 1981 to 1990, so Gorbachev put all his chips on the Twelfth Five-Year Plan (1986–1990). Work on that plan had not yet started, presenting him with an opportunity to put pressure on Gosplan to guarantee a substantial increase in the share of projected capital investment for agriculture.

Gosplan argued that it was too early to set the sectoral shares of capital investment for the Twelfth Five-Year Plan since the total amount of investment was calculated in the course of compiling the plan, and that the whole determines the parts rather than the other way around. However, Gosplan's arguments met with Gorbachev's political bullheadedness. His political mentality at that time was typically Soviet—political will transcended common sense.[23]

I was a member of a special task force which at the end of 1982 drafted a memo to the government on this subject. If my memory is correct, the memo was roughly entitled 'The Volume and Structure of Capital Investment in the Twelfth Five-Year Plan' and contained the following basic points:

- A huge number of construction projects has already been started; the share of gross investment in the Soviet GNP is one of the highest in the world.
- Investment is metal-intensive, and therefore dependent on the ferrous metals sector. The USSR is already the world's biggest producer of pig iron, steel, and rolled metal. Investment growth will require further increases in production of these materials.
- These and other considerations limit the feasible increase in investment to 5–7% in 1986–1990.
- Given this modest rate of growth, the three major sectors—agro-industrial (Gorbachev), military-industrial (Ustinov), and fuel-energy (Dolgikh)—would swallow up to 85% of all investment in production. The remaining 15% would be insufficient even to sustain the existing level of output in other branches of the economy (metallurgy, chemical, civilian machine-building, transportation).
- The problems of agriculture should be solved not by throwing more investment into this sector, but by balancing livestock numbers with the availability of feed and by improving the processing of raw materials.

Gosplan skillfully pounced on the opportunity to pit the interests of the military-industrial lobby in the Party against its agricultural counterpart. There was a story circulating in Gosplan that Baibakov, when rebuked over the telephone by Gorbachev and Ustinov for the lack of funds, employed each one's arguments against the other. He would cite Gorbachev's demands to convey to Ustinov the political need to bolster the material-technological base of the agricultural sector, which called for huge investments. In speaking with Gorbachev, he would allude to Ustinov's arguments supporting a strong national defense.

The Projection Toward the Year 2000

The special Party and government decree on the preparation of the projections to the year 2000 and the Twelfth Five-Year Plan marked a shift in the relationship between Gosplan and the top political leadership. This project, which started in 1983, involved several consecutive stages.

First, the AN, Gosplan, and the GKNT were to develop a set of technological and socioeconomic forecasts to the year 2005, broken down into four five-year periods. Next, Gosplan, together with the AN, GKNT, and

Gosstroi, as well as other agencies, were to develop a 'Concept of Economic and Social Development to the Year 2000,' with the Twelfth Five-Year Plan (1986–1990) delineated in greater detail. The Concept was to be reviewed and approved by the CM.

After that, Gosplan, the ministries and other agencies as well as the Union republics were to develop the 'Draft of the Main Directions for Economic and Social Development in 1986–1990 and to the Year 2000.' The Draft was to be adopted by the Congress of the CPSU. The final stage involved the compilation of the detailed Five-Year Plan broken down into annual plans.

This scheme emerged during the period of Chernenko and Andropov, neither of whom showed any inkling for reform. The reigning idea of that period was to improve socialism, to fine-tune the economic mechanism based on planning. The ideology of acceleration was not in the air. The leadership entertained more modest ambitions, especially since Reagan seriously scared them by the Strategic Defense Initiative. For the most part, the economic-political elite stuck to the commonsense principle "slow and steady wins the race."

At that time my career took a new turn. After a few months on the job as the head of the Department of Long-Range Social and Economic Development, Anchishkin suffered a heart attack. Vorobiev was appointed my new boss. I became the virtual leader of the team in charge of drafting the Concept.

The Concept was conceived not as a traditional plan document loaded with figures disaggregated along ministerial, departmental, and territorial lines, but as a political-economic statement outlining various government policies (prices, social, technological, foreign trade, industrial, agricultural). It was a very generalized document, brief and to the point.

The leitmotif of the initial version of the Concept was the deteriorating prospect for the Soviet economy caused by natural and demographic factors as well as by the obsolescence of fixed capital. The replacement of the latter would take several five-year periods because of the low expected rates of growth of investment. The Soviet economy approached the late 1980s bearing a heavy burden of unresolved problems, including the quality of labor; the quality of goods; the wasteful utilization of resources; a huge number of unfinished construction projects; backward agriculture; exports heavily skewed toward a few raw materials; and strong dependence on the import of grain, consumer goods, and technology.

While listing the symptoms, we rarely named their causes. The ideological taboos were impossible to overcome. The planned system and its flaws could not be named as the main causes of economic backwardness and

stagnation. Instead we focused on the mistaken policies of the previous decision makers and their lackadaisical attitude toward their responsibilities. Nevertheless, the Concept did acknowledge that the negative economic trends
continued and the burden of unresolved problems kept on growing. This cliché
statement was followed by equally banal recommendations: "we must live and
build within our means," "wages must be earned," and "the economy must be
economical." In short, the trends and phenomena were recognized but their
reasons were either swept under the rug or discussed implicitly, while the
suggested solutions represented mostly a set of tautologies.

Yet one important point was incessantly underscored by Gosplan—the
oil price boom was over and world fuel prices were likely to drop. It was
imperative that the 'holy cows' of the Soviet economy, defense and agriculture, find less expensive ways to sustain themselves. 'Fraternal' aid to
Cuba, Vietnam, and the European CMEA member countries had to be
scaled down. The economy had exhausted its capacity to support external
expansion, and it was necessary to limit noneconomic and ideological aspects of economic decisions.

The first version of Gosplan's Concept (dating to about January–February
of 1983) focused on defending the low projected rates of GNP growth to the
year 2000. For instance, the report sent to Baibakov in February 1983 used
the following arguments:

> The average annual growth rate of utilized national income is projected to be
> in the 2.8 3.2% range in 1986–2000. The Department of Long-Range Plan-
> ning studied the sources of growth of national income for the Tenth Five-
> Year Plan and concluded that about 0.8–1.0 percentage points of the growth
> rate was due to the lower quality of foodstuffs, growth in the sale of vodka
> and other alcoholic beverages, and an increase in world prices of fuel ex-
> ported to Western countries during 1979–1980. Discounting these factors,
> the real economic growth rate for 1976–1980 was about 2.8–3.0%, as op-
> posed to 3.8% published by TsSU.
>
> The projected average annual growth rate of the national income for
> 1981–1985 is 2.9%, which means that the real annual rate of economic
> growth for the 1976–1985 period is under 3%. One of the objectives set in
> the Concept is to sustain the current rates of growth for the entire 1986–2000
> period.

The first official version of the Concept, sent to the government in September 1984, projected the average annual growth rate of national income
as 2.8–3.2% for 1986–2000. The growth of investment for each five-year
period was estimated at no more than 7–9%. Converting these figures to the
method used by the CIA would imply a rate of GNP growth no higher than
1.5% p.a. for 1986–2000. Since I was personally responsible for macroeco-

nomic calculations and had a vast amount of information from the various sectoral departments at my disposal, I argued (and I still stick to my words) that this alternative of development of the Soviet economy was feasible. The proposed course was the maximum that could be achieved by the command system in its decline.

The Changing Official Reaction to Gosplan's Projection

The Concept was considered at the Presidium of the CM in September 1984. The participants in that meeting included Tikhonov (then chairman of the CM), Gromyko, Dolgikh, and Baibakov. According to Vorobiev, the discussion proceeded smoothly (I ranked too low to qualify for such meetings). Gromyko spoke a lot, but nothing really important was said and the resolution called for the revision of the Concept. I am not certain about Gorbachev's personal position with regard to the Concept, but I do know he had the document on his desk.[24] Once Gorbachev became the general secretary, the Concept underwent major revisions.

Andropov announced straight out that he had no ready prescriptions on how to improve the centrally planned economy's performance significantly. As a result, he emphasized discipline, holding officials responsible for the assigned tasks, a kind of general tightening of the screws of the loose government and economic machinery. Essentially, Andropov built on Gosplan's recommendations for greater centralization of the economy in order to eliminate or curtail many ruinously expensive practices (grain imports, proliferation of investment projects, growth of wages). One can only guess Andropov's motives, but his choice of strategy was logically consistent for three reasons: as chairman of the KGB he was much better informed than Gorbachev about the true state of the Soviet economy; he trusted Gosplan and kept the likes of such dilettante economic advisors as Aganbegian, Shatalin, Abalkin, and Petrakov at a distance; unlike Gorbachev, he did not suffer from the disease of narcissism.[25] A pragmatic thinker concerned with the survival of the Soviet empire, he had an inborn imperial mentality.

On the other hand, Gorbachev's provincialism surfaced already during the preparation of the Food Program. From the outset, Gorbachev dreamed of the empire surging ahead, rather than merely surviving. He saw himself as the new Messiah, the creator of the new socialist thinking. Gorbachev's rise to power dramatically changed the tone of the Concept and the 'Main Directions' which were still on the drawing board. The 'modest figures' projected by Gosplan began to grow like mushrooms. Khrushchev's fancy to catch up with the United States in terms of development and labor productivity was revived. Gorbachev's pet idea of acceleration shifted Gosplan's efforts toward the rates of growth of the national income.

The head of a section of the CC Economic Department, V.F. Karachkov, in a private conversation with me chided Gosplan for allegedly lacking faith in the potential of the Soviet economy, for assuming a defeatist posture, and for failing to recognize the political significance of the motivating role of a taut plan. I tried to argue that it is not the growth rate per se, but the real goods behind it that matter. If the Soviet economy continues to increase the output of pig iron, steel, cement, tractors, tanks, and harvesters, it might formally grow at a higher rate. But this will be attained at the cost of lowering the efficiency of resource utilization, skewing the structure of the economy toward extractive industry, and making it even more grotesque. All these arguments were rejected by the *apparatchik* from the CC. He demanded an all-round economic upsurge, including better quality of goods, higher rates of growth, a shift of exports from fuel to processed goods, full balance among the flows in the economy, and so on and so forth.

The September 1984 version of the Concept began to crumble under Ryzhkov's pressure. As secretary of the CC for the economy, he demanded from Gosplan 'good figures' for all indicators. The first line of defense, which was put up by Gosplan already during the rule of Chernenko-Andropov—the very low growth rate of investment (5–7% for 1986–1990)—was breached immediately. Planned investment growth was increased to 12–15%, and then to 20–22%.

The 2.5–fold target growth rate of labor productivity in 1986–2000, later incorporated into the draft 'Main Directions,' had a purely political origin. TsSU estimated that in the early 1980s labor productivity in the USSR was 40% of that in the United States, that is, it lagged behind by 2.5 times. In effect, the 2.5–fold targeted growth of labor productivity was a political directive aimed at attaining by the year 2000 the U.S. labor productivity of the early 1980s.

Gosplan's work on the Concept and the 'Main Directions' in 1985–1986 became politicized and ideologized in large measure due to Ryzhkov, who was the Secretary of the CC for the economy [before he became chairman of the CM in September 1985]. He came to Gosplan in 1979 never having overcome his production engineer's mentality. Perhaps it was Vorobiev's mistake to discuss his ideas regarding long-range economic prospects only with Baibakov, to whom he had access and whose personal trust he enjoyed.[26] Vorobiev did not particularly try to convey his understanding of the situation to the vice-chairmen of Gosplan—Ryzhkov, Lalaiants, Sitarian, Sliun'kov, Paskar', and Vanchikov—nor to Baibakov's other deputies.

Under pressure from Ryzhkov, Gosplan prepared materials for the 'Main

Directions' which were insufficiently elaborated, poorly coordinated, and suffered from numerous discrepancies. It was becoming clear that the days of the old Brezhnev-Kosygin guard—such as Tikhonov, Arkhipov, Baibakov, and Garbuzov—were numbered, and that a new generation was vying for power. Ryzhkov's transfer to the CC increased the influence of Sitarian and Vid. Ryzhkov trusted both of them and took their suggestions seriously. Both had the same servile mentality and espoused the 'your wish is my command' principle.

Aganbegian, who was newly transferred to Moscow, together with Sitarian and other members of the team drafting the documents for the upcoming Party Congress, were inventing new sources of acceleration of the Soviet economy in a dacha in Volynskoe. I recall having to recalculate the balance of the national economy several times at the request of the Economic Department of the CC. We then had to submit the results, presented as Gosplan's figures, to Volynskoe, where further 'improvements' were made.

The key ideas of the acceleration program were definitely born outside Gosplan. Gosplan was unfortunate and guilty at the same time for operating like a huge iron which irons indiscriminately everything that is put on the ironing board. In the old Soviet way, Gosplan was a pliant and obedient body in the hands of the political leadership, and was incapable of standing its ground and resisting pressure exerted from above. This was the established practice under Stalin, Khrushchev, and Brezhnev. It persisted under Gorbachev as well.

4.4 The Changing View from the Top

4.4.1 Under Andropov and Gorbachev
Vadim Medvedev

Realization of the approaching economic disaster grew in certain circles of Soviet society even in the last years of Brezhnev's rule. Economic growth slowdown, declining efficiency, proliferating shortages, hidden decline in the real value of the ruble, and worsening of social problems, could not go unnoticed. The gradual expansion of business, tourism, and information contacts with the West led to increasingly unfavorable comparisons of our standard of living. More and more frequently, sharp warnings about particular issues appeared in the press, as memoranda to the governing bodies, or in conference reports (in particular by economists). However, these signals were lost in the false picture of well-being that was painted in the leadership's speeches and in the chorus of praise for "the outstanding leader and fighter for peace" Brezhnev. Proposals to discuss some of the more critical problems of the country's development within the Party encountered the leadership's misunderstanding and its inability to formulate and solve these problems. The intention to hold a plenum on technological progress was announced several times, and the preparations for the plenum were said to be under way. However, it was never actually conducted under the Brezhnev administration.

Only with the coming to power of Yu.V. Andropov did the CC initiate an honest analysis of the situation in the country, primarily in the economy. Andropov entrusted this work to Gorbachev, who under him became practically the second in command, and to Ryzhkov, the newly elected secretary of the CC for economic issues. The analysis was conducted with the cooperation of the leading national centers for economic research, with active participation of Academicians A.G. Aganbegian, L.I. Abalkin, T.I. Zaslavskaia, G.A. Arbatov, P.N. Fedoseev, A.A. Nikonov, A.N. Lukinov, E.M. Primakov, and O.T. Bogomolov, and of the well-known economists S.A. Sitarian, R.A. Belousov, G.Kh. Popov, G.A. Egiazarian, and V.A. Medvedev. A.N. Yakovlev also joined this work from 1983.

By that time, economic growth in the Soviet Union had fizzled out. During 1981 and 1982, even according to official statistics, the growth rate of industrial production fell almost to zero. The growth of the real incomes of the population also ceased.[27] For the economists who worked with Gorbachev on the analysis of the situation and the development of a new economic policy, it was sufficiently clear the official statistics distorted many indicators of the growth and structure of the economy, and the level and dynamics of incomes. For example, the share of basic sectors in the economy was underestimated, because the prices of their products did not include capital cost, and undercounted current cost. Neither was it taken into account that net income was mainly concentrated in the prices of final products.

No serious economist believed the data on military expenditures as indicated in the state budget. While no breakdown was ever published, the professionals knew that the reported number related to the expenditures for the maintenance of the personnel of the armed forces only, without expenditures for acquiring weapons and military materiel, research and development, and other items. The alternative estimates of the size of the Soviet economy relative to that of developed Western countries, prepared by the Institute of World Economy and International Relations, differed significantly from the official ones. Many of the mistakes of the official statistics were due to the false assumption about the absence of inflation in the Soviet Union.

This is why we proceeded from the assumption that at the beginning of the 1980s the growth of industrial production had stopped, and the real income of the population had actually declined, even though this was not confirmed by the data of the TsSU.

The academics and experts were practically unanimous in their diagnosis.[28] The economic stagnation resulted from the exhaustion of the possibilities for extensive economic growth, and the slow transition to intensive growth based on technological progress. This was especially evident from comparisons with the fundamental changes experienced in the economies of developed Western countries, directed toward resource saving, structural change toward technologically advanced production, low pollution and ecological soundness, and a new quality and high skill of the worker.

Militarization occupied a special place among the reasons for the backwardness of the Soviet economy. Military industry was a privileged sector, separated by a high wall from the civilian economy. It represented a different world, a different technological level, concentrating the best workers, engineers, and scientists, and getting the most valuable resources without constraint. For a long time, even high officials of the CC, such as heads of departments and CC secretaries, had no access to information on military and military-economic issues, which was surrounded by a strict taboo. National defense was regarded as the holy of holies. It was widely argued that the people would forgive the leadership anything but a repetition of the tragedy at the beginning of World War II, and that this was the primary political priority. We remained under the spell of such arguments under Andropov and even for some time after Gorbachev came to power. Only gradually, under the pressure of extremely acute economic problems, did the scales fall from our eyes. It became obvious that without a reduction in the burden of military expenditures it would not be possible to resolve the urgent socioeconomic problems. This, to a large extent, stimulated the development of a new military doctrine and a new foreign policy aimed at stopping the arms race.

The economic crisis was temporarily delayed by favorable world market conditions. World prices of petroleum and petroleum products increased approximately tenfold from the early 1970s through the early 1980s. The opening up in the 1960s of rich fuel reserves in Western Siberia permitted the country to export 207.6 billion rubles (more than $300 billion) worth of petroleum and petroleum products in 1971–1985. This windfall turned into a real misfortune. While the West in response to the growth of energy prices turned to resource saving and alternative sources of energy, the Soviet economy was debauched by the abundance of apparently cheap fuel. However, from 1982, oil prices started to decline, falling by 3 to 3.5 times in the next six to seven years. The oil bonanza continued for some time, thanks to increasing production and export of fuel. But at the end of the 1980s the slowing of the rate of increase and then a fall in petroleum production, combined with declining petroleum prices, resulted in a sharp decrease of hard currency revenue from the sale of petroleum and petroleum products.

4.4.2 Under Chernenko
Igor Prostiakov

The reforms of 1965 and 1979 did not bring the expected results. This is particularly true of the 1979 reform, planned by a very small group of people headed by Kosygin, who was increasingly falling into Brezhnev's disfavor. Other leaders had no stake in the reform, and when Kosygin left [in 1980], it was practically abandoned. Why, despite this, were new reform measures proposed in 1984?

Apart from poor economic performance, there were flaws in the command system that could no longer be ignored. Many regional functionaries objected to their subservient role and complete dependence on Moscow. The regions no longer wanted to settle for a situation where the central government concentrated in its hands all the financial resources and then doled them out arbitrarily. As a result, the regions' prosperity depended on their relationship with the central institutions and individual high-ranking officials rather than on their economic efficiency. Enterprises belonging to the sectoral ministries disposed of 70–80% of the financial and other resources in a region. Yet the ministries frequently ignored the interests of the regions where their plants were located, making investment and hiring decisions without consulting with the regional authorities.

The labor collectives and managers of enterprises simply executed orders handed down from above, no matter whether they were reasonable or absurd. Perhaps the main scourge of the system was the indifference and apathy of the great majority of the working population, their inability to think independently, social parasitism, and a low level of discipline. Many people no longer saw any link between their income and their personal effort. People lost a sense of reasonable expectations and began to think that the government and society are obliged to support them regardless of whether it has the means to do so.

Notes

1. In 1987, TsSU was renamed Goskomstat. What is written in the text about TsSU is also relevant for Goskomstat.
2. The top leadership received detailed reports on the military industry directly

from the VPK ministries, and aggregated data from the special (i.e., military) department of Gosplan. TsSU had access to the total output of the military industry in value terms, and some other data needed for compiling the main macroeconomic aggregates (gross social product, national income, industrial output).

3. By the Resolution of the CM of 6 September 1957. Exception was made for the production of defense equipment in physical terms.

4. The reports of the ministries did not encompass all the enterprises in a given sector, since enterprises in a given sector would often be subordinated to different ministries.

5. The ministries' production plan fulfillment and other reports were often exaggerated. To avoid complications, many ministries and agencies would clear their data with TsSU in advance.

6. In some cases they clearly did not. On one occasion, when Brezhnev wanted information on food prices at the Moscow markets, he did not request it from TsSU. Instead he turned to his son-in-law at the Ministry of Internal Affairs and asked him to prepare a report on the subject. This was quickly done and sent to Brezhnev (Churbanov 1992, p. 76). In 1971, Kosygin refused to accept the official data according to which real wages then were eight times higher than in 1913. Himself born in 1904 and the son of a skilled worker who had lived in a three-room apartment and supported himself, his wife, and three children out of his wages, he realized that this official statistic could not be true (Fetisov 1997, pp. 231–232). Similarly, the leaders and their economic advisors in 1985–1987 were skeptical of the macroeconomic statistics of TsSU (Medvedev, Chapter 4.4.1). This skepticism was one of the factors leading to the 1987 decree discussed below. [Ed.]

7. See *Vestnik statistiki,* no. 8, 1987. [Ed.]

8. 'Self-repayment' means the generation at enterprise level of sufficient revenue to cover full costs (including normal profit). The revenue may be transferred to a higher body. 'Self-financing' means the generation and retention at enterprise level of sufficient revenue to cover full costs (including normal profit). [Ed.]

9. Corrected data were subsequently published in the statistical yearbook for 1988.

10. The growth of national income was more exaggerated than that of gross social product due to the systematic underestimation of the growth of material cost, so as to show a declining material intensity of production. Our calculations revealed that the growth of material cost actually outpaced that of the gross social product.

11. The results of the reevaluation, along with a report which contained a thorough analysis of the Soviet economy for the thirty–year period, were presented to the management of Goskomstat by the director of Goskomstat's Institute of Statistics, E.B. Yershov. The estimates for industry and construction were published by me in Eydelman (1992, 1993).

12. These results were eventually published in Khanin (1991). For an English-language survey, see Harrison 1993. [Ed.]

13. At the beginning of the 1980s, after a thorough examination of Soviet history, I realized that the most likely outcome would be a reversion to some form of Stalinist economy.

14. Certain details have grown dim in my memory. I did not save any documents pertaining to these events since I did not consider them all that valuable. Therefore, my account may not be entirely accurate.

15. See also Ellman and Kontorovich 1997, p. 260. [Ed.]

16. We have been unable to find this reference. [Ed.]

17. I do not remember whether or not I wrote to A. Kosygin.

18. See Zoteev in Chapter 4.3. [Ed.]

19. Baibakov 1993, pp. 129–132. See also Ellman and Kontorovich 1997. [Ed.]

20. Ernst Henry was a pen name. He told me that his real name was S. Rostovsky. It has recently been uncovered that this name was also a pseudonym. In the last few years, the Russian as well as the Western press has published allegations of E. Henry's ties with the NKVD and his role in spying for the Soviet Union in England before the war. There is probably some truth to these reports.

21. A few years later, I discovered that Aganbegian presented this idea as his own in Moscow.

22. In 1975 and again around 1977, Gosplan submitted warnings to the leadership about the deteriorating economic situation. See Baibakov 1993, pp. 126, 128–133. [Ed.]

23. There was a famous Stalinist slogan, "There are no fortresses which Bolsheviks cannot storm." [Ed.]

24. The September 1984 version of the Concept was classified, like most materials produced by Gosplan. One of Gorbachev's assistants requested that the Concept be sent to his office, and [the Gosplan official] Vorobiev dispatched the document by courier but did not request a delivery receipt. Later, when Gorbachev moved his office in the CC building, the Concept must have gotten stuck in some safe, and all attempts on the part of Vorobiev's secretary to have the documents returned to Gosplan proved futile.

25. Several memoirs contradict the first and second of these assertions. See Ellman and Kontorovich 1997, p. 260. [Ed.]

26. Vorobiev was the Gosplan official who prepared the critical Gosplan report discussed at the Presidium of the CM around 1977. See Baibakov 1993, pp. 129–130. [Ed.]

27. According to a passage in the unpublished part of the paper written for this project by V.P. Mozhin, "Thanks to high petroleum prices, exports contributed one quarter of the total increase in national income in 1981–1985 (compared to less than 6% in 1966–1970). Without counting this contribution and also the increasing sales of alcoholic beverages, the average annual growth rate of NMP produced was no higher than 1%, instead of the official 3.1%. The country had reached the verge of economic stagnation, where the living standard stops growing and for the majority of the population even erodes." [Ed.]

28. As V.P. Mozhin put it in the unpublished part of his paper for this project, "By the middle of the 1980s, the necessity of changes in the economy was generally recognized." Similarly, O. Yun', in Chapter 5.2.1, states that in 1985–1986 among Gosplan and CM officials, "Everyone recognized the need for change." [Ed.]

5

Early Attempts at Change,
1983–1987

5.1 Economic Reform in the Interregnum Between
Andropov and Gorbachev-Ryzhkov
Igor Prostiakov

The Interregnum

An unusual situation arose in the USSR in early 1984. A state that for centuries had been based on strictly centralized rule suddenly found itself without a strong central authority. Little change was visible on the surface. The nation's main political institution, the Politburo, continued to approve all major international, economic, and social decisions. The legislature, the Supreme Soviet, kept operating, as did the top executive institution, the CM. Yet it became obvious to the insiders that these institutions were beginning to break down. The primary manifestation of this was a reluctance to make decisions on urgent matters and to change the established way of doing things.

A long-overdue generation shift was taking place in the Politburo, the highest party body which regulated the activities of all of the major government and economic institutions at both the central and the regional levels. Approximately half of this body's posts were occupied by members of the older generation who had been promoted during the 1950s and 1960s: the chairman of the CM, N.A. Tikhonov; the Moscow City Party Committee first secretary, V.V. Grishin; G.V. Romanov, in charge of the military-industrial complex; the Ukrainian first secretary, V.V. Shcherbitskii; and the Kazakhstan first secretary, D.A. Kunaev. All of these people were very influential. They represented the most developed republics and regions as well as major economic sectors. No decision could be made without the support and good will of these politicians. People in this group tended—sometimes consciously, and often by force of habit—to preserve the existing system for governing the country and its economy, perhaps with minor modifications. In support of their views they pointed to the attempts to reform the economy in 1965 and 1979, which often failed to yield the desired results.

The other part of the Politburo consisted of the proponents of reform, although each of them had his own vision of the purpose and essence of the impending changes. This faction increasingly gravitated toward M.S. Gorbachev. Although during this period Gorbachev's group had fewer votes than the conservatives, the support of many local party functionaries and its superior standing in public opinion made it quite influential. Some rapidly ascending secretaries of the CC CPSU, first of all N.I. Ryzhkov and E.K. Ligachev, were drawn to this group, which in turn actively promoted them and boosted their image as modern-thinking people. Selecting and nominating candidates for the posts of regional Party secretaries fell within the responsibilities of the group's sympathizers. This played an exceptionally important role in what was to follow.

Since neither faction could make its adherent the general secretary after Yu.V. Andropov's death, they settled on the compromise figure of K.U. Chernenko, devoid of leadership qualities and in bad health. This kept the *status quo* between the factions. Soon Chernenko's health deteriorated further, and he could no longer actively participate in the work of the Politburo. This is when the top Party and government bodies started to malfunction. The general secretary had the last word on the issues discussed by the Politburo. With Chernenko incapacitated, there was no one to break the deadlock between the factions, which were about evenly matched. As a result of this, the agenda of the Party and government bodies began to be filled with secondary issues on which both factions were in agreement. The important problems were being left unsolved.

The impasse, with its relative 'power vacuum,' ended with the creation of the Politburo Commission for the improvement of economic management. The need for its creation was first discussed in February 1984 after a meeting of the Presidium of the CM attended by Gorbachev. About ten days later, there was a special larger meeting attended by two representatives of the CM, Tikhonov and G.A. Aliev (both members of the Politburo). The CC was represented by Gorbachev, Ryzhkov, Dolgikh, and one or two others. It was at this meeting that the decision to create the Commission on economic management was reached. It began its work immediately. In late April 1984, the Politburo adopted a resolution simultaneously formally setting up the Commission and adopting the first fruits of its work, the Concept of improving the management of the economy.

Although its name suggests that the Commission ought to have dealt with a strictly limited range of issues, from the very beginning, it took on the task of solving all the most important economic problems. Moreover, while the work of the Politburo and the CM was stalled, the Commission largely replaced both of these organizations. In some respects it was even superior. This is not surprising considering the fact that the Politburo was split into two factions, and the CM did not want and could not assume the responsibility for resolving the major problems. The Commission included Tikhonov (chairman), Gorbachev, Gromyko, Aliev, Ryzhkov, Ligachev, Romanov, Dolgikh, and Kapitonov. These were the highest of the top leaders who resided in Moscow and had the opportunity (especially in view of the general secretary's illness) to decide any issue since there was simply no one to contest their power. Sometime in the fall of 1984, at the suggestion of Tikhonov, the Commission was renamed in accordance with its real functions—the Economic Management Commission of the Politburo.

An Early Draft of the Radical Reform Program

The Commission's first move was to elaborate the Concept for improving the management of the economy and to prepare the groundwork and implement a series of economic experiments. The Concept was prepared by the first deputy head of the CC Economic Department and subsequently Union Minister of Finance B.I. Gostev, the head of the group of consultants at this department Sarkisiants, and myself. At the same informal meeting where the creation of the Commission was discussed, the participants gave us their directives on all the principal issues to be dealt with in the Concept.

These directives were very general. They were the fruit of 'collective wisdom' marked by compromises and the reconciliation of various points of view. Tikhonov, who presided at the meeting and called the tune, underlined the necessity of keeping the sectoral [i.e., ministerial] system of economic management and increasing enterprise autonomy. Others, including Gorbachev, were also stingy with words, limiting themselves mostly to platitudes. Ryzhkov, who was then a CC secretary, threw questioning glances at his advisors. One got the impression that the leaders did not know what should be done and how.

Not having been given any rigid guidelines, the three of us had seemingly complete freedom of action (or of thought, to be more precise). In reality, our freedom was highly restricted. We had only ten to fifteen days in which to draft the Concept, the accompanying memo, and the draft resolution for the Politburo. So, we really had no time to ponder the issues. We were unable to summon the assistance of other specialists since we were given direct orders "not to expand the circle of those in the know."

We also recognized that our proposals regarding the economy were constrained by the entrenched stereotype of what was subject to change and what was 'untouchable.' Overly 'bold' proposals could provoke the rejection of the entire idea of reform. On the other hand, half-hearted measures, which would just create an illusion of reform without altering the basic underpinnings of the Soviet economy would only promote ossification. Our proposals had to be sweeping without being unacceptable to the leadership.

According to the Concept, state ownership was to be preserved and gradually differentiated into Union, republican, and municipal property. The role of cooperative property was to increase, and limited private property without the use of hired labor was to be permitted.

Cooperatives and individual labor activity were to remedy the near absence of small and medium size enterprises, making the economy more flexible and open to innovation and changes in consumer demand. Cooperatives and individual labor activity were also intended to strengthen labor incentives. We understood that cooperatives could legalize the existing informal sector of the economy. However, the realization of this possibility hinged on the tightening (or loosening) of government regulation of the cooperatives. The Concept, which was designed to lay the cornerstones of the economic reform package, could not encompass such details. We were familiar with the experience of the creation of small enterprises in Bulgaria and the development of individual activity and private property in Hungary, as well as the experience of cooperatives in Sweden and Italy.

The leading role of the plan was to be preserved. However, the plan was to become more flexible (especially medium- and long-term plans) and less binding, for instance, by introducing state orders and gradually reducing their share in output to 40–60%. The role of the market—resting on a socialist basis—would be strengthened. A significant share of output would be determined by contracts between buyers and sellers.

The regions would enjoy greater independence and have more responsibility for meeting the demands of the local population for social and cultural amenities and consumer goods and services. A two-channel tax structure was to be introduced by which some tax revenue would go directly into the local budgets according to preset standard rates and remain at the disposal of the regions. The sectoral [i.e., ministerial] system of control was to be retained in heavy and defense industry as well as national transportation and communication. Light industry and food production (with the exception of a few monopolies which served the army or the entire population) and agriculture were to be transferred to the control of the regions.

The enterprises would get much more discretion in determining their production program, the use of their revenue, and fixing wages. For the majority of enterprises, the interaction with the administrative agencies would gradually be limited to state orders and various budget payments based on rates determined by law.[1] There would remain environmental and certain other regulations, although here also the role of economic considerations was to be strengthened.

The state monopoly of foreign trade would be gradually lifted, as most authority over this activity would be transferred to the republics, regions, and enterprises. The number of ministries would decrease and some of them would be merged. At the enterprises' initiative, intermediate-level institutions of economic coordination would be formed. The government's control over the composition and size of the enterprises' management personnel would gradually be lifted.

The 1984 Concept differed from the 1965 reform both in its overall conception and with respect to the situation in the country. The notion of the socialist market guiding our work on the Concept had no affinity to the reform of 1965. The 1965 reform focused upon establishing new economic indicators to measure economic performance and new vertical 'state-enterprise' relations. These initiatives were carried out within the framework of the entrenched and rather narrow view of the notion of socialist property and its possible transformation.

In 1984 the idea was to introduce qualitative shifts allowing for elements of the market that would have been regarded during the period of the 1965 reform as inherently capitalistic. Another key difference was that in 1984 it was aimed to transform the entire system of economic relations, both vertical and horizontal (center-republic-locality), including more regional autonomy, coordinated improvement of the planning, management and organizational systems, restructuring of industry, etc.

Our version of the Concept was discussed by the Politburo in April 1984 (if I remember correctly, either on 24 April or 26 April) and adopted without any revisions. The text of the Concept was distributed to the members and candidate members of Politburo, the secretaries of the CC, the first secretaries of the Party, and chairmen of the Councils of Ministers of the Union republics, and three to five other people.

For a long time following the approval of the Concept, all the top officials avoided offering their personal vision of the impending reform as a whole, both at public appearances and at closed meetings. At best, one of them, most often Gorbachev or Ryzhkov, touched upon some isolated aspect of the reform, and even then only in passing. I think that the explanation of this was lack of the professional training and experience required to grasp the subject. This also explains the contradictory and even confused subsequent actions in the area of economic reform. They were often initiated and conducted on impulse and based on narrow considerations, without a program developed ahead of time and directed toward clear objectives.

In the early fall of 1985, M. Gorbachev decided to test his views on the reform before a reasonably competent audience. While the chairman of the CM, Tikhonov, was on vacation, Gorbachev unexpectedly addressed the CM apparatus. Unfortunately, at that very time I was called away for a couple of days to a meeting with Tikhonov in Sochi. Therefore, I was not present at Gorbachev's speech. At the time, I was struck not only by the suddenness of his speech and his timing (during Tikhonov's absence) but also by the fact that Gorbachev forbade anyone to see the record. Nonetheless, I took a look at it upon my return to Moscow. The speech was still a rough draft rather than a consistent system of ideas. He touched upon the reform in a fragmentary fashion, generally following the Concept.

Yet the speech also contained certain new features, compared to the Concept. A special emphasis, although without any elaboration, was put on using market levers and expanding the incentive role of wages. However, he did not oppose the market to central planning. Instead, he regarded them as two components of a single mechanism, metaphorically comparing the plan to the sails of a ship and the market to the wind that fills those sails. Gorbachev's speech and other pronouncements of the top leaders at the time suggest that they envisioned the future reform as a means for accelerating economic development within the framework of the socialist system (or at least pretended that they did).

The New Rulers' First Steps

Almost immediately upon returning from his vacation in the fall of 1985, Tikhonov met with Gorbachev to negotiate a voluntary retirement. In exchange, he received a promise that he would retain for the rest of his life all the privileges he had enjoyed as chairman of the CM—personal guards, personal physician, government dacha, government car, and so on. After his departure, everything fell into place. Gorbachev and Ryzhkov were able to implement their plans.

Initially, they pursued two key directions. First was the gradual reform of the economy and its structure, the implementation of global changes in the economy's control system. Second, they were preparing personnel changes which also encompassed the Politburo, which would make it possible to implement perestroika not only in the economy but in society as a whole.

The division of labor in the Gorbachev-Ryzhkov team became more and more pronounced, although, of course, it was not absolute. The former focused on the modernization of the Party and the government. The latter headed the reform of the economic system. He was able to embark on this task fairly independently, without having to defer to other high-ranking members of the Party and the government, except for Gorbachev. This marked the end of the short period of the 'power vacuum.' The Economic Management Commission of the Politburo ceased to work. No one formally disbanded it, but Gorbachev and Ryzhkov avoided giving powers to its members.

At the first meeting of the CM which Ryzhkov attended as chairman, he formed a powerful economics department in the CM apparatus and subordinated to it (formally granting it supervision rights over) all the major economic (and not only economic) institutions, including Gosplan; Gossnab; GKNT; Gosstroi; Goskomstat; the State Labor Committee; the Finance Ministry; the State Committees on Standards, on Inventions, and on Petroleum Products; and even a few subdivisions of the KGB and the Ministry of Internal Affairs. As a result, the role of the branch secretaries of the CC was drastically diminished. Strict limitations were imposed on the number of people, including those at the top level, who were admitted to the meetings of the CM and its Presidium.

I had been observing closely the work of the nation's top leadership since January 1978, when I was appointed assistant to the chairman of the CM, A. Kosygin. I do not hesitate to state that with the coming to power of the Gorbachev-Ryzhkov tandem the opinions of experts came to be valued less than ever before. Here is just one example.

Kosygin always thoroughly acquainted himself with all the basic documents presented by various government institutions and research institutes to be discussed at the meeting of the CM or its Presidium. However, he realized that even his very rich experience (Kosygin had worked as a minister of the USSR since 1939) does not guarantee true insight into all issues. At the meetings of the CM, with many speakers expressing opposing points of view, there was no time to delve into all the intricate details. Therefore, prior to each meeting Kosygin held a preliminary meeting with the relevant specialists working in the CM apparatus (production engineers, other kinds of engineers, economists, organizers, ecologists, etc.).

During these preparatory meetings the specialists briefed Kosygin on the essence of the issue, possible ways to resolve it, and the pros and cons of each solution. There was a very lively exchange of views during which the specialists could defend their position and even argue back. Kosygin asked many unexpected questions, which sometimes impelled even the specialists in a given field to look at the approach they proposed from an entirely new perspective. New solutions were often found, and sometimes issues were removed from the agenda because of not being properly prepared. As a result, Kosygin walked into the CM meeting well informed. He easily discerned which ministers were guided by the interests of the state and which failed to rise above the narrow interests of their branch. In Kosygin's absence, all those who presided over the meetings prepared for them in exactly the same manner (with the exception of minor details).

Having risen to the post of chairman of the CM, N. Ryzhkov started out by preparing for the government meetings in a similar way. However, fairly quickly the preparatory meetings began to lose their previous significance. Ryzhkov listened very little, preferring to speak himself. He did not like the arguments of the experts (and later the experts themselves) if they did not match his opinion. In such instances, he was quite capable of insulting remarks, after which many experts decided to keep their views to themselves. Later, the preparatory meetings were terminated altogether. Instead, Ryzhkov was briefed for the meetings by two or three of his closest aides. These were people personally loyal to Ryzhkov, often promoted in return for services they had rendered him in the past. They were ambitious but very mediocre specialists, frequently with only a vague understanding of the issues on which they briefed Ryzhkov. As a result, they gradually came to adapt their 'advice' to what Ryzhkov wanted to hear from them.

Neither Gorbachev nor Ryzhkov had any clue as to the role of the market and almost no understanding of financial issues. A particularly significant confession was made by Ryzhkov already at the twilight of his career as chairman of the CM. Summing up the activities of the government that he headed, Ryzhkov announced, "Whereas before we were reluctant to use terms such as 'cost,' and perceived the word 'profit' as almost a foreign term, now we are talking about 'self-financing.' " I remember thinking that he was probably telling the truth, since as an engineer he had rarely encountered economic concepts and had become accustomed to them only upon becoming the chairman of the CM.

The new rulers' first, and perhaps the most decisive step toward economic reform was the large-scale experiment.[2] The anti-alcohol campaign was the second major new policy. While failing to eradicate alcoholism, it seriously undermined the consumer-goods market and antagonized the general public by making buying a bottle of wine or vodka extremely inconvenient. The campaign also presented the new reform-minded rulers with a peculiar dilemma. Alcoholic beverages accounted for up to half of all food purchases, and for 20% of retail sales. The crackdown on alcohol depressed retail sales, national income, and real income per capita. A statistical report showing a decline in the standard of living would be a bad way to start reforms. Therefore, on 31 January 1986, Ryzhkov signed Order no. 210, changing the reporting procedure. The amount by which sales or production of alcohol fell in a given year was also subtracted from the data for the previous year for calculating annual growth rates.[3] Sliun'kov, who was promoted to the Politburo by Gorbachev himself, opposed this falsification and stated that he would not sign papers containing cooked numbers. Apparently, this independent stand cost him his seat in the Politburo. (Similarly, V. Dolgikh lost his post as candidate member of the Politburo because of his independent-mindedness.)

The new leadership's third major step, adopted with great pomp, was the resolution on reducing the number of deputy ministers and members of the *collegia* of ministries and agencies. The number of these officials in many ministries—both in Moscow and in the republics—exceeded all reasonable limits, because they were entitled to the use of special government clinics, priority access to resorts and sanatoria, and a few other privileges. Therefore, as soon as a new relatively important area of concern would appear (and often without it), a new post for a deputy minister or *collegium* member would suddenly spring up. Such a practice made the management pyramid top-heavy, reducing its flexibility and robbing middle management of responsibility and independence.

The top leaders demanded that the proposal for new staffing standards be compiled within a few days. Therefore, the same staffing numbers were adopted for whole groups of ministries: one for all the machine-building ministries, another for all the fuel ministries, and so on. Thus, the relatively small Ministry of Electrical Equipment and the vast Ministry of the Machine Tools Industry were both permitted to have six deputy ministers.

Conclusion

In 1984–1986 the top government and economic leaders, particularly Gorbachev and Ryzhkov, saw fairly clearly the issues facing the country at the time. However, the methods they chose to resolve these pressing problems generally turned out to be inconsistent and contradictory and, as a result, often led to the very opposite of the intended result. The situation was adversely affected by the fact that these two leaders lacked the necessary experience. Their backgrounds prior to coming to power were in areas in which such experience is not acquired, and even if acquired, it is totally inadequate for managing a country, especially such a vast one as the USSR. Unfortunately, their lack of experience was exacerbated by excessive ambition.

5.2 The Large-Scale Experiment

5.2.1 A Promising Departure
Oleg Yun´

The Idea

In the 1980s Gosplan used 400 material balances in developing the five-year plans, and close to 2,000 balances for the annual plans. Essentially Gosplan operated with 400×400 and 2000×2000 product matrices, although the actual input-output table used was 260 × 260. In Gossnab the list of goods to be produced and distributed was disaggregated down to between 15,000 and 16,000 items, and at the ministries to 50,000 items. In the process of attaching customers to suppliers, supply organizations disaggregated the list of items a further 10–15–fold. Hence the total nomenklatura of goods embraced by centralized planning at various levels was of the order of 500,000–750,000 items. However, already in 1972, according to the all-Union classification of industrial and agricultural output, the total number of items produced in the economy was 12 million. By 1982 the number had doubled to 24 million. This means the plan covered only 2–3% of the range of goods actually produced, that is, it was simply impossible to calculate the real demand for all items. This flaw was magnified as product diversity increased.

The planning mechanism could not be improved by extensive computerization due to the technological backwardness of production, particularly in the electronics industry. The only feasible alternative was to expand horizontal, market relations among the enterprises by granting them greater autonomy.

To address these problems, a large-scale economic experiment was begun in 1984. Its principles originated in the analysis of the implementation of the Decree of the CC and the CM 'On the Improvement of Planning' of 12 July 1979, undertaken in 1981 with my participation and with the help of academics, and ministry and enterprise officials.[4] Our findings, repeatedly discussed in Gosplan, the CM, and the CC, were that the Decree had had no noticeable impact on economic performance due to its piecemeal nature. Growth rates continued to decline.

Following a discussion of Gosplan materials on this issue at the CM in February 1983, first deputy chairman of Gosplan L.A. Voronin proposed to test the approaches to greater enterprise autonomy in a number of industries. The main principles of this experiment were to apply to all the participating industries, but some details were to be industry-specific. Enterprises subordinated to the Ministry of Heavy Engineering, the Ministry of Electrical Engineering, the Ministry of Food-Processing Industry of Ukraine, the Ministry of Light Industry of Belorussia, and the Ministry of Local Industry of Lithuania were selected to take part in this experiment.

Under the experiment, the compulsory targets of the five-year and annual plans were to be confined to the most important final results and to limits for centralized investment and construction work. Enterprises were to be evaluated by their record of contract fulfillment. The maximum number of employees of the enterprises had to be agreed upon with the local authorities. The norms mandated by the five-year plan were not subject to review.

The income earned by the enterprise and allocated into its incentive funds according to the norms could not be taken away. Enterprise annual plans were to be based upon economic norms specified in the five-year plan and contracts.

In July 1983, a Commission of the CM headed by L. Voronin was set up to oversee this large-scale economic experiment. I headed the research council of this commission. The results of the experiment confirmed the advantages of the enacted program. The enterprises started to assume plan targets higher than the control figures communicated to them. Enterprises became more sensitive to the demands of their customers. Contract fulfillment improved significantly, increasing from 96.7% in 1981 to 98.6% in 1986 for industry. Resource utilization improved as users started turning down previously ordered products, and enterprises began to curtail their workforces. Costs were cut and profits grew. After falling for many years, growth rates were going up: the years 1985–1986 became the inflection point.

The experimental system of management had certain flaws. The norms for the rates of growth of [wage and incentive] funds used in the experiment allowed enterprises to keep the basic wage funds and the incentive funds shaped under the old system, so as to convert to the new mode of operation without endangering employees' income. However, the norms were so taut compared with the former system that some enterprises preferred to keep the existing funds with little effort rather than expend great effort to see them grow only marginally. Also, the newly established norms favored technologically backward enterprises since they were in a better position to achieve improvements. As backward enterprises caught up with more productive ones, wages and benefits at the former outstripped those at the latter.

The large-scale experiment did not address the basic system of sectoral and regional management and planning, supply, the financial system, and price setting. It had little impact on technological innovation, capacity utilization, product quality, or the magnitude of input inventories. Construction, transport, and trade still operated under the old system.

The experiment confirmed the benefits of giving enterprises more autonomy and responsibility for the final results of their work. Its implementation revealed the need for a more radical restructuring of the economy.

The Experiment and Acceleration

The experiment had been in effect for over a year and had begun to bear its first fruit when Gorbachev became the leader and immediately sought to change radically the situation in the economy. The objective of significant acceleration in socioeconomic development by using the latest results in science and technology was announced.

According to a 1988 survey only 16% of production capacity was up to world standards and half of all production capacity was physically worn out by at least 50%. Huge investments and efforts were needed to eliminate the lag. The technical reconstruction of the economy was to be accomplished in a "historically short time" by some kind of a 'great leap.' By 1990, the retirement of obsolete capital was to double, more than a third of the capital stock was to be replaced, and the share of new technologies in it to reach 50%. Investment in machine-building was to increase by 80% compared with the previous five-year plan. At least half of the investment was supposed to be channeled into the retooling and reconstruction of existing plants.[5]

The CC and CM Decree of 12 July 1985 changed some of the experiment's conditions to marry it with acceleration.[6] Starting in 1986, the cost of introducing new products covered by the centrally allocated funds was counted toward meeting the enterprise's sales contract compliance targets. Wholesale prices of producer goods in the 'highest' quality category were marked up by up to 30%, while the goods in the 'first' category were discounted by 5% in the first year, 10% during the second year, and 15% during the third year. If a repeated quality certification did not promote the product to the 'highest' category, it was to be discontinued. Of the wholesale price discount on lower quality goods, 70% was to be at the expense of the producer's material incentives fund (but not to exceed 20% of the fund's planned size). Equipment, machinery, instruments, and spare parts for them, exported for hard currency received an additional markup of up to 20% of their wholesale price. The production development fund was to be based on stable economic norms for the five-year period, depending on the level of capital utilization and the enterprises' performance. The enterprises themselves were to plan their reequipment using this fund. Retooling and reconstruction of existing enterprises financed by the production development fund or bank credit was given top priority in the allocation of supplies.

In December 1985, the CM set up the Commission for the improvement of management, planning, and the economic mechanism, headed by the candidate-member of the Politburo, first deputy chairman of the CM, and (from mid-1985 till February 1988) chairman of Gosplan, N. Talyzin. The Interdepartmental Commission of Gosplan and the Commission for the general direction of the economic experiment were dissolved. The primary duty of the newly formed Commission was to develop the large-scale experiment. The Commission's authority was broadened and the rank of its members was higher than that of its predecessors. It included the heads of all the central economic agencies, the chairman of the RSFSR Gosplan, the secretary of the AUCCTU, the vice-president of the AN, the president of the Academy of Agriculture, and later a few leading scholars. The Commission's research section was headed first by D. Gvishiani and from February 1987 by A. Aganbegian. I became a member in March 1988.

Task forces of the Commission were set up in every sectoral department of Gosplan. They were headed by the chiefs of the respective departments and composed of specialists from the central economic agencies and academics. These teams, in collaboration with the respective ministries, prepared the conversion of the respective sectors to the new mode of operation. The teams also examined the results of the experiment and made recommendations to the Commission on all pertinent issues. I headed a general task force of department heads from the central economic agencies, and individuals who were in charge of reform implementation in their respective spheres (finance, prices, labor, supply). Our team analyzed the proposals made by the sectoral teams and functional departments and then introduced its own proposals to the Commission.

The implementation of acceleration overlapped with the work on changing the economic mechanism, posing unrealistic objectives before the 'experimenters' and in some cases distorting the conditions of the experiment. In keeping with the new methods of management, the number of binding targets in the state plan for 1987 was cut by more than 50% compared to the plan for the previous year.[7] However, as enterprise managers pointed out, enterprises still received a tremendous number of plan assignments. At the Novolipetsk Metallurgical Works the number of targets exceeded 500, as the Ministry reclassified many targets from obligatory to 'indicative.'[8]

The simultaneous operation of different economic mechanisms created difficulties both for the economy and for those who administered it. Given the incremental spread of the large-scale experiment, these problems were unavoidable.

The Leadership Criticizes Gosplan

G. Popov proposed to shift the supervision of reform from Gosplan and the Finance Ministry to a commission headed by the general secretary, since "the primary driving forces of perestroika are the Party organs and the enterprises."[9] While this proposal was not accepted, Gosplan was subjected to systematic criticism by the political leaders. At a meeting on the problems of improving the economic mechanism, the newly appointed chairman of the CM Ryzhkov accused Gosplan of clinging to its old mode of operation and eschewing active involvement in the large-scale experiment. At the same time Ryzhkov emphasized that Gosplan was responsible for implementing the experiment, and pointed out that his opinion was also that of Gorbachev's.[10] N.V. Talyzin agreed with Ryzhkov's criticism.

At first glance, this criticism might seem justified. However, this was not really the case since the various departments and deputy chairmen at Gosplan were called upon to take part in the discussions of the large-scale experiment only as new sectors were being drawn into the experiment. At the beginning of 1986 only one-third of industry, some transport enterprises, consumer services, and communications operated under the new mode of management.

The agency heads and the experts working for the Commission and its task forces were deeply involved in the discussion of the results of the experiment and in drafting resolutions. Each participant was thoroughly familiar with the problems of the sector under his supervision. Everyone recognized the need for change. There was a wide range of opinions which, as a rule, would converge during the discussion. The members of the Commission and the task forces freely challenged the opinions of their chairmen, since they were not administratively subordinate to them. Instead, the members would, as a rule, expound the position of their own agency. However, on the political level, it was the prerogative of the meeting's chairman to sum up the discussion and pronounce the 'ultimate truth.' Of course, some bureaucrats avoided assuming an active role in the reform. However, since the reform was 'blessed' by the Party and the government, they simply carried out the decisions of the superior organs.

On 2 July 1986 V. Mozhin, the head of the Economic Department of the CC, briefed the deputy chairmen of Gosplan on the recent meeting on economic reform held by the general secretary. There, Gosplan had been harshly criticized for the slow pace of its own internal restructuring which, according to the CC, was stalling the changes in the economy. The task set was to spur major improvements in the technology and methods of centralized planning so as to create the conditions for increased enterprise autonomy. At a Politburo meeting two weeks later, Gosplan was branded an enemy of all innovation and an organization trying to shape the economy in its own image rather than adapt to the new methods of management, according to the deputy chairman of Gosplan, S. Sitarian. It was said at the meeting that this denunciation applied not so much to the top echelon of Gosplan as to the heads of its departments. Yet no personnel changes took place at Gosplan.

I believe the main reason for this criticism of Gosplan was the leadership's desire to see the results of its economic policy as soon as possible. The impatience of the rulers reflected their failure to comprehend the inertia inherent in economic processes. Instead of waiting patiently for the results of the experiment and subsequently adjusting the economic mechanism, the leadership would alter the rules of the game without really analyzing the results of the experiment or giving enterprises a chance to adjust to the new conditions.

The research unit of the Commission, which included the most progressive economists of the time (L. Abalkin, A. Aganbegian, O. Bogomolov, P. Bunich, A. Egiazarian, I. Lukinov, V. Martynov, and later G. Popov and others) just generated ideas, with each scholar staking out his own position. The head of the unit evaluated those positions and formulated conclusions and recommendations. At a March 1986 meeting the chief of the CM department for economic reform, P. Katsura, noted that scholars' recommendations were rarely implemented because they lacked a feasible transition mechanism.

In December 1986, summing up the Commission's work for the year, Talyzin justly noted that he had received no assistance from the research unit, and therefore all the Commission's recommendations were purely empirical. As a result, five of the unit's members (Abalkin, Aganbegian, Egiazarian, A. Miliukov, and Popov) were made members of the Commission. The research unit was charged with analyzing the proposals drafted by Gosplan in response to its critics.

Cadres Decide Everything

I think that perestroika's most vulnerable spot was its personnel policy, which failed to undergo any major overhaul. Real shifts occurred only in the top political leadership. Personnel changes at the lower levels were very slow. Of course, it was impossible to replace the entire administrative staff. Retraining of incumbent officials of various ranks took place at the Academy of the National Economy of the CM, at Advanced Economic Courses at Gosplan, and at the branch institutes for advanced training. Still, real-world experience could be gained only by actual immersion in the new mode of management. However, the rapid changes in the economic environment produced constant modification of numerous regulations and procedures, making it very difficult for specialists to develop models of sustainable and effective enterprise development.

Also left intact was the rigid system of hierarchical subordination. Although there was an appearance of collegial discussion, in fact the system of one-person decision making was preserved. Under these circumstances success largely depended on the individual qualities of the leaders. Let us take a brief look at them.

N.V. Talyzin, who headed Gosplan and the Commission on Improving Methods of Planning and Management until February 1988, was clearly out of his league at this critical time. For many years he was in charge of the communications sector. Although his thinking was not confined to official categories, he was confused when it came to the most rudimentary economics and was certainly not in a position to lead the restructuring of the economic mechanism. As a result, he looked up to his superiors for guidance, which he flaunted publicly: "Ligachev is more important than Marx." "What is wrong with this document is that it proposes no real mechanism and Ryzhkov demands we come up with a mechanism." The substance of the proposals was worked out under the leadership of the deputy chairman of Gosplan and of the Commission, S. Sitarian, a veteran of reforms who really understood the deep problems of the Soviet economy. An advocate of innovation, he was also attentive to the views expressed by the bosses, including those less qualified than himself.

N.I. Ryzhkov would probably have been a good manager of the nation's economy under stable conditions. However, he was ill equipped to handle the problems of transition. Even in 1981 he avoided economic issues. Having been appointed to Gosplan as the first deputy chairman for general questions, Ryzhkov assumed the responsibility for managing the material balances, while entrusting the very important aggregate (*svodnyi*) task to N.P. Lebedinsky. Later on, when as the head of the Government he chaired discussions of draft proposals, extra perseverance was required to explain to him the complexity of economic interrelations and the drawbacks of the proposed solutions.

From the Experiment to the 'Radical Reform'

Under the terms of the experiment, revenue retained by the enterprises according to the norms provided for less than half of that needed for retooling and reconstruction and less than one-third of that needed for social purposes. The centralized investment transfers covered the shortfall. The demand for free government funds was still enormous, and the economic mechanism favored those who spent more.

In order for the norm-based revenues to finance all the projects stipulated in the plan, it was necessary to switch from norms for fund growth to norms for fund formation. This was tried out for the first time in 1985–1986 at the Sumy Machine Works and the Volga Motor Works at the initiative of their directors. I was in charge of development and implementation of the Sumy project. The Volga Motor Works experiment was conducted by V.A. Rzheshevsky, another deputy chief of the Gosplan department for improving planning and economic incentives.

Investment for retooling, reconstruction, and expansion was financed from the enterprises' own profit and depreciation. At the Sumy factory, norms for payments to the budget and the economic incentive funds were set as percentages of profit. At the Volga Motor Works the norms were percentages of the value added (*khozraschetnyi dokhod*). The results of both experiments were so impressive that Gorbachev spoke about them at the CC Plenum held in June 1986.

At a meeting in January 1986, the deputy head of the CM Department of Economic Reform, A.I. Miliukov, proposed extending self-financing to entire sectors. He received unanimous support from the task force supervising the Sumy experiment (deputy director of the enterprise V. Moskalenko; corresponding member of the AN, P. Bunich; and myself). The discussion centered on whether to make economic norms enterprise-specific or uniform for the entire sector. Eventually, we all agreed on the latter. A report analyzing the results of the Sumy experiment, proposing its further development and testing self-financing at sectoral level was submitted to the CM before the end of February. After approval by Ryzhkov, Gosplan and the branch ministries jointly elaborated the proposals.

Starting in 1987, enterprises of five industrial sectors were transferred to full *khozraschet* and self-financing. Yet in June 1987, the CC Plenum approved the blueprint for the radical reform mandating all enterprises to convert to full *khozraschet* and self-financing in 1988–1989. In his speech at the Plenum, Gorbachev noted that five to six months were not sufficient to reveal the advantages and the drawbacks of the new system of management. However, the decision was made. It took me by surprise. All the preliminary proposals which I helped draft or with which I was familiar focused on more testing of full *khozraschet* in designated sectors of the economy, and comprehensive conversion to the new system in 1991–1995. Perestroika took into account only the desire for fast change of the existing system, while completely overlooking the capacity of even the active part of the population to implement change.

The economy worked under the conditions of the large-scale experiment for only one year and was far from exhausting its opportunities. The personnel at the enterprises, ministries, and agencies were just beginning to master the new managerial methods when they were forced to adopt another, much more complex mechanism without due training.

5.2.2 Bad Design and Fraudulent Implementation
Igor Prostiakov

The financial aspect never received sufficient attention during the preparation of the experiment, which ensured that it would be essentially useless and even to some extent harmful. The participating enterprises were to receive significant additional financial resources, including an increase in the wage fund, irrespective of their actual financial standing. Even if the enterprise's financial situation deteriorated, additional money, ostensibly for improving its performance, would still have been appropriated by the budget. In other words, an experiment intended to improve the government's financial position inevitably aggravated it.

Prior to the meeting of the Commission of the Politburo, which was to examine the terms and goals of the experiment, the chairman of the CM and the chairman of the Commission, N.A. Tikhonov, received a memorandum [from me] about the completely erroneous design of the financial side of the experiment. Having read it, Tikhonov immediately distributed the memorandum among the members of the Politburo who were to decide on the implementation of the experiment, including M.S.Gorbachev and N.I. Ryzhkov. The latter immediately called me and, having admitted the reasonableness of the memo's suggestions and conclusions, asked me not to dwell on this issue at the Commission's meeting. At that meeting, he again agreed with the memo's conclusions and proposed postponing the work on these issues to a later date, clearly meaning the second stage of the experiment. Everyone agreed with him, but later forgot about his proposal and did not attempt to correct the glaring mistake.

The results surfaced fairly quickly, especially since the five ministries that first began to operate based on the new system of management were soon joined by the enterprises of twenty-one other Union, Union-republic, and republic ministries. The new system was imposed upon them rather mechanically, without any analysis of the initial results of the experiment and changes in its conditions. Not that such analysis was impossible. The opportunity was there, but by that time certain leaders were already eager to demonstrate their input into perestroika. They simply would not allow the time required for analytical work and insisted on moving further ahead without looking back.

The other weakness of the experiment was the extremely simplified, if not naive, organization of its implementation. Designed to substitute economic methods for administrative ones, the experiment itself relied exclusively on command methods. The enterprises participating in the experiment enjoyed a preferential supply of inputs because the territorial administrations of Gossnab and other supply organizations were ordered to provide one. The supply organizations simply diverted supplies from enterprises not included in the experiment. The experiment produced an artificial improvement in one part of the economy at the expense of others. From this perspective the economic experiment was reminiscent of Potemkin villages.

5.3 Searching for an Economic Policy

5.3.1 Summoning the Experts
Vadim Kirichenko

During the 1970s and early 1980s new ideas had no significant impact on economic practice. This dormant academic potential came to the fore at the beginning of perestroika.

In 1982–1984, Gorbachev (at that time a secretary of the CC and responsible for agriculture) arranged a series of meetings of economists and the leading officials from the economic departments. I participated in these meetings. The discussion was open-minded, without any taboos imposed from above (the only exception was price reform). When Gorbachev became the general secretary, N. Ryzhkov (at that time a CC secretary and the head of the Economic Department of the CC) took over the meetings. Following the discussions, research institutes were given a deadline to prepare reports and submit them to the secretaries of the CC or to its Economic Department. In 1984 alone, Gosplan's Research Institute (of which I was the director) drafted nine reports on different topics.

The first meeting took place on 31 July–1 August 1982. Almost seventy people participated, which was more than at any subsequent meeting. Gorbachev was getting acquainted with the economists from the main research centers and university departments (mostly Muscovites). The results of the numerous previous attempts to improve the economic mechanism were critically assessed, including the most recent Decree of the CC and the CM No. 695 of 12 July 1979 'On the Improvement of Planning.'[11] The decline in the efficiency of production was identified as the main reason for the economic growth slowdown and the deep economic disequilibrium, especially concerning investment. Inefficient structural policy, the sluggish pace of innovation, and excessive centralization of management were also cited. The key issue was the lack of economic incentives. The highly skilled personnel suffered the most from a distorted wage system. Also discussed was the need to integrate economic and social policies.

The meetings held in 1984 were more narrowly focused on the preparation of the Twelfth Five-Year Plan and on the economic mechanism that would ensure its successful implementation. The meeting held by M. Gorbachev and N. Ryzhkov on 16 March focused on the need for comprehensive rather than partial improvements in the economic mechanism. A. Aganbegian proposed to bolster centralism by delegating greater authority to Gosplan in the realm of price policy, wages, and economic norms. In addition to compiling a plan, this body would also be concerned with the economic means to implement it. Intersectoral committees were to be set up to facilitate coordination among sectoral ministries.[12] To strengthen regional management, the country was to be divided into ten–twelve superregions, each with its own planning commission and with responsibility for current direction of the enterprises, including those directly subordinated to Moscow. The enterprises were to be merged into large production associations.

The idea of greater enterprise autonomy and of *khozraschet* on the basis of stable, long-term norms was defended by A. Egiazarian (of Moscow University), V. Mozhin (head of the Council for the Study of Productive Forces), and others. L. Abalkin (chairman of the political economy department at the Plekhanov Institute) was the most outspoken proponent of radical change.

Five more narrowly focused meetings were held in July 1984: on the rate and structure of economic development (2 July); on improving utilization of fixed capital, its modernization, and improvement of investment policy (4 July); on price policy and subsidies (6 July); on the standard of living, wages, and pensions (16 July—chaired by Ryzhkov); on the machine-building industry, the energy and fuel complex, the output of construction materials, and reducing material intensity of production (23 July).

Putting price policy on the agenda for open discussion (at the 6 July meeting) was in itself out of the ordinary, as the following incident demonstrates. At the end of the 1970s, the academic council of Gosplan's Research Institute was preparing to discuss the issue of retail prices. A draft report for the discussion was sent to a number of research organizations and individual specialists on price policy. The leading officials of the CC Economic Department and Gosplan took the intention of the Institute's academic council as seditious and insisted that the discussion be canceled and the circulated copies of the report be returned. They feared that the issue of retail price reform would arouse public opinion. The director of Gosplan's Research Institute was ordered to put an end to such freewheeling ways in the future.

At the meeting held by the CC in July 1984, there was no unanimity on price policy for the Twelfth Five-Year Plan. The deputy chairman of Gosplan, S. Sitarian, advocated keeping prices unchanged and laying the conceptual groundwork for price revision by 1990. Yu. Yakovets, head of a department in the Academy of National Economy and a former director of Goskomtsen's Research Institute, called for a program to stabilize and reduce prices by cutting costs and strictly regulating incomes. Trade Minister G. Vashchenko also suggested cutting prices, except on fashionable and luxury items; even these items were to be targeted for price reduction eventually. Finance Minister V. Garbuzov commented that the possible increase in retail prices should be compensated for by various transfers.

Retail price increases to restore equilibrium in the consumer goods market were supported by Gosbank, Gosplan's Research Institute, and TsEMI. That proposal met with stiff resistance from representatives of the AU-CCTU, the CC apparatus, and the Ministry of Trade, which was unusual for the normally amicable atmosphere of the meetings. It should be noted that the issue of free prices was not raised—only state-set prices were discussed. The prevailing attitude toward the price issue was not grounded in economic reality. Rather it reflected fear of social, and possibly political, repercussions of retail price increases.

Gorbachev supported the idea of working out a "new formula" for price policy for the Twelfth Five-Year Plan, but wanted to proceed cautiously, saying that the issue was not purely economic, but predominantly sociopolitical. He said that it was necessary to find ways of halting the growth of prices, to stress cost cutting and quality improvement without raising prices. This persistent ambiguity and vacillations (depending on which group of economists he paid attention to at the time) were one of the main reasons for the inconsistencies of the future economic reform.

The budget deficit and its financing, credit and monetary matters, emission, and inflation, were never discussed at the meetings between the country's leaders and the economists. One reason for this is that, at the time, all information regarding these problems was classified, accessible only to a few economists in the government, and off limits to academics. Consequently, any discussion with academic economists would have been useless. Secondly, the prevailing mindset (except perhaps for a few specialists in finance and money) considered output in physical units, capital goods, production capacities, and labor resources to be the main factors in the Soviet economy. As for money, the Ministry of Finance and Gosbank would invariably allocate any amount needed. That was purely a technical question.[13] The notion of inflation was considered to be inapplicable under socialism. It was only much later that financial and monetary problems were recognized to be important.

5.3.2 Rulers Did Not Know What to Do
Vladimir Mozhin

Even prior to becoming general secretary, Gorbachev began to elaborate his own position on the necessary changes. The problems in the economy and ways to escape the impending crisis were openly discussed at meetings (in which I participated) in a small circle of people. The proposed measures boiled down to imposing stricter plan and labor discipline, creating various new administrative bodies, converting enterprises to self-financing, accelerating technological progress, and improving the structure of production. While opinions varied, no one at that time cast doubt on the economic system based on total state ownership. At the Twenty-Seventh Congress of the CPSU, Ryzhkov (1986, p. 4) stated that it was necessary "to reinforce and improve the centralized planning mechanism—it is a great triumph and a fundamental advantage of socialism. On this issue, we have not justified, and never will justify, the hopes of the bourgeois ideologists for our deviation from this fundamental principle."

Unlike other members of the Politburo, Gorbachev—even prior to the Twenty-Seventh Party Congress—stressed the need for radical change in the economy in his speeches. At Politburo meetings he justified this position by referring to major social tension in the country due to the persistence of socioeconomic problems. Most cities suffered from food shortages, millions of families had to queue for decades for an apartment, and initiative in the workplace was stifled. Gorbachev received his information from various sources and cited personal impressions gathered while touring the country and talking to people.

However, Gorbachev did not have a well-thought-out alternative model of the socioeconomic system, still less specific methods for moving toward it. He spoke in generalities, and his suggestions remained within the existing system.

At the same time the possibilities of using command methods of control were getting less as a result of the liberalization of the political system and the emergence of a new generation free from a fear complex. The command-style system had lost its political backing. As a result, labor discipline plunged and a general apathy and inertia set in. Without repression and in nonemergency (nonwar) situations, Stalin's model of the economy was not viable. This is the main reason for the collapse of the Soviet economy.

Furthermore, the issue of the immense military spending was not addressed [in 1983–1987] in spite of the fact that overall military spending at that time reached 34–36% of NMP produced (Pavlov 1993, p. 15). Militarization deformed the structure of the economy, prompting a huge waste of resources and distorting the structure of output. Hence, the main reasons leading to the economic crisis were essentially not discussed.

A commission created in 1985 and headed by Ryzhkov drafted a proposal on "developing an integral system of managing the economy."[14] I participated in a working group of this commission, along with the future Prime Minister, V. Pavlov, and others. Even our timid attempts to question the rigid centralization were met with resentment. "Do you want to return to NEP?" was the response of the Party leadership. This reveals the real extent of their 'radicalism' at that time. The commission's report recommended a more integral approach to planning, with the creation of new agencies to manage related sectors of the economy (the Fuel-Energy Complex, Agro-Industrial Complex, etc.), and some improvements in the economic mechanism.

The course adopted by the Twenty-Seventh Party Congress did not deviate from the usual voluntaristic command methods of the initial years of perestroika. At the same time, certain theoretical propositions expounded in Gorbachev's report at the Congress helped dispel some established ideological dogmas and stereotypes. This cleared the ground for subsequent concrete proposals that gave a specific content to the vague reform-minded statements. In particular, I mean Gorbachev's statements on the need to reexamine the concept of ownership, to lift restrictions on cooperative ownership, and to overcome misconceptions regarding market relations. This gave the green light to work on a new concept of economic reform.[15]

The creation of the state quality control system announced in 1986 was a command-style change.[16] It was modeled after the 'military representatives' at defense plants, who were independent of the management and could reject substandard products. About 70,000 inspectors were recruited, but their activities started causing production delays and conflicts. This innovation was soon discarded. All quick-fix proposals were seized upon. For instance, the Leningrad Regional Committee of the CPSU came forward with the idea of round-the-clock utilization of the main production equipment at the enterprises.[17] This was viewed as an alternative to new construction. Meetings at the CC were held and resolutions passed. However, the project stalled because there were hardly enough workers to operate all the machines in one shift. At the beginning of 1986 there were about 6 million unfilled vacancies in industry.

5.3.3 Society Was Not Ready for a Radical Reform
Vadim Medvedev

Under Andropov the leadership still lacked a comprehensive program of economic measures. The Party's leader did not have sufficient experience and knowledge for that. The practical actions of that time stressed improving discipline, establishing order, and increasing the responsibility of officials for carrying out their duties. This led to some excesses. Analytical work continued during 1984 when the entirely uninspiring and hopelessly ill Chernenko became the supreme political leader. The transition toward practical measures in the economic field proved even more difficult. Chernenko and the chairman of the CM, Tikhonov, foiled the already planned plenum of the CC on science and technology policy, which would have included Gorbachev's report. The main conclusions from the analysis of the economic situation were presented by Gorbachev in his speech at a conference held in December 1984, before he became general secretary.[18] It stated that "the main task of our time is to strive for a significant acceleration of social-economic progress."

At that time [1985–1986] the country's leadership, the government and economic structures, as well as society at large, were not yet ready for profound changes in the economic mechanism, not organizationally, not psychologically, and not in terms of social science recommendations. There took place a search, a slow and difficult liberation from the stereotypes of the past.

The economic reforms were viewed through the prism of the interests of various layers of the ruling elite. Enterprise management heartily supported enlarging their autonomy, but this was often understood in a one-sided way and did not include earning one's own keep. Ministry and local government officials ardently defended the rights of their institutions, resisting wider autonomy for enterprises and still more so the release of enterprises from subordination to them. Party organs defended their right to directly manage the economy, which was undermined by enterprise independence. To this were added the ideological stereotypes concerning the priority of statist methods of economic management. Hence a suspicion toward any other, even if more efficient, forms of management.

Back then, only academics, primarily economists, as well as journalists and writers, supported deep and decisive reforms of the economic system. A good mutual understanding formed between them and the Gorbachev leadership, but this was not enough. The political leadership felt not only the influence of the intellectuals, but of the whole spectrum of moods found in the economic, government, and Party environments. This explains why its actions in changing the methods of running the economy were, in that period, inconsistent and contradictory.

Gorbachev's speeches reflected the views of academics and progressively inclined managers and government and Party officials. On the other hand, government resolutions, even those that went through the Politburo and were labeled joint decisions of the CC and CM, and often even the actions of the CC Secretariat, wrapped up new political directives in a web of tasks, instructions, and commentary which often emasculated the content of the original ideas.

Gradually, two approaches to the economic reform developed. One maintained that the reconstruction of the economy on a modern technological basis was impossible without profound changes of the economic mechanism, from the forms of property to the specific methods of management, and without rejecting the command system in favor of economic methods and incentives. The other approach preferred the retention of the mobilization model, solving the country's problems by means of willpower, directives, and administrative control, and by appeals to [political] consciousness and discipline. The economic policy of those years rotated in a circle of contradiction between these two approaches.

The first approach was primarily expressed in the experimental system of economic management known as "the three Ss" (self-dependence, self-finance, and self-management), introduced first in three, then in all sectors of industry. New forms specific to particular sectors were created in construction (planning and evaluation according to final output), retail trade and light industry (working to customers' orders), and R&D organizations. On the initiative of Nikolai Travkin, collective contracting (*kollektivnyi podriad*) was introduced first in construction and then in the other sectors. Individual labor activity, up to then in effect forbidden, was legalized.

Measures to improve external economic activity, adopted in mid-1986, spelled the end of the outdated state monopoly of foreign trade. A number of large associations and enterprises were permitted direct access to the world market, bypassing the Ministry for Foreign Trade.[19] The opportunity of setting up links with partners in socialist countries was offered to all enterprises and organizations. Despite inconsistency and insufficient depth in a number of these steps, they slowly created a new situation in the economy and clearly indicated the direction of its future development.

The other approach, aimed at preserving the command methods of managing the economy, was exemplified by the introduction of state quality control.[20] It was impossible to tolerate the low quality of products any longer, and the idea of state quality control, borrowed from defense industry practice, was jumped at. When the controllers carried out their duties honestly, social tension arose in the worker collectives [because workers would lose part of their wages for rejects and poor quality]. To resolve these conflicts, pressure was applied on the controllers through Party and other channels so that they would not be too stringent. In other cases, enterprise management began to find a common language with the controllers, especially since, in the majority of cases, they were former employees of those same enterprises. The system of state quality control became polluted by bribery. As a result it became totally discredited and had to be abolished within a few years.

Other attempts to solve real problems by purely voluntaristic methods included the movement for multishift operation of machine-building plants and the introduction of special bodies governing multisectoral complexes: the agro-industrial, fuel and power, and machine-building complexes. Both were unsuccessful in reaching their announced goals. Another example was the notorious anti-alcohol campaign. Although drunkenness and alcoholism were serious social problems, the attempt to deal with them by voluntaristic campaign methods discredited perestroika. The campaign was in due course abandoned and by the late 1980s remained just a bad memory.

The policy that was most at odds with the progressive trends of economic change was the fight against non-labor incomes decreed in May 1986. It concerned a wide range of phenomena: "mercenary behavior," "the struggle against persons living above their means," "rejection of private ownership psychology and money-grubbing," "eradication of non-labor incomes, foreign to the nature of socialism." A crusade was announced against all that did not fit the mold of traditionally understood socialist ways of management and distribution. However, the concept of 'non-labor income' was not defined with any precision. Anything could be described by this term. The concept of 'speculation' was also used without clarification. At the same time the necessity of increasing control over the operation of collective farm markets was stressed, which meant a ban on middlemen. Controls over the use of excess living space were suggested, obviously hinting at a negative perception of the renting out of excess living space by citizens. Transactions in excess of 5,000 rubles by individuals and enterprises were to be made by bank transfer rather than cash. The whole spirit of these decisions, as well as many of their details, contradicted steps toward developing individual labor activities and cooperatives that were being taken at that time.

The developments of 1985–1986 pointed to the conclusion that serious changes in the economy could not be reached without a complex and radical restructuring of the economic mechanism. This conclusion was reached in March 1986 at the Twenty-Seventh Congress of the CPSU. However, another year of searching, of trial and error, was necessary before fundamental reform of the economic mechanism began. We were lulled by the fact that economic growth remained positive, and in some cases improved, in 1985–1986.

Was the leadership acting in a rush when it decided on the radical reform, not having waited for the results of the investment maneuver embodied in the Twelfth Five-Year Plan, and of the large-scale economic experiment in a series of industries? Not at all. On the contrary, we were late in starting the economic reform, having let at least a year go by, which was, moreover, the most favorable from the point of view of political conditions in the country. We should have included the radical reform already in the Twelfth Five-Year Plan, and built the plan around the reform. The redistribution of investment in favor of machine-building, the core of the Twelfth Five-Year Plan, should have been tied to the reform. Instead, we hoped to move this heavy load with the help of the old mobilization methods, political directives, and administrative pressure.

From the very beginning Gorbachev and his associates considered deep, serious economic reform unavoidable, but they were afraid that society would not immediately accept it. They held that it was necessary to approach it gradually, using a series of transitional stages. As a result, the structural changes got separated from the institutional reorganization and turned out to be doomed to failure.

5.4 The Acceleration Strategy and the Twelfth Five-Year Plan

5.4.1 The Official Concept
Vadim Medvedev

The concept of acceleration of social-economic development was presented by Gorbachev at the first Plenum (April 1985) of the CC after he was elected general secretary, and at the June 1985 conference on technological progress. It formed the basis for the new leadership's political program, as reflected in the resolutions of the Twenty-Seventh CPSU Congress and the Twelfth Five-Year Plan approved at the congress.[21]

It was intended, on the basis of the latest stage of the technological revolution, to retool major sectors of the economy, increase economic efficiency, and create the preconditions for a qualitative improvement of the standard of living. The second component in the strategy of acceleration was structural change in the economy: priority development of sectors defining the technological level of society, de-emphasizing extractive sectors and stressing resource-saving technologies, overcoming the hypertrophy of heavy industry, and establishing a modern consumer sector and a modern social infrastructure.

The third component of the acceleration strategy was improving the system of management and the economic mechanism so as to facilitate the implementation of the first two components. The center was to play a more important role in carrying out economic strategy, while giving up operational involvement in economic activity. The independence of enterprises was to expand decisively. The price system, finance, and credit were to be improved. Optimal coordination between regions and branches of the economy was to be ensured. Comprehensive democratization of management was envisaged to increase the role of the worker collectives, control from below, and the accountability and openness of economic units. Questions were raised of improving property relations, and of overcoming the underestimation of market relationships, which were necessary to create effective incentives for economic activity. However, all this was meant to happen within the framework of improving economic planning. Traditional concepts and ideological dogmas still weighed heavily on all of us.

Even under the best of circumstances, this strategy would have yielded results only after several years. Meanwhile, progress could be achieved only by tapping reserves that did not require considerable expenditures and that could give a quick and substantial return. This meant overcoming waste; enforcing elementary order in the economy; strengthening planning, technological, and labor discipline; and improving the quality of output. Andropov's short-lived rule had shown that a lot could be achieved by such measures.

5.4.2 Dolgikh's Alternative
Yurii Belik

According to the established practice, each department prepared its own draft of the relevant sections of the CC report to the Twenty-Seventh Party Congress. The materials were delivered to a group of the general secretary's speech writers, who were putting together the report. An innovation was introduced into the preparation of the CC report to the Twenty-Seventh Congress. CC Secretary V. Dolgikh was charged with preparing an alternative draft of the economic section.[22] The Economic Department played the leading role, aided by the Departments of Heavy Industry, Machine-Building, Agriculture, and Light and Food Industries.

In his speeches Gorbachev announced the goal of accelerating economic growth.[23] There were no calculations or economic arguments to prove the feasibility of the task.[24] Specialists from the departments and V. Dolgikh himself were not inclined to interpret the thesis of accelerated growth literally. Our previous experience showed that the growth of the country's industrial potential was accompanied by a decline in growth rates. The highest average annual rate of industrial growth in Soviet history occurred during the First Five-Year Plan (over 23%), and it had been declining ever since, although the absolute increase for each 1% of growth naturally grew substantially.

Hence, the acceleration of growth was not feasible. The draft of the economic part of the CC report presented by Dolgikh did not include "higher growth rates" among the major objectives. It is not surprising that our draft was turned down since it did not conform to the general secretary's slogan of acceleration. Party discipline required that the latter be embodied in the CC report to the Congress and in the report given by Premier Ryzhkov. At least no sanctions were applied to Dolgikh and his group! Of course, Gosplan incorporated 'acceleration' into the Twelfth

Five-Year Plan and its long-range projections, and the government presented them at the Party Congress.

After a few years it became obvious that no acceleration had taken place. This was first said out loud by the delegates to the Nineteenth Party Conference in June 1988. It was stated with particular sharpness at the CC Plenums of February and March 1990 where, in connection with the preparation for the Twenty-Eighth Congress, the results of five years of perestroika were discussed. When the main tasks of the Thirteenth Five-Year Plan (1991–1995) were discussed in October 1988, acceleration was not even mentioned.

The Economic Department was powerless to interfere with unrealistic decisions made in the upper echelons of the Party hierarchy. Another example of this was the resolution to combat drunkenness approved in May 1985. People in the Economic Department, as well as a number of other departments in the CC, realized that there was no quick fix for the problem and that the budget would suffer a serious blow. These problems were also recognized in the government, Gosplan, and the Finance Ministry. Gorbachev was unable (and probably did not wish) to oppose Ye. Ligachev and M. Solomentsev—the zealous initiators of this measure. The resolution was 'collectively' approved by the Politburo.

5.4.3 Acceleration by Command
Vladimir Mozhin

The acceleration of economic growth—a weapon from the command arsenal—emerged as the primary solution of all socioeconomic problems before the Twenty-Seventh Party Congress. Higher rates of economic growth for the Twelfth Five-Year Plan (1986–1990) were set by putting pressure on Gosplan and the ministries. The increase in the share of investment in NMP, a one-third increase in overall investment, and an 80% increase in investment in the machine-building sector were to support these targets. These measures aimed to overhaul the basic industries and sharply raise labor productivity.

Gorbachev, with the support of Ryzhkov, was the chief proponent of the acceleration strategy. The branch departments of the CC were keen supporters of it. Experts from Gosplan and the ministries were rightly skeptical of these proposals. Financial resources necessary for such a leap were lacking, and there were no designs or technological solutions which would raise industry to the new technological level.

The financial aspect merits special attention. In 1971–1985 domestic revenues of the state budget fell short of plan targets by 153 billion rubles, while expenditures exceeded plan estimates by 303 billion rubles.[25] The Twelfth Five-Year Plan for 1986–1990 contained a state budget deficit of over 127 billion rubles. The actual budget deficit in 1986–1988 alone reached 184 billion rubles, that is, more than triple the deficit for the previous three five-year plans combined.

Characteristically, at the quarterly briefings of the Politburo on the course of plan implementation, the financial issues were dealt with at the end and were hardly discussed at all. On the other hand, the health of specific industries and the attainment of various physical targets were given a considerable amount of time. The (underestimated) magnitude of the budget deficit was first made public as part of the draft budget for 1989. During the first few years of Gorbachev's rule, all attempts on the part of the Economic Department of the CC to address the fiscal situation were virtually ignored. The Finance Ministry was diligently executing the obviously unfeasible objectives of the country's leadership, the members of which had no understanding of financial or monetary issues.

Command methods were also deployed in planning the rates of growth and quality improvement in machine-building. On numerous occasions I witnessed the CC secretary and member of the Politburo, L.L. Zaikov, summon the Ministers of the Machine-building, Instrument-building, and Electronics industries. Reluctantly they would promise in writing that 85–90% of the output of their sector would meet international quality standards by the end of the Five-Year Plan. The head of the Machine-Building Department of the CC, Arkady Volsky, understood that such promises were preposterous, but nevertheless incorporated them into the plan draft.

Only during the first year of the Five-Year Plan (1986) was the rate of growth somewhat higher than before. Soon afterward, however, all the major indicators began to plummet.

5.4.4 Planning Techniques, Feasibility of Targets, and Outcomes
Vadim Kirichenko

The main role in defining the conceptual basis for the Twelfth Five-Year Plan was played by researchers at the Institute of World Economy and International Relations, TsEMI, and some empirically oriented researchers at the Institute of Economics (all of the AN), Gosplan's Research Institute, and a number of other departmental institutes.

The basic aims of the Twelfth Five-Year Plan were determined by the 'Main Directions of Social and Economic Development of the USSR for 1986–1990 and for the Period up to 2000,' adopted at the Twenty-Seventh Party Congress in March 1986. The draft Five-Year Plan was endorsed at the June 1986 Plenum of the CC. The plan was adopted at the fifth session of the USSR Supreme Soviet, also in June 1986. The plan aimed at the acceleration of economic growth, to be achieved primarily by improved labor productivity and more efficient resource use. This, in turn, was to be brought about by accelerating the pace of technological change, retooling, and technical reconstruction. The spotlight was on the high-technology sectors, especially on the accelerated growth and qualitative restructuring of machine-building. At the same time, social policy and the need to combine economic growth with social development were stressed.

The technical side of the development of the Twelfth Five-Year Plan was much better than in previous years. By that time, the planning agencies had overcome their ideological aversion to the use of forecasts at the stage of drafting the plan. The biggest economic forecasting project involving dozens of academic and agency research institutes was the voluminous 'Comprehensive Program of Scientific and Technological Development' for a period of ten–fifteen years, broken down into five-year segments. The conclusions of this work were not binding for the planners. Rather, the work presented a broad overview of desirable changes in the economy and alternative solutions to various economic, structural, and technological problems.

The formerly controversial programming approach had also gained recognition.[26] The drafters of the Twelfth Five-Year Plan could build on the long-range programs, such as the Food Program, the Energy Program, and the Housing Program. Gosplan's Chief Computer Center was equipped with modern computers and had vast experience of calculating plan parameters. Many ministries had their own networks of computing facilities. The preliminary stages of planning incorporated mathematical-economic models, including factor models and large input-output tables in both value and physical terms. Optimization models were being tested in sectoral planning calculations. Mathematical models were widely used at the pre-plan stage for determining the trends and structure of household incomes and expenditures and the structure of consumption.

However, no scholarly, methodological, or technical innovations could compensate for the declining capability of the plan-distributive system and recurring arbitrariness in planning and managing the economy. These efforts were akin to equipping an old machine with a computerized control system, which does little to raise the efficiency of the whole system. The planners continued to rely on command methods to resolve radically new and urgent problems.

The plan presumed strict adherence to administratively set prices; obligatory assignment of customers to suppliers based on the established centralized supply network; channeling as much of the enterprises' net income as possible through the state budget; massively subsidized prices of agricultural products; and narrow limits on the discretion of the republican and local administrative bodies. The redistribution of resources (notably, investment) remained the primary tool of economic control.

The 1986–1990 Five-Year Plan was designed to reverse the declining growth rates of the previous decade. As the draft of the plan traveled through the various stages toward its approval (Twenty-Seventh Party Congress, June 1986 CC Plenum, the Supreme Soviet), the targets and resource utilization norms got more and more taut. In the final version, the target growth rates of the national income, industrial output, investment and its efficiency, labor productivity, and real per capita income were all higher, and targets for the metal- and energy-intensity of the national income were lower, than the same indicators in the 'Main Directions' adopted by the Twenty-Seventh Congress.

As one of its merits, those involved in drafting the Twelfth Five-Year Plan pointed out the year-by-year breakdown of the key targets, designated as guidelines for the annual plan targets. The plan envisioned a steady year-by-year increase in the rates of growth.

The plan aimed to accomplish everything at once, and many of its goals were incompatible. The rate of investment (as a share of the national income) was to increase at the same time as defense spending and real personal income. Key industries were to undergo large-scale reconstruction and also to increase output at a rate higher than in the previous five-year plans. Consumer goods imports were to be cut in order to free up hard currency for investment goods imports, yet the supply of high-quality consumer goods was to expand. One of the objectives was to curtail the production and sales of alcoholic beverages (the anti-alcohol campaign), which would deprive the budget of a significant part of its revenue. Retail sales (alcoholic beverages excluded) were to increase by more than a third, the budget subsidies to agriculture were to be kept intact, and budget expenditures on wages were to grow. National income, industrial and agricultural output were to grow faster than in 1981–1985, while the numbers of those employed in the productive sectors and the fixed capital stock were supposed to grow more slowly. Output was supposed to grow faster than the input of factors of production.

Targets for economic efficiency[27] bridged the gap between the rather realistic assessment of the possible growth of factors of production and the euphoric performance expectations. As in previous five-year plans, efficiency targets were the least justified part of the plan. In 1986–1990 the efficiency of investment was planned to increase by 16%, even though it fell by 12% in 1981–1985 and had been falling for many years before that.[28] Even at the time, this was unrealistic. The plan was doomed not to be fulfilled, which only aggravated the imbalance in the economy.

As always, when the Twelfth Five-Year Plan was being drafted, the planners were pressured by all kinds of Party directives. This explains the many complex and formidable tasks incorporated into the plan. It was normal for various long-term programs (for developing a particular region or industry, constructing large manufacturing plants, major infrastructure projects) to be approved by the Party and government during the course of the current five-year plan. In most cases, the resources for the programs were to be found in the next plan period. The planning agencies were instructed to incorporate the proposed projects in their draft of the next five-year plan. Preliminary calculations would reveal that all these programs and resolutions together required more resources than were forecast for the next five years. Sometimes, the production capacities that were to go into operation could not be staffed because of labor shortages.

As [each] five-year plan was being drafted, its parts were considered by the CC Secretariat or the Politburo, and additional instructions were issued. Sectoral departments of the CC examined the parts of the plan dealing with their sectors and wrote their recommendations. In effect, the demands of the sectoral ministries were validated by the Party. The 'lobbying effort' of the local Party and government officials to ensure investment and new construction projects in their respective regions was also very important. The Gosplan chairman, [usually] not being a member of the Politburo, could not always withstand the pressure and had to compromise with sectoral and regional demands.

Notes

1. That is, it was intended to end the practice by which ministries determined the amounts which individual enterprises had to pay the center and used these payments to redistribute resources from high-profit to low-profit or loss-making enterprises. [Ed.]

2. On the experiment, see Chapter 5.2 below. [Ed.]

3. That is, the denominator was being decreased to make a ratio—the growth rate—look larger. See also Eydelman in Chapter 4.1. [Ed.]

4. For the text of the Decree see 'Ob uluchshenii . . .' 1982. [Ed.]

5. Gosplan together with the ministries revised the 'Main Directions of Economic and Social Development for 1986–1990' [to accommodate the new policy]. However, it was unable to arrive at a consistent set of targets even at the macro level. The capacities of the construction sector, and of the industries producing cost-effective and heat-treated metal products, high-grade materials, plastics, industrial ceramics, and composite materials, could not support the targets of acceleration. In 1986–1988 investment in industrial construction was 1.4 times higher than for the first three years of the previous five-year plan, the share of new products in the machine-building output increased from 4.3% to 11.4%, and the average annual growth rate of machine-building was 1.5 times higher than the rate for industry as a whole and reached 5.6%, as compared to 4.0% in 1981–1983. Yet there was no breakthrough in the performance of the machine-building complex and no major retooling of the industrial base. The quality of domestic machinery and equipment was still inadequate; only 5% of it was exported. Imports remained high. Toward the end of this period the term 'acceleration' ceased to be used.

6. '*V TsK KPSS i Sovete Ministrov SSSR*', *Pravda* 4 August 1985. [Ed.]

7. It was cut by half in industry, by 1.8 times in the agro-industrial sector, by 3.7 times in construction, and by 2.3 times in the R&D sector.

8. As noted by the Works' chief economist V. Breus at the round table organized by the journal *Kommunist* in July 1986. In his words, "Acceleration can mainly be seen in the growth of paperwork."

9. At that same round table.

10. This criticism was conveyed by Talyzin to the 'reformers' *(perestroechniki)* at Gosplan on 5 December 1985.

11. See '*Ob uluchshenii . . .*' 1982. [Ed.]

12. This was later realized as Agroprom and the Machine-Building Bureau. On their role in the initial Gorbachev strategy, see Medvedev in Chapter 5.3.3, below. [Ed.]

13. For the historical background to this point of view, see Ellman and Kontorovich (1992b) pp. 110–111. [Ed.]

14. 'Integral' *(kompleksnoe)* management and planning were to transcend sectoral divisions and hence to forestall suboptimization by sectoral ministries. [Ed.]

15. V. Medvedev, A. Aganbegian, L. Abalkin, and V. Mozhin were directly involved with the economic aspects of Gorbachev's report to the Twenty-Seventh Congress. In addition, the work of numerous academics and practitioners was used. [See, for example, Tsipko in Chapter 7.2. Ed.]

16. Introduced in January, 1987. [Ed.]

17. Two- or three-shift operation. [Ed.]

18. '*Zhyvoe tvorchestvo mass*', *Pravda* 10 December 1984. [Ed.]

19. See Kurierov in Chapter 9.4. [Ed.]

20. See the resolution of the CC CPSU and CM '*O merakh po korennomu povysheniiu kachestva produktsii*' of 12 May 1986 [*Pravda*, 2 July 1986].

21. The need for acceleration had been stressed in Chernenko's speech of September 1984 at the jubilee meeting of the Union of Writers (Pechenev 1996, p. 93). [Ed.]

22. By this time, the secretary for the economy, N. Ryzhkov, had become chairman of the CM, and no one had taken his previous position. Dolgikh, more familiar with macroeconomic issues than the other secretaries, was assigned to lead the project.

23. Starting with the April 1985 plenum of the CC.

24. This was not the only populist cry to come from the mouth of the general secretary. In May 1985 in Leningrad he stated, "We need labor productivity to grow by 6%, 7%, or better still 10% annually, and in many sectors even faster. Without this we will not reach the highest world level. . . . The goal should be to make all goods made in Leningrad and the Leningrad region competitive in the world market." In April 1986 at the Togliatti car factory he challenged the workers to become the trendsetters in the world automobile market.

25. 'Domestic revenues' probably exclude revenue from foreign trade, which increased enormously as a result of the increase in world oil prices and hence of the corresponding imports. [Ed.]

26. Analogous to the 1960s American PPBS (planning, programming, budgeting, system) method. [Ed.]

27. This refers to labor productivity and the output/investment ratio. [Ed.]

28. Efficiency of investment is the ratio of the increment of output to investment in the same period. [Ed.]

6

'Radical' Economic Reform, 1987–1989

6.1 The Preparation of the Reform: Views from the Central Committee

6.1.1 Compromises at the Top
Vadim Medvedev

The serious economic disruption of early 1987 finally shifted the balance of forces and opinions toward radical economic reform.[1] The CM and Gosplan explained it by a sudden shortage of ball bearings and of certain types of chemicals, and by increased difficulty in importing components due to the growing tension in the balance of payments. All this was possibly so, but more important was the general increase in the instability of the economy, and its unhealthy condition.

During the following months the situation got back to normal, to a certain extent even compensating for the January disruption. This was achieved by, among other things, increasing oil exports to countries with convertible currency, though this was not easy, because by this time the growth of oil production had already stopped. Gold sales on the world market were also increased. In March 1987 at a Politburo meeting, Gorbachev bluntly posed the question of preparing and conducting a radical economic reform. It was decided to call a special CC Plenum on this question. Preparation for the Plenum started immediately.

Taking into account the lessons from the past, and, especially the sad experience of Kosygin's reform, creating a new economic mechanism on the level of the enterprises and associations formed the basis of the reform. It was intended to go considerably further than was mandated in the large-scale economic experiment. Enterprises' property and finances were to be clearly separated from those of the state. Relations between the state and the enterprise were to be set on an economic basis, and enterprise self-management widened. The primary units of the economy were to be commercialized, based on market relations among them.

The Law on the State Enterprise was supposed to underpin all the other measures of economic reform: restructuring of the financial and banking system, of the supply system, and of the price system. Central planning was to be subordinated to macroeconomic policy, freeing the planners from operational functions. The economic ministries were to be merged into fewer units, with the possibility of a future transition to a nonministerial system of economic management.

Taking into account the complexity and acuteness of all these problems and the need to work out compromises among conflicting interests, the development of the reform was divided into three parts. The main conceptual burden was borne by Gorbachev himself and his closest aides (including the present author), with participation by some leading economists. They wrote the main points for preliminary discussion of the framework of reform by the Politburo, prepared the presentation of the subject to the CC Plenum, and finally prepared Gorbachev's speech. Another group, consisting of heads of several ministries, agencies, associations, and enterprises, along with Party officials, prepared the draft Law on the Enterprise. The government, led by Ryzhkov, prepared a package of specific decrees concerning the different topics of the economic reform: planning, financial system and banking, price formation, supply, and others. Gorbachev coordinated the work of the three teams at the regular working sessions and during discussions at practically every Politburo meeting. For several months, these questions remained the center of attention of the Party, government, social organizations, and the press.

Dominant in the outline of the report to the Plenum and the report itself was the drive to free the economy from administrative pressure, to give space for economic laws and incentives while preserving centralized control only to the extent necessary for the social reorientation of the national economy and support of technological progress and structural programs. Yet there was also a view of the reform as an aggregate of half-measures, doing away with only the more odious arbitrary methods, while preserving the command system.

Sharp discussions surrounded the replacement of centralized resource distribution, that is, the supply system, by wholesale trade. The leaders of Gossnab agreed with this idea, but immediately attempted to limit it to satisfying one-off needs of the enterprises, while preserving the main flows of resource allocation along centralized channels. While many academic economists argued for the transition to free prices, others tried to dilute this idea by proposing transferring price setting powers to local authorities and limiting free prices to seasonal and local goods. At the meetings of the Politburo, Ryzhkov and other members of the CM constantly bewailed the underestimation of the ministries' role. There were even attempts to put forward a slogan about 'increasing the role of the ministries in the new conditions.' The alleged motivation was fear of losing the levers of control over the economy.

The struggle around the relationship between the enterprises and the superior administrative organs was the most protracted. It focused on the role played by the control figures and state orders handed down to enterprises. The government leaders insisted on making the control figures and state orders obligatory, arguing that without this a state plan was unthinkable, and the economy would fall apart. The reformers, on the other hand, thought that control figures of production volume should serve only as a guide for voluntary contracts between enterprises. The production plan should be formed as the sum of these contracts. The state orders should be used only for production purchased by the government for military or social programs. Forming a relatively small fraction of total output, state orders should be attractive and profitable for enterprises.

This controversy was a matter of principle and continued up to the last day before the Plenum. Literally on the eve of it, at a meeting in Volynskoe, Gorbachev and Ryzhkov, with the participation of the present author, discussed the final materials for the Plenum. There, the formulation along the lines of the reform position, which Gorbachev shared, was agreed upon, but with some compromises and concessions.

In hindsight, taking into account subsequent developments, many components of the 1987 reforms now seem insufficient and even naive. Gorbachev's report and the document 'Main Propositions of the Fundamental Restructuring of the Management of the Economy,' on the one hand, and the concrete decisions concerning certain aspects of the reform, as well as the Law on the State Enterprise, on the other, differed in their approach to reform, reflecting the struggle of opinions. Nevertheless, it was a serious, profound, and complex review of all questions, which could initiate change and serve as a solid basis for the beginning of fundamental economic transformation.

6.1.2 It Was About Enterprise Autonomy
Vladimir Mozhin

The idea of a Law on Enterprises was put forward by me in a March 1986 memo addressed to Gorbachev. The thrust of the proposal was to grant enterprises economic autonomy and legally shield them from superior administrative bodies interfering in their operations. The functions of ministries and other administrative bodies had to be redefined accordingly. This was to be facilitated by the pressure exerted by the newly autonomous enterprises themselves. Gorbachev was supportive of the idea of such a law and instructed that it be elaborated by the government.

As long as just the general principles of reform were discussed, the attitude of the leadership was calm, if not unanimously supportive. The confrontation started with the drafting of the Law on the State Enterprise and the resolutions of the June 1987 Plenum of the CC.[2] Conflicts centered on the system of mandatory plan targets for the enterprises. Our group, supported by Gorbachev and Medvedev, advocated the abolition of mandatory gross output targets. Ryzhkov, supported by Vorotnikov, Dolgikh, and Biriukova, was dead set against our proposal. This seemingly minor controversy reflected two vastly different approaches to economic reform. One aimed to grant real economic autonomy to the enterprises, the other to preserve one of the cornerstones of the command system. All participants realized what was at stake. This issue was heatedly discussed at three Politburo meetings, each lasting several hours, and again when the final draft of the report was being prepared.[3] Ultimately the adopted version provided for the enterprises to receive indicative targets and state orders as the basis of their plans rather than mandatory output targets.

The Enterprise Law that was approved by the Plenum and subsequently by the Supreme Soviet stated that enterprises would operate on the basis of full *khozraschet* and complete self-financing. An attempt was made to curb the power of the economic ministries over the enterprises. At the same time certain elements of the old system were preserved, including the rationing of producer goods, price controls, official determination of the suppliers an enterprise should use, and resource redistribution through the ministries.

The resolutions on reform passed by the Plenum were also half-hearted. The leadership still subscribed to the basic framework of the planning system founded upon state ownership. Not a single word was said about the transition to market relations, not to speak of a market mechanism in general. I would venture to say that even the leading and certainly progressive economists (Aganbegian, Abalkin, Anchishkin, Popov, and others) were not as yet ready to discuss the transition to a market mechanism based on private property, unregulated prices, and no centralized planning. Such issues were not raised even in confidential conversations.

However, the resolutions adopted by the Plenum in 1987 departed in many respects from the economic postulates of the official ideology. The principle of unchanging prices was repudiated, competition, bankruptcy, and the necessity of ending the rationing of producer goods were recognized, and the role of the financial system was stressed. The new mind-set was conducive to subsequent work on the reform and its legislative basis.

6.1.3 It Was About Planning
Yurii Belik

The staff of the CC's Economic Department were unanimous in recognizing that the command system of economic management, built on all-embracing centralization, extensive development, and gross indicators, a system ignoring the law of value, had fully exhausted its potential as early as the beginning of 1980s. The situation called for drastically new approaches, and the documents of the radical reform undoubtedly presented such an approach. A group of the Economic Department's specialists (about twenty people) labored over their own part of the 'package.'

A hierarchical system of planning was proposed. The Concept of social and economic development with a sliding fifteen-year horizon was to serve as the foundation for more detailed Main Directions for the next fifteen years and the next five years. The Main Directions, in turn, was to serve as the foundation of the five-year plan, which was to become the primary tool for implementing the long-term strategic social and economic objectives. Annual planning would be delegated to the enterprises themselves. The planning mechanism represented the cornerstone of the entire program for improving the mechanism of management. However, the radical reform went no further than good intentions since it was never implemented.

6.2 The Preparation of the Reform: Economists' Views

6.2.1 The Rush
Oleg Yun´

While I was not directly involved in drafting the reform adopted at the June 1987 Plenum of the CC, its approach coincided with my own views nurtured for many years and developed in my book (Yun´ 1986). The goal was to switch from mainly administrative to economic methods of management at all levels of the economy, and to democratize management. Enterprises could set their own five-year and annual plans based on the state orders, orders placed by enterprises and organizations, and consumer demand.

Economic levers of state control and the initial data for the compilation of enterprise plans included control figures, long-term economic norms, state orders, and quotas (*limity*).[4] Enterprises were to pay the government for the capital, labor, and natural resources they used. The scope of centrally-set prices was to be drastically reduced, and they were to be integrated with the five-year plan so they could embody the conditions and the objectives of the economy for the planned period.

To coordinate the reform with socioeconomic policy, as well as to bring together all the central economic agencies, in July 1987 a new body, the Economic Council, was formed. Headed by the chairman of Gosplan (from February 1988, Yu.D. Masliukov), it included the heads of the economic agencies. I was appointed executive secretary of the Council. Masliukov, who had previously worked at the VPK, was a wise manager with a good knowledge of the economy, who was fast mastering the principles of the market mechanism. He was soon elected alternate member, and then full member, of the Politburo.

The new economic mechanism was to be tested as the Thirteenth Five-Year Plan (1991–1995) was being drafted, in order to enter the new plan period with a well-oiled system. However, the Law on State Enterprises demanded that all enterprises switch to full *khozraschet* and self-financing in 1988–1989, when the economic mechanism for assuring all enterprises equal starting conditions was not yet in place.

The enterprises were to be given norms, which by using they would develop their five-year plans. In reality the conversion to full *khozraschet* and self-financing was undertaken during the Twelfth Five-Year Plan period. Norms for incentive and investment fund formation and payments to the state had to be made to fit the current plan. Most ministries calculated the norms backward from the results planned for the remaining years of the plan. The sum of planned investment in retooling and expansion, construction and maintenance of social projects, and all bonus funds, determined the amount of profit to be retained by the enterprise. Its ratio to planned profit determined average norms of allocation to the various funds. The remaining profit was to be remitted into the budget as payments for the use of capital and payments out of profits. Payment for the use of assets varied between 2% and 8% depending on the amount of profit to be paid to the budget. The shortfall, that is, the annual difference between the payments into the funds and the amounts needed, was to be covered by borrowing.

Since plan targets and profitability varied across enterprises, all norms for profit allocation and distribution among the incentive funds were calculated individually for each enterprise. Essentially, the norms became just another form of enterprise-specific obligatory assignment. Audits indicated that many ministries took advantage of this 'flexibility' to revise the norms, eroding the stability of the economic environment and undermining enterprises' responsibility and incentives. The revised system of prices was to be developed together with the new five-year plan. This made impossible the precise comparison of the social cost and benefit of the enterprises' activity under the new system.[5] Payments for the use of natural resources intended to collect rent arising as a result of differences in natural conditions were never instituted. Hence a significant portion of the rent was retained by the enterprises controlling these resources.

The new mechanism was designed to induce enterprises to earn profit to be used for innovation and for their economic and social development. Yet conversion to free trade in producer goods was supposed to be completed only by 1992. While the opportunity to make money for investment was unlimited, the opportunity to purchase investment goods was rather limited. Quotas on contract work and the centrally distributed investment goods were supposed to be granted only for the purpose of fulfilling state orders. This created the danger that the enterprises' earnings might become worthless, especially in view of the fact that many enterprises had to work at full capacity just to fulfill state orders.

These and other inconsistencies and the ways to remedy them were addressed in my memo sent to the Economic Department of the CC and to the deputy chairman of the Commission and Gosplan S. Sitarian as early as August 1987. The same topic was explored in my article.[6] Neither got any response. Implementation had already begun.

Finally, it was proclaimed that: "Everything is permitted which is not explicitly forbidden by a law." All decrees, including the ministries' regulations, were to be repealed if they contradicted the Law on the State Enterprise and other new regulations. This was done promptly. However, new regulations were not yet established. This gave rise to a complete lack of discipline.

The *ad hoc* and inconsistent nature of the economic reform stemmed from the diversity of views in government as well as in academic circles. This diversity of opinion was not bad per se since it made for a more objective analysis of the issue. However, at any given moment, only one course of action can actually be implemented. The greatest flaw of all the economic transformations in our country was that the most important issues were decided in an authoritarian manner rather than on the basis of dialogue and converging points of view. In order to expose and correct mistakes in a timely manner it is necessary to let them surface. This is incompatible with a rushed implementation of the reform within such a brief period of time.

The success of the large-scale experiment would have been reinforced and the result of perestroika might have been different if the enterprises had converted to full *khozraschet* and self-financing based on carefully worked out control figures for 1991–1995, a mutually consistent set of economic regulators ensuring equal starting conditions for the enterprises, and a comprehensive and consistent set of laws and regulations.

6.2.2 The Hubris
Gennadii Zoteev

Under Gorbachev, Gosplan was still a well-oiled reliable machine in the bureaucratic sense of the term. This machine was obviously ill equipped to deal with reform, but it was in good working order as far as the system's survival was concerned. However, Ryzhkov, Aganbegian, Sitarian, Vid, and other dilettantes misused the machine, thus discrediting Gosplan, perhaps inadvertently, in the eyes of Gorbachev. In any case, Gorbachev's relations with Gosplan were tense since his tenure as the secretary of the CC for agriculture. This was one reason why Gorbachev was so susceptible to the idea of a radical restructuring of the Soviet economic system.

The initial development of a reform package was delegated to Gosplan in 1986. To this end, Ryzhkov invited Gvishiani and his team to Gosplan to prepare a detailed proposal on improving the economic mechanism.[7] Around August 1986 Gvishiani and his entire team suddenly vanished from Gosplan. There were rumors that an angry Ryzhkov called Gvishiani an impotent scholar who failed to prepare quality documents for the reform package and the acceleration of technological progress.

Baibakov's retirement and his replacement by Talyzin marked the end of the command-like image of Gosplan. Baibakov was not a habitual watchdog and had a very natural and straightforward demeanor, but inside he was a typical representative of Stalin's guard. Here is just one example. At a meeting of the Gosplan *collegium*, one of the department chiefs collapsed. He was taken to the waiting room of Baibakov's office, and after fifteen minutes the doctor pronounced him dead. The secretary whispered the tragic news to Baibakov, who did not bat an eyelash and calmly, as if nothing had happened, continued to lead the meeting of the *collegium*.

In 1988, while still working as an advisor to Ryzhkov, Baibakov invited me for a discussion. For almost two hours I tried to explain to Baibakov the past, the present, and the future of the Soviet economy. He listened rather lethargically, probably because he simply failed to comprehend many of the things I was saying. At the end of the conversation he snapped out of his slumber and asked a rhetorical question: "How can all this be happening? We worked so hard and accomplished so much. We have such a powerful industry, the energy sector, and here you are coming up with such gloomy assessment and forecasts." The mentality of a petroleum engineer and the Minister of the Petroleum Industry kept prevailing.

The same fate awaited Gosplan. Never homogeneous or monolithic, it was torn by the same conflicts as the CC and other government bodies.

Gosplan's solutions were generally adequate and well grounded for concrete, technical, engineering, or sectoral problems. But as soon as the issue infringed on the vital political interests of the system, Gosplan was totally inept as the central managerial body. It was powerless against the arbitrary actions of politicians and the onslaught of dilettante economists with their miraculous prescriptions. This limitation of Gosplan was also a major flaw of the Soviet system. The system was too cocky and it overestimated its potential.

I would not rule out, at least as a working hypothesis, that the Soviet system could, as a result of lengthy rationalization (three to four five-year periods), have adjusted to the new conditions and eventually transformed itself. This process would have entailed getting rid of certain flaws, first and foremost putting an end to the Party's arbitrary political intervention in the economy. However, history was to take a different course. The top-ranking Party officials were infused with nihilism and skepticism toward the planned system and cultivated this attitude by 'flirting' with dilettante scholars like Leonid Abalkin, Stanislav Shatalin, Nikolai Petrakov, and Abel Aganbegian. It was this group which defined the opposition to Gosplan during the initial stage of Gorbachev's rule. They accused Gosplan of narrow-mindedness and conservatism, and regarded Gosplan's conception of a very cautious movement forward as plain wrong.

I recall the debates at one of the meetings of the research council (of which I was a member) of the Institute of National Economic Forecasting at the end of 1987. My thesis was that academic economics, as represented by its 'generals,' played a dangerous game when it presumed to know how to reform the Soviet economic system. Even Western economics had not provided any clear-cut solutions to this problem. Gosplan needed the help of academic economists not to concoct new myths, but to debunk them. Since academic economists now had a much greater influence on Gorbachev, they should honestly admit to him that they did not have (at least yet) any quick-fix solutions, nor could they predict the consequences of reform for the Soviet economy. My arguments met with a sharp rebuttal from Shatalin and Yaremenko (Aganbegian pretended to be editing some text and did not partake in the discussion). The crux of their argument was that I represented the standard Gosplan approach which denied new scientific developments, and that Gosplan was simply incompetent and unable to digest scientific recommendations. I retorted that Gosplan did indeed suffer from incompetence but that the academics should also have admitted that Soviet economics was bankrupt and was getting lost in its own backyard.

6.2.3 Getting the Details Wrong
Yevgenii Yasin

The Gestation of the 'Radical' Reform

The year 1986 seemed to end successfully. Propaganda proclaimed the reversal of the economic growth slowdown. Official statistics announced that the growth rate of national income had increased to 4.1%, which should have testified to the success of the acceleration policy. In reality, the situation was not as good as it seemed. The improper accounting for growth in construction alone inflated the rate of growth of the national income by 1.5–2%. Where growth did occur, it had an unhealthy character. To improve upon the enterprises' gross indicators, their managers would occasionally be made to perform completely useless work.[8]

The architects of the 'acceleration' policy themselves realized that it had failed, and were considering what to do next. No one doubted the necessity of deep institutional reforms. The question was what they should be. In 1986 there were disparate attempts to improve the economic mechanism based on the conceptual framework of the still unfulfilled 1979 reform, and also on 'the large-scale economic experiment' initiated under Andropov and embodying the same ideas.[9] The experiment aimed at providing incentives to the enterprises to fulfill their customers' orders rather than pile up gross indicators. (In this sense the 'acceleration' was actually a deviation from this course.) The other objective was to give enterprises more autonomy, in particular in allocating their income. Instead of setting the targets for all revenues and outlays in absolute terms in the enterprise finance plan, the state would set the shares of profit which should be allocated to particular uses.

During 1986, these innovations spread to a variety of sectors, with the peculiarities of each one taken into account. Over 100 decrees were issued to enact these changes in particular sectors. At the same time, at the initiative of certain enterprises, such as the Volga car plant in Togliatti and the Frunze Machine-Building Association in Sumy, Ukraine, new experiments were started in the hope that they would reveal more effective ways to manage the economy.[10] These enterprises used the experiments as an occasion to win concessions and privileges, as a result of which the experiments always proved successful.

Amidst this bustle the country's leadership began to think that the time was ripe for something more fundamental. Hence, from the beginning of 1987 preparations started for a 'radical' economic reform. The brightest economists, including Academicians L. Abalkin, A. Aganbegian, and A. Anchishkin, and the more educated members of the staff of the CC and the CM, were summoned to work on the main directions of the reform.

The main idea of the reform was 'socialism with a human face' along the lines of Hungary and Yugoslavia, a third way, neither capitalism (i.e., a normal market economy), nor 'barracks socialism' of the type previously epitomized by the USSR. In other words, something beautiful, humane, and more efficient. There was never talk of repudiating the entire system, but only of modernizing and reinvigorating it. It was expected that enterprises with a somewhat greater autonomy and guided by stronger and more effective economic incentives (established, naturally, by the government) would perform more efficiently. The old socialist idea of self-management by the workers' collectives would provide strong incentives for productivity growth.

The theoretical framework of the 1987 reform was fashioned by the most progressive Soviet academic economists out of the stock of ideas which they had accumulated over the twenty years of Brezhnev's rule under strong ideological pressure and in isolation from the main currents of Western economics. It could not have been otherwise. The people who were enlisted to lay the foundation of reform had been criticizing the existing system and presenting proposals for steering it in a market direction throughout the entire Brezhnev period. There simply was not anyone better.

There were two main schools of progressive Soviet economists: the traditional Marxist political economists who thought 'market socialism' was feasible, and the adherents of the theory of the optimally functioning economy brought up on the ideas of L. Kantorovich, V. Novozhilov, and V. Nemchinov.[11] The latter group was closer to Western economics and worked primarily in TsEMI in Moscow and the Institute of Economics and the Organization of Industrial Production in Novosibirsk. The leadership was ready to accept everything they proposed. Of course, the academic ideas were transformed and brought down to earth by the practitioners from the CC and CM apparatus, Gosplan and Gossnab, who had a closer knowledge of the realities of Soviet economic life.

The enterprise was thought of as the key element of reform. The best possible conditions must be created for its successful performance. The next step was to create an environment (the administrative control structure, the finance and credit system, and the organization of supply) capable of supporting these favorable conditions. The word 'market,' which had long circulated in academic circles, was still unpronounceable to the political leadership.

An intensive process of dismantling Communism's ideological dogmas went on during the period in question. It constituted one of Gorbachev's greatest accomplishments. This process seemed exceedingly slow to the reformist participants, even though they themselves at times could not keep up with what was already permissible and what was still not, or what was the meaning of the ever-accelerating changes.

The Law on the State Enterprise

Introduction

At the core of the reform was the Law on the State Enterprise, passed in July 1987. It embodied the main ideas of the 'new' Soviet model of social-ism with a human face. It also set the stage for the future collapse of the Soviet economy. To implement the law a package of eleven decrees of the CC and the CM on restructuring Gosplan, Gossnab, the Ministry of Fi-nance, the sectoral ministries, the banking system, and other economic agencies was immediately adopted.[12]

The Law on the State Enterprise bore little resemblance to an ordinary law. To a large degree it was a political statement, which was evident even in its language. For example, part 3, paragraph 1, of the Law states that "the main objective of an enterprise is to fully satisfy the social needs of the economy and of citizens with its products while maintaining high quality, at minimum cost, and increasing its contribution to the acceleration of the socioeconomic development of the country." It is hard to imagine similar wording which does not oblige anyone to do anything in the statutes of another country. The fundamental principles of the reform, which stem from the Law on the State Enterprise and the related decrees, are described below.

Democracy in the Workplace and Self-Management

While this was not the main aspect of the reform, its results were probably the most destructive. At the time the law was adopted political democracy was out of the question since Gorbachev's political reforms were still a year away. Democracy in the workplace was offered instead. Although privatiza-tion was not even mentioned, the law proclaimed that: "the workers' collec-tive, being a fully-fledged master at the enterprise, shall resolve all questions of production and social development independently" (O korennoi . . . 1987, p. 6). The managers of the enterprises and their subdivi-sions, down to the level of foremen and team leaders were to be elected. The directors would be elected for a five-year term by the labor collective. True, the superior body (ministry) retained the right to confirm or reject the election results, and in the latter case to hold a new election. Still, under these circumstances the director ceased to be the representative of the gov-ernment as the owner, but rather had to cater to the workers and their moods. He was forced to take into account factors that had nothing to do with the rational conduct of business and even more so because the law provided for the early removal of the director if the collective did not find him satisfactory.

Councils of Labor Collectives (CLC) were elected at the enterprises to act as the organs of self-government with broad powers. The representatives of the administration could occupy no more than one quarter of all the seats on the CLC. However, participation by directors was not forbidden.[13] As a result, the directors ended up heading the CLC at many enterprises. But in most cases other people came forward and soon a struggle for power between the management, the CLC, and the unions ensued (the division of responsibilities between the two latter bodies was not well defined).

In all this could clearly be seen the influence of the Yugoslav variant of socialism, which by this time had already demonstrated pretty clearly its inadequacies. It is enough to say that the high rates of inflation, which the Yugoslav system of socialist self-management had experienced for years, were to a considerable extent caused by the orientation to consumption of self-managed enterprises. In the USSR the negative features of this system manifested themselves in 1988–1990.

State Orders and Direct Links Among Enterprises

The reform was *not* about a rejection of the Soviet mode of planning and a transition to a market economy. It was about making planning less rigid and providing more autonomy for the enterprises. For this purpose, obligatory plan targets for all aspects of the enterprises' performance were replaced by the state order. Along with control figures and long-term economic norms and limits, the state order became the plan's tool for steering the enterprises. The control figures were recommendations or nonobligatory targets for the enterprise's total output in monetary terms, profit, hard currency revenue, and some aspects of technological innovation and social development.[14] State orders were mandatory and in this respect differed little from the old planning methods. All Soviet reforms engaged in semantic games, when terms associated with negative phenomena were replaced by more fashionable and progressive ones, while the substance remained the same. However, it soon became clear that this change had taken on a life of its own, independent of the wishes of its initiators.

If the traditional plan targets covered the entire output of the enterprise, the state order set targets only for major products, as well as for the commissioning of new production capacities and 'social' projects financed by centralized investment.[15] The collapse of the planned system essentially started when the state orders were limited to only *part* of the output. The logic of planning requires completeness. The mandatory state order, just like the plan target, makes sense if the government also provides enterprises with the material resources needed to fulfill the order. This is precisely what the government did by allocating *fondy* and *limity,* documents entitling the enterprise to raw materials, parts, and subassemblies which were also produced to meet plan targets. Those who produced them in turn demanded rations of inputs. In the end, either the planned system had to encompass the entire economy or it could not function effectively.[16]

Establishing state orders for only a part of the output meant that some necessary inputs had to be obtained by the enterprises on the free market, without government rations. However, with prices set by the government, it often turned out that these resources were in short supply. Because the enterprises could not secure the necessary materials, they had grounds to reject the state order even though it was supposedly compulsory. Or the enterprises would demand that the government allocate them a quota for the materials, which meant that the producers of these materials would have to receive a state order. An insoluble contradiction was emerging: either every unit received a state order for everything it manufactured, which meant a return to the old system, or free prices would have to be introduced and state orders cease to be mandatory, with the government competing with other buyers. The latter option would have meant a real transition to the market, which was definitely not envisioned by the 1987 reform.

The state orders limited to only part of the output had to be supplemented by direct exchange between enterprises without government interference. While the market was not explicitly mentioned, that is what was meant by direct ties between enterprises and wholesale trade. Direct ties had always existed between enterprises, but they had been considered illegal since they were not under government control. Permitting these ties legitimized direct trade between enterprises. However, from the very beginning this trade developed under the perverse conditions of government-set prices and a highly monopolized economy. Therefore, exchange mainly took the form of barter, when prices did not perform their function and had to be supplemented by other incentives in order to achieve mutually agreeable contract terms. For example, one enterprise would agree to provide its supplier with some part of its material incentives fund or some scarce commodity which began to perform the role of quasi-money. Items in high demand, like construction materials and cable, frequently played this role.

All this entailed countless abuses and undermined the system of state orders, from which the enterprises wanted to escape by any means, since direct exchange was more lucrative. The market came into direct confrontation with planning and began gradually to squeeze it out. Yet the very form assumed by this process was detrimental to the economy as a whole, leading to a drop in output, increasing costs, and the destruction of the existing economic links and mechanism of resource allocation.

Distribution of the Enterprises' Income

Long-term economic norms—the third lever for directing enterprises' activities according to the plan—were to regulate the uses of their revenue. The enterprises were to convert to full *khozraschet* and self-financing, which meant to cover all their outlays including investment from their own revenues. Replacing the planned distribution of revenues by economic norms was to give enterprises more freedom and incentives to increase revenues: the more an enterprise earned, the more it retained.

The law allowed enterprises to pick one of two models of *khozraschet*. The first model was based on normal accounting of cost and profit. Economic norms determined the shares in which profit was divided between the enterprise's contribution to the state budget and its funds for development of production, social development, and material incentives.[17] Under the second model economic norms applied to the distribution of the 'self-financing income,' calculated by deducting the nonlabor cost from the revenue. The wages fund was determined as a residual after making payments into the budget and the three enterprise funds mentioned above according to economic norms.

The presence of two alternatives in the law was the fruit of ideological discussions concerning the form most consistent with socialist principles. It was argued that the second model alone was consistent with socialist ideals since it created greater interest on the part of the workers in the performance of their enterprise. The concept of profit was not appropriate for socialism with a human face. The first model was defended by the argument that profit is not an ideological notion and that labor compensation should be included with other costs of production, for otherwise no one would try to minimize it. It was decided that this dispute ought to be resolved experimentally. Actually, the only substantive difference between the two models was that the second one provoked a faster growth of incomes and aggravated inflation. The main problem was, who was to determine the economic norms and how?

At that time the USSR had practically no taxation system and the 1987 reform did not envision its creation. The population paid income tax at a single 13% rate. The tax was deducted from wages by employers, and the tax was invisible for the people: they were simply paid less money. Enterprises contributed part of their profit into the budget at a rate determined by the superior organ: higher profits meant higher liability while losses were covered by state subsidies. Therefore, the shift to economic norms for payments to the budget was a certain step forward toward creating a tax system in the USSR. In other respects it not only failed to justify itself, but also greatly fueled the crisis.

Since Soviet enterprises for decades had been shielded from natural competitive selection, their profitability, costs, and investment varied enormously. To suddenly impose a uniform system of norms, along the lines of a single tax schedule, was practically impossible. Moreover, the system of fixed government prices left enterprises with no room to maneuver. As a result, the uniform, long-term economic norms quickly degenerated into individualized norms calculated specifically for each enterprise based on its performance in the past in absolute terms, with a few minor adjustments. Attempts to get around this stumbling block by basing the norms on the rate of growth of some indicator, such as the wage fund in relation to the growth of sales, failed. The reformers immersed themselves in details, though the idea itself was not viable.

Yet it did have a visible practical effect. Wages went up and so did the various enterprise funds which were being spent less and less rationally. The final result was the acceleration of inflation, deterioration of the government's fiscal situation, and mounting shortages of consumer goods.

Emasculation of the Sectoral Ministries

The planned economy's strictly hierarchical system of management had its own logic. The sectoral ministries played a key role in this hierarchy by providing a link between the enterprises and the highest echelons of planning. The rotting of the Soviet system during its decline manifested itself, among other things, in the ministries turning into giant departmental monopolies which not only failed to carry out the will of the Center, but increasingly imposed their own interests upon the Center. The more powerful the ministry (for example, Sredmash, which united the entire nuclear industry), the more the government danced to its tune.

From the very beginning of perestroika the sectoral ministries came under fire from all sides. They came under fire from the enterprises, on whose autonomy they encroached; from the local Party authorities with whom they perpetually competed for influence; and from liberal economists who saw the ministries as the main stronghold of the old system.

Already in 1986, at the insistence of the enterprise directors, Gorbachev eliminated one level of the hierarchy, the All-Union Industrial Associations. The associations, which had replaced *glavki* (chief administrations), were in charge of specific subsectors within the sectoral ministry. For example, the Ministry of the Automobile Industry included the 'Autodiesel' association, in charge of all enterprises making diesel engines or their major components. Eliminating the industrial associations was perhaps Gorbachev's first move as a reformer, and a characteristic one at that. He always listened to advice, but only acted on the advice which happened to reach him at that particular time and which did not require extraordinary effort.

The Law on the State Enterprise was the next step in disarming the sectoral ministries, that cornerstone of the planning hierarchy. It did not eliminate the ministries themselves, but significantly changed the nature of their relations with the enterprises. Prior to the reform the relationship was simply one of subordination on the part of the enterprises. Now the ministries were responsible for expanding the enterprises' autonomy, guiding them primarily with economic tools. The ministries were forbidden to issue any commands that were not on the government-approved list. An enterprise could appeal in court to have any of the ministry's orders that exceeded its jurisdiction fully or partially annulled and demand damages for any loss suffered as a result of these directives or any other inappropriate action of the superior body. Subordination was thus strangely mixed with the legal relationship of equal parties, the only relationship proper in a court of law.

The power of the ministries was greatly undermined. They continued to perform their functions primarily because, as it turned out, the enterprises needed them. In the absence of a market, the ministries arranged all intrasector cooperation, financed research and development projects, trained personnel, and lobbied the central government on behalf of the enterprises. However, the ministries' influence continued to decline, destroying the principal coordination mechanism of the planned economy. Nothing came along to take the place of the ministries, at least not until 1992.

Laws on Cooperatives and Leases

Along with the Law on State Enterprises, the laws on Cooperatives and Leases, passed in 1988, played an important role in the reform. They marked the beginning of the rebirth of private property and entrepreneurship in Russia. At the time, these laws did the most to bring Russia closer to a market economy. Technically, both laws also had an ideological justification. Lenin once stated that cooperatives are acceptable under socialism, even though they had greater autonomy and could act like normal market agents. To stay within the framework of 'the socialist choice' while using some of the advantages of the market, the reformers recalled the notion of cooperatives and decided to use them to augment the state enterprises by filling the niches unoccupied by the latter.

The important thing was that essentially cooperative property was, or could be, private; state enterprises could become partners in cooperatives; and the prices of cooperatives' output were not fixed except when they were fulfilling state orders and receiving government entitlements to inputs. While cooperatives did not have the resources of state enterprises, they enjoyed much greater independence. Taxes on cooperatives were initially low, and their opportunities enormous. Literally within a year or two, under the guise of cooperatives, private enterprise was born.

Cooperatives paid much higher wages and salaries than state enterprises, and needed the resources that only the latter possessed. A symbiosis between the state enterprises and the cooperatives quickly emerged. The cooperatives were like parasitic fungi preying upon the state economy and decomposing it. This became another front in the struggle between planning and market, where planning suffered total defeat. This could not but hurt the economy at some stage.

Leases represented another method of privatizing the economy while preserving the socialist facade, like oral sex for virgins. State enterprises were rented out to their employees, who formed a special legal entity, an organization of tenants. These organizations got the rights of possession and use of government property if they fulfilled certain conditions stipulated in the lease. The lease could also contain an option to buy, so that in a few years an enterprise could become the property of its workers. Leased enterprises were not fully independent like cooperatives, but still enjoyed more discretion than state-run organizations. They were no longer subordinated to the ministries or other agencies, and were bound only by the lease. The period from 1988 to 1990 was full of conflicts between employees who wanted to lease their enterprises and ministries which were supposed to play the role of landlord but did not want to give up their power.

6.3 It Was Not Tried

6.3.1 There Was No Real Effort to Implement the Resolutions
Vladimir Mozhin

Propagandistic babbling surrounding the reform was soon in full swing, but practical steps were lacking. In fact, certain seemingly reform-oriented measures were very superficial and served only to confuse the system of economic control. For instance, in the fall of 1987 a commission was set up, composed of several members of the Politburo and chaired by Ryzhkov. Its job was to define the new functions of the central agencies and the organizational structure of the ministries in accordance with the adopted resolutions. The commission held meetings twice a week. Piles of paper were accumulated. The ministries were given instructions on the number of deputy ministers, the number of directorates, and so on. However, the crucial issue of the real functions of the ministries was virtually ignored. A similar commission headed by Ligachev examined the structure of local administrative bodies. The two commissions continued to operate for an entire year, until the fall of 1988. Their work was endorsed by the Politburo, although it produced no positive results.

In the light of the political sensitivity and complexity of the situation, in June of 1987 our group proposed setting up a state committee for economic reform, headed by Gorbachev. We resorted to a historical analogy. After several unsuccessful attempts, serfdom in Russia was abolished only when the committee responsible for it was chaired by the country's highest authority, Emperor Alexander II. Unfortunately, Gorbachev rejected our proposal. Moreover, he increasingly shifted the work on the reform to Ryzhkov and the CM.

One year after the Law on the State Enterprise was adopted, the Economic Department of the CC sent a memo to the Politburo. It stated that the former system of mandatory plan targets had been preserved under the guise of state orders. In order to fulfill gross value of output targets, enterprises were still producing goods that were not in demand. Ministries continued to control the resources of the enterprises, redistributing them from the more efficient to the less efficient ones in order to keep the latter afloat.

Very little changed also in the upper rungs of management. This was inevitable, since the reform of each system was assigned to the agency in charge of it. For instance, Gossnab was drafting the proposal for the transition to wholesale trade in producer goods, the State Committee on Prices for reform of price setting, and the Finance Ministry for reform of the financial and credit system. All these agencies resisted innovations and clung to the established practices.

The government was reluctant to make decisions on the most controversial issues. Thus, the reform of price setting was constantly postponed, as neither Gorbachev nor Ryzhkov took a definitive stance on it.

Meanwhile, the economic situation in the country continued to deteriorate. By the mid-1980s energy prices on the world market had declined. At the same time economic decentralization expanded, due in part to a substantial growth of the cooperative sector after the adoption of the Law on Cooperation in 1988. The rate of growth of personal incomes increased sharply. Yet the economy, with its hypertrophied raw materials and military sectors, was unable to respond with a higher output of consumer goods and services.

The growing budget deficit necessitated printing more money, since one-third of budget outlays went to pay wages. In the Eleventh Five-Year Plan the average annual net emission of new cash money totaled 3.6 billion rubles, but in 1987 it was 5.9 billion, in 1988 it grew to 11.7 billion, and in 1989 it grew to 18 billion rubles. The resulting inflationary pressure manifested itself mainly in the growing shortages of goods. (Since prices were fixed by the government, the price level was growing at only about 2.0–2.5% annually.) Every passing day witnessed store shelves becoming more and more empty.

The economic reform adopted in June 1987 came to a halt as no practical steps, apart from the Law on the State Enterprise, were taken to implement it. This paralysis amid the deteriorating economic situation discredited the idea of economic reform and played into the hands of its opponents.

6.3.2 Conservative Resistance
Vadim Medvedev

After the Plenum, the struggle over the practical interpretation of its resolutions resumed, increasingly dominated by conservative forces on the one side and by growing radical opposition on the other. Already after several months, during the compilation and discussion of the plan for 1988, the planners tried to make control figures obligatory. Many instances of enterprises being pressured by planners, ministries, and local soviet and Party organs came to light. For example, orders for light industry enterprises from trade organizations were 3 billion below the plan estimate. Instead of encouraging producers to offer the retailers high-demand goods, the government and Gosplan raised the alarm. They stopped just short of accusing the trade organizations of forgetting society's interests, of being unwilling to attain a balanced plan and to lead the struggle for completion of the Twelfth Five-Year Plan. The state order was widely used as a hidden form of preserving state planning, applied not only to production used by the state, but to any important output. As a result, in many enterprises the share of state orders in total production reached 90–95%.

In the new system of relations between enterprises and the budget, the formation of wage funds, economic incentives funds, and other aspects of the economic activity of enterprises should have been regulated by uniform and stable economic norms. In practice, they were neither uniform nor stable. Instead of being a means to facilitate the transition from command to

Table 6.1

Main Economic Indicators, Average Annual Rate of Growth (%)

	1981–1985	1986–1988
GNP	3.7	3.9
Industrial output	3.6	4.0
Agricultural output	1.0	3.0
Consumer goods production (excluding alcohol)	3.7	5.0
Labor productivity	2.7	2.8

economic methods of management, they became a means to preserve ministe-rial control, ensnaring enterprises by numerous restrictions and conditions.

As a result of all this, already at the end of 1987 and the beginning of 1988, the reform gradually began to lose shape. The aggravated political struggle, the emergence of opposition to perestroika from both the left and the right, obviously took the attention of Gorbachev and his aides away from the practical implementation of economic reform.

6.4 It Failed Because of Poor Design

6.4.1 Contradictions of Reform
Oleg Yun´

Although I myself was actively involved in the reform I have no clear-cut answer as to why real-life implementation deviated from the officially pro-claimed principles of reform. Gorbachev clearly saw these contradictions. In his speech at the June 1987 Plenum he pointed out the difficulty of transition to full *khozraschet* and self-financing when the Five-Year Plan was already in progress. However, apart from the vague statements that "history has not given us much time to solve this problem" and "this ought not to stop us from implementing the new principles of management," there was no explanation for this conscious discrepancy between theory and prac-tice. In 1987 the power of the general secretary was still practically absolute and unchallenged. There was no democratic discussion and decision mak-ing in the economic and political fields yet, although the process of general democratization had already begun. As a result, the implementation of the resolutions passed by the Plenum began in spite of all their contradictions.

Prior to 1988 the economy was rebounding (see Table 6.1).[18] The con-version to new methods of management was an important contribution to the economic recovery.

Table 6.2

Comparative Performance of Enterprises Under the Alternative Systems of Management in 1988

System	Labor productivity growth rate (%)	Profit growth rate (%)	Cost reduction per ruble of output (%)
Full *khozraschet*	5.7	11.4	1.0
Large-scale experiment	3.6	9.4	0.5

The year 1988 gives us a glimpse of the reform's potential. In 1988, 60% of industry and selected other sectors operated under the new system, while 40% of industry and some other sectors remained under the large-scale experiment.[19] Both groups were in comparable conditions: the same supply and pricing environment, and no privileges for the enterprises operating under the new system. In 1988, the enterprises that switched to the new system of management significantly outperformed the others (see Table 6.2). For each 1% of labor productivity growth, average monthly wages at the enterprises on full *khozraschet* grew by 0.2 percentage points less than those at enterprises working under old rules. Enterprises that switched to the new system were cutting down their work force twice as fast as the others.

However, as early as 1988 an excessive growth of wages (especially disbursements from the material incentives fund) relative to the growth of output and labor productivity emerged. The planned ratio of average monthly wage growth to labor productivity growth in industry was set at 0.78 for 1986–1990 (a 1% increase in labor productivity should have generated a 0.78% increase in wages). In 1986–1987 this ratio held firm, but in 1988 it rose to 1.7. The average ratio for 1986–1988 was 1.06% rather than 0.78%. In 1989 enterprises shoveling their earnings into wage increases pushed the ratio up to 2.0, that is, the growth of wages outpaced labor productivity growth twofold.

The explosive growth of wages was ignited by the competition on the labor market resulting from the rapid expansion of cooperatives following the adoption of the Law on Cooperation in May 1988. To encourage the creation of cooperatives the Supreme Soviet imposed a purely symbolic tax on their income, allowing them to pay wages twice as high as at state enterprises for the same work. Skilled workers began to flock to the cooperatives, and the managers of state enterprises had to raise the wages of their employees to stem the outflow.

Table 6.3

Imbalance in the Consumer Goods Market, Annual Growth Rates (%)

	1987	1988	1989	1990
Consumer goods industry output (group B)	4.1	5.4	4.9	4.4
Producer goods industry output (group A)	3.7	3.4	0.6	−3.2
Household income	3.9	9.2	13.1	16.9
Retail sales	1.1	6.9	8.4	10.3

The actual gains in personal income were rather modest, but still they could not be turned into goods or services. Beginning in 1987, output of consumer goods grew faster than that of producer goods (see Table 6.3). Still, money incomes increasingly outpaced retail sales. Inventories dwindled and shortages worsened. Social tension rose and there were rumors of a monetary reform.

There was also a pronounced disequilibrium in the producer goods market. The state order in 1989 accounted for about 70% of enterprises' capacity. Enterprises began to determine part of their production program based on prices, norms (tax rates), and the tax concessions. They would often adopt output and profit plans much less demanding than the control figures. Production of unprofitable or low-profit-margin goods was terminated, causing problems for the consumers. Sometimes, enterprises would refuse to accept a state order (compulsory under the Law on the State Enterprise) for a low-profit-margin item. In most cases enterprises simply would not enter into a contract with the user for whom state order was intended. As a result, physical flows of supplies in the economy started to rupture. Price reform was urgently needed.

6.4.2 Unintended Consequences at Work
Yevgenii Yasin

Freeing prices was, of course, unthinkable in 1987. The most the liberals were able to accomplish was a directive that government prices should be set together with other indicators of the five-year plans.[20] Contract and free prices appeared, and it was promised that their use would be allowed to expand. A comprehensive review of all prices and tariffs—yet another administrative prices increase—was planned. When rumors of the hike filtered into the press in the summer of 1988, a campaign against it began. Even though the price increase was necessary for financial stabilization, the authorities balked at acting against popular sentiments. The government was already showing its weakness, promising the public virtually un-changed prices until the end of 1990, that is, the end of the Twelfth Five-Year Plan. And this at a time when all the planning and distribution structures were being revamped [see Chapter 6.5, below, for more detail on price reform].

The introduction of economic norms for payment into the budget pre-cluded arbitrary exactions from the enterprises' revenue, resulting in a chronic shortfall of budget receipts. Meanwhile, surging enterprise revenues were increasingly being used for wage payments. At the same time, the branch lobbies' appetite for government investment did not diminish. The government was afraid to tread on the privileges of three powerful blocs—the Fuel-Energy Complex, the Military-Industrial Complex, and the Agro-Industrial Complex. It hesitated to infringe upon the interests of any social force no matter how essential such moves were to stabilize the economy. Perhaps there was some feeling of goodwill: "We want to make everyone happy, so everyone should also make everyone else happy, and everything will turn out fine."

In 1988, there were certain signs of an economic upswing, as is usually the case when inflation starts heating up. Thanks to the Law on Coopera-tives, private enterprise appeared out of thin air and started to grow. The first Russian entrepreneurs remember with gratitude N. Ryzhkov, contrast-ing him with the strict monetarist Ye. Gaidar. At the same time, their good feelings for that period stem from the fact that the conditions were then ideal for looting state property.

Despite the Law on the State Enterprise, the old mechanism was still largely operational in 1988. The ministries, already deprived of their power, continued coordinating the interaction among the enterprises on the bases of inertia and of enterprises' consent. Gossnab could no longer allo-cate or ration inputs. But it tried to use the legally recognized control figures and ceilings (*limity*), to force the enterprises to use its services in distributing that part of their output that they could now sell independently. All this kept the system afloat for a while. The situation really began to deteriorate in mid-1989.

The worsening shortages of consumer goods combined with the budget deficit and significant loss of centralized control over resource allocation forced the Union government to transfer more powers to local authorities, especially the republics. This was the basis for the growth of economic and political separatism among the regions. The latter started to curb 'exports' to other areas in order to provide for the needs of their own population.

The 'blossoming' of democracy in the workplace led to a significant slackening of work discipline. Overly demanding directors were removed.

Others, trying to win favor with the collectives, became more permissive. Still others, while flirting with the employees, began to grab more and more for themselves and their cronies in anticipation of privatization. Labor collectives would often become a director's weapon in his struggle with the ministry and superior organs. A struggle with his competitors in the market was usually unnecessary because there weren't any.

6.5 Price Reform: The Missing Link?

6.5.1 Failure of Political Will
Vadim Medvedev

The decisive blow to the 1987 reform was to its heart—price reform. The government, Gosplan, and Goskomtsen had, to say the least, no enthusiasm for this work.[21] A period of 2.5–3 years was allocated to preparing price reforms. Society would have had to live in a state of acute tension for such a long period of time! Soon after the Plenum, the government, Gosplan, and Goskomtsen began to reject the principle of conducting the reform of all prices at once.[22] The idea crept up that first only wholesale prices had to be reviewed, not touching retail prices till later. However, this meant an even greater imbalance in the price system, increasing still more state subsidies. The negative view of price reform united conservative and radical forces. The government was able to excuse itself: "We are not against price reform, but look at the popular reaction." The national political leadership of the time still had a large reserve of political trust and authority, which should have been used to implement unpopular measures for the sake of creating favorable launching conditions for economic reform. Gorbachev made a series of calming statements, and the problem of price reform was removed from the agenda. Reform of the economic mechanism lost its linchpin and headed off track. That chapter of economic history was closed toward the end of 1988 and the beginning of 1989. The first attempt to change radically the economic mechanism ended up in failure. My belief is that it was not a result of deficiencies within the 1987 reform itself, which it of course had, but a result of political factors.

6.5.2 Passing the Buck
Oleg Yun´

At the end of 1988 a number of leading scholars (Abalkin, Shatalin) spoke against price reform arguing that it would result in a reduced buying power of the ruble and might lead to social unrest given the situation on the consumer goods market. They proposed to postpone a comprehensive price reform by two–three years, creating, in the meantime, an economic environment conducive to its implementation. Yet the delay exacerbated economic chaos. Citing the resolutions adopted in 1987, the State Price Committee headed by V. Pavlov insisted upon introducing new wholesale prices starting on 1 January 1990.

N.Ya. Petrakov and Ye.G. Yasin advocated a three- to four-stage price review to be completed by 1995. Each stage was to be bolstered by strict control over enterprise and personal income, dismantling of the rationing of producer goods, reducing wasteful state expenditures, and improving investment policy. This approach ignored the need for stable norms in the Thirteenth Five-Year Plan. A.G. Aganbegian insisted that the new five-year plan be compiled in new prices, and that wholesale price revision had to be coupled with the general reform of price setting to expand the use of contract [free] prices. He further argued that price reform was essential to creating wholesale trade instead of the supply system and overcoming the fiscal crisis.

In April 1989 the Economic Council recommended to the government either to proceed with the price reform starting on 1 January 1991 (in conjunction with the overall economic reform package) or to begin a step-by-step review of the centrally-set prices while expanding the scope of free and flexible prices. The Economic Council supported the Politburo's decision to keep retail prices fixed for two–three years. In December 1989 the Congress of People's Deputies resolved to complete all preparatory work required to implement the review of wholesale and procurement prices by July 1990 and enact the new price structure at the beginning of 1991. There was no talk at the Congress of a comprehensive reform including retail prices. Ryzhkov's government did not have the spirit to go ahead with this unpopular measure.

6.5.3 Vox Populi
Yurii Belik

The price-setting reform included a review of wholesale and procurement prices, freight transport tariffs, and estimate prices.[23] It was to be carried out fast, because the Thirteenth Five-Year Plan would be based on the new prices. A retail price reform was also intended.

In 1987, the CC received nearly 1,400 letters complaining about consumer prices, and the number did not go down in 1988. Prices were rising under a variety of pretexts, reform or no reform. People were alarmed by the proposed increase in retail prices on foodstuffs and asked that the promise made by Gorbachev at the Nineteenth Party Conference—that implementing retail price reforms would not be done in a way detrimental to the standard of living—should not be abandoned. As they visited different regions of the country, high-level Party officials had to respond to a barrage of questions about prices. [On one occasion] speaking at a meeting of the Secretariat, its chairman Yegor Ligachev said: "I was almost torn to pieces."

At that same meeting, the Economic Department together with other departments of the CC were instructed to study the price situation and report to the CC within two months. Two teams composed of representatives from the Economic, Light and Food-Processing Industry, Agriculture, and the Trade and Services Departments were to study the price situation in the Moscow and Rostov regions. Additional data conforming to the guidelines of this project was obtained from five other regions. The Bureau for Social Policy of the CM, Goskomtsen, the AUCCTU, and the Union People's Control Committee also took part in the study. Analysis of the data confirmed that the country was experiencing a sustained rise in prices and tariffs for practically all goods and services.

Since 1984 official increases in retail prices had been limited to bread and alcohol. However, hidden price increases affected other goods as well. Unsatisfied demand was estimated at more than 70 billion rubles, and retail trade inventories were below the norm. All this affected retail prices and the assortment of goods produced. Rather than expanding production and improving the quality of mass-produced goods, enterprises focused on the more expensive items. In 1986–1987 more than 90% of the growth in retail turnover was due to price hikes, particularly on allegedly new products. Increased production of new higher-priced goods was accompanied by the disappearance of inexpensive quality products consumed primarily by people with low to average income. A similar drop in output afflicted products geared toward children, young people, and senior citizens. As prices rose, the increased monetary value of output was accompanied by a drop in real output sometimes by as much as 20–25%.

Food items were subject to direct as well as hidden price increases. The quality of certain meat and dairy products went down, and the prices of potatoes, vegetables, and fruits went up (especially after the maximum prices were abolished). The service sector also experienced significant price increases resulting from its enterprises being switched to complete khozraschet.

These findings were incorporated into the memorandum presented by the Economic Department and four other departments of the CC. The memorandum suggested, as a transitional policy, stabilizing the consumer market, ensuring effective control over prices, and limiting inflationary phenomena.[24] In particular, it was recommended that the state order handed down to individual enterprises stipulate the share of relatively inexpensive goods in total output. The reform of wholesale prices should make the production of cheap goods as profitable for the enterprises as that of the expensive ones. More stringent specifications were to be imposed on goods labeled 'new' and especially on fashionable items, in order to limit high prices to truly new and quality products. It was also recommended to make price setting reflect supply and demand not only by price hikes but also through price reductions resulting from, say, substituting inputs that lowered the quality of the good. Also proposed was setting up an All-Union Consumer Protection Association under the auspices of the AUCCTU and speeding up the introduction of a unified national system of price monitoring. The report was accompanied by a sizable addendum entitled 'Workers' letters concerning the reform of retail prices and price-setting.'

The report was submitted to the CC Secretariat (to Ye. Ligachev, who commissioned the report). It was assumed that the report together with the recommendations would be discussed at one of the meetings of the Secretariat where some members of the department would present it. Instead, the departments' report was circulated among the members of the Politburo and discussed at its meeting on 29 October 1988. The Politburo's decision affirmed "the essential social, political, and economic role of carrying out a retail price policy aimed at improving the welfare of the people, reinforcing the principles of social justice, and spurring labor productivity." The Politburo agreed with the basic findings and conclusions of the report and recommended (i.e., explicitly recommended rather than 'ordered'!) to the CM that it address this issue and take appropriate steps.

Around the same time one of the central newspapers published a penitential article by Academician S. Shatalin, in which he renounced his former position regarding retail price reform and advocated postponing it until certain important preconditions were met.[25] The conclusions arrived at by the departments and supported by the Politburo were further strengthened by his authority.

Notes

1. In January 1987, output of many industrial goods fell below the level of January 1986. See '*O rabote promyshlennosti SSSR v ianvare 1987 goda*', *Ekonomicheskaia gazeta*, no. 7, 1987. [Ed.]

2. The law was drafted by the Council of Ministers. The resolutions of the Plenum were drafted by Aganbegian, Abalkin, Anchishkin, Mozhin, V. Pavlov, G. Popov, and others. Among the members of the Politburo, Medvedev, Yakovlev, and later Sliunkov directly took part in the work.

3. Apparently, Gorbachev's report to the Plenum. [Ed.].

4. These probably refer to maxima for centrally financed investment. [Ed.]

5. Because of the flaws of the existing system of prices. [Ed.]

6. '*Sistema ekonomicheskikh normativov*', *Ekonomicheskaia gazeta*, no. 39, September 1987.

7. Gvishiani, Kosygin's son-in-law, headed the All-Union Institute for Systems Research of the AN USSR and the GKNT.

8. The official growth figure was also inflated by the creative accounting applied to the decline in state retail alcohol sales. [Ed.]

9. The former was enacted by the Resolution of the CC and the CM 'On the Improvement of Planning and Strengthening the Influence of the Economic Mechanism in Increasing the Efficiency of Production and the Quality of Work' of 12 July 1979. See *Sovershenstovanie* . . . 1982. [Ed.]

10. See Yun´ in Chapter 5.2.1. [Ed.]

11. Prominent scholars who introduced the ideas of the price mechanism and opportunity costs into Soviet economics and initiated 'the mathematical revolution in Soviet economics.' [Ed.]

12. For the text of the law and the decrees, see *O korennoi*. . . 1987.

13. The director was the boss of the enterprise. [Ed.]

14. Long-term norms are addressed below. [Ed.]

15. Another difference from the old system was the ambiguous clause in the law to the effect that government orders could be placed on a competitive basis, with contractual responsibility on the part of the producer and the buyer. Competitive bidding for government orders was a myth because of the monopolization and closed nature of the Soviet economy. The mutual responsibility of the parties made little sense since the buyer was a superior state body which could issue commands but had no assets, and so could not cover damages if liable.

16. Chinese experience was different. [Ed.]

17. Providing for investment, collective consumption, and monetary bonuses, respectively. [Ed.]

18. The data in Tables 6.1, 6.2, and 6.3 are official Soviet statistics. [Ed.]

19. From 1989 the entire production sector switched to the new mode of management.

20. This was one of the recommendations of the theory of optimal planning.

21. This is misleading. In 1987, in the light of the decisions of the June Plenum, new wholesale prices were calculated by Goskomtsen and distributed to the localities for introduction from 1 January 1988. At the end of 1987, however, the political leadership decided not to introduce them (Pavlov 1995, pp. 78–85). [Ed.]

22. This statement blames subordinates for the hesitations of the Party leaders. The latter suffered from what Pavlov describes as a 'Novocherkassk syndrome' (see also note 40 in Chapter 3). At the end of 1982 they drew back from the increase in the price of bread and other food products scheduled for introduction on 15 January 1983 (Pavlov, 1995, pp. 70–71). The problem was not that Goskomtsen sabotaged Gorbachev's price reform, but that Gorbachev repeatedly hesitated and wavered on this issue. [Ed.]

23. Procurement prices applied to the state purchases of agricultural products from the farms. Estimate prices were used in construction and investment planning. [Ed.]

24. This oblique formulation means: "keep and even strengthen administrative price setting, and do not raise the price level." [Ed.]

25. *Sotsialisticheskaia industriia*, 30 October 1988. The article was entitled 'I Want to Admit My Mistake' and was presented as an interview with the Academician.

7

Political Reform, 1988–1991

7.1 Getting the Party Out of the Economy

7.1.1 The Motives for Change and the Weakness of Opposition
Vadim Medvedev

The genealogy of political reform dates back to the efforts at reform of Soviet society during the Khrushchev thaw: the criticism of the cult of personality and its consequences, the disassociation from the most odious manifestations of totalitarianism. It is true that this effort was broken off midway, or even at its very beginning. But the ideological and intellectual sources of the political reforms of the 1980s lie exactly in that period, and it is not at all accidental that the banner of perestroika was raised by those 'men of the sixties,' of whom Gorbachev was one, who had felt the strongest influence of the Khrushchev thaw.[1] An understanding of the necessity of political reform was strengthened even more in the Gorbachev leadership after the first steps of perestroika. It became clear that without political reorganization in the country the whole process of reformation would be impossible.

At the Nineteenth Party Conference and at subsequent plenums of the CC the following characteristic situation usually arose. In the debate a significant part, if not a majority, of those present would sharply criticize the leadership, but then vote by an overwhelming majority to support the decisions and resolutions proposed by Gorbachev. This peculiarity of Party forums most clearly manifested itself at the Twenty-Eighth Party Congress. Thus, Ligachev, the idol of the conservative forces, who enjoyed the vocal support of the delegates at the Congress, received no more than a quarter of the votes in the election for deputy general secretary of the Party. The reformist version of the Program statement of the Congress, which I proposed in the name of the editorial commission of the Congress, was accepted by 90% of the delegates' votes.

In some situations courage failed the critics at the decisive moment. In other situations prudence prevailed, an understanding of the danger of chaos and confusion which might ensue as a result of voting against the Party leadership. The Party's traditional attitude of obedience, which had been cultivated for decades, as well as the psychology of mandatory support of ideological-political unity around the Politburo and the general secretary, also had its effect. Gorbachev skillfully used this for carrying out the reform policy. And this produced results, up to a certain moment.

7.1.2 The Party and the Economic Reform
Vladimir Mozhin

The Party was the backbone of the command economic system. The most insignificant economic decision could not be made without Party approval. No individual could hold even a minor executive position at an enterprise or the lowest position in the state apparatus without being a Party member and passing through the Party 'filter.'

Gorbachev was confronted with a formidable task. In order to dismantle the command system, he had to get rid of the Party dictatorship in the economic realm. Yet it was impossible to conduct perestroika without taking Party interests into account. Gorbachev tried to preserve the Party and reform the economic system at the same time. Life has proved this to be impossible. Initially, when reform did not yet diverge from the usual administrative methods, the Party establishment supported economic changes. As the reform became more radical, particularly after the emergence of the concept of transition to the market, the attitude of the Party officials toward Gorbachev's policy became more reserved, and then outright hostile. Soon after the Law on Cooperation and the Law on the State Enterprise were passed, the Party apparatus and the state structures dependent on it started to resist the economic reform. More and more reports of sharp criticism of the reform measures at Party meetings came from the provinces. Demands were made to shut down the cooperatives, strengthen discipline, and restore order.

One of the key reasons for the slow implementation of the reform was that Gorbachev had to take heed of other members of the Politburo. He could count on the support of only three or four Politburo members (Yakovlev, Medvedev, Shevardnadze, and, to some extent, Sliunkov). Fundamental reforms required a broad social basis. But there was no force in the country capable of giving real support to the reform. The Soviets were helpless and powerless. The state apparatus was generally antagonistic toward any innovation. The labor unions were completely in the hands of the Party committees and had no position of their own. In the CC apparatus itself, the initially reserved attitude eventually became more and more wary.

The atmosphere at the plenums of the CC changed. At first dissatisfaction with Gorbachev's actions was not openly voiced from the podium, but if one sat in the hall where the plenum of the CC assembled one could sense the atmosphere of disapproval which manifested itself in the remarks and general mood of the delegates. Gorbachev persistently stressed the impossibility of implementing fundamental economic reform without changing the political system.

The Nineteenth Party Conference marked the start of such changes. One of the key issues addressed at the Conference was the separation of powers between the Party and state bodies. It was not the first time the Party's role in the economy was questioned. It was not unusual for Party organizations to issue direct orders to the enterprises or other economic structures. The CC adopted numerous resolutions to curb such practices, but to no avail. The CC itself was engaged in economic micromanagement. The Politburo and the Secretariat discussed a multitude of purely economic questions and issued decisions that were mandatory for the CM and other government agencies. Naturally, this was a thorn in the side of the leadership of the CM.

On the basis of the resolutions passed by the Conference, the departments of the Central as well as local Party committees responsible for particular economic sectors were liquidated. Party committees were forbidden to pass resolutions containing direct orders to government, economic, or public organizations.

I do not think Gorbachev anticipated the full consequences of the political reform. Judging from his statements, he counted on democratic changes to boost the lower echelons of the Party and thus overcome the resistance of the apparatus, which was hampering the economic changes. However, the economy was hit hard by the consequences of the political reform. Party organs were dislodged from the reins of economic control at a time when the reform was making its first steps and economic levers of coordination were lacking. Without the support of the Party organs and strong Party discipline, the state apparatus was unable to successfully manage the economy. The Soviets continued to demonstrate complete helplessness. Having gained freedom and lacking any directives from above, many enterprise directors were disoriented.

Gorbachev's appeals for renewal and the use of political rather than coercive methods fell on deaf ears. The Party apparatus could not and did not want to reform. Stiff opposition to economic reform was brewing, was gaining strength with every plenum of the CC, and was clearly formulated at the Twenty-Eighth Party Congress. The reference to private property was included in the Congress policy statement only after being termed 'labor private property' and following a very animated discussion. A number of CC delegates openly accused Gorbachev of deviating from Marxist-Leninist ideology. It was hoped that after the Congress, which approved the transition to a market economy, the Party would experience reconciliation. However, debates about transition to the market raged at the October 1990 Plenum as well as at subsequent plenums all the way until the collapse of the USSR and the dissolution of the CPSU.

7.1.3 Changes in the Central Committee Apparatus
Yurii Belik

The Party's excommunication from governing the economy started with the innocent-sounding decision taken in January 1988 on Gorbachev's initiative to reorder the work practices of the Secretariat and the Politburo. The Secretariat had been in charge of all current affairs related to appointments of officials and compliance with the decisions made. Attendance at its weekly meetings by the chiefs of the departments in the apparatus of the CC CPSU was mandatory. On the one hand, the work of the departments was coordinated by the Secretariat and, on the other hand, the departments were used by the Secretariat as tools in implementing quarterly and monthly plans. The Secretariat performed all the preparatory work on the issues to be considered by the Politburo. Its meetings at the time were chaired by Ligachev.

On 7 January 1988 it was ruled that issues to be subsequently approved by the Politburo would no longer be on the Secretariat's agenda. This resolution effectively nullified the Secretariat's historically active role.

The Party's complete withdrawal from guiding the economy took place in accordance with the Politburo's September 1988 resolution concerning the reorganization of the Party apparatus (based on Gorbachev's memorandum). All the sectoral departments of the apparatus were eliminated, and their functions in directing the economy were to be taken over by government agencies established specifically for that purpose. The number of departments in the CC was reduced from twenty to nine.

In the same fashion, Party committees at all levels—republican, regional, and so on—were marked for restructuring. The managerial role of these links had been very important in view of their close ties to actual production. The sectoral principle of Party control of the economy was replaced by faceless, nebulous structures in the CC's apparatus where everyone was responsible for the 'political' supervision, which in reality meant nothing at all. The economy spun out of control and started to disintegrate rapidly.

The memoranda regarding the Secretariat and the dissolution of the branch departments of the CC were not really discussed. They reflected the position of Gorbachev and his closest ally A. Yakovlev, who was probably the one who raised the issue and prepared the memoranda. Individually, many members of the Politburo were against the proposal, but as a group they voted for it (a peculiar flaw of the so-called collective leadership). Complying with Party discipline, the departments' staff and heads went along with the restructuring while cursing the authors of these reforms in confidential discussions with colleagues. The Party's divorce from the economy was necessary, but it happened too fast. The newly formed government economic departments were ill prepared to assume the functions previously fulfilled by the Party.

In September 1988 the Socio-Economic Department effectively became the apparatus of the Commission on Social and Economic Policy (the commissions were a novelty in the restructured CC apparatus). At the end of 1990 the Socio-Economic Department was transformed for the last time into the Department for Social and Economic Policy. Its staff actually increased (while overall, the CC staff was reduced significantly). By that time, the Department had long lost control over the economic agencies it used to supervise, becoming a kind of research center.

The restructured Department was still part of the apparatus of the Commission on Social and Economic Policy, whose membership actually expanded to fifty-four people, all at the level of members of the CC. The Commission was characterized by a 'conference' style of work. At first the heads of the Union Ministries and agencies—such as Gosplan, the Ministry of Finance, the Ministry of Health, and the State Labor Committee—and the chairman of the Bureau of Social and Economic Development of the CM were all involved in the work of the Commission. The agenda at the meetings was diverse (in keeping with the makeup of the Department itself): improvement in retirement benefits, increasing the efficiency of investment, improving the economic mechanism in construction, the main directions of housing policy, and so on.

The Commission's decisions were mostly of a directive nature, that is, the Party continued to encroach on the jurisdiction of the government agencies (probably because of the system's inertia). Bewilderment regarding this issue was openly voiced. With each new meeting of the Commission the rank of the participants went down and the heads of the agencies stopped coming altogether. The effectiveness of the Commission's decisions was very low as practically all of them were ignored. Certainly by the beginning of 1991 the Party was completely dislodged from the reins of economic control.

7.1.4 How the Chinese Path of Reform Failed in the USSR
Yevgenii Yasin

The comparatively free elections to the Congress of People's Deputies in the spring of 1989 and the Congress's proceedings, where the democratic opposition for the first time presented its position, were key factors in undermining the established political regime and dethroning the Party. Liberal democrats and followers of Gorbachev were euphoric, while Communists sustained major defeats and retreated.

Influenced by his radical associates, Gorbachev had already contemplated political reform in early 1988. He was convinced that democratization would help him break the nomenklatura's resistance to economic reform. The efforts of A. Sakharov and his associates in the opposition led to the removal from article 6 of the Constitution of the formulation which declared the Communist Party to be the guiding force of Soviet society.[2] The one-party totalitarian system started to come apart at the seams. No one expected that the unraveling would happen so quickly and easily.

Party organs, standing above the law because they controlled the levers of power, were the last authority capable of maintaining the operation of the collapsing economic machinery. They could fire any director and appoint a new one, or instantly change the social status of any senior official, all of whom were Party members. This allowed them to control resources and to force any enterprise to produce required items at its own expense. Up till 1989, Party organs were literally flooded with letters and telegrams from enterprises requesting that they lean on an unreliable supplier or delinquent customer, help obtain more inputs, etc. The Party even complained that such entreaties distracted them from their primary duty—political work. Actually, this management function was the Party's most useful activity.

The Party's influence was especially strong in agriculture, where collective farms were officially not subordinate to a higher administrative agency. The Party organs organized planting and harvesting, imposed agricultural products procurement agreements, and constantly cajoled collective farms' chairmen and state farms' directors. The Party would try to fix all the leaks sprung by the economic system. When its influence began to wane, the impact on the economy was immediate, no matter what the effect of other reforms was. After this, any kind of Chinese-style gradual reform became impossible.

Why remove such a cornerstone? The Party's extensive role in managing the economy was common knowledge. However, anti-Party sentiment among the people was so strong and the Party's own actions so clumsy that after a certain time any attempt to preserve its power, including its control over the economy, became completely futile. Apart from the purely emotional reasons, it was widely accepted that any attempt to preserve elements of the old political and economic structure to smooth out the transition would only either prolong it or even halt the reform altogether. The only way for the reforms to go forward was for the Communist true believers to be completely demoralized. In general, it is hard to comprehend this period of Russian history if one attempts to find a rational explanation for all that took place.[3] Events unfolded spontaneously and in many respects irrationally, which is normal for periods of major social upheaval.

The 1987 reform was in many ways an attempt to implement the Chinese model in Russia. It envisioned a two-sector economy, where the cooperatives, leased enterprises, and joint ventures would constitute the free sector, existing alongside the state sector, with its mandatory state orders, fixed prices, and centralized allocation of inputs. The outcome is well known. Perhaps a 'humane socialism'-type model, while not particularly stable, would have provided for a gradual transition to a market economy, allowing the society a less radical and painful departure from socialist ideals. The secret police and censorship would perpetuate the old ideological cocoon, within which a new economic system would be developing like a butterfly. Tried in Hungary and Yugoslavia, this possibility was basically abandoned in Russia in 1968, when the 'Kosygin reform' was terminated. The last chance was lost in 1989, when Gorbachev's political reform removed the Communist Party from power. Afterward, events unfolded spontaneously, no longer under the control of the government or the Party.

7.2 The Collapse of Marxism-Leninism
Alexander Tsipko

The Making of an Anti-Communist

My articles in *Nauka i zhizn'* [Tsipko, 1988–1989] were widely regarded as braving the bastion of official ideology. They represented the first attempt to openly challenge Marxism and were written from a White perspective. I wrote nothing about Marxism or the Bolshevik Revolution that hadn't been said by the *Vekhi* contributors in their books (for instance, in *Iz glubiny*).[4] However, I managed to get my views published in the official press in a country that just a year earlier had celebrated the seventieth anniversary of the October Revolution and remained the stronghold of world Communism. I did this while not only being a Party member, but also working as a consultant for the International Affairs Department of the CC.

When I entered the spotlight of the national and Western press following the publication of my articles in *Nauka i zhizn'*, I found it difficult to answer the questions about when and where I broke with Marxism. Ever since I was a child I have experienced awe for everything pre-Revolutionary—books, journals, and even household items such as an old refrigerator with ice, still functional in the 1950s, which my family inherited from my grandfather. These things represented a myth, a paradise lost which captured my imagination and guided my judgment about what is good and what is bad. It was obvious that life before the Revolution had followed a normal, natural course; that people had enjoyed greater freedom; and that this world had been lost forever. When I watched films about the Civil War I always supported the Whites. I did not like these films, because the side I supported always lost.

I came to associate Marx's theory with the endless suffering of the people which I had been hearing about since childhood: collectivization, the famine of 1932–1933, and the atrocities of 1937. As children, my generation knew that the country homes of many academics were occupied by widows whose husbands had been shot, and that executions took place in the shooting range inside the Alexander Barracks on Kanatnaia Street in the evening, with airplane engines turned on.

Most families in the suburbs of Odessa, where I lived as a child, made a living by buying and selling; renting out rooms; growing tomatoes, grapes, and aubergines; and so on. A person with such a background is simply unable to accept the idea that private property is evil, or that people are collectivist by their very nature, or that the market is doomed to perish.

When I was sixteen I published an article-letter about happiness in life in the journal *Iunost'*. It shows how we found an escape from the contradiction between what we knew about our country and what we read in the history textbooks. We focused on those aspects of Komsomol (and later Party) activity that were grounded in reality and independent of ideology: learning to help friends who are in trouble, to be good students, not to steal or lie. Children are probably taught the same things at Catholic schools.

I was always a principled opponent of the covert struggle with the law that permeated our life in Odessa. I liked to do everything by the book and to defend the interests of the state. If we were sent to harvest corn at the collective farm, I was a shock worker. For me, the Komsomol, and later the Party, was a tool in the struggle for labor discipline, and against theft and cheating in trade, which I strongly disliked. This spontaneous state-minded[5] position helped me reconcile my non-Communist world outlook with life in the ranks of a Communist political organization.

Never, even as a student [at the Philosophy Faculty of Moscow State University], did I utter a single word in defense of class struggle, dictatorship of the proletariat, atheism, collectivization, Red terror, or Stalin's ter-ror. I pursued, especially in the early 1970s, those facets of Marxism—such as cooperative socialism and the free development of the individual—which went against the grain of the Marxist theory of the socialization of labor. I detested the Marx who championed the "bonfire of the revolution," as well as his teachings concerning the dictatorship of the proletariat.

Not a single student in my class (at least among those who were popular with their peers) specialized in the Marxist theory of revolution or the theory of atheism. The most gifted students tried to escape from ideology by transferring to the departments of mathematical logic or the history of philosophy. For those who, like me, were immersed in politics, the only option was the Department (*kafedra*) of Historical Materialism.

Had my classmates who committed suicide for political reasons—Abaev, Rumin, Skop, Kolzhikov—known that a quarter of a century later the crime and the insanity of the Marxist ideology and the Bolshevik experiment would be exposed, they would have opted to live and witness the day. However, at the time the hope for change was dim. Even in the mid-1960s—the most liberal period between the Twentieth Party Congress and perestroika—Stalin's rule could not be called 'criminal' and 'totalitarian.' 'Personality cult' was the harshest characterization permitted.

Like many of my classmates, I was infatuated with the young Marx, particularly his theory of alienation. The most gifted scholars at the Institute of Philosophy—our idols Genrikh Batishev, Oleg Drobnitsky, Yury Davidov, Alexander Ogurtsov—found a 'sanctuary' in elaborating upon Marx's theory of alienation. They tried to use it to show that the socialist world we lived in perpetuated the same old alienation described by Marx. Moreover, Communism as practiced had nothing to do with the Communist future envisioned by the young Marx. This kind of game posed no real threat to the Soviet regime. It 'mythologized' Marx, forging an illusion of 'another' Marx, one somehow concealed from us.

My anti-Stalinism was commonplace in my class. Among the twenty most academically advanced and politically active students in my class, only two were convinced Stalinists.[6] In nostalgia for pre-Revolutionary Russia, however, I was exceptional among my classmates.

In 1965, a course providing a broad overview of late nineteenth–early twentieth century Russian idealism was introduced at the department. Hav-ing read Sergei Bulgakov's works *From Marxism to Idealism* or *Karl Marx as a Religious Type,* I found it simply impossible to remain a believing Marxist. Pyotr Struve's *Marx's Theory of Social Development* proved even more 'cleansing.' No student familiar with such seminal works of Russian philosophical thought as *Vekhi* or *The Meaning of Creativity* by Nikolai

Berdyaev can in good conscience take seriously dilettante works by Lenin, such as *Materialism and Empirio-Criticism*. Whether intentionally or not, our professors, who had released Russia's pre-Revolutionary philosophical wealth from special collections *(spetskhrany)*, nudged us to an anti-Marxist world outlook. It was at the suggestion of the cautious Igor Narsky, my supervisor at the Student Academic Society, that I read Struve's *Marx's Theory of Social Development*. Narsky's own bitter battle with Il'enkov and his attempt to show that dialectical logic cannot exist was, in effect, a challenge to Marx's *Capital*.

In the ideology espoused by the authors of *Vekhi* and in the works of Sergei Bulgakov, Nikolai Berdyaev, and Semen Frank I discovered my own brand of liberal patriotism, which echoed my own intuitive nostalgia for the pre-Revolutionary Russia that is forever gone. Thanks to the study of pre-Revolutionary Russian philosophy, I felt myself to be a Russian. This was not because I was a baptized Orthodox Slav, but because I belonged to Russian culture and was proud of Russian culture, because we Russians had something to be proud of. The patriotism of Pyotr Struve became my patriotism. It was in 1965 between my second and third years at the university that I became the man I am today—that same man who wrote the articles in *Nauka i zhizn'* in 1988–1989.

I never even dreamt of the restoration of the intellectual climate enjoyed by Russia prior to the Bolshevik Revolution. I did believe a level of intellectual freedom on a par with [post–1956] Poland to be attainable. During the mid-1960s Adam Schaff and his bold, as we perceived it, book *Marxism and the Individual,* were really popular among students.

The Career of a White Expert

This was the worldview that I brought with me to my first job at the newspaper *Komsomol'skaia Pravda* in the fall of 1965. There, I fashioned a style of using the traditional philosophical issues and quotations from the classics to challenge the Marxist-Leninist stereotypes. An example of this was a collaborative work, *Sermon Through Action* (Molodaia gvardiia, 1968). In my own contribution, I used pronouncements of Marx and Lenin to prove the existence of a universal, timeless, and classless culture and morality. Vladimir Kokashinsky, a department head at *Komsomol'skaia Pravda* who hired me, used Lenin's statements on the dangers of bureaucratization to show that we lived in a bureaucratic state. Igor Klyamkin used Marx's criticism of the alienation of labor under capitalism to show that labor is just as 'alienated' under the Soviet system. Today, these texts, with their endless quotations, are difficult to read, but at the time, they felt like a breath of fresh air breaking the monotony of Marxist regurgitation.

This game with the official ideology did achieve some serious results. Professor Sokolov's statement at a roundtable discussion that Lenin's teaching on the conflict between materialism and idealism is "a feeble foundation" for studying the history of philosophy slipped through the censorship and was published in *Komsomol'skaia Pravda* in December 1967. Using my own column, 'Seminar with Our Correspondent Alexander Tsipko,' I managed to get into the press the banned Gregory Pomerants. Professor Kosichev threatened to expel me from the Philosophy Faculty [I was still only an intern] for publishing the subversive statements by Sokolov (who by that time had recanted, claiming that his views had been distorted). However, they couldn't really touch me once I had been transferred to the Propaganda Department of the Komsomol Central Committee. At a graduation party where we had quite a bit to drink, Professor Shkurinov, who was probably a KGB informer, just as Kosichev was, told me that if it were not for my new job, I would certainly be 'diagnosed' and sent to a mental institution.

My transfer to the Komsomol Central Committee took place during the relative ideological thaw which lasted from October 1964 to August 1968, when our troops entered Czechoslovakia. The chief of the Propaganda Department, Valery Ganichev, had the ambitious plan, supported by [the Komsomol first secretary] Sergei Pavlov, of setting up an alternative system of youth political education, more lively than the arid Party-run one. Programs of study had to be created, seminars conducted, and new textbooks written. Fresh people who knew how to write were needed. I happened to catch the eye of the leaders of the Propaganda Department (many of whom graduated from the same Philosophy Faculty as I did).

Many of them apparently believed that the methods of teaching Marxism-Leninism mattered, that if discussion of ideological issues were permitted, the 'truth of Marxism-Leninism' would win out. My boss, Victor Skorupa, a professional Komsomol official, envisaged a youth program devoted to moral issues. He wanted to go beyond the repetition of official clichés, to appear a progressive person. On the other hand, he did not understand that, as we professionals knew, Marxism and universal morality are incompatible. [Many years later] Gorbachev, who was of the same generation as my bosses, and himself a former Komsomol official, made the same mistake.

However, Gorbachev was a social democrat and a Westernizer, while my colleagues at the Propaganda Department were Red Slavophiles. The ideology of Red patriotism was formulated in the pages of the journal *Molodaia gvardiia* in the late 1960s, and its founders Victor Chalmaev, Mikhail Lobanov, Anatoly Lanshchikov, and Dimitry Balashov—that is, all the 'heroes' of the much publicized article by Alexander Yakovlev in *Literatur-naia gazeta*—were active in the Propaganda Department of the Komsomol Central Committee. Like me, these people missed the Russia that was destroyed by the Bolsheviks and sympathized with the Orthodox Church. Among themselves, they would hold entirely White conversations—two decades before perestroika began. However, I was dead set against the Red patriots' worship of Stalin, whom they regarded as a great statesman and Russia's savior.

The view of the future in the mid-1960s was more optimistic than in the early 1980s when it seemed that there was no hope for positive change (particularly during Chernenko's reign and yet another campaign against anti-Communism). Survival, even at the Komsomol Central Committee, was not a problem if one simply stuck to White patriotic views. The head of the Propaganda Department once joked about my being a White specialist in the [Komsomol] Central Committee. "If Lenin hired White specialists, then why shouldn't we have one follower of *Vekhi*?" Still, I was the only staff member to be blacklisted for travel to the West. In my three and a half years at the Komsomol Central Committee, I was granted only one trip abroad—to Bulgaria—and then reluctantly.

Starting in the fall of 1968,[7] denunciations against me began to stream into the Komsomol Central Committee. I found out afterward that they were written by employees of the Philosophy Department of the Academy of Social Sciences at the CC at the request of their boss, Felix Momdzhian. The chief policeman of philosophy Gregory Kvasov [of the Academic Affairs Department of the CC] called for my expulsion from the Party for upholding revisionist ideas and Christian morality in the pamphlet I wrote entitled *Conversations on Morality* (*Molodaia gvardiia*, 1968). The Academic Affairs Department of the CC engineered a 'trial' which took place in June 1969 at the Philosophy Department of the Academy of Social Sciences of the CC. The 'jury' was composed of people from the Institute of Marxism-Leninism and from the Ethics Section of the Philosophy Institute of the AN. I am grateful to the people at my department who helped me avoid really dire consequences. Rather than the more severe offense of committing ideological errors, I was accused in the official records of negligent editing that resulted in ideological errors. I received a reprimand and had to keep my mouth shut for half a year until the penalty was lifted, to avoid being blacklisted.

Had I chosen to remain quiet, I could have stayed at the Komsomol Central Committee as long as I wanted. Tiazhelnikov, who was wary of me after reading the denunciations, still appreciated the work I was doing. However, I wanted to go into the academic world and asked to be transferred from a part-time *(zaochnaia)* graduate program to a full-time one. In early January 1970 the journal *Kommunist* published an editorial fiercely critical of my ill-fated brochure *Conversations.* . . . Luckily for me, the senior professors and, most important of all, Dean Ovsiannikov bailed me out and allowed me to defend my Candidate of Sciences dissertation.

My former Komsomol colleagues appreciated the fact that I did not succumb to the pressure to 'serve' Tiazhelnikov, disliked by the 'old guard.' In time, they went to work for the Molodaia gvardiia publishing house and the journal *Molodoi kommunist,* which provided me with an outlet for my writings. The Academic Affairs Department of the CC, where my mortal enemies worked, had relatively little sway over the publishing houses. Kvasov and Pilipenko could pull an article of mine from an academic journal or cancel the defense of my dissertation (which they actually did when I tried to sidestep their embargo of my Polish diploma[8] and defend my Doctor of Sciences dissertation at the Institute where I worked). But banning my book once it was included in the publishing house's plan was simply outside the scope of their jurisdiction. Only the CC's Propaganda Department could do that, and it didn't appreciate the Academic Affairs Department's meddling.[9] Good personal relations with the director of the publishing house (first Ganichev and then Vladimir Desiatirek) allowed me to publish three books in the 1970s. The third one, *Socialism: The Life of Society and the Individual,* stirred up a scandal, but by then I was an established author and it would have been difficult for the CC Academic Affairs Department to hurt me much, thanks to my old Komsomol friends.

In 1982 the publication of my already typeset book *Some Philosophical Aspects of the Theory of Socialism* was postponed and the situation seemed hopeless. Kvasov, Pilipenko, and Rutkevich were on guard. Luckily for me, Boris Pastukhov had already been appointed the director [*sic*] of the State Committee on Publishing and my old friend Yuri Stel'makov was his assistant. After I filed a complaint, the cunning Pastukhov recommended that the manuscript be sent for review to the Institute of Marxism-Leninism of the CC and to the Academy of Social Sciences at the CC. I sent the chapter on Marx to the former and the chapter on Lenin to the latter, where they drew good reviews from Bagaturiia and from Yuri Krasin, respectively. My own CC Department,[10] so as not to be left behind, concocted a two-page memo, signed by the consultant Nikolai Kolikov, recommending the book for publication. After about ten more reviews the book was published, leading to yet another brawl.[11] The material that in two short years was to become the philosophical precondition of perestroika, became a part of open scholarship.

Gorbachev to the Rescue

While I was trying to save my book, *Some Philosophical Aspects of the Theory of Socialism,* fate introduced me to Gorbachev, then secretary of the CC for Agriculture. In early 1983, I was briefing my colleagues for an Academic Council meeting meant to rebut Mikhail Rutkevich's review, written on the orders of the CC Academic Affairs Department and charging the leadership of the Institute [the Institute of the Economics of the World Socialist System of the AN where I worked] with recommending a politically harmful book for publication. At this time I became better acquainted with the Institute's agricultural economists Gelii Shmelev and Nikolai Buzdalov, who had written their share of manuscripts (on cooperatives in Eastern Europe) that were then buried. They advised me to try to gain access to Gorbachev, with whom they had worked closely on the report for the June 1982 Plenum of the CC. Gorbachev had strongly impressed them with his openness and—by the standards of the time—progressiveness. When Shmelev and Buzdalov suggested that the report should support family contracts, which had proved very successful in China, Gorbachev replied: "Don't rush things. In due time, we shall raise more important issues than family contracts."

In early 1983 I managed to get by without Gorbachev's help. When the book finally came out in December 1983, I sent a copy, signed with something like "With deep respect," to Gorbachev. Also, together with Bogomolov we sent a copy to everyone in the CC who was instrumental in getting the book published, above all to Georgiy Shakhnazarov. In early 1984 Alexander Yakovlev, who was preparing his own book, *Panamerika,* for publication by Molodaia gvardiia, was in close contact with the editor of my books Raissa Chekryzheva. Following his trip to England with Gorbachev, Yakovlev told Chekryzheva that somehow my name came up in the conversation on board the plane and that Gorbachev mentioned that "it is necessary to support such creative Marxists as Tsipko."

Soon after, Gorbachev had to act on his word. In January 1985 my book once again became the focal point of the behind-the-scenes confrontation between Peter Fedoseev[12] and Richard Kosolapov (then the editor-in-chief of *Kommunist*). As vice-president of the AN, Fedoseev blackballed Kosolapov at the November elections for corresponding members to the Division of Law and Philosophy. Kosolapov, at the time regarded as Zimyanin's likely successor to the post of Secretary for Ideology at the CC, repaid Fedoseev by accusing him of "abetting revisionism at the Academy of Sciences." My book, published by the Nauka publishing house, where Fedoseev headed the editorial board, was used as an example of revisionism. Kosolapov enlisted the help of his buddy and my enemy from the Komsomol Central Committee days, A. Roganov, who at that time was the Moscow city Party committee secretary for ideology. The deputy director of Nauka, who authorized the book's publication, was fired and reprimanded. Kosolapov commissioned three biting reviews, for which he recruited the most zealous participants in the ideological trial of my book at the Moscow University Economics Faculty in the spring of 1984, militant opponents of the market Melentiev and Eremin.[13] They were joined by Moroz, a Ukrainian philosopher from Dnepropetrovsk. At the instigation of Kosolapov, Mikhhail Zimyanin called on the First Secretary of the Cheremushki District Party Committee to investigate the matter and requested my immediate expulsion from the Party.[14]

Kosolapov's task was complicated by my book's overt criticism of his philosophical dogmatism and his claim that it is the theoretical prognosis made by Marx rather than the practical results of its implementation that has great cognitive significance. To fend off subsequent charges that he was using his official position to settle personal scores with his opponent, Kosolapov convened the editorial board of *Kommunist* on 20 January. He called for a show-of-hands vote to defend his actions as purely political, aimed at "unmasking views opposed to Marxism-Leninism." By the way, the subsequent leader of 'Democratic Russia'[15] Yuri Afanas'ev (at the time a member of the editorial board) was one of the first to support the ideological vigilance exercised by his friend and boss Kosolapov.

That same evening I received phone calls from Genrikh Volkov and from the editor-in-chief of the journal *Iuridicheskie nauki,* Yuri Piskotin, whom I had never met. They conveyed in detail all that had gone on at the editorial meeting and advised me to take precautions. Only the CC could curb Kosolapov. I resorted to a method used many times by my immediate superior, the department's chief Anatoly Butenko—writing letters to the CC secretaries accusing Kosolapov of seeking to monopolize social sciences and hampering criticism and self-criticism. Letters written along these lines with the help of Butenko were sent to Rusakov, Zimyanin, and Gorbachev. To be on the safe side, I asked Buzdalov to deliver by hand the copy of the letter addressed to Gorbachev to his chief aide Anatoly Lushchikov.

My hunch proved correct. Gorbachev, who was acting general secretary for the hospitalized Chernenko, never received my letter sent through normal channels. Chernenko's chief of staff Vadim Pechenev controlled (with Chernenko's permission) the first department and all incoming mail addressed to Gorbachev. At the time (the end of January 1985), both Kosolapov and Pechenev had just started betting on Grishin as Chernenko's possible successor. My complaint against Kosolapov could have been exploited by Gorbachev for his own political purposes, which is why it was intercepted.

Fortunately for me, my archenemy was also engaged in a struggle with Gorbachev. The complaint against Kosolapov delivered to Lushchikov was exploited by Gorbachev immediately with amazing political finesse. According to Lushchikov, Gorbachev read the copy of my letter, asked his secretary to connect him to Kosolapov and said: "Richard Ivanovich, I happen to have a copy of Tsipko's letter regarding the critical reviews that are about to be published in no. 3 of the journal. I really don't know anything about the book or the reviews but it seems to me that it would not be advantageous to the Party to have an ideological discussion right on the eve of the Party Congress." Gorbachev told me many years after this incident that he regarded my boss Butenko and myself as important allies in the academic community in his struggle against Kosolapov. Gorbachev's support couldn't have come at a better time for me or for the Institute. However, as far as my official status was concerned, this incident had no major repercussions.

Undercover Advisor to the Ruler

In December 1986, when I was in the office of Gorbachev's aide Georgi Smirnov, he took from the bookshelf my book, *Some Philosophical Aspects of the Theory of Socialism.* "Just leaf through the book," he said, "and pay attention to the marked pages. Your book really served our purpose for the Congress. We squeezed it for everything it was worth." Looking at the highlighted paragraphs I saw what I had already discovered when watching Gorbachev on TV delivering the political report at the Twenty-Seventh Congress of the CPSU. I was euphoric then. Gorbachev had adopted my concept that human life and human civilization are the cardinal values of mankind![16]

Gorbachev and Smirnov got me involved in working on the materials for the Party Congress in a strange way, so that nobody would find out that I was honored to write for the general secretary himself. In early January 1986 I received a call from N.I. Lapin, who became the director of the Institute of Philosophy after Smirnov vacated the post. I was intrigued by Lapin's request to meet with me right away, and agreed since the defense of my dissertation depended on him. He proposed that we meet somewhere on neutral ground and picked the passage of the Lenin Prospect subway station. There, during an evening rush hour I was told that Smirnov, "at the leadership's request" (Gorbachev's name was not mentioned) had asked for a rush job to be done by Monday. I was to prepare a text on the social and economic efficiency of cooperatives for the report team.[17] Referring to the instruction given to him by Smirnov, he mentioned, "You can use the ideas from your book as much as you want. The main thing is that the argument be convincing." As we said our goodbyes at the stairway leading to the exit from the station, Lapin asked me not to tell anybody, including my colleagues at the Institute, about this assignment.

This was my chance to use Gorbachev's report to rehabilitate many of my own ideas. I worked with a graduate student on Saturday and Sunday in the poorly heated building of the Institute, and we edited the text and even typed it. After all, secrecy was requested. I didn't want to wait till Monday, so I met Lapin at that same Lenin Prospect subway station on my way home late on Sunday and handed the text over to him.[18] On 25 February Gorbachev said a few phrases about cooperatives bearing little verbal resemblance to what I had written.[19]

Usually the names of the experts enlisted to draft Party documents were not kept secret. They were included in the report team, which bolstered their position in dealing with the leadership of the AN as well as with the commission of the CC authorizing foreign trips. Arbatov, Bovin, Bogomolov, and Primakov were the regular members of the report team under Brezhnev. Under Gorbachev, Gavriil Popov, the late Academician A.I. Anchishkin, [Otto] Latsis, and later Yegor Gaidar, joined the report group on the advice of Vadim Medvedev. These people belonged to the nomenklatura, albeit unofficially, and were a kind of academic elite.

However, in spite of the April [1985] Plenum and all the changes that took place in the country, and despite the fact that my works influenced the ideology of perestroika, Gorbachev and Smirnov would have me stay in the shadows. Of course, in philosophical circles, particularly at the top level, it was well known that Gorbachev personally forbade Kosolapov to criticize my works until after the Party Congress and that one of the reasons for Kosolapov's dismissal was his use of his position to purge "such creative interpreters of Marxism as Butenko and Tsipko." When Smirnov told us about this in April 1986, I was struck by his admission that Butenko, Gorbachev, and myself had a common enemy, and that Gorbachev needed our assistance in his struggle with Kosolapov.

The first time I was invited to Smirnov's office it was together with Butenko, but soon I was turned into a guinea pig (probably one of many) to test Gorbachev's then secret reflections on the fate of socialism. I am still not clear about which ideas that we discussed with Smirnov belonged to Gorbachev and which to Yakovlev. It seems that immediately following the Party Congress they had a common ideology. The ideas underlying perestroika were fostered by the same group that assisted Gorbachev at the end of 1984 in the preparation of his report at the All-Union scientific-practical conference, entitled 'The Living Creativity of the People.' Besides Smirnov and Yakovlev, the group included Medvedev and Bikenin.

I began gradually to be included in the work of this group, but my formal status did not change. So, when my old foe Felix Momdzhian, the chairman of the Philosophy Department at the Academy of Social Sciences of the CC, decided to sabotage my second Doctor of Sciences defense, scheduled for June 1986, I had no allies. No one could make him give his approval, at the department meeting, for the review of my dissertation. Smirnov, who had confided to me Gorbachev's secret designs, did not respond to my call for help. Anatoly Yegorov, the director of the Institute of Marxism-Leninism and, in effect, my mentor since early 1985, followed suit. The Academic Affairs Department of the CC, which controlled the fate of AN employees, still perceived me as an 'anti-Soviet' element and an 'agent of Solidarity.'

On a personal level, my handlers—Leonid Moiseev at the CC and the KGB personnel working at our Institute—expressed no animosity toward me. However, Bogomolov still could not confirm my appointment as the head of a sector, and travel to the West was still off-limits for me. As late as October 1986, the new head of the philosophy section at the CC's Department of Academic Affairs crossed my name off the list of people going to a scientific conference that was to take place in Poltava, hosted by Morgun, the then-popular first secretary of the Regional Party Committee.

I hold no grudges. Gorbachev and Smirnov did the best they could to help me and others being persecuted by the old regime. Even following the Twenty-Seventh Party Congress Gorbachev and his team still did not have a firm hold on power and did not entertain any ideas of burning the bridges leading back to conservatism and dogmatism. The most convincing testimony of this is Gorbachev's own speech at the Twenty-Seventh Party Congress. Every group could find something in his report that supported its position.

In March 1986 Smirnov asked me to write a general essay about perestroika and Soviet socialism for Yakovlev.[20] Apparently this was a test of my seriousness and truthfulness. I quickly wrote a stylistically polished twenty-four-page text, hoping that Yakovlev would hire me to work in his department. I mentioned Gorbachev's failure to show ordinary people the advantages of perestroika, and the lack of any tangible improvements as a result of his policies. "The complexity and gravity of the moment is that we do not have time for lengthy deliberations. The history of the Party will not witness another Congress like the Twenty-Seventh Congress. The people and the Party's rank-and-file are running low on patience. Countries of the [socialist] commonwealth, especially Poland and Hungary are on edge." I appealed to the secret readers of my essay to go beyond trite declarations and to "revolutionize our own worldview; to heed the gravity of the social situation; to lay bare the underlying causes of our past failures; and not to brush aside the many pressing problems that need to be addressed."

When Smirnov called me to his office sometime in early May, he seemed satisfied. My essay was short on loud anti-Soviet rhetoric, but it did articulate the social ills and the inherent flaws plaguing our system and the destructive consequences of class struggle and Civil War. I gathered from Smirnov's comments that Yakovlev was most impressed by my plea to go farther ahead and expose the root causes of the crisis of socialism, and by the argument for reexamining pre-Marxist socialism and expanding the conceptual range and the values underlying perestroika, for instance, by paying heed to the criticism by Dostoevsky and Plekhanov of state socialism and the nationalization of land.

When Smirnov invited me and Butenko to his office at Staraia Ploshchad'[21] for the first time, he asked us to be as open as possible. He would say several times: "Don't think that Gorbachev does not recognize the gravity of the situation. Sixty years have gone down the drain. Turning away from NEP, the Party lost its only chance. People suffered in vain. The country was sacrificed in the name of scholastic conceptions of Communism that had nothing to do with real life." Of course, such talk left the main holy cows, Lenin and the October Revolution, unscathed. Still, in 1986 I perceived the CC as the bastion of loyalty and dogmatism. It was not long ago that Mikhail Suslov and his successor Mikhail Zimyanin walked these corridors, mercilessly punishing anyone who dared to question the sanctity of Soviet history. Now we hear that the general secretary is almost 'anti-Soviet' and rejects practically the entire epoch of socialist construction. And this was the same Gorbachev who just two short weeks before had argued so eloquently that "the history of our country, its economic, social and cultural achievements are a convincing proof of the viability of the Marxist-Leninist teaching and of the great potential of socialism embodied in the progress made by the Soviet people. We are justifiably proud of everything we have accomplished during these years of tough struggle and hard work."[22]

When I was confided these blasphemous thoughts and doubts attributed to the general secretary, I could not help but feel that now my own heretical ideas no longer lived in a vacuum but were inexorably linked to the thoughts of the very leader of the Party. This certainly alleviated fear for my own ideological sins, but at the same time it was constricting. Well, their plan worked out perfectly. By confiding to me (naturally, with Gorbachev's permission) his heretical thoughts, Smirnov realized full well that I would not advertise the fact that the general secretary was saying one thing and thinking something very different. Smirnov did not need to spell it out that the time for coming out with these ideas in public had not yet come and that we needed to exercise caution and support Gorbachev.

So I was not surprised when Smirnov, acting on behalf of Yakovlev, asked me to go one step further and probe into the fundamental flaws of Soviet socialism. This was my chance to explain to the leaders of the Communist Party my understanding of the fundamental cause of our tragedy, the destructive nature of Marxism. In order to play it safe, I used the words "philosophy of uniformity" instead of "Marxism." This was the only compromise I allowed myself in that paper. After I handed it to Smirnov, there was a three-month pause in our contacts. I rewrote the paper to soften it, and submitted it for publication in *Sotsiologicheskie issledovaniia*. The late chief editor, Anatoly Kharchev, understood perfectly well what was meant by "the philosophy of uniformity," but risked it (Tsipko, 1986b).

Now I wish that I had raised the question of the philosophical roots of Stalinism in that paper. The topic of Stalinist repressions provided significant leeway in legally criticizing almost the entire Soviet period. By 1986, the intelligentsia realized that both Gorbachev and Yakovlev were anti-Stalinist and that at the very least a replay of Khrushchev's thaw was forthcoming. However, I did not concern myself with that issue. I was still living and breathing 'stagnation [i.e., Brezhnev-Chernenko] period' concerns. Dogmatic Soviet Marxism, the philosophical justification for the class struggle and state ownership of the means of production, remained my main antagonists.

My article was used by Nikolai Kosolapov, an aide to Alexander Yakovlev, in drafting Yakovlev's acclaimed report on the state of social science in the Soviet Union. It was presented in April 1987 at a meeting of the Economics Division of the AN USSR Division as a research paper written by a corresponding member of the AN (Yakovlev 1987).[23] I was present, and as Yakovlev was reading his report he (and then Bogomolov) kept pointing to me as a victim of persecution by these "dogmatists" and "retrogrades."

These ideological games had little to do with true social science. A scholar who has come to the realization that the king has no clothes, that the so-called theory of Communism is stillborn, must openly state so. Nothing would have happened to me back in 1986 if I had honestly and forthrightly explained my views on Marxism, the Bolsheviks, and the Revolution. Still, the game I played and my brand of revisionism did make sense in spite of its vulnerability on moral grounds. The non-Marxist brand of Marxism drew the intelligentsia away from the greatest threat of all, the true dogmatic Marxism and faith in the healing powers of the Revolution. It was not an accident that in 1983 and 1984 my revisionist books had the widest circulation among the philosophical literature.[24]

Perhaps the most important thing to remember about that time is that I never believed that the USSR could quickly and peacefully free itself from Communism, even when perestroika had begun. The ban on the CPSU and the dismantling of the KGB were beyond our expectations. I know of no intellectual in the USSR or abroad who anticipated such a dramatic capitulation of Communism in the Soviet Union. Our inner fear deterred us from even dreaming about such things. Our only hope was the emergence of a new leader, who would come and liberalize the system from above.

An Anti-Communist in the CC Apparatus

When, at Shakhnazarov's request, Gorbachev finally took me into the Department of Socialist Countries in November 1986, I felt as if I were one of the initiates. I realized then that there was no limit to Gorbachev's ideological flexibility. Still, what prompted me to write the anti-Communist articles published by *Nauka i zhizn'* in late 1988 and early 1989 was not my cat-and-mouse game with Yakovlev and Gorbachev, nor the internal affairs of the CC, but the rapidly changing intellectual climate in the country and the new opportunities to speak and write the truth.

As soon as the floodgates were opened, it was an instinctive reaction on my part to spill out all the dormant ideas that I had nurtured over the course of many years. I had not realized it at the time, but the November 1988 issue of *Nauka i zhizn'* marked the last test of the ideological resolve of the CC. I wrote that faith in Communism is not merely a weakness or a romantic infatuation, but is "a great sin before man and one's nation." A critical analysis of Soviet history should go beyond Stalin's repressions. The Red Terror instituted by Lenin and Trotsky, one of the most horrendous crimes against the Russian people, cannot be justified. Our entire social structure is predicated upon false premises. Collectivization and the Bolshevik-inspired self-genocide of the Russian people have their roots in Marxism. This was the first time I spoke as a free man and said what I thought (although not throughout the entire text) about the 'great theoretician' Karl Marx, his faithful pupils the Marxists, and their 'great' October Revolution. My articles, particularly the last two, provided ample ground to throw me in jail under Article 71 of the Criminal Code (subversion of the constitutional order).

Decades of waiting to speak the truth about the Soviet regime informed my (or rather our) passionate desire to topple the very foundation of the official ideology and the official version of Soviet history. If we had known the high price that the average Soviet citizen would have to pay for our vehement denunciation of the official ideology, we would probably have been more cautious in our assault on the Soviet past. However, at the time we believed that the main impediments to a normal life were the vestiges of Stalinism and the shackles of the official ideology.

All the while, I remained a regular employee of the CC doing mundane tasks. My first appearance on television went down well in the CC. "He is one of us and speaks as smoothly as the 'democrats.' He can hold his own," they said. In the CC and its International Department I was surrounded by the graduates of the Moscow State Institute for International Relations who knew that Marx's prognosis had proved wrong and that the entire socialist experiment was a futile endeavor. Only the unhappy late Jan Šmeral, the son of a Comintern leader and a founder of the Czechoslovak Communist Party, could not break with Marxism. All the other people who surrounded me in the CC were quite indifferent to the fate of the doctrines of Karl Marx. They were, however, afraid of what subsequently happened, that perestroika might lead to total chaos with unpredictable consequences. This possibility was discussed among my colleague-consultants as early as the beginning of 1987.

Of course, if instructions had come from above to condemn me, then no one would have dared to defend me. The staff at the CC was never monolithic, for each Department was a law unto itself. Still, I felt that even in other departments, which had traditionally been opposed to our International Department, no one wanted to do me in. These people did not care about the fate of Marxism and its scholarly merits. However, following the publication of my articles I became popular in the CC and was invited to give evening lectures to the people from—allegedly the most conservative—General Department and the newly formed Department for Ethnic issues. Just as in the Komsomol twenty years earlier, I felt that no one in the CC perceived me as an enemy, a renegade, or a devil.

If I had not been a consultant at Medvedev's department of the CC, my articles in *Nauka i zhizn'* would not have been published. The journal's deputy chief editor, Khrushchev's daughter Rada Nikitichna, did not rush to assume the responsibility for publishing my articles. First, she investigated my standing with the powers that be, my relationship with Medvedev, and my political reputation in the CC *apparat*. Rada Nikitichna later told me that the conservative leadership of the censorship office was relieved after discovering my close ties with Medvedev, who, unlike Yakovlev, was perceived to be neither a democrat nor a liberal.[25]

My argument with Communism and Marxism became legal and open and my struggle with the Soviet regime was conducted according to the Soviet rules of the game. This is why no one in the CC touched me, setting a precedent and, in effect, legitimizing anti-Communism. The anti-Communist worldview and the rationale behind it began to emerge from underground, eventually gaining the status of a legal worldview on a par with others, such as the official ideology of the CPSU. As Soviet society became accustomed to legal anti-Communism, even the orthodox Reds of the CC's Organization and General Departments started to sympathize with my articles. Nikolai Portugalov, whom I met regularly at 4:00 P.M. in the cafeteria, had a habit of greeting me by raising his hand and saying, as he got close, "Sasha, you are a genius. It took you four articles to say what could be said in a single sentence: "Marxism is bullshit and the Bolsheviks led by Lenin are a bunch of criminals." He would add, smiling, "Still, you are a genius. It takes guts to say flat out that Marxism is bullshit." Starting in the fall of 1988 these conversations were not out of the ordinary in the CC. Nikolai Portugalov was a close associate of Falin.[26]

At the press conference about my articles, Western journalists did not believe me when I told them that people at the CC were treating me well. Yet two days before that I gave a one-hour lecture before some propaganda officials of the CC apparatus on the key mistakes made by Marx and the reasons why Marxism had failed to 'deliver.' Vladimir Vishnevsky, the deputy secretary of the Party Committee of the CC apparatus, opened the lecture. Just five years earlier, when Vishnevsky worked as a consultant to the Ideology Department, he had banned the publication of my pamphlet on the concept of the way of life. Back then I was ostracized for writing the truism that a study of the life of society must begin with an analysis of the way of life of its members: how they work, live, what they think, and what they hope to achieve. Now, this same Vishnevsky calmly listened to me telling the terrible truth about the doctrine that he had spent all his life defending. I said that in every single country the introduction of Marxism had led to a reduction in the standard of living and to the destruction of its culture and traditions; that in no country and at no time has the collectivist mode of production been proved superior to the one based on private property. I called on my audience not to link any more the fate of the country with that of Marxism, but to concern themselves with saving the state.

Not a single interruption or call to order was made during my hour-long tirade. There was not a single question from the audience after I finished my lecture. But as soon as the end of the lecture was announced, many people from the *apparat,* especially from the transformed Ideology Department, came over to shake my hand and to say encouraging words to the effect that it was about time that all these myths of the Leninist guard and 'pure Marxism' concocted by intellectuals were finally dismantled.

In practice since 1988 the CC apparat was actually more anti-Communist, at least potentially, than the opposition formed from the ranks of the intelligentsia. This is evident in the quick switch made by the Party apparatchiks in every single Soviet republic from Marxism-Leninism to national anti-Communism. By contrast, the great majority of the first wave of democrats, including Elena Bonner, Galina Starovoitova, Mikhail Batkin, Mikhail Berger, and Vladimir Bibler, who were united under the banner of *Moskovskaia tribuna,*[27] did not challenge Communism or Marxist-Leninist ideology per se, but rather the 'Stalin-Brezhnev' regime and the Russian statist perversion of the ideals of the October Revolution and socialism. They aimed not at the rebirth of the country destroyed by the Leninists, but at the rebirth of the Bolshevik happiness destroyed by Stalin.

The Party apparatchiks were more receptive to anti-Communism and White ideology. The great majority of them were nationalists (*pochvenniki*) and avid admirers of the legal anti-Communist 'country-prose' authors such as Valentin Rasputin, Vasilii Belov, Vladimir Soloukhin, Viktor Astafev, and Sergei Zalygin. They did not care which state they served, White or Red. The state-centered idea (*derzhavnichestvo*) was used to justify (to oneself) one's collaboration with the CPSU and all the privileges bestowed by the *apparat.*

Even prior to perestroika, a significant part of the CC *apparat* regarded Communism as a facade. These people weren't really the guardians of Communism, as much as they were the guardians of the rules of the game handed down from above. When the leadership chose to tighten the screws, the dogmatic zealots, such as Oleg Rakhmanin, Richard Kosolapov, and Gregory Kvasov, would come to the fore. When, at the highest level, the wind started blowing from another direction, then the pragmatic majority espousing more liberal rules of the game, such as Medvedev, Yakovlev, Shakhnazarov, and Bikenin, would gain the upper hand.

I was the first and only member of the perestroika team to advocate a gradual process of restoring pre-Bolshevik Russia and 'relegitimizing' the Constituent Assembly. My views displeased the social democrats in Gorbachev's circle, including Georgii Shakhnazarov and Ivan Frolov, who warmly supported my decision to leave the CC. Yakovlev, on the other hand, would not let me go, leaving the final decision on this matter to Gorbachev. I was in limbo for about half a year, but as soon as Gorbachev set his mind on revamping the CPSU along social democratic lines, my letter of resignation was accepted. I left the CC in March 1990.

7.3 Politics and Enterprise Behavior
Lev Freinkman

The most important source of economic stability under traditional socialism was the mechanism that, in the absence of a market and free prices, supported a certain balance between monetary flows and real output. In the financial sphere, this mechanism was the direct withdrawal of excess money from the economy (via the withdrawal of the residual profit of the enterprises, monetary reforms, and one-time price increases) and control over the consumer market (rigid planning of the wage fund and closing off all other channels of cash emission).

Stability of real flows was attained by direct coercion—strict administrative sanctions for not fulfilling the plan and, in many cases, even stricter sanctions for violating the delivery schedule. The supply system was supported exclusively by the political pressure of the ministries and the CPSU regional committees on the enterprises. In the 1960s and 1970s, people were no longer executed for shipping paint to a customer who did not have a centrally approved ration. Still, a routine sale of scarce (i.e., virtually any) goods to a customer without a ration could have resulted, under unfavorable circumstances, in the loss of one's Party card and consequently one's position.

Beginning in the second half of the 1960s, a certain expansion of the enterprises' autonomy and political liberalization led to a significant increase in the volume of output which was sold (actually bartered) by the enterprises themselves. Such operations were either not provided for in the plan or were incorporated into the plan at the initiative (often under the pressure) of the enterprises themselves.[28]

This new phenomenon did not change two basic facts. First, the overwhelming share of the enterprises' independent operations was directed toward the fulfillment of the plan or, more broadly, toward creating a positive image of the enterprise in the eyes of its superiors. Economic autonomy was subordinate to the plan at the stage of plan implementation.[29] The plan still defined the composition of the real flows, while barter supplemented and reinforced the planned allocation of resources.

Second, the limits of the semilegal independence of the enterprise were ultimately determined by the personal relationships between the director and his branch or Party bosses. As soon as these personal relationships went sour (if, for example, the director became 'too independent' from the point of view of his superiors), an unplanned audit initiated by the superiors would 'reveal' all kinds of previously known breaches of economic discipline and the delinquent individual would be subject to severe sanctions.

That such punishments were fewer and less severe in the 1970s than in the 1930s did not change the essence of the mechanism of economic control. The power to take away the Party card of any manager without citing the performance of his enterprise (profits, output, or even the extent of plan fulfillment) was the universal tool for reconciling economic interests in the system. The punishments signaled to the economic agents what the system's demands were (attain the required level of output, sell it at set prices to designated consumers, and use the income generated to pursue the prescribed goals). While often economically irrational, these actions were perceived by the directors as necessary for their own political survival. Such a mechanism of coordination was the only thing keeping the system together.

In the course of a few years the system was deprived of the mechanisms maintaining the balance of real and monetary flows. Control over financial flows was destroyed by the straightforward miscalculations in economic policy such as the normative method of profit distribution or the 'Abalkin' tax.[30] The destruction of the controls over real flows (the supply system) had a more fundamental character. Not only were the rules for forming the enterprises' production plans and for the distribution/sale of their output changed. The very institutions directing the flows of goods and services (primarily the corresponding subdivisions of Gossnab and the sectoral ministries) were destroyed, often irrevocably. The degradation of the fundamental institutions of the system and the sharp decline in their effectiveness as a result of ill-considered and inconsistent reforms radicalized public consciousness. It became politically feasible to demand the complete liquidation of these institutions, while the contrary idea of their full restoration turned out to be unacceptable, at least to the majority of the political elite.

I am unable to fully explain the breakdown in political control over the enterprises, to answer the question: "When, why, and how did the threat of taking away one's Party card lose its universal power?" I would only point out several factors that may help us understand why the political foundation of central planning dissolved so easily and comparatively fast.

The significant expansion of regional autonomy in the mid-1980s appears to be one such factor. Regional authorities received significant new freedoms in organizing the production of consumer goods, in developing agriculture, in housing construction, and in the social sphere. Using these rights required that local enterprises from different sectors cooperate under the auspices of their CPSU regional committees in solving regional problems. The redirection of real resources from the center and sectoral ministries to the regions was also required for the new rights to be realized. As a result, powerful regional coalitions arose for lobbying and defending the redistribution of resources. From that moment on, the enterprises, especially large ones, could count on the support of the regional authorities in their negotiations with the sectoral ministries much more than before, using the slogan 'caring for local interests.' Since the regional Party leaders were traditionally recruited from among the directors of the largest enterprises, they were socially closer to the enterprise directors than 'the Moscow bureaucrats removed from real life.' The local coalitions were also strengthened by the traditional patriotism of the Russian provinces.

The enterprises' opportunities to exploit the differences between the regional and central authorities expanded greatly. However, the regional authorities possessed effective levers to influence the behavior of their enterprises which were not purely political. They regulated the enterprise's access to the local infrastructure, and its workers' access to public services, new housing, and consumer goods. For this very reason, regional administrative control over the enterprises, which had been less pronounced in the mid-1980s, turned out to be more stable in the medium term than that of the central authorities [whose only levers were political—Ed.].

The 1987 Law on the State Enterprise created yet another support for directors' independence by making the position elected rather than appointed. Firing a director who displeased his superiors but enjoyed the support of the workers under conditions of glasnost required that the person be seriously discredited politically or be shown to have committed a real economic crime.

At that time, the administrative system's defenselessness in the face of 'suddenly' empowered directors became clear. Control over the use of state property based on noneconomic coercion did not require elaborate formal procedure or legislation. Under the new conditions of 'the expansion of democracy' and relative protection from blatantly arbitrary actions of superiors, experienced directors had the opportunity to extract personal profit from the primitive condition of business law, the accounting and taxation system. The weaker the system became, the more damage was inflicted by the opportunistic conduct of the directors, further undermining the system and expanding the opportunities for self-seeking behavior.

The inconsistent implementation of the reforms appears to be the fundamental factor that dispelled the directors' fear of authority. Gorbachev's team was constantly discrediting itself and its policy by repeatedly making erroneous and half-hearted decisions, then quickly reversing and publicly condemning them. The state quality control, the campaign against unearned income, and the anti-alcohol campaign were the most notorious policies of that type. At the same time, dozens of less important measures [discussed in Chapter 8] were being enacted to change the long-established way of doing things, only to be revoked, left unfulfilled, altered.

The contradictory nature of the new regulations gave executives at all levels, and directors in particular, great opportunities to serve their own interests. Old rules could be ignored since they were officially revoked, and the new ones need not be followed because they were expected soon to be changed or forgotten. Numerous poorly designed experiments (such as renting the plant with an option to buy, or intersectoral state concerns), intended to promote the autonomy of individual enterprises but without imposing a hard budget constraint, raised directors' expectations and increased their call for further economic liberalization.[31]

The open conflicts between Gorbachev's and Yeltsin's administrations over the control of the enterprises in 1990 were the apotheosis of the destruction of the political component of the economic mechanism. The enterprises could choose which of the two centers of power to obey and which rules to follow. Both administrations competed in bestowing privileges and vague promises of economic autonomy on directors. After this critical moment it was probably no longer possible to save the traditional economic system.

7.4 Local Party Organs and the Economy During Perestroika
Yurii Kuznetsov

This study is based on interviews with former leading local Party functionaries conducted in 1994–1995 following the informal methodology of Belanovsky (1993). Among those surveyed were two former first secretaries of regional Party committees, the secretary of a regional committee for agriculture, the first secretary of a city committee, and the first secretary of a city district committee who held a brief appointment as second secretary of the regional committee.[32] Interviews conducted by the AN Institute for Economic Forecasting team headed by S. Belanovsky in 1991 and those from other projects were also used.

The local Party organs fulfilled four critical economic functions: implementation of the priorities set by the central Party and government organs (Naishul 1991, p. 20); intraregional coordination (Kordonsky 1992, p. 42; Rutland 1993); assisting economic actors in establishing and maintaining supply ties and enforcing contracts; and conflict resolution within the framework of customary law. We shall begin by examining these functions as played out during the classical Soviet period and then discuss how they evolved during perestroika.

The Regional Party Organs in the Classical Soviet Economy

Priority Implementation

When asked "What were the economic functions of the Party organs?" Leonid Khitrun, first secretary of the Ryazan Regional Committee, stated, "the main task was to elaborate and implement the strategic course in line with the general economic policy of the state."

Yuri Ganin, secretary for agriculture of the Gor'ky Regional Committee, responded to the same question: "prior to perestroika the Party played the role of a state mechanism which governed all aspects of social and political life. . . . One had to keep a close eye over the bureaucratic machine, since state officials have different labor motivation than people in industry. For instance, the official's salary did not depend on output or some other objective indicator. I believe the historical situation dictated that control be exercised via the Party."

Other respondents also mentioned priority implementation as one of the Party's functions, though in a different context.

Q: "It is widely held that the regional Party committees were a transmission belt of the central party organs or the Politburo. Is this a fair statement?"
A (Gennady Khodirev, first secretary of the Gor'ky Regional Committee): "Absolutely. Say, the CC passes a resolution calling for higher output of fertilizers. The projects where the increase will be produced are determined. The regional Party committee staff spends time in Dzerzhinsk at such a construction site. Since the decision is made jointly by the CC and the CM, the responsibility for meeting the deadline is borne by both the minister and the relevant regional committee of the Party."

In order to implement the priorities handed down from 'above,' the Party organs employed such traditional tools as personnel policy, and supervision of the implementation of the assigned tasks. Generally they kept a close eye on the activities of the officials. No less important is the fact that the local Party organs also took these priorities into account in fulfilling other functions. Paying heed to the established priorities in coordinating regional economic activity was quite natural, for the allocation of resources to a region hinged on complying with the priorities.

Priorities were also taken into account in deciding upon the allocation of supplies. Every Party committee had a limited amount of time available and limited administrative 'clout' and had to decide which deliveries to take care of first. Apparently, enterprises belonging to priority sectors of the economy were served first. Khodirev's examples of the regional Party committee's intervention in supply problems concerned an automotive plant, an oil refinery, and a large defense enterprise, all from the strategically important sectors (see pages 194–195).

Many of our respondents contended that rather than meddling in the operation of the enterprises, Party organs were responding to the enterprise directors' appeals for help in resolving their problems. Naturally, the director faced a difficult dilemma, whether or not to appeal to the Party, and if so, at which level.

Q (to G. Khodirev): "What happens if everybody starts complaining to the regional committee regarding every matter?"
A: "One can recognize the crux of the problem right away and decide if it can be solved by the enterprise director himself or whether he truly needs help. If someone comes with a trivial request, he will be shown to the door so fast, he will never make similar requests again. The directors were well versed in such matters."

Q (to Alevtina Aparina, secretary of the Volgograd central district committee): "What informed the director's decision on whether to appeal to the Party bodies, and at which level?"
A: "Party organs enjoyed considerable authority. Real decision-making power was in their hands. Therefore, the director will not just turn, he will run to the Party, because there is nobody else to turn to. . . . As far as which level to go to with his grievances, the director had to decide that based on the nature of the problem."

This suggests an unwritten code, which defined the scope of issues that could be appealed to the Party committees at various levels of the Party hierarchy. It seems that this unwritten code did bear the stamp of the priorities established by the Party.

Intraregional Coordination

L. Khitrun: "It is essential to coordinate activities on the level of the region. These are not merely administrative units, they are also basic economic building blocks. . . . The regional Party committee was the integrating force which elaborated, arranged, and coordinated economic policy. . . . It organized the entire chain of production composed of economic, managerial, research, and cultural links. Whether it did it well or poorly, the Party committee took all the various interests into account as it worked out an economic policy for the development of the region. . . . A locality, be it a city, a district, or especially a region, must have a powerful economic body which coordinates and controls all the local administrative bodies. It is no accident that these functions were fulfilled by the regional Party committee. . . .

Another branch of power was the Soviets—the CM, Republican Council of Ministers, regional executive committee.[33] These bodies were responsible for economic issues. However, since the regional and district executive committees were not directly subordinate to the CM, the territorial units of the ministries and agencies could not take orders from the regional executive committee. They could only interact with it. The political organ was forced to do this work, that is, to coordinate the activities of all these economic units. . . ."

Vera Rafikova, first secretary of the Nefteyugansk City Committee, argued similarly:

Q: "What was the economic function of the city committee?"
A: "Its role in the Party hierarchy and its basic function was to provide the socioeconomic basis for the city or the district in which it was located. . . ."

Q: "What distinguished the role of the city Party committee from that of the city executive committee?"
A: "Executive bodies of the local Soviets carried out the decisions handed down by the superior bodies, while the Party organs provided organizational and political support for the implementation of economic policy. This is the difference. The bureau of the city Party committee would convene all key economic executives and assign them their respective responsibilities. For instance, asphalting the roads in the city was not in the plan. Yet, this had to be done. . . . The bureau of the city Party committee would invite the enterprise directors, explain the situation, and request their assistance. At first, the directors would cite a lack of funds, but eventually, following a joint discussion, they would come around and propose a solution. The bureau of the city Party committee would draft the appropriate resolution. The time frame and other specifics were also ironed out at the bureau meetings.

"The executive committee is an economic body. It faces plenty of immediate, current problems. The Party organ stood above all this. It was a superstructure built on top of the executive committee and it set the course of development."

In his memoirs, B. Yeltsin (1990, pp. 63–64) gives an example of the Sverdlovsk regional committee successfully coordinating local bodies in construction of the 350–kilometer highway from Sverdlovsk to Serov, which Moscow would not fund.

Intraregional coordination by the Party committees was a peculiar way of resolving the free rider problem when public goods were produced within the respective regions. Fulfilling a plan by a region or district was such a 'public good' for economic units as well as for the officials of the locality. When "a secretary of the rural district Party committee restrained the public prosecutor so that the collective farm's chairman could illegally hire labor-only sub-contractors (*shabashniki*), which helped both the collective farm and the district fulfill the plan" (Naishul 1992, p. 71), the public prosecutor appeared in the role of a potential free rider, who might put bureaucratic interests before the common interest to produce public goods.

The Party officials' power to solve the free rider problem "stemmed from their position as the unchallenged repository of political authority in the region" (Rutland 1993, p. 92). Party compulsion did not always entail direct force, though, as a rule, regional organs of the CPSU could set the law-enforcement authorities against a transgressor or one who violated an agreement. The Party could even organize a boycott against anybody, as its tentacles permeated the entire economic fabric of Soviet society.

Establishing and Maintaining Economic Ties and Contract Enforcement

According to some of our respondents, establishing economic relations and organizing delivery of certain material resources was the primary economic function of the regional Party organs, which demanded much time and effort from the officials.

Q: (to G. Khodirev): "What were the economic functions of the Party regional committees during the Brezhnev era?"
A: ". . . regional committees were squeezing parts and raw materials out of the suppliers. For instance, if there was a lack of metal at a motor works, it either had to be imported, or found somewhere in the Soviet Union. In this case, the regional committee would contact the ministries, Gosplan, Gossnab, or other regions. When oil for the oil refinery in our region (with an annual output of 20 million tons) was in short supply, there were the Tiumen or Krasnoyarsk regional committees to turn to."

Q: "Weren't the ministries supposed to care about all these problems?"
A: "They did care and, apparently, issued appropriate orders. But each enterprise faced specific problems which could, in most cases, be solved by

the local Party organs. Sometimes a manager would defer to the secretary of his regional Party committee more than to his minister."

Q: "Can you recall a case when the request was addressed to the regional committee rather than the appropriate ministry?"
A: "The factory I worked in [before taking the Party job] was the only one in the country which made important assemblies for military use. The casing for them was made at the Volgograd factory. The Ministry would set deadlines for the production of a new kind of casing, send its representatives to the factory, but to no avail. Our enterprise turned to the regional Party committee, which via the CC pressured the Volgograd regional committee. This is when they started moving: organized several work shifts, set up a continuous production schedule, established incentives for the workers.

"Of course, it should have been the job of the Ministry, but sometimes a minister did not have enough good specialists. The functions of shop superintendents or factory managers, let alone foremen, cannot be discharged from Moscow. On the other hand, there are political levers to help organize a labor collective, holding a meeting, explaining how important the work is and the need to meet the deadline. As a rule, that kind of approach was effective."

A. Aparina: "Our main function was to dislodge, to push through, to obtain something from somebody. If there were no railroad cars to transport the output or if they faced difficulties with delivery and contractual obligations, we would try to assist them."

Q: "What would you do when some organization asked you for, say, railroad cars?"
A: "Since we could not issue orders, we contacted the managers and helped them to reach an agreement. We invited them to the district committee and called for an open discussion. . . . We coordinated the work, appealed to the transportation department of the regional executive committee, Soviet organs—we begged, demanded, and pushed."

The Party's ability to solve supply problems, as with regional coordination problems, was determined by the fact that its organs embraced the whole economy, and by its access to coercion.

Conflict Resolution Within the Framework of Customary Law

Customary law in the Soviet Union has only recently attracted the interest of researchers (Naishul 1992, p. 70). The norms of customary law may be unwritten and enforced without recourse to the state law enforcement machinery. The Party's activity in intraregional coordination, including interdepartmental arbitration, and in supporting contract compliance may be characterized as a (at least partially customary) legal system at work. Apparently, one of its most strictly observed norms was the fulfillment of obligations undertaken as a result of Party arbitration.

One could argue that there were several legal systems in operation in Soviet society with both complementary and competitive jurisdictions, including what was called in late Soviet journalistic writing "departmental, clan, and telephone 'law' " (Panin and Lapkin 1991, p. 168). Consequently, the official Soviet law and the legal system of the CPSU coexisted alongside other legal systems.[34]

In addition to the matters described above, the Party had legal authority in the resolution of intraenterprise and intraindustry conflicts. According to a respondent, "Previously, a factory director could be brought to justice through the Party committee; now he is an absolute master."[35] Party organs took part in settling the conflicts between enterprises or departments and their branches, as the story of Nikolai Travkin and his innovations in construction demonstrates (see Konovalov 1987, p. 106).

Party committees at every level were the body citizens usually appealed to when seeking justice. B. Yeltsin remembers being unfairly expelled from secondary school because of a conflict with his class leader. At that point he "realized for the first time what the Party city committee really was" (Yeltsin 1990, pp. 22–23). One of our respondents gives another example (from the perestroika period) concerning the Party's role in a dispute between private citizens.

V. Rafikova: "A girl in our town took too many tranquilizers and died. She was a problem child. . . . The school principal made her come to the teachers' council several times. After being reprimanded at one such meeting, the girl took an overdose of tranquilizers. . . . The parents brought an action against the school principal. When the trial began, the community, the parents, and the chairman of the city court pressured me to expel the principal from the Party before a legal verdict was reached. The understanding at the time was that a Party member should not be tried. I believed that only the court could decide whether a person was guilty or not, and refused to expel the principal before the trial ended. On the other hand, it was believed that a Communist would get a milder punishment. A complaint about me was filed with the regional Party committee. I could have been punished or even relieved of my duties. In the end, the principal was acquitted."

The Party's Withdrawal from the Economy

The directives of the Nineteenth Party Conference (June 1988) about the separation of functions among the Party, the Soviet organs, and the economic management played the main role in the Party's withdrawal from the economy. On 10 September 1988, the Politburo adopted a resolution 'On the reorganization of the apparatus of the local Party organs,' stating that "The reorganization of the Party apparatus requires radical change in the functions, substance, and working methods in every subdivision of the Party committees. Command methods, parallelism, duplication, substitution for the Soviet and economic bodies, and technocratism must be eradicated."[36] The Party's withdrawal from the economy had an organizational and an ideological component.

The former consisted in the reorganization of the apparatus in such a way as to hinder the Party's participation in the economic life and discharge of the functions described on pages 191–196. Departments dealing with specific economic sectors in the apparatus of the Party committees at every level were abolished (except for the agricultural one). Some regional committees used to have more than ten such departments, which served as the main link between the territorial organizations of the CPSU and the enterprises. The abolished departments were superseded by a single socioeconomic department. In the fall of 1988, 1,064 departments and 465 sectors were abolished in the Central Committees of Union Republics and regional and district committees. The number of departments was cut by 44%. Only departments and sectors concerned with priority sectors, such as agriculture and, in part, defense industry, still remained (by the end of October 1988, forty-two Party committees at regional, district, and republic levels still had departments of defense industry and another ten had sectors for it).[37]

The ideological component of the Party's withdrawal consisted of destroying the consensus among the heads of economic and state entities that it was necessary to obey the decisions of the Party committees and their bureaus. The decline of the Party's authority and influence among the Soviet people apparently began with the campaign for disclosing 'the errors of the past' which commenced at the April 1985 CC Plenum and intensified after the January 1987 Plenum. The Nineteenth Party Conference, in conjunction with the subsequent decisions made by the leaders of the CPSU, accelerated the decline of the Party's authority and provided legal grounds for the economic managers' natural drive for greater autonomy.

Our respondents describe 'withdrawal of the Party from the economy' as a continuous and long-term process, rather than one related to particular organizational and ideological decisions. According to G. Khodirev, "because of the democratization within the Party, its liberalization, and the general withdrawal from economic affairs ordered by the general secretary, our influence had been waning."

Q: "When did this withdrawal begin?"
A: "I think already in 1989 our say in economic matters was much weaker than that of our predecessors."

Q: "Did this happen because of some resolution?"
A: "It was proclaimed at plenary sessions, in reports and resolutions. It was stated that the Party must give up inappropriate functions, that is, do more political work and let the ministries, agencies, and local executive committees deal with economic matters. But this is easier said than done. There were no structures in the executive committees to take our place, yet they were told 'to manage the economy.' How would they manage it?

"The chairman of the executive committee had in his subordination the departments of education, public health, municipal services, and agriculture. So who were to take care of industry? They did not have a single person for that. The best thing to do under the circumstances would have been to move the appropriate departments from the regional Party committees to the Soviet organs in order to maintain management of industry. But this was not done. Almost all the industrial departments were disbanded, whereas the Soviets did not build up anything similar."

Q (to L. Khitrun): "What happened in 1988?"
A: "It did not take place *in 1988*. It would be inappropriate to pinpoint an exact date for this process. Attempts to assign economic functions exclusively to the economic bodies were being made continuously. In 1988, it was just done more decisively. It was no doubt the right decision, but the reality of the situation dictated another course of action. It was not just a matter of a power struggle. Life is much more complicated. If in the region things are not getting done, the organization is not up to the task, and the political system just looks on and takes notes, this cannot last long."

Yu. Ganin: "Of course, in 1988 Party leadership was not as strict as before, but it was still there. . . . half the sessions of the bureau of the regional committee were devoted to agriculture."

Q: "How did the demands of the CC on the regional committee and its secretaries for various sectors change from 1988 to 1991?"
A: "During my tenure the demands never ceased. Official reports were

regularly filed. I was summoned to the CC Secretariat, and to conferences and seminars held in the CC."

Q: "Were you held responsible for agriculture in 1991 as strictly as in 1988?"
A: "It's hard to say. You feel strictness when you are summoned to the CC Secretariat or to the first secretary of the regional committee. Former Minister of Agriculture Nikonov was the Secretary of the CC for Agriculture at the time. He conducted teleconferences and said that our regional Party organization did not take proper care of agriculture, and failed to make industry inject resources into the rural economy. He always talked figuratively, like 'the region can always find stainless steel for a vessel with submarine wings, but never for a trough for a dairy factory.'"

Q: "Is that the way it was till the very end?"
A: "I think so. Actually, the Party never withdrew from agriculture. It could not have been otherwise. You remember the bare shelves in the food stores. . . . The demands increased because the Party had assumed the responsibility of providing the people with food and employment."

Apparently, that was characteristic not only of the Party, but also of the Soviet hierarchy till the end of 1991. Thus, N. Kondratenko, chairman of the Krasnodar krai Soviet, speaking in the summer of 1991: "A manager is becoming more and more independent. He is told to 'keep on trading.' You applaud this in Moscow, and do not see that this is bad, because it is me, the head of the regional government, not the manager, who bears the entire responsibility. He has the land, labor, electrical power and other means of production and is now getting freedom of action. I have none of these. Nonetheless, I am still responsible for deliveries to Cheliabinsk, Moscow, Leningrad and so on. On top of that, I have to provide this manager with the necessary supplies. If Gorbachev and Yeltsin are such supporters of the market, they should declare that local Soviets are no longer responsible for providing the population with foodstuffs, since the market will take care of it. But they do not make such a declaration, and then wonder where the 'itch to give orders' comes from."[38]

The above quotations suggest that though the influence of the local Party organs over the economy decreased rapidly and had actually ceased by the time of the August coup [except in agriculture], they were still responsible to the supreme bodies of the CPSU for the state of affairs in their region. These conditions must have led to critical disorganization of the entire apparatus and disorientation among its staff. Following the Party's withdrawal from the economy, the local organs of the CPSU no longer fulfilled the functions previously assigned to them.

The Effects of the Party's Withdrawal

The withdrawal of the CPSU from the economy, together with the collapse of the hierarchy of the industrial ministries, weakened the transmission to the lower levels of the priorities of the highest echelon of state power.[39] The weight of these priorities, that is, the individual preferences and expectations of top level officials, in determining the economy's product mix declined considerably compared to the individual preferences and expectations of ordinary consumers. Large-scale reallocation of capital, which is still going on, was the necessary result of this change.

The local committees of the CPSU ceased to function as a regional coordinator, but the need for coordination did not disappear. Of course, coordination between ministerial structures was no longer necessary after the industrial ministries had been liquidated and their enterprises struck out on their own. But the problem of the territory's common resources used by many enterprises remained. There were numerous agencies, including economic ones, with territorial subdivisions: the Central Bank, the State Committee on Land Use, the Prosecutor's office, tax inspection, the MVD, KGB, and many others.

The lack of regional coordination was quickly felt, judging by the interview with Mikhail Karakai, chairman of the city executive committee of Krasnodar, in the fall of 1991.

Q: "What are the relations between the city executive committee and the enterprises located within the city's jurisdiction, but not subordinate to either the city or the regional Soviets?"
A: "Officially, the city executive committee cannot force the enterprises to do anything, as the only thing they have to do is to pay fixed taxes into the city budget. Before, the city Party committee could influence them, but this lever no longer exists. Therefore we have to develop personal contacts with the enterprises' managers."[40]

Stripping the local Party organs of the responsibility for establishing and maintaining economic ties and contract enforcement contributed to the rather poorly explored phenomenon known as 'the breaking off of economic relations.' Enterprises had to find new ways of enforcing delivery agreements and contractual obligations.

A. Visgolin, head of the Kaluga city administration [former city executive committee), said, in the fall of 1991, "We have to deal with various kinds of problems, some of which are outside our authority. For instance, breach of contract should be adjudicated in the arbitration court, but instead, people appeal to us. The plaintiff is a deputy of the city Soviet, which is a real torture. When we say that we are not supposed to handle such complaints, he comes back with, 'We voted for you, so get to work.' "[41]

The city administration was now expected to fulfill the former role of the city Party committee, as it was believed to be a successor to the committee's economic role.

Some observers talk about a *de facto* paralysis of the state legal system during the period of economic reform. This was caused, among other things, by the dismantling of the institutions involved with the 'informal' ways of resolving legal conflicts. The ineffectiveness of the state machinery in ensuring protection of private rights and contract enforcement caused the assumption of these functions by the legal and illegal coercive bodies, such as the 'mafia' (organized crime), registered security and law firms, police and other official armed agencies providing protection.[42]

The Role of Local Party Organs in Some Events of Perestroika

Elections of Enterprise Directors

The campaign for electing enterprise directors was launched when the Law on the State Enterprise came into effect in 1988. Election of directors by the employees threatened to undermine the line of command in the sectoral hierarchies, so the ministries attempted to get 'their' people elected. The Party committees, with their ability to influence workers through the primary Party organizations at the enterprises, could play an important role in this campaign.

Q (to G. Khodirev): "In 1988, when you became the first secretary, the Law on the State Enterprise was being implemented. What was the regional committee's role in this process?"
A: "The election of directors was a dumb thing. I think the law played a negative role in this respect. Demanding, but highly professional, managers were very likely to be kicked out at the elections. Directors were replaced, but things did not get any better. Our regional committee monitored the situation at the enterprises. Every such law or resolution was handed down to enterprises by means of a directive issued by the respective ministry. This was transformed into an enterprise director's order listing specific steps to be taken. We kept an eye on the implementation of these steps to make sure they were for real."

Q (to L. Khitrun): "Did the Party organs try to influence the election of directors?"

A: "Election of directors was a measure imposed by a person or a group of persons and there was no rationale behind it. Yes, democratic principles require taking into account public opinion, but a manager has to be trained almost since childhood. . . . That is why the election of directors was a far-fetched measure. Competition between two or three candidates evaluated by experts is one thing. A worker, however, can never assess if a given candidate is adequate for the job of enterprise director."

Q: "How were directors elected?"

A: "Things were simply left to drift and we lost some key managers as a result. . . . Together with the ministries and agencies we dealt with the problem and organized the elections. For example, take the Ryazan Machine Tools factory, the largest in the industry. Naturally, we kept in touch with the Minister of the Machine Tools Industry. It so happened that when the time to elect the director came, a very good director got promoted to be first deputy minister.

"We could not afford to make a mistake, but we wanted to abide by the established guidelines. . . . In three days I went around the whole enterprise to meet people and discuss the issues with the specialists. Then we joined forces with the Minister and discussed a number of potential candidates with the workers. As a rule, the workers did not like stricter, more demanding individuals, and consequently, they enjoyed less support. We had to explain the situation and try to convince the workers.

"There were three candidates during the elections, each with his own program. . . . I attended the workers' meeting together with the Minister, and when they asked for our suggestions, we told them we had someone in mind, but we would not name anyone so as not to pressure the workers. Discussions went on, but the workers did not ask for our opinions, since they knew our position from previous meetings. . . . When we were asked afterward whether their decision matched ours, both of us thanked the workers for having elected the right leader."

Q (to V. Rafikova): "Please describe in detail the elections of enterprise directors."

A: "Many people did not agree with this idea and I did not agree with it either. Negative attitudes toward the idea were often expressed at seminars and meetings. But according to our democratic centralism principle, once a decision was made, everybody had to follow it. Elections were held everywhere, and the very idea was widely supported by ordinary workers. It was like some kind of contagion. They all began demanding reelections and electing a director from their midst. It became absolutely necessary to stabilize the movement and calm their passions. That is what we were doing for the most part, especially where the elections were unavoidable, because the employees had already held meetings and decided that the work of their manager was unsatisfactory and it was necessary to replace him. We tried to organize this process. We created committees which attended the meetings and examined the candidates for the leading posts. Certain rules of eligibility for the post, in keeping with the law on elections, were introduced."

Q: "What motivated your actions in the election campaign?"
A: "It was decided at the top that we had to take part in this whole thing. . . . Being entrusted with the task, I realized that it was entirely my responsibility to do this job. So I became engaged in preparing the election conference. We were looking for a kind of person who would not irritate the labor collective and be able to organize rather than disorganize production. . . ."

Q: "Did your candidates always win?"
A: "Yes, except for Yuganskneftegaz. I never nominated anyone who would clearly be opposed by the workers. . . ."

Q: "Was the nominee usually someone recommended by the ministry?"
A: "Yes, in most instances. But we discussed possible options with the people from the ministry in advance."

Q: "Were you ever instructed by the regional committee?"
A: "We were never instructed to support any given candidate, but we did receive general instructions on how to organize the election process. . . ."

The interviews confirm local Party organs tried to assist ministries in their attempts to get their people elected.

Interregional Barter

The Party's pullout from economic affairs coincided with the rise of barter relations in the Soviet economy (Naishul 1992, p. 73). In the following interviews the respondents describe the role of the regional Party committees in the operation of the regional barter economy.

Q (to G. Khodirev): "Was the region engaged in barter?"
A: "Yes, sure. We never had enough meat and dairy products of our own.

Every year the government supplied us with 25,000 tons of meat products, about 100,000 tons of milk, 5,000 tons of butter, and 10,000 tons of cheese from state reserves. The rest of our needs we had to obtain by barter. We had an oil refinery, an automobile plant, a glassworks, where glass for every automobile model was manufactured, and we produced washing machines and television sets. Hence we had goods to exchange. For example, our corn was not good for baking, so we had to supply the region with about 600,000 tons of corn for bread products and with fodder grain for feeding cattle and poultry. Because state-imposed discipline was becoming more and more lax, our deliveries from state resources declined, and in the last year ceased altogether."

Q: "This was in 1991?"
A: "Yes. They still existed on paper, but everyone tried to save himself and ignore everyone else. Therefore we had to develop barter."

Q: "Was the regional Party committee or the Soviet's executive committee in charge of these transactions?"
A: "It was the executive committee acting through the trade administration."

Q: "Where did the resources for barter come from?"
A: "It was not easy because of the vestiges of plan discipline. For example, the GAZ [Gor'ky automobil'nyi zavod, that is, Gor'ky auto plant] motorworks had its whole output allocated to customers ahead of time. If the agreement was breached, the plant had to pay a fine. So we asked the government to leave about 5% of the region's output at *our* disposal. Some share of that was left to the producers, so that they could barter for their own needs. The rest went for the region's needs. Teachers, doctors, and pensioners found themselves in a much more difficult situation than the workers. Some directors did not want to recognize this, and fights ensued. If we could not reach an agreement with the enterprise, we would go through the CM, Gosplan and Gossnab, asking them to lower the enterprise's obligatory shipments so as to leave some output in our region.
    ... We could exchange television sets, washing machines, and other output produced in our region. Besides, we smelted metal—Krasnoe Sormovo made rolled metal used in construction."

Q: "Was it you or the chairman of the regional executive committee who appealed to the CM?"
A: "We always filed requests together. The chairman of our regional executive committee was a very respected, experienced man. He knew everyone,

but he preferred to work together with the first secretary, because then things were much easier. Consider the following minor detail. I could just show my pass and proceed into the office of the chairman of the CM. But the regional executive committee chairman needed to secure a pass in advance in order to see him. It was really absurd—he could not see his own boss. But when he was with the 'first [secretary],' nobody asked him for a pass."

Q: "When did you become fully engaged in barter, in the supply and acquisition of resources?"
A: "From 1988. The situation then was already clear. For instance, Kalmykia had to deliver meat, but did not. Neither did Krasnodar krai. You scratch my back, and I will scratch yours."

Q: "Even in spite of the withdrawal of the Party from the economy?"
A: "Well, life in the region did not just stop."

Q: "Was there anyone in the regional committee who dealt specifically with barter?"
A: "No. The regional executive committees, city executive committees, and district executive committees organized barter transactions. They would only consult with us about what goods were to be exchanged. If we had nothing against it, they would go ahead with the exchange. Also, they tapped our knowledge of the market conditions, which we knew well. For instance, the chairman of the regional executive committee would come and say something like, how about two hundred Volgas for so many thousand tons of corn shipped from some region. If we approved the idea, they carried out the transaction. We never got directly engaged in barter."

Q (to L. Khitrun): "How did the regional Party committee participate in the process of interregional barter?"
A: "The regional committee never participated in barter."

Q: "Did it take part in organizing barter?"
A: "The regional committee furthered the process of exchange. . . . It was the deficiencies of planning, on the one hand, and the absence of free market relations, on the other, that spurred barter between the regions. By the way, barter had always existed and played an important role in our economy even before perestroika."

Q: "What role did the regional Party committee and regional executive committee play in these relations? How did their roles differ?"
A: "Of course, the regional executive committee was directly involved with

this, as well as with the budget and the plan. . . . But interregional barter effected strategy. When it came to strategy, the regional executive committee needed help. So they asked us to exert some pressure, to pull some strings and make the necessary decisions."

According to our respondents, the functions of the regional Party committees in interregional barter included establishing commercial ties, assisting regional authorities with securing a greater say over the allocation of resources, and resolving conflicts between the executive committees and enterprises concerning local taxes in kind, which were the main source of 'revenue' used by the local authorities for barter.

During 1988–1991, the conditions surrounding barter operations reveal a gradual shift of regional power from the regional Party committees to the executive committees of the regional soviets. The need to have resources for exchange increased the administrative pressure exerted by the local administrations upon the enterprises. This trend was highly pronounced in the agricultural sector.

Agriculture

Throughout the late Soviet period, agriculture was at the center of attention of the Party organs. According to G. Khodirev, who worked in the Organizational Department of the CC before being appointed first secretary of the regional committee, agricultural issues occupied a significant share of time of the CC functionaries, and not just those at the Agriculture Department. The fact that during the reorganization of the apparatus of the regional committees in 1988, almost every branch department was abolished except for the agricultural one, indicating just how important agriculture was in the eyes of the Party. The attention paid to agriculture was apparently due to the leaders' belief that political stability in the regions depended on how well the population was supplied with food. Also, agricultural products were the staple goods in barter in the last few years.

The secretary for agriculture of the Gor'ky regional committee, Yuri Ganin, describes the activity of his department during the 1988–1991 period: "What were we doing? You visit a farm, and milkmaids complain they cannot buy bread or candy for children. So we call a meeting at the district committee and invite the chairman of the district consumer cooperative to find out why trade is so poorly organized. After the meeting, a mobile shop begins to arrive every day at a fixed time. If there was no mobile shop, a *kolkhoz* car would arrive and take orders. Once I even had to try to get a consignment of rubber boots, so I called my friends in Moscow to get them."

Q: "When you were the secretary, did you ever have to deal with procurement of the kolkhoz output into the state funds?"
A: "No, already by that time we did not do this. We made forecasts regarding what and how much would be procured. I was in charge of agriculture and retail trade. Every day, I had to know how much sugar, butter, or meat we had in store. . . . There was barter. We did not do it ourselves but we had control over the operations."

Q: "Did the executive committee perform this work?"
A: "Yes, only the executive committee. But we maintained control. These issues were discussed at the bureau meetings and other meetings in order to avoid blunders.
. . . We were in charge of ensuring vegetables for the winter, of getting ready for the winter."

Q: "Was this demanded by the CC?"
A: "The CC was also involved in this work. This was the established practice. It was the Communist Party that was responsible for the social and political situation in the country."

Q: "Was the Party responsible to the very end?"
A: "To the very end. If something critical took place, it was immediately reported to the first secretary of the regional committee or to the general secretary at the Politburo."

Withdrawal of the Party from the economy undermined the Party's administrative control over the agricultural enterprises. Simultaneously, however, for the above-mentioned reasons, the executive committees strengthened their pressure on the agricultural enterprises.

N. Kondratenko (chairman of the Soviet of Krasnodar krai commented [summer 1991]): "People wonder where this 'urge to command' comes from. I simply have to do it. My orders have never been as strict as they were during the last four years. Today the consumers in our krai pay 2.5 rubles per kilogram of corn, whereas I have to send it to Moscow for 30 kopecks per kilogram. Moscow does not allow us to give orders. At the same time, they expect somebody to feed them."

Conclusion

The local committees of the CPSU were an important component of the Soviet economy. The Party's withdrawal from the economy during perestroika caused an institutional vacuum which resulted in serious disorganization of the economy.

All the traditional economic functions of the Party committees (except the first one) are characteristic not only of the Soviet economy, but of a market economy as well. This suggests that, technically, it might have been possible for the Party organs to adapt to the new conditions as purely economic structures. S. Kordonsky (1990) proposed to 'de-ideologize' and commercialize the system of Party organs, so as to make it function like "a stock exchange and a joint-stock bank." At the time, such recommendations seemed very far-fetched. In fact, the CPSU leadership did the exact opposite. It deprived the Party of economic functions and tried to turn it into a purely political and ideological formation analogous to Western political parties.[43]

Notes

1. This was also the view, although with an opposite evaluation, of Molotov. Already in 1973–1974 he anticipated, and explained sociologically, the emergence of a Gorbachev-type figure (Chuev 1991, p. 375). "Also in the future there will be struggle in the Party. Khrushchev was not an accident. The country is a peasant one, the right deviation is strong. Where is the guarantee that they will not rise to the top? It is entirely possible, that in the near future anti-Stalinists, probably Bukharinists, will come to power." [Ed.]
2. In February 1990. [Ed.].
3. This paragraph is a response to the editors' insistent questions along the lines: "If policy X was known to be harmful, why was it proposed, accepted, and implemented?" [Ed.]
4. *Vekhi* (1st ed., Moscow, 1909 [English translation—Armonk, NY: M.E. Sharpe, 1994]) is a famous book of essays on the intelligentsia and the future of Russia. It criticizes the intelligentsia for too much faith in 'the revolution' in the perfectibility of society and in socialism, and for adherence to Marxism. It argues that the intelligentsia should pay more attention to spiritual values, individual moral development, legal norms, and the Russian Orthodox church. Its contributors included N.A. Berdyaev, S.N. Bulgakov, and P.B. Struve. The first edition of *Iz glubiny* was ostensibly published in Moscow in 1918. [Ed.]
5. *Gosudarstvennicheskaia,* a position in Russian politics which stresses the importance of the state and its interests and rejects revolution and anarchy. [Ed.]
6. One of them, Valery Legostaev, Alexander Zinoviev's best student, later became Ligachev's aide.
7. That is, after the Soviet invasion of Czechoslovakia, which had a significant influence on the ideological climate in the USSR. [Ed.]
8. This probably means that they prevented it from being recognized in the USSR as equivalent to a Soviet Doctor of Sciences degree. [Ed.]
9. It was the opposition on the part of my supervisor (*kurator*) at the Propaganda Department, Mikhail Gabdulin, that kept Kvasov from expelling me from the Komsomol Central Committee and blacklisting me.
10. Presumably the Department of Propaganda. [Ed.]
11. Michael Rutkevich in his review labeled my book an epitome of "shameful revisionism" and propaganda for "capitalist commodity production." Gregory Kvasov in

his memo to the CC Academic Affairs Department described the book (which was banned from the shelves at the academic libraries four months after publication) as anti-Leninist and as directed against the Marxist teaching of the revolutionary mission of the proletariat.

12. Chairman of the social sciences division of the AN since 1971, director of the Institute of Philosophy of the AN in 1955–1962, and director of the Institute of Marxism-Leninism in 1967–1973. [Ed.]

13. This second 'trial' took place at an open meeting of the Economic Society chaired by Professor N.A. Tsagolov, the founder and patriarch of the political economy of socialism.

14. M.V. Zimyanin was head of the Agitation and Propaganda Department of the CC in 1976–1985 and a CC Secretary in 1976–1986. In 1965–1976 he was the chief editor of *Pravda*. [Ed.]

15. This was the main anti-Communist political movement in Russia in 1990–1992. [Ed.]

16. "What distinguishes the Communist worldview is its focus on the people, their aspirations and concerns. Lenin stressed that human life and the opportunity to fully realize oneself is the highest value. Social development is our top priority. . . . We will not take 'no' as an answer to the question: is there to be a future for mankind. We profess that social progress and civilized life must and will go on" (*Materialy XXVII s''ezda* 1986, pp. 20–21). In this roundabout way, Smirnov introduced into Gorbachev's report the main idea of my book, that the recognition of the absolute value of human life constitutes the foundation of true humanism and social science. It is hard to say whether Gorbachev realized all the political and ideological ramifications of his statement, which, in effect, is not Marxist. However, the evolution of what Gorbachev dubbed the 'new thinking' and the greater focus in his subsequent speeches on universal human values suggest that Gorbachev *did* comprehend the full implications of this argument.

17. This means the team writing Gorbachev's report to the Twenty-Seventh Party Congress. [Ed.]

18. For the published version, see Tsipko, 1986a. [Ed.]

19. "There should be full clarity on the issue of cooperative property. Its ability to contribute to the socialist mode of production and to the better satisfaction of the people's needs is far from being exhausted. Many collective farms and other cooperatives have demonstrated their efficiency. The creation and development of cooperative enterprises and organizations should be fully supported where needed. They should be widely developed in the manufacturing and processing sectors, residential and small-farm construction, consumer services and trade" (*Materialy XXVII s''ezda* 1986, p. 40).

20. Even after I became a consultant to a CC department, Yakovlev did not wish to advertise our relationship, and my primary link to him was the editor in chief of the journal *Voprosy filosofii*, Vladislav Lektorsky.

21. The Old Square where the office complex of the CC was situated. [Ed.]

22. *Materialy XXVII s''ezda* 1986, p. 4.

23. For a slightly different version see Yakovlev 1990, pp. 214–235. This was actually a report at the Social Sciences Section of the presidium of the AN. [Ed.]

24. This is based on a study of the library checkout cards in the academic libraries in the RSFSR conducted in 1984 by a team from the Sociology Institute of the AN.

25. The reader of Hough (1997, pp. 260–261) may get the impression that the famous *Nauka i zhizn'* articles were written on the instructions of Yakovlev. According to Tsipko this is not the case. The "assignment" from Yakovlev referred to by Hough was in May 1989, after the last of the *Nauka i zhizn'* articles had been published. (Oral communication from Tsipko, 8 September 1997.) [Ed.]

26. V.M. Falin was first deputy head of the International Information Department of the CC in 1978–1983, political commentator for *Izvestiia* in 1983–1986, head of the International Department of the CC from 1988, and a CC secretary in 1990–1991. [Ed.]

27. A discussion club of Moscow intellectuals, which began its meetings in February 1989. [Ed.]

28. During this period the plan itself was to a large extent the result of trade (i.e., negotiations and exchange of bureaucratic favors, sometimes known as 'plan bargaining') between the enterprises and the system, as V. Naishul has convincingly described.

29. The changes were more significant at the stage of plan formulation. The plan began to be geared more toward the real interests of the enterprises. It also became easier to revise the approved plan targets.

30. On the normative method of profit distribution, see Yasin in Chapter 6.2. On the Abalkin tax, see Abalkin 1991, pp. 116–119.

31. Many of these experiments were not vehicles of economic reform, but rather weapons in the political struggle within the leadership, designed to attract the most active directors to Gorbachev's side.

32. The same word, "region," has been used to translate two Russian words, *oblast'* and *krai*. [Ed.]

33. According to the Soviet constitution, executive organs of government at various levels were formed by the corresponding Soviets. The CM and republican Councils of Ministers were formally established by the Union and republican Supreme Soviets, and local government was discharged by the executive committees of the regional, district, or city Soviets. Prior to perestroika, the Soviets, unlike their executive arms, played a largely perfunctory role. [Ed.]

34. Parallel and competitive legal systems were characteristic of Europe in the eleventh–fifteenth centuries (Berman 1983).

35. Author's interview with a pensioner in Nizhnii Novgorod in 1993 for the Public Opinion Foundation study of the political consciousness of Russian citizens.

36. *Izvestiia TsK KPSS,* No. 1, 1989, p. 87.

37. Ibid., p. 89.

38. Interviewed by I. Verkhovtseva for the project of the Institute of Economic Forecasting of the RAN under the direction of S. Belanovsky in the summer and fall of 1991.

39. For evidence on the collapse of the hierarchy of industrial ministries, see Belanovsky 1991.

40. Ibid.

41. Ibid.

42. On the phenomenon of the 'roof,' see Racket 1994.

43. The economic functions were frequently taken over, at least partly, by local government bodies. The latter often continued to deal with them even after the collapse of the USSR and 'the transition to a market economy.' For example, in the late 1990s the Moscow city government had a Department of Science and Industrial Policy whose functions overlapped with those of the old economic committees of the Moscow city Party organization. See the interview with its deputy head in *Moskovskaia Pravda* of 20 October 1997, p. 2. [Ed.]

8

Attempts at Market Reform, 1989–1991

8.1 Coping with the Consequences of the 'Radical' Reform
Lev Freinkman[1]

The Factors and Mechanisms of the Financial Imbalance

The reforms [of the late 1980s] destroyed the old system's mechanisms for control of financial flows [see Chapter 7.3]. Enterprises received significantly greater financial resources than before to be used at their own discretion; erosion of the separation between noncash transactions between enterprises and the cash in the hands of the population allowed the enterprises' money to filter into the consumer market; and the income of the population grew as the leadership initiated a series of large-scale social programs in order to support trust in perestroika.

As of 1 January 1988, the new law on state enterprises introduced to the greater part of the economy a new system of distribution of enterprises' revenue based on stable rates that imitated a tax system [see Chapter 6.2]. In 1987 the self-financing enterprises produced only 20% of industrial output, and in 1988, about 60% (Shmelev and Popov 1989, p. 231). As a result, in 1988 the percentage of enterprises' profit retained by the enterprises increased from 54% to 61%. In 1987 only 20% of the profits generated by the enterprises or 37% of the profits retained by them was directed into the economic incentive funds. In 1988 the corresponding numbers were 49% and 80% (Goskomstat 1989, p. 617). At the same time the share of depreciation kept by the enterprises increased sharply from 12% to 90%. By the beginning of 1989, the total amount of money held by the enterprises approached 100 billion rubles (*Izvestiia*, 14 December 1989).

During the early 1989 transition to normative rates of productivity and wages, the norms were greatly delayed in getting to the enterprises, and for a good part of the year the enterprises distributed wages without any control. Monetary resources not spent by the enterprises (since no goods were available) were no longer transferred to the budget, but rather became a source of credit expansion. Through the system of commercial banks this money entered circulation, which further intensified the imbalance.

The structural policy of the Twelfth Five-Year Plan exacerbated inflationary tendencies. [The annual plans in the acceleration period made the situation worse.] For instance, 19 billion rubles were earmarked for capital investment in 1988, in addition to the appropriations stipulated in the Five-Year Plan (*Ekonomicheskaia gazeta,* 1989, no. 5, p. 5). The attempt at acceleration led to the growth of external debt and the stagnation of investment in the consumer-goods industries. In the next few years the government undertook desperate measures to rectify the situation. In 1989 centralized investments had to be cut by 7.5 billion, and in 1990, by 8 billion rubles (*Finansy SSSR,* 1989, no. 8, p. 5). However, these cutbacks were more than made up for by higher investment on the part of enterprises that were desperately trying to spend their accumulated money. The growth of decentralized investment that continued until 1990 resulted in an increase in the overall volume of unfinished construction and additional pressure on the consumer market for building materials.

In 1989 the value of building and installation work grew by 2 billion rubles instead of being reduced as planned. The volume of unfinished construction projects grew by 27.6 billion rubles, and inventories increased by 51.9 billion in the first nine months of 1989. In 1990 the government planned to curtail centralized capital investment in construction work in the productive sector of the economy by 27 billion rubles relative to appropriations stipulated in the Five-Year Plan (not in comparison to the previous year).

In 1988 the imbalance shifted from the sphere of noncash transactions to the consumer market. In response, the government reanimated the traditional administrative levers of control in the 18 January 1989 letter of Gosplan, the Ministry of Finance, Goskomstat, and the State Bank, entitled 'Calculating the Ratio Between Wage Increases and Labor Productivity for 1989–1990.' For enterprises and organizations that were operating on the basis of the first model of self-financing, this ratio would be determined by comparing the rate of growth of the average wage and the rate of growth of labor productivity. For enterprises and organizations operating under the second model of self-financing or under lease-based contracts, this ratio was to be calculated by comparing the rate of growth of payments from the wage fund with the rate of growth of their revenue.

The Ministry of Geology's industrial subsectors were first to convert completely to the second model of self-financing. In 1988 the average wage there increased by 19%, while labor productivity grew by 28%. It appeared that a very positive effect of introducing progressive methods of management was achieved. In reality, this was not so. The first problem was the time lag. Deposits discovered today are not going to materialize into consumer goods any time soon, if ever. At the same time wages have already been paid out and yearn for goods to buy. The economic mechanism governing the operation of the geological industry aggravated the situation because it failed to induce the industry to explore deposits which were truly beneficial to the economy. The work was evaluated based on the quantity rather than the value of the discovered reserves. This pushed prospectors to search for bigger deposits/fields. According to the data published by the Government Commission on Reserves under the CM, the already discovered reserves of a number of nonmetallic minerals in the Magadan region would have been sufficient for the next 300 years, but this did not stop the search for new mineral deposits.

The use of normative ratios between labor productivity and wages did not contribute to equilibrium between the cash income of the population and the volume of consumer goods and services. It only regulated the wage fund as a share of the enterprise's income (under the second model of self-financing and leases) or of its volume of output (under the first model). We could say with certain qualifications that the established rates impeded the growth of wages as a percentage of GNP. The share of wages in Soviet GNP was only about half that in all civilized countries.

In August 1989 the first session of the Supreme Soviet ratified the 'Changes and Addendum to the Law on the State Enterprise' and the decree 'Taxation of the Wage Fund of State Enterprises' which changed the system of taxing the wage fund in proportion to the enterprise's output or revenue, to taxing the overall amount paid out of the wage fund—the so-called Abalkin Tax. The new tax did not apply to increments in wages resulting from higher output and sales of consumer goods and services. However, nothing was said about which goods should be considered consumer goods. In practice all goods categorized as consumer goods in the list compiled by Gosplan were treated as such. This led to serious conflicts. For example, the Pushkin Hardware Factory (in the Moscow region) produced automobile oil filters and uppers for footwear. The uppers were delivered to the shoe factory, whereas the oil filters were sent straight into retail sale. It turned out that neither of these products was included in the Gosplan list of consumer goods—they were considered to be producer goods, which meant that the higher wages resulting from their increased output were taxable (Liberman and Freinkman 1991).

The tax curtailed production and employment, for this allowed the growth of average tax-free wages. It ought to be noted that it took the government just four months after the tax was introduced to recognize the repercussions of their own regulations. The government then introduced corrective coefficients to adjust for the base wage level depending on the dynamics of the volume of output produced (*Izvestiia,* 9 February 1990). As a result, from the beginning of 1990 wages were regulated by some sort of hybrid 'tax-normative' method.

There was an inevitable erosion of Gosplan's list to which goods having nothing to do with consumer goods were gradually added, "as soon as the decree went into effect, a stream of requests for favorable treatment and relaxation of the rules flowed into the CM. The government was forced to make some concessions. As a result, in the fourth quarter of 1989 when the tax went into effect it generated about 0.5 billion rubles—which was only half the amount expected" (*Izvestiia,* 9 February 1990). There is evidence that concessions were extended even to the manufacturers of space technology.

In 1988 the economy's wage fund grew by 6%. In 1989 it grew by 9%, a figure that in former times had been achieved only over the course of an entire Five-Year Plan. Moreover, the growth of the population's cash income surpassed the growth of its expenditures on consumer goods and services by almost 40%. The gap between the population's cash income and its expenditure on consumer goods and services [after adjustment for various other payments, contributions, and increases in savings bank deposits] was reflected in the issue of new cash money—18 billion rubles in 1989 alone.

Those who were closer to budget appropriations than to the final consumer achieved the most powerful results in mastering the new methods of management, such as self-financing. While geology had already advanced to the second model of self-financing, its companion industries still lingered under the first model of self-financing. They were still not driven to a rational use of resources, such as extracting the most oil from the well, all-round efficient refining, and saving of fuel. There was no sense in searching for new deposits since it was not at all clear whether the marginal output attained owing to colossal efforts and generous budget appropriations would ever reach the consumer. This kind of growth only aggravated disequilibrium.

With significant resources accumulated by 'non-self-financing' enterprises, the emergence of a large number of self-financing enterprises—lease-based, cooperatives, joint-ventures—in industries far removed from the consumer market led to large-scale transfer of money from the noncash sector to the cash one. Sharp increases in expenditures on computer programming, research, consulting, and design were not accompanied by any significant progress in productivity and only intensified the overspending characteristic of the economy.

Attempts to Curtail State Orders

Every year (1987, 1988, and 1989) the government attempted to curtail significantly directive planning and to provide more opportunities for enterprises themselves to sell their output. It was assumed that the free exchange of goods would automatically lead to a viable wholesale network and the market.

However, these measures were undertaken in an economy suffering from a very weak financial system. As of the summer of 1990 the overall inflationary gap on the producer goods market was estimated to be in the range of 300–500 billion rubles; that is, it [the gap] almost reached one-half the volume of industrial output (Anisimov 1990). The ratio of the enterprises' total monetary resources to total inventories in the economy grew from 30.2% in 1984 to 62.6% in 1989 (Danilov-Danilian and Freinkman 1992). This greatly strengthened the dictate of the supplier. Fixed prices rendered the production of many product lines unprofitable. At the same time, the labor collectives had no incentive for wage growth since the wage fund was controlled, while the noncash incentive funds could hardly be converted into real goods. The most blatant evidence for this is the increase in unspent incentive funds, which reached 120 billion rubles by the summer of 1990 (or 26% of the annual wage fund).[2] The distribution of these funds among the enterprises was very uneven. For example, in less than 1.5 years the accumulated investment fund at the Moscow Artistic Clock factory that operated under self-financing reached 70% of the value of its fixed assets (Medvedev, Nit, and Freinkman 1989a). Furthermore, the norms governing payments into the incentive funds were unstable and were directed against the most active collectives. In many cases an increase in profits led to a reexamination of the norms set by the ministries and a reduction in the real income left to the enterprises.

As a result, the enterprises lacked real opportunities to interact independently. Their alleged independence in distributing their output turned into contract violations and disorganization of production. Every so often the government was forced to interfere in the economic activities of the enterprises and expand centralized planning and distribution.

A very typical situation arose during the latter half of 1988 when the 1989 plan was formulated. While in 1988 state orders exceeded 90% of the industrial output target, the 1989 state orders were supposed to be cut by an average of 30% in monetary terms and almost six times in terms of the number of products (Samarina 1990). 'The Temporary Resolution on the Procedure for Working Out State Orders for 1989–1990' proposed that serial and mass-produced goods as well as items of intersectoral use should not be included in the state order. This immediately sparked two factors that produced unprecedented delays in concluding economic contracts. In the first place, massive failures in managing the national economy began to take place. To develop a plan for 70% of total output proved too difficult a task (see Yasin in Chapter 6.2). The handing down of assignments and other economic information from Gosplan and Gossnab to the ministries and, in turn, to the enterprises, occurred with great delays and misunderstandings.

Given the rather ineffective economic mechanisms, the curtailment of state orders resulted in so-called dead spots in the economy in which neither the old administrative nor the new economic levers of control were operational. In these sectors of the economy the production of unprofitable goods was being scrapped, output prices were on the rise, and overall output curtailed. At the completion of the contract campaign for 1989 (the deadline was 15 October 1988) only 76.3% of the contracts had been concluded (*Izvestiia,* 13 December 1988). According to the statistics provided by the TsSU, as late as 9 January 1989 this figure was only 96.0%.

Toward the end of 1988, judging by all the traditional indicators used in directive planning, economic paralysis threatened the economy. The 1989 output targets for the majority of enterprises were not defined. Lack of agreements for supplying even a small share of the resources required generally implied the complete inability to guarantee the output of the final product. This called for an almost complete restoration of the centralized allocation of resources. This was legalized by the joint decision of Gosplan and Gossnab, No. 80/80 of 11 October 1988, which specified additional products that were to be allocated by the center. According to this document, in November 1988, out of 107 types of products used in oil and chemical machine-building that were originally turned over to the enterprises for sale, only two maintained that status. In other words, in most cases even that part of the enterprises' output that had formally ceased to be included in the state order, and the production of which the enterprises had to plan for themselves, continued to be distributed as before, that is, based on the decisions of the central authorities. For example, at the Ural Compressor Factory the state order's share in the production plan for 1989 was 80%, and the remaining 20% was distributed by a centralized quota system. At the Moscow 'Kompressor' and 'Borets' factories and at the Industrial Concern 'Iskra' the proportions of the state order and the quotas were 60% and 40%, 0% and 100%, and 30% and 70%, respectively.[3]

The legal basis for the memo of Gosplan and Gossnab was provided by

Resolution No. 889, passed by the CM on 25 June 1988. This resolution allowed for the centralized allocation of certain items that had been omitted from the state order. This step completely contradicted the original conception of reducing the state order by automatically delegating to the enterprises all decisions that were not part of the domain of centralized planning. The resolution passed by the CM introduced an intermediate notion of not centrally planned output which was nevertheless centrally distributed. And the memo issued by Gosplan/Gossnab greatly expanded the share of such output. Consequently, although the state order was formally reduced in 1989, the enterprises did not gain any new rights. The situation of the previous year repeated itself albeit under a different guise.

It was likewise promised that state orders would be reduced in manufacturing industry to a level below 50% of the volume of output. However practical implementation was delegated to the branch ministries, which extended the orders to cover almost 100% of output. The same thing happened in the following years. Even in 1990, the official state orders placed with the enterprises comprised almost 90% of their output (Popov and Shmelev 1991, pp. 76–78). By the end of 1991, on the eve of Gaidar's reforms, wholesale trade was calculated by Goskomstat to be only 14% of total sales (consumer goods excluded).[4] This is much lower than in even the most centralized East European countries on the eve of the reforms (Bulgaria— 25%, GDR and Czechoslovakia—30%).[5]

These kinds of repeals and revisions of government resolutions are very typical of the economic reforms of 1988–1990. Among the grave ramifications of this vacillating policy was uncertainty in the enterprises and inability to develop and implement a coherent economic strategy. The limits of independence, never clearly marked in the first place, were always shifting without any underlying strategy. For example, at the Moscow Concern 'Mosrentgen' in 1988 the state order covered the entire output, in 1989 only consumer goods were included (i.e., less than 10% of the output), and in 1990 all medical equipment was included, which made up the bulk of the enterprise's output.[6]

Even an insignificant exclusion of specific items from the state order led to an additional imbalance due to the disruption of complementary technologies. For example, in the railroad construction industry the state order covered only rails and ties, while the planning and production of the hardware required to fasten these parts was left to the discretion of the enterprises. This quickly led to a significant reduction in the production of the hardware and delays in completing construction projects. Another problem was the discrepancies in the size of the state order for technologically related branches, the reason being that the various poorly coordinated cutbacks in the state order were implemented in isolation by different subdivisions of the administrative system. For instance, the state order for autos was set at 91% of their annual output; the corresponding percentage for tires was only 71%.[7]

Therefore, the growing imbalance that surfaced over the course of the reforms was immediately linked to those areas in which the loosening of administrative control took place. Economic freedom without consumer control over the producers not only failed to stabilize the economy, but increased the chaos significantly.

The incentives given to the producers of items included in the state order—incentives which were introduced only in 1989 and directed at improving the production of goods deemed most important by the government—proved totally inadequate. The essential flaw of this approach was the fact that these incentives had a tax-like character and given the meager purchasing power of money they failed to make the fulfillment of the state order attractive for the enterprises. Consequently, the quality of planning worsened, the control over the fulfillment of state orders became weaker, and the incentives for complying with the orders were not strengthened.

Similar problems surfaced most prominently as the enterprises engaged in the output of consumer goods. Traditionally, consumer goods were included in the state order in full and the plans provided for higher rates of growth of their production. However, after the introduction of a tax on increases in the wage fund in the summer of 1989 (the so-called Abalkin Tax—see above) additional problems with providing the resources needed in the production of consumer goods arose. For example, in 1990 the enterprises of the concerned Kvantemp planned to increase the output of batteries by 34.3% for which they needed to acquire 26% more zinc powder. Yet the supplier of this raw material agreed to increase the output by only 3% because the above-mentioned tax limited the tax-free growth of wages to exactly 3% per year (*Material'no-tekhnicheskoe snabzhenie,* 1990, no. 2, p. 10). The government demanded higher output of final products from the enterprises but, at the same time, hindered the acquisition of all the necessary materials and components.

Decentralized Implementation of Reforms and Recoil

One of the central reasons for the failure of the economic reforms of the 1980s was the extremely decentralized character of the reform process. Since there wasn't a general strategy for reform implementation, its separate aspects were dealt with in isolation by different ministries and agencies, each guided by its own self-interest. The reform of the supply system was typical in this respect. In principle, it was understood that the growth of wholesale trade, that is, the narrowing of the traditional domain of resource distribution by Gosplan and Gossnab, required changes in planning, price setting, and income distribution. However, Gossnab, which was in charge of introducing wholesale trade, didn't have the authority to interfere in the domains of other departments. Nevertheless, Gossnab had to create at least the semblance of radical transformation in its own domain. The result was 'fake' reforms and the distortion of ideas.

For example, Gossnab cut the number of centrally distributed product types from more than 13,000 to 618, that is, by more than 20 times, over the course of two years (1987–1989). In monetary terms the reduction in centrally distributed items turned out to be far less—from 290 to 195 billion rubles, or about a third.[8] The reduction in the number of items distributed by Gossnab was achieved mainly by aggregating goods rather than by ending centralized distribution. However, the aggregation of the assortment made the process of centralized distribution totally meaningless. Under aggregate planning, the detailed breakdown of orders within the bounds set by the allocated quotas took place via direct interaction between the user and the supplier. As a result, the supplier could dictate completely the terms of the contracts, and shifts which took place in the economy were skewed in favor of the supplier. Users lacked any real levers of influence over the supplier. The money the users were willing to spend was not much of an incentive for suppliers since suppliers could not spend it as they saw fit. Greater freedom in setting the output program was not supported by freedom in the utilization of income.

In order to dampen the uncontrollable destruction of the remnants of economic equilibrium caused by such measures, at the end of 1988 a new decree was adopted by the CM which allowed users to prolong for 1989 the existing distribution contracts. Buyers could resort to arbitration and thus force on the manufacturers the previously agreed-upon terms (including the assortment of goods). Instead of being managed by Gossnab, some areas of the economy became regulated by Gosarbitrazh (the State Arbitration System), a mere change in the form of traditional bureaucratic control.

There was yet another departmental aspect to the problem of implementing economic reforms. The ministries, which were obliged to report regularly to the Party and the government regarding their accomplishments in 'the creation of the socialist market,' were forced to make numerous, albeit purely cosmetic, changes and improvements. In this situation, the way almost invariably chosen by the departments was to conduct constant reorganizations of their administrative structure. For example, the secretary of the Party committee of the Lauristin Machine Works in Tallinn stated at the end of 1988 that the main result of perestroika in the Ministry of Chemical Machine-Building for his own enterprise was that it had been transferred four times from one chief directorate to another. These transfers resulted in a complete loss of interest by ministry officials in the current difficulties of the factory (Medvedev, Nit, and Freinkman 1989b).

Such superficial restructuring had significant macroeconomic consequences. During the short period from mid-1987 to the end of 1988, all the basic economic institutions that had supported the established economic ties between enterprises were 'reformed.' This concerned, first and foremost, the territorial and product chief directorates of Gossnab, the banks, and the chief directorates of the branch ministries. The flow of new reforms accelerated and, toward the fall of 1988, was so overwhelming that the directors of the enterprises could no longer orient themselves in this maze of new procedures for 1989, for supply, sales, and the determination of production programs. First of all, the procedure for making economic contracts was not clear. For example, the Novolipetsk Metallurgical Works was supposed to increase the share of inputs it received via direct economic links from 10% to 90%. Within a very brief time period, this enterprise had to conclude more than 1,000 contracts with suppliers. The suppliers, on the other hand, refused to sign the contracts, since the money that the Metallurgical Works offered to pay for the raw materials lacked any real buying power. Everyone was interested in some kind of barter service or product, especially metal. But the enterprise was not authorized to distribute independently even a single ton of its metal, since the state order exhausted 100% of its output capacity. The situation was further complicated by the fact that the exact size of the state order became known to the enterprise much later than the deadline for concluding the contract campaign. Therefore, the enterprise was able to conclude fewer than one-fifth of the necessary contracts within the time allotted. In order to make sure of their inputs, the supply agents of the enterprise sent the same supply requests and orders simultaneously to three or four potential suppliers (Medvedev, Nit, and Freinkman 1989b). This kind of conduct served to distort the perception of the economic needs of the enterprises and deprived the central agencies of the opportunity to work out some reasonable solution using the old administrative methods.

At the Lipetsk Machine-Tool Factory the aforementioned 'contractual' problems were exacerbated by the lack of reliability of the supply arrangements. The factory was the sole buyer of a number of special brands of steel, and its performance hinged upon proper coordination with the Voronezh Chief Territorial Directorate of Gossnab. While the Lipetsk region was within the 'sphere of influence' of the Voronezh Directorate, things were more or less fine. But with the reorganization of Gossnab into single-region chief directorates in 1988, the Voronezh suppliers were no longer interested in the needs of the Lipetsk enterprises. To make things worse, the new Lipetsk chief directorate had neither the resources, nor the storage facilities, nor the experience to accommodate the production schedules of the enterprises. There was not a glimmer of hope for help from such traditional sources of emergency assistance as the chief directorate of the Ministry of Machine-Building or the metals section of the Union Gossnab, all of which were also subject to reorganization (Medvedev, Nit, and Freinkman 1989b).

Full-scale centralized distribution was completely restored at the end of 1988. Gossnab again started distributing goods which had already been allocated as part of the earlier contracts signed by the enterprises themselves. These contracts had to be quickly amended or dissolved altogether and new contracts with new users, who had acquired centrally allocated quotas, had to be made. At an average industrial enterprise such changes affected 20–40% of the contracts.

The old supply system with its cumbersome quota procedure fully discredited itself by incompetent interference in direct links between the enterprises, incentives for the growth of stocks, and so on. At the same time the gravity of the situation and the role of Gossnab in the old economic mechanism rendered major changes in its structure and mode of operation extremely problematic. Despite all its deficiencies, this body solidified the economic mechanism. Being the monopolistic supplier of all the users, it was in a position to hold departmental and local ambitions in check. For example, the State Industrial Concern 'Iuzhmetallurgprom' (in Donetsk) produced output based on direct contracts with the users. Besides the contract, all deliveries of metal to the clients required the permission of Gossnab. However, by May of 1988 permissions for only 20% of the concern's annual production program had come in. Something failed in the old administrative mechanism, which had been suddenly reorganized. As a result, it was impossible to deliver the metal that had been produced to the consumers, and the output piled up at the concern's warehouse while the users stood idle (Medvedev, Nit, and Freinkman 1989b). Moreover, the stable economic cooperation that had existed for many years under the barter-type market depended on the personal 'horizontal' relationships among the directors of the enterprises, the officials of the branch ministries, and the regional departments of Gossnab. These relationships had been based on informal mutual assistance that had existed for many years. Numerous reorganizations inevitably destroyed these powerful, informal, informational ties which were based exclusively on mutual trust.

It is clear that the problem was not the number of territorial administrations subordinated to Gossnab, but rather the principles underlying the operation of these administrations. Yet the departmental logic of reform implementation dictated a different course. For example, to transform the intrasectoral structure was simpler and faster than changing the economic mechanism, and consequently made it easier to report on one's work in implementing the goals of perestroika. As a result, the main objectives of shifting to economic incentives were not attained. The weakening of the vertical ties between the enterprises and the ministries in 1988–1989 proceeded much more slowly than the destruction of the horizontal ties in the economy. This disrupted the rhythm of economic life and compromised the ideas behind the reform.

In failing to create firm incentives for the expansion of production or for taking buyers' interests into account, the government, by chaotic dismantling of the established methods of direct bureaucratic control, initiated the uncontrollable destruction of existing economic ties and atomization of the national market into closed, regional segments. Consider the example of the timber industry. In 1990 state orders made up 95% of the output of this sector. At the same time it was subject to self-sufficiency in terms of hard currency. Given the prevalent deficit of spare parts for imported equipment, this drove the industry to export the bulk of the output left with it (i.e., not included in the state order), since it was the only way to finance these vital imported items. Consequently, the free supply of lumber in the country diminished. At the same time the local authorities, which received considerably more rights during the course of the reforms, began to demand the expansion of exports from the timber industry operating in their territory to the detriment of complying with domestic contracts stipulated in the state order. In response, the regions and republics that didn't have their own timber and faced severe shortages took countermeasures to curtail the delivery of goods to timber-producing regions (*Rynok,* 1990, no. 3, p. 7).

'Barterization' of the Economy

As a result of inconsistent government policies, an uncertain future, and a general crisis of central authority, the enterprises began virtually to ignore the orders of traditional institutions. Regional authorities, particularly in the union and autonomous republics, assisted them in this. The most important indicator of the loss of government control over the actual performance of the economy was a drop in the fulfillment of contract terms for the delivery of output. In the first nine months of 1990, the official shortfall in deliveries of industrial output relative to signed contracts was 11 billion rubles—a 35% increase over the preceding year.

The strongest blow from the disruption of promised supplies was experienced by the economically weakest buyers—the social sphere, the enterprises located in remote regions, state, and collective farms.[9] For example, in the first half of 1990, gasoline and diesel fuel production in the USSR surpassed plan targets. However, the supply of these products to the agricultural sector was only 79–82% of the planned amount, which aggravated the serious problems of crop harvesting.[10] The shortfall in the delivery of foodstuffs to the large cities which began after this could be regarded as a kind of retaliatory step on the part of the rural producers. In a sense, the observed fall in directly sold grain (the share of state purchases of grain fell from 38% of the total harvest at the beginning of the 1980s to 28% in 1989) may serve as a measure of the expansion of barter (*Argumenty i fakty,* 1990, no. 45, p. 5). The producers of grain rejected the traditional government channels of 'marketing' grain and preferred to barter it.

Formerly, the ministries and Gosplan could dictate their terms to the enterprises since they possessed real material resources and they could guarantee a minimal stability in logistic support. Now, the ministries were unable to help 'their own' enterprises and the enterprises were forced to resolve their problems independently, through barter. Consequently, the enterprises no longer felt the need to comply with all the administrative instructions and rules.

The most obvious reason for the collapse of traditional economic ties was the fall of output. In 1989, the output of 64 out of 144 basic industrial product categories fell, and unfinished construction increased by 20 billion rubles. In 1990, the volume of industrial output fell by 1.2%.[11] Contract defaults due to the weakening of administrative control and the fall of production were exacerbated by the widespread plant closures forced by ecological regulations. In the chemical industry alone, in 1989–1990 more than 600 enterprises and production facilities stopped operating because of public outcry, and for the industry as a whole, production capacities with an output totaling 2 billion rubles annually were shut down (more than 2.5% of the annual output of this branch).

The reduced import of complementary products caused by the higher foreign debt and the fall of oil exports was another destabilizing factor. For example, in the first half of 1990 the Lenin Komsomol motorworks in Moscow received only half of the imported rolled steel it had requested and the delivery of plastics dwindled to almost zero. Similar situations occurred at the other large automobile factories in the Soviet Union (*Argumenty i fakty,* 1990, no. 24, p. 4). According to Gosplan's estimates, the sharp reduction in imports created an emergency situation in many branches of light industry (where 60% of the enterprises worked with imported raw materials), metallurgy (the production of zinc and galvanized steel, oil pipes), and the chemical industry (the production of soda-based products, materials for the leather and varnishes/stains industries, reagents used in drilling for oil and gas).[12]

The intensification of interrepublic and interregional disagreements also led to major breakdowns in supply contracts for such goods as food and agricultural raw materials. Moldavia, for example, in 1990 delivered to the Union fund only one-third of the fruit and less than 60% of the vegetables it was supposed to (*Izvestiia,* 6 October 1990). The Supreme Soviet of Ukraine demanded that the enterprises first fulfill the needs of the republic's economy and reexamine their contracts with enterprises from other regions. An analogous process of growing territorial autarky took place at the level of individual regions within the republics. By the decision of local authorities, a significant redistribution of output took place, especially timber, building materials, food, and consumer goods in general. As noted in Chapter 7.3, the crisis of authority that afflicted the central authorities exerted considerably less impact on the local administrations which, as it turned out, possessed more stable levers of control over the enterprises.

The uncertainty and inconsistency of the relevant regulations and the constant changes that were introduced by the Union parliament and the government impaired economic discipline. Entirely characteristic in this regard were two presidential decrees issued in the fall of 1990 and concerned with the stabilization of economic ties and the introduction of contractual prices ('*O neotlozhnykh* . . .' 1990; '*O pervoocherednykh* . . .' 1990). On the one hand, the goal of one of the decrees was understandable and justified: to try to prevent a further collapse of economic ties, since by the end of 1990 the situation in this area was catastrophic. The conclusion of delivery contracts for the following year (1991) proceeded even more slowly than they had in the previous year. According to Gossnab's data, by the beginning of September 1990 only 23% of the contracts had been concluded, as opposed to 43% in the previous year. By 11 October the figure was only 33%. At the raw materials for light industry fairs held in the fall, users could secure only 60% of the resources they required. On the other hand, the other presidential decree called for the expansion of the scope of contractual prices which exerted an opposite effect on the economy. By driving up prices, the established suppliers could force the buyers to 'willingly' refuse their products.

The waning of administrative control under conditions of a nonfunctioning ruble made barter the only vehicle of economic cooperation. Enterprises altered their output mix in order to lessen their dependence on suppliers as well as to expand their opportunities for bartering. The pervasiveness of barter manifested itself in two complementary phenomena: an increase in the share of barter operations and the expansion of autarky.

The growing autarky increased the gap between the main sectors (primarily between the enterprises producing consumer goods and their suppliers in the producer goods sectors) and aggravated the scattering of resources in situations that required their concentration on the most vital tasks. In some situations this tendency turned out to be for the better since it undermined monopoly and expanded competition. For example, the Cherkassk Research and Production Association 'Rotor' opened a department for making radioelectronics since their low-quality supply hampered the production of its main output. Analogous decisions were made at the Minsk watch factory, the Vilnius factory 'Sigma,' the Minsk tractor factory and other enterprises. The 'Odessatranstroi' trust obtained the transfer to it of the unprofitable Berezovo lumber enterprise in the Tiumen' region and planned to raise its output to designed levels within one year. As a result, a significant number of the enterprises of the Ministry of Transport Construction located in the Southern European part of the country could be converted to economic self-sufficiency (Medvedev, Nit, and Freinkman 1989a).

In the majority of cases, however, increased barter and autarky resulted in a less effective use of resources. For example, with brick factories operating considerably below capacity, new ones were being built. In a number of regions genuine trade wars flared up, as local authorities prohibited the shipment of goods beyond the borders of their region.

Sometimes a spontaneous cooperation among the parties was mediated by the various price substitutes, primarily by direct transfers from the buyer's material incentive fund into the seller's fund. Actually, this form of transfer was used by the buyers as a surcharge added to the officially set prices. The main advantage of such markups, in comparison with officially permitted contract prices, consisted of the fact that every ruble that was immediately transferred to the material incentive fund maintained its full value for the supplier: it could be 100% used to pay the employees. This was the real benefit of such transfers, for both the seller and the buyer. For example, in order to attain higher quality and better delivery of the foil it ordered, the Ust'-Kamenogorsk condenser factory transferred to the supplier (the Mikhailovsk non-ferrous metals processing factory) 5,000 rubles from its incentive fund as well as shipping to its employees 200 extremely hard-to-get electric heaters which it produced at its own factory. However, these success stories are rather rare (Medvedev, Nit, and Freinkman 1989a).

Price Reform

Price liberalization could have normalized the circulation of goods. However, the idea was extremely unpopular throughout perestroika because of its political costs. Palliative solutions such as contract prices or isolated price markups did not suffice, while creating an opportunity for additional abuse linked with the reclassification of products and disguised shifts in product mix. The only attempt to resolve the situation came at the end of 1990. Even in the face of an impending political crash, Gorbachev's team was unable to change its habitual strategy of piecemeal bureaucratic decisions, which failed to respond to the new political-economic reality.

The resolution of the CM 'Conversion to a New System of Wholesale Prices and Tariffs,' adopted on 25 October 1990, introduced [from 1 January 1991] new wholesale prices for all the key products of the industrial, transport, and communications sectors. It allowed the remaining products to be exchanged at freely agreed prices, subject to limiting the maximum rate of profit and making certain provisions for regulating the actual level of profitability. The maximum level of profitability in industry (it varied by branch) was 25–30%; for transport, communications, and publishing it was set at 40%.

In conjunction with the new taxes and social security contributions, the reduced size of state orders and curtailed centralized distribution of resources which took effect from January 1991, and also the deformities caused by the breakdown of established economic ties between enterprises and regions, the new prices created a radically new financial and economic situation which was very difficult to foresee.[13]

As stipulated in the appendix to the decree, fixed prices were preserved for vital product categories: fuel, rolled metal, and electric power, but also railroad ties, cord fabric, quartzite, radio components, semifinished goods made from optical glass, and so on. The breakdown of some categories was supposed to be determined by subsequent decisions of the ministries. Later on, the republican authorities were also granted the right to define items whose price was not subject to bargaining. In order to evaluate the magnitude of what was to take place, consider that, already in 1988, 5% of the final output of the machine-building industry was sold at contract prices and that this figure was growing quickly. The decreed maximum rates of profit undermined further the measures that had been undertaken. The ceilings again forced enterprises to increase their costs, to expand (mainly on paper) mutual trade, and to invent (taking advantage of the weak tax agencies) new ways of concealing income.

The decree failed to address the most critical question: what would the new fixed prices be? It was already impossible to introduce the prices that had been set in 1988 and kept under strict secrecy in the files of the State Committee on Prices. In the meantime many other financial parameters had changed, for example, social security deductions had increased. The actual precise prices were communicated to the enterprises virtually on the eve of their going into effect.

The reform presupposed changes in wholesale prices only. It took a few early months of 1991 with industry operating under the new prices and a deep financial crisis in the consumer branches for retail price policy to be reexamined (Kolosnitsyn et al. 1991).

8.2 The New Stage
Vladimir Mozhin

At the end of 1989 the struggle surrounding economic reform spilled over from the offices of the members of the Politburo to the podium of the Palace of Congresses. In December 1989 the government submitted to the second Congress of Peoples' Deputies the report 'On Measures for Economic Recovery and the Stages of Economic Reform,' prepared under pressure from the deputies. For the first time it announced the goal of transition to a market mechanism, while preserving government price controls, planning, and other forms of government regulation. In presenting the report, Ryzhkov (1989, p. 2) announced that the government could not agree to the introduction of private ownership or to large-scale denationalization of state property, including the sale of small and medium-size enterprises.

By that time the Economic Department of the CC was removed from direct involvement in drafting the reform. However, we sent our proposals directly to Gorbachev. After he was elected president of the USSR in March 1990, we tried to use 'the first 100 days' to jump-start the reform through a series of presidential decrees. In collaboration with the president's assistant, N. Petrakov, and with Ye. Primakov, we produced a number of documents and draft decrees. However, Gorbachev failed to respond to our initiative.

In spite of all the efforts, Gorbachev was unable to introduce any major economic reforms. Essentially, the perestroika years were spent elaborating the concept of economic reform, which ultimately boiled down to a market economy. The first major reform action was taken at the beginning of 1992, after the collapse of the Soviet Union. From the very inception of perestroika, Gorbachev had no fully fleshed-out alternative socioeconomic model. He realized that the country was about to go downhill, and decided to utilize models that had proved effective in Western countries, but without renouncing the Soviet version of socialism. It turned out that such a symbiosis was impossible. But the realization of this fact took some time. It would seem that Gorbachev himself had to overcome his own entrenched preconceptions. While he lacked any insight into economics, he ought to be commended for grasping the essence of the situation and moving, albeit slowly, in the right direction.

Academic economists were of little help in the reform. They were ill prepared for such a drastic turn of events and often limited their advice to generalities. Prolonged ideological isolation also took its toll. Only the very young had any theoretical knowledge of the market system, and at that time they were not close to the leadership.

The reform decisions were largely confined to general principles. Their implementation depended mostly on the CM and Ryzhkov, who was very cautious. His half-measures often nullified the reform-oriented changes, as was the case with the Law on the State Enterprise and the restructuring of the ministries. However, the key player that shaped and controlled the pace of the economic reform was the Party, with its vast apparatus. Gorbachev could not ignore the Party's ideological platform and predominant position in the economy. He was forced to look over his shoulder, sometimes, I believe, hiding his true intentions.

8.3 The Parade of Market Transformation Programs
Yevgenii Yasin

The First Concept of Market Reform

By the middle of 1989, it became clear to experts that the economic model of 'socialism with a human face' in its Gorbachev version, thought up two years earlier, had proved inviable and significantly exacerbated the economic crisis. By that time, moreover, public opinion was better prepared for a movement in the direction of a normal market economy. In July 1989, N.I. Ryzhkov presented his new cabinet, which included the economist-reformer L.I. Abalkin as vice-premier, to the Congress of People's Deputies. Abalkin was also the head of the newly formed State Commission on Economic Reform, charged with developing a program for the transition to a market economy. Pro-market economists like G.A. Yavlinsky, who were very critical of the reforms enacted so far, were on the commission's staff. The commission as a whole was reform-minded. The obstacles to change, created by the other, more conservative agencies, were often discussed at its meetings.

The first result of the commission's work was a background report for a conference in October 1989, describing a plan for further reforms.[14] The document was drawn up by Yavlinsky and Yasin. Its outline and content were discussed with and approved by Abalkin. In the course of drafting the document, all the ideas were discussed with Abalkin and as a rule met no objections on his part. Ryzhkov and other members of the government did not give any directions. The premier completely relied on Abalkin. It was only later that disagreements arose. No ideological taboos were imposed from outside. However, the authors grew up in Soviet society and knew the do's and don'ts as perceived at the time by the establishment. Self-censorship assured that for the most part only acceptable changes were proposed. The main constraint was to stay within the bounds of the 'socialist choice.'

While preserving some ideological clichés, this report differed fundamentally from the principles of the 1987 reform. It still spoke of diverse forms of public ownership and did not directly discuss private property. But the use of the form of ownership best suited for each situation was advocated. The objective was not yet privatization, but *destatization*. The rejection of the dogma that property income is illegitimate was recommended (only labor income had previously been considered legitimate). For the first time the market was viewed as the chief mechanism for the coordination of economic activity and the command economy was rejected. The need for free prices and competition was affirmed. The conflict between economic efficiency and social justice was acknowledged, implying the utopianism of the goal of building an efficient economy on the basis of social justice, understood in the socialist sense.

Government regulation was still allotted a significant role. Yet the report proclaimed, "We are not talking about improving the existing economic mechanism, nor about merely replacing its out-dated parts. One internally consistent system must be dismantled and replaced by another one, also internally consistent and thus incompatible with the previous one."

The report examined three variants of transformation—conservative, radical, and moderate radical. The conservative variant preserved the old system with a few changes that were to be slowly implemented. Naturally, it was rejected. The radical variant was also rejected, but it met with a more interesting fate. Presented to demonstrate the dangers of radicalism and bolster the case for the third, moderate strategy, it became the basis for the '500 days' program in 1990 and was almost fully implemented by Gaidar in 1992. Its essence was the rapid liberalization of prices and economic ties, financial stabilization, and energetic privatization. The consequences of following the course of radical reform described in the 1989 report were very similar to the ones later observed in practice.

The 'moderate radical' variant proposed roughly the same steps as the radical one, but taken gradually. Significant administrative control over the economy would initially be preserved. The share of state orders, regulated prices, and state property in the economy was to be reduced over time. Since this variant was never tested, it is hard to judge its viability. Its piecemeal incremental model of transition to the market appeared quite logical. Yet given the conditions of that period, incrementalism was doomed to failure, as the subsequent events confirmed.[15]

Discussion of the Abalkin commission's report was accompanied, probably for the first time, by a political demonstration. Near the building where the conference was being held, orthodox Communist protesters raised signs reading "Down with the Abalkinization of the country!" These people worried in vain.

The 'Revitalization' Program

After the conference the government discussed the report, and apparently gave it high marks. It ordered that the reform be combined with the Main Directions of the Thirteenth Five-Year Plan being worked out by Gosplan, as well as with the urgent measures for reviving the economy that were being worked on by yet another group headed by the first deputy vice-premier, L.A. Voronin. People with very different views on life and reforms in the country were working on each of these issues. The result of the fusion was that the efforts of the pro-reform people were practically negated. The final document still retained the name of the moderate-radical variant, but behind this facade was hidden the conservative variant. Gosplan's ideology won the battle over the direction of reforms.

The 'Revitalization' Program, introduced at the Congress of People's Deputies in December 1989, fused absolutely irreconcilable views and theories.[16] Its main idea was to postpone all reforms for two years, and meanwhile (in 1990–1992) not only keep but reinforce the old administrative planning mechanisms. These mechanisms would help revitalize the economy, balance the budget, and saturate the consumer market. From this improved and more balanced position the country could later start moving toward the market. New administered prices (retail, wholesale, and state purchase), prepared by V. Pavlov back in 1988, were to be introduced in 1991. The incentives for accepting state orders were to be strengthened, investment demand reined in, and a number of programs aimed at augmenting the capacity of the construction industry carried out.

At the Congress, democratic deputies (e.g., G. Popov) openly ridiculed the program's authors for planning 1995 egg production, as had been done in all the previous five-year plans. However, the Congress approved the program. Its resolution did not contain even the faintest premonition that from that moment on, despite all the energetic pronouncements, the Soviet economy would inexorably go downhill.

Hardly a month had passed after the Revitalization Program was passed when even its proponents realized that it could not be implemented. It was no longer possible to govern using the old administrative methods, because commands did not reach those who were supposed to execute them, and if they did, they were not followed. Ministers convened in the Kremlin, orders were issued, quotas for material and financial resources were allocated, but none of it worked any more. Market mechanisms did not work either. The ruble did not work because the monetary system was practically demolished by irresponsible fiscal and price policy.

At the same time, certain circles in the government started talking about a 'recoil.' While the Revitalization Program was itself a step backward, it became clear that mere declarations were not enough, that the old levers of power had to be made to work again. But restoring the old order without returning to totalitarianism and repression was impossible. As an important government official said at the time, to return the economy to its 1985 state, politics would have had to be rolled back to 1937.[17] To understand the processes at work in the Soviet Union in this period it is important to realize that already in early 1990 the political and economic crises had practically spun out of control. From that time onward it became pointless to argue for stronger government regulation of the economy.

Meanwhile, Poland was implementing the Balcerowicz plan.[18] Reform-minded economists who visited Poland were of the opinion that this was just what the doctor ordered for Russia. Discussion within the small group of reform-oriented economic advisors led to the conclusion that changing economic conditions made the moderate-radical and the radical variants about equal in terms of their negative consequences. The radical variant now looked more attractive because liberalization did not require much in terms of organizational effort and worked fast. The program of 'prudent' gradualism, carried out through government regulation, raised more and more doubts due to the progressive weakening of the state.

In January–February 1990 a group of economists inclined toward the radical variant emerged in the president's apparatus and in the government, including G. Yavlinsky, N. Petrakov, B. Fedorov, Y. Yasin, and S. Aleksashenko. Outside the apparatus, the radical approach was championed first and foremost by the younger people from Gaidar's team, as well as by A. Mikhailov and M. Zadornov, who worked with Yavlinsky. The radicalization of their views resulted from the pressure from society and from the evolution of their own ideas, driven by their analysis of economic conditions and trends. It was becoming perfectly clear that the government's reluctance to significantly deregulate and stabilize the economy was only making matters worse.

The radicalization was also prompted by the growing ranks of the proponents of a 'rollback,' such as the future member of the State Committee for Emergency Rule A. Tiziakov and his Association of State Enterprises.[19] L.I. Abalkin played an important role during that period, speaking at the internal government meetings against the rollback and for accelerating market reforms.

N. Ryzhkov's Program for Transition to a Regulated Market

In January–February 1990 the leadership began to recognize the new realities. N.I. Ryzhkov, who had up to then almost single-handedly determined economic policy, came under pressure from Gorbachev's team, which demanded more vigorous implementation of the reforms. Within the government, the debate between the proponents of a rollback and the advocates of a faster move toward the market ended with the victory of the latter (L. Abalkin, Yu. Masliukov, V. Pavlov, and S. Sitarian). These were, of course, very moderate reformers, but at the time they were the first to realize that the country had no choice but to accelerate the pace of reform, whatever the consequences might be.

It was decided to commence work on a new program for a rapid transition to a market economy. In spite of the quick and complete failure of the previous program, the prime minister demanded that the matter be presented as if everything were going according to plan, namely that the new program was not new at all, but merely a development of the old one. Actually, it was a completely new and much more radical program rejecting virtually all the main ideas of the previous one, approved just two months ago.

In April, the Presidential Council considered and rejected the first version of the new program, significantly more radical than the October 1989 report. This document, which was never published and remained practically unknown to the public, opened with an almost open acknowledgment of the failure of the government's policies and a formulation of fundamentally new objectives:

> The economy cannot long function under an artificial combination of the fundamentally incompatible command and market structures. Practically all attempts at transition to economic methods of control run into powerful resistance from a monopolistic non-market environment, which discredits the general idea and concrete goals of reform. . . . This environment prevents the economy from noticeably approaching equilibrium, thereby condemning a country with great potential to chronic shortages and disequilibria. Attempts to reduce mechanically the scope of centralized planning and distribution, to develop direct ties and wholesale trade without changing the system of price

setting and under conditions of excess money supply, only undermine production incentives, aggravate disequilibria, and encourage barter. . . . The government deems it expedient to implement in 1990–91, to the maximum degree possible, the measures for transition to the market scheduled in the Program for revitalizing the economy for 1992–93.

For the first time, the task of macroeconomic stabilization was given top priority. Free prices were recommended for most economic sectors.[20] This was expected to fill the store shelves with goods, something that otherwise would be impossible to achieve. Energetic measures for developing free enterprise and destatization were suggested. Several hundred of the largest state enterprises would be turned into joint-stock companies within a year by selling shares to legal entities and individuals. Small-scale privatization was also planned. All proceeds from the sale of state property were to be used for paying off the state debt and reducing the budget deficit. For the first time, the April program included calculations simulating the consequences of its implementation (incomplete at the time of the presentation to the Presidential Council).[21] The text spoke of the inescapable doubling or tripling of the price level; a drop in production of at least 15–20% (more in heavy industry and construction); the closing of inefficient enterprises; the emergence of unemployment; the standard of living falling by 20–25% at the first stage of reform; and increased inequality of income and wealth in society.

Now, when reality has far outstripped all these forecasts, these figures do not seem so ominous. But at the time, they undoubtedly became the main reason for rejecting the April program. Let us remember that prior to this the prevailing notion was that reforms must immediately improve all indicators. The incompetence of the majority of Soviet economists, not to speak of the leadership, was one source of this fallacy. Another was the experience of the reforms in Hungary, Czechoslovakia, and the USSR in the 1960s, where certain immediate gains were achieved within the framework of the partially liberalized socialist system. Somehow it did not occur to many people that conditions had changed, making the replication of the past impossible.[22] Finally, the leaders who had decided to go ahead with the reform had themselves to disseminate and share the illusion that they would be relative painlessness, otherwise it would have been hard to decide on anything and to convince others of the necessity to act. It made it much easier to accuse one's opponents of indecisiveness or adventurism.

Margaret Thatcher was visiting the USSR around that time. In his meeting with her, L.I. Abalkin expressed, for the first time I believe, the view that the reforms would be painful. Mrs. Thatcher was glad to see that this was understood and cited her own experience as confirmation of the economy's inevitable initial deterioration following institutional transformation. Still, no one save a very small circle of economists expected the crisis to be so deep.

Within a week of the rejection of the April program, Gorbachev, speaking in Sverdlovsk, declared that he would not allow reforms to bring about a lower standard of living for the people. Boris Yeltsin, elected chairman of Russia's Supreme Soviet, said the same thing two months later in connection with Ryzhkov's speech presenting the second version of his market program to the Supreme Soviet on 24 May 1990. The Presidential Council was scared by the radicalism of the April version. It is plausible that Ryzhkov, who can hardly be suspected of radical leanings, intentionally suggested the radical version to Gorbachev to scare him and to stop further accusations of not wanting to proceed with the reform. If this assumption is true, Ryzhkov managed to achieve his goal and got the opportunity to reshape the program to his taste, which, like that of V. Pavlov, favored an administrative price revision. This point was actually the primary distinction between the May and April versions. However, now all the other sections of the program—which had been watered down to the point that even the innocent word 'destatization' disappeared—looked like hollow declarations when compared to the concrete and very convincing figures indicating higher prices of bread and other foodstuffs and the much less inspiring figures on compensation.

The prime minister refashioned the program as he saw fit, and paid for it dearly. The 24 May speech virtually marked the end of his career. The effect was so strong that in a matter of hours, almost all goods had been cleared out of the stores, even though the suggested price increases were only to go into effect six months later. No one would listen to any explanations. The Ryzhkov-Pavlov price reform may have been not such a stupid idea from a strictly economic point of view, as a way to reduce inflationary pressure. But politically and psychologically, it was an unforgivable mistake. The state of the Soviet economy began to deteriorate with every passing day. Inflationary pressure had been building up rapidly since 1988, suppressed only by the government-fixed prices and the state orders, which proved less and less effective. Shortages were getting worse and the ruble was losing ground, weakening the producers' incentives. Ryzhkov's speech provided a psychological push which sent the economy tumbling down. People started buying whatever they could to redeem their money. The shortage of consumer goods became much worse.

The '500 Days' Program

Economic programs have been fashionable in Russia from the fall of 1990 up to the present day. The most common accusation against the government is that it does not have a program. If one says, "Excuse me, but we do have a program," the response would be: "What kind of program is that, we need another one." The programs are routinely measured against the standard of the '500 Days' program, apparently because of the latter's early, loud success with the public and its quiet death on a dusty bookshelf. Such programs have always been a tool of politics first and foremost, and only then served the needs of economic reform. This was doubly true of the '500 Days.'

In May 1990, as Ryzhkov was speaking at the USSR Supreme Soviet, at the nearby Russian Congress of People's Deputies a chairman of the parliament was being chosen in a down-to-the-wire race. B.N. Yeltsin, elected with a majority of only six, needed visible political initiatives, and the deteriorating economy provided a good opportunity for political maneuvers. But what specific actions could he undertake in Russia without the cooperation of the Union? At the initiative of Yavlinsky and Petrakov, an attempt was made to bring Gorbachev and Yeltsin together so they could work in concert for the victory of reform and democracy. The effort succeeded. For a while the alliance between the two leaders seemed fruitful to both of them. They agreed to develop a joint economic program. N. Ryzhkov turned out to be the scapegoat in this program, especially since he had set himself up with his price reforms.

The new economic program was elaborated in parallel with the government's program, which the premier was supposed to present to the parliament in early September after some finishing touches had been applied. No one remembers the government's program anymore, while the '500 Days' program, created under the patronage of Gorbachev and Yeltsin, is still being talked about. The reason for this is that the country needed to be shown a way out of the hopelessly persistent economic crisis, and it pinned its hopes on market reforms. And the country then trusted the initiator of perestroika, Gorbachev, and the tough fighter for democracy against totalitarianism, Yeltsin, and rejoiced that they had come to an agreement.

The '500 Days' program (*Perekhod* . . . 1990) was a decidedly radical version of the transition to the market. There was no other way out by the summer of 1990. The only issue was courage and political will to accept the inescapable severe consequences in order to avoid even greater losses from a prolonged decay and complete demise of the economy. The debate between radicals and gradualists is endless, but perhaps all can agree that there are rare times when the radicals turn out to be right. These are times when a breakthrough or qualitative shift is needed, and gradual, delicate actions are no substitute. Such a time had dawned in Russia, and the '500 Days' program was its banner.

Naturally, no one thought that a market economy could be built in 500 days. But the old genotype could be destroyed and replaced by a new one, from which the market could grow. Breakthroughs are never accomplished over long periods of time. The most important thing was a daring polemical slogan, and B. Yeltsin seized upon it instantly. The '500 Days' was in many ways similar to the April program, but without ideological limitations: the words 'socialism' and 'capitalism' were not mentioned even once.

The basic idea was that over the course of three months (through the end of 1990) the government was to implement a series of impressive institutional changes (privatization of small establishments, strengthening the right of private property, and demonopolization) and, most importantly, financial stabilization to lower inflationary pressure. Starting 1 January 1991, a gradual deregulation of prices would begin, accompanied by tight financial constraints. By the end of the first 400 days, about 70–80% of prices of goods and services were to be freed.[23] During the same period, the ruble would become convertible for current account transactions. By the end of the 500 days, up to 70% of industrial enterprises and 80–90% of construction, trucking, and wholesale and retail enterprises were to be sold or leased.[24]

Of course, these were fantastic time frames. It is interesting to note, however, that when economic liberalization actually began, it took roughly 500–600 days. Government controls on the prices of petroleum, coal, and grain were lifted by the fall of 1993. Partial convertibility of the ruble was achieved even faster. By the beginning of 1994 (over a period of 16 months) up to two-thirds of all state enterprises had been converted into joint-stock companies and privatized. Rapid financial stabilization was not achieved, but then it could not have been achieved that quickly in Russia. The '500 Days' as the program of a radical breakthrough was, in the final analysis, carried out, although late and based on a somewhat altered scheme (liberalization without prior macroeconomic stabilization).

The program's section on the economic union became a subject of sharp conflicts. Some argued that the authors were destroying the Soviet Union by giving too much power to the republics. Others thought that this was the way to save the Union, because the republics' push toward sovereignty and independence had grown so strong that it could only be stopped by force. The concept of an economic union was based on the belief that even with broad political autonomy, the republics' economic interdependence was a fact of life, making cooperation advantageous for all. As became apparent in the not too distant future, political leaders could not, or no longer wanted to, be guided by such ideas.

In September 1990, the program was considered by the parliaments of the USSR and Russia. The latter, under Yeltsin's pressure, approved it in a week. In the former, the program got tied up by the opposition of Ryzhkov and his cabinet, as well as of the entire old Party-government establishment. They realized that things were coming to a head politically: either they, or the '500 Days' program and real reform, would prevail.[25] Gorbachev was put under intense pressure, which he could not resist. Yeltsin did not seem to be very upset by the end of his alliance with Gorbachev, which had raised such high expectations. He clearly saw new political opportunities in Gorbachev's being guilty for the failure of their joint program. In a fiery speech before the Russian Parliament, Yeltsin predicted harsh consequences resulting from the rejection of radical reforms by the Communist Union center, and thus freed himself to work actively against it.

8.4 The Party Learns About the Market
Yurii Belik

The Department was charged with learning how the market economy was regulated in the countries that had much experience in this respect. By that time the Department had been renamed the Socio-Economic Department and was slowly becoming a kind of quasi-research organization. Starting in mid-1989, teams from various economic agencies headed by representatives from the Socio-Economic Department went abroad on a quest to learn about market experience in Sweden, France, the Federal Republic of Germany, Belgium, Finland, Japan, and the United States. The problems of transforming the Soviet economy into a market economy were extensively discussed with experts from the International Monetary Fund (IMF), the World Bank, the Organization for Economic Cooperation and Development (OECD), and the European Community (EEC), and also with a number of prominent Western scholars. We had a great opportunity to learn a thing or two and to obtain valuable knowledge.

The reports of all the groups were consolidated into a single report that was submitted to the leadership. Here are some key points from it:

> The market can produce a powerful socioeconomic impact only if accompanied by an appropriate government policy. An inept transition to the market mechanism may lead to crisis phenomena. The need for government regulation of the market was stressed by almost everyone. . . . It can be implemented via economic, exchange rate, fiscal, investment, and R&D policy.
>
> A modern market mechanism is a flexible system of adapting production to consumer needs. At the same time it is a system of stringent government oversight over the principles of fair competition and social protection.
>
> The joint-stock company must be the dominant form of state and private property. . . . It permits a natural fusion of individual, group, and state interests.

Incomes policy is an effective tool for stimulating economic growth while protecting the interests . . . of the main social groups of workers and entrepreneurs (including the state sector). Almost all Western economists (including W. Leontief and G. Shultz) recommended that wholesale and retail prices be more closely aligned to world market prices.

According to the experts, the Soviet transition to the market system must be preceded by market equilibrium and a balanced budget. In order to avoid hyperinflation with a drop and a sharp differentiation in the standard of living, preemptive changes in prices and incomes must be implemented that will create the requisite market equilibrium at the macrolevel.

A necessary condition for effective systemic reforms is the socioeconomic support of the majority of population and also maintenance of financial and labor discipline at the microlevel.

A report entitled 'Government Regulation in Japan,' compiled in December 1989, compared that country's experience of postwar economic recovery to the initial stages of perestroika. The government's role in the economic recovery in Japan was extensive: indicative planning (twelve [*sic*] five-year plans!), extensive consideration of social policy, particularly at the early stages of recovery, priorities in structural policy.

8.5 Foreign Advice
Philip Hanson

The Soros Initiative

In October 1988 a Western team of six economists went to Moscow, under conditions of some secrecy, to advise the Soviet government on economic reform. The team was sponsored and led by the financier, George Soros. Its advice was intended to assist, not partial reform in the Gorbachevian style, but a transformation to capitalism. The effort went on into the summer of 1989. It included meetings with a number of senior Soviet officials, of whom the highest placed was the prime minister, Nikolai Ryzhkov. The exercise did not perceptibly change Soviet policies. In late 1989, after waiting some time for an official Soviet response to the group's proposals, Soros declared the venture dead.

The team did achieve one thing. George Soros wrote, a few months later: "I did not consider . . . the time . . . wasted. I had learned a lot about the disintegration of the Soviet economy and the paralysis at the decision-making center" (Soros 1990, p. 30). As a member of the team, I can say the same. My aim in this section is to set out what I observed in the course of this attempt to advise the government, and the conclusions that may be drawn about the making of economic policy in Moscow in the last years of the USSR.

George Soros was born in Hungary, studied in London, and has based his remarkable career in New York. In Hungary he experienced the Nazi occupation, but very little of the subsequent Communist regime. In London, as a student of Popper, he began to develop ideas of his own that originated with Popper's notion of an open society. In New York, he made very large amounts of money. His first Open Society Foundation was set up in Hungary in 1984. He turned his philanthropic attention to the Soviet Union in 1987, when he set up a foundation there.

It was in 1988, by Soros's own account, that he put the idea of a particular strategy for Soviet economic transformation to Moscow's Ambassador in Washington, Anatolii Dubinin (Soros 1990, p. 28). My understanding is that around this time he consulted two outstanding economists, Wassily Leontief and the late Ed Hewett, about the idea, and that they played a part in formulating the initial, outline proposal. Dubinin sounded out his government, and an invitation came from Vladimir Kamentsev, the head of the State Foreign Economic Commission (GVK), for Soros to come to Moscow to discuss the idea of what came to be known as the Open Sector (hereafter OS) proposal. The Soviet side stipulated (I was told) that the exercise was to be conducted secretly, in the sense that no information about it was to be given to the media, Western or Soviet, and that the participants should keep the number of people to whom they revealed the project's existence to the minimum.

The GVK was a creation of perestroika. Set up in 1986, it was one of several 'overlord' bodies that Gorbachev's reforms added—curiously—to the Soviet hierarchy. It had oversight of all agencies engaged in foreign economic relations, including the Ministry of Foreign Trade and the State Committee for Foreign Economic Relations (GKES). Ivan Ivanov, a deputy chairman of the GVK, a former academic, and the coordinator of the Soviet side in our OS discussions, has given a detailed account of the reorganization in question and the thinking behind it (Ivanov 1987). In principle, Kamentsev was a senior member of the government.

The OS advance party included the Hungarian economist Marton Tardos, Soros himself, Hewett, Leontief, the recently retired IMF economist Jan Mladek, and myself. Hewett, perhaps the outstanding Sovietological economist of his generation, was in effect Soros's deputy. At that time, Hewett was at the Brookings Institution; he later served on the National Security Council, before his tragic, early death from cancer.

Leontief, who was greeted at the first meeting with a patriotic round of applause from the Soviet participants, had the unique advantage, for the purposes of the project, of being a Nobel prize-winning economist who had been born, and had grown up, in Russia. The fact that he had emigrated even before Stalin came to power was not, in right-thinking Moscow circles in the late 1980s, held against him. Rather, it added to his status.

Tardos, who has more recently been a prominent Free Democrat deputy in the post-Communist Hungarian parliament, had not merely lived under Communism in Hungary, but had studied in Leningrad for his doctorate toward the end of the Stalin period. He, more than any of us, I believe, could read at once the doubts and questions that arose in the minds of the Soviet officials during our discussions. Mladek brought to the discussions the perspective of an international economic organization (IEO), or, rather, the perspective of an economist with long experience of an IEO. He also had an East European background. I was, I suppose, the token West European.

The initial discussions with Kamentsev, Ivanov, and an array of senior officials and economists led up to a four-hour meeting on 31 October with Prime Minister Nikolai Ryzhkov. He gave his blessing to the project. Meetings were resumed in Moscow in January 1989, with an expanded Western team that included the economists Anders Aslund, Herb Levine, Mario Nuti, Gur Ofer, and Vladimir Treml (from Sweden, the United States, Italy, Israel, and the United States, respectively); the academic lawyer Bill Butler; and two bankers based in Western Europe. In this and subsequent rounds of discussions there was a mixture of plenary sessions and separate working groups dealing with various aspects of the OS scheme.

There were also meetings in New York and London but, as Soros put it, "they were deteriorating into tourism." (Soros 1990, p. 30.) The plan was for a final, agreed report to be presented in May 1989 to the government, the Communist Party leadership, and the Soviet press. Ivanov, for the Soviet side, sought a postponement, and eventually the whole effort ended in a typically Soviet fashion. The OS scheme, as a strategy for beginning the transformation of the Soviet economy, was never explicitly rejected or accepted. The Kremlin simply never called back. Late in the year, George Soros informed members of the expedition that he considered the episode to be closed.

We were then free to reveal that there had been an attempt to advise the Soviet government. Soros himself had concluded that "the body of the centrally planned economy had decayed too much to be able to nurture the embryo of a market economy" (1990, p. 30). The notion of the OS as the embryo of a market economy was at the center of our proposal for a transformation strategy.

The Open Sector Idea

Members of the Soros team were united in the belief that what was needed was not reform but transformation to a capitalist economy, and that such a transformation was not impossible but faced enormous obstacles. To make a breakthrough, part of the economy should be transformed so that it was based on private enterprise and market rules of the game. The success of this 'Open Sector' would have a demonstration effect for the rest of the society. In addition, the relations of the OS with the rest of the economy would be designed in such a way as to gradually draw the rest of the economy into the market sector by creating powerful incentives for 'ordinary' enterprises to transform themselves into what Soros succinctly called 'real firms.'

The OS would be composed of certain selected territories in which market rules would prevail, together with existing real firms wherever they might be located: at that time, joint ventures and cooperatives.[26] The OS would have a separate, convertible currency to which the ruble would be connected by a floating exchange rate. All firms inside the OS would be free from any planning intervention whatsoever. Foreign direct investment would not be restricted to the 49% maximum foreign equity stake that was imposed on joint ventures in the 1987 legislation.[27] Trading with the outside world would be decentralized and free from administrative constraints.

In retrospect, this scheme looks visionary. But then, so is the whole idea of transforming the former Soviet Union to capitalism, whatever strategy is pursued. That such ambitions are easily dismissed as overoptimistic does not mean that they are unattainable. I think all of us saw the successful economic transformation of the Soviet Union as immensely difficult, and perhaps unachievable. Nevertheless, we considered that the slim chance of success might be increased by focusing initial, radical change on a narrow front. This narrow front was to be the OS.

All in all, the OS project cannot but look, in retrospect, like a naive endeavor. But those involved knew it was a long shot. Subsequent developments have not demonstrated that it was impossible. One thing, however, that hindsight suggests we gravely overestimated was the capability of the Soviet state. The proposal was perhaps most utopian in the presumptions that it entailed about policy implementation. It assumed that if we could have convinced key members of the leadership, they could have got such a scheme implemented.

The selection of specific regions for the OS was something we said was for the Soviet side to arrange, though we hoped to gain agreement on criteria for that selection. One such criterion was that there would be a wide mix of economic activities within such regions (taken as a whole, not one by one). Another was that economic activity in the OS should be as little dependent on inputs from the rest of the economy as was possible, though nobody supposed that regionally self-contained clusters of input-output relations were available in the Soviet Union.[28]

To implement the scheme required central legislation to insulate the OS from planners' intervention and to formulate the broad rules of the game that would operate within it. The two key questions, given that premise, were: what would be the mode of interaction between the Open Sector and the rest of the economy? What would be the basis of its monetary system? Other matters could be considered after those two questions were addressed.

The question of how the OS would interact with the rest of the economy was particularly tricky. The OS currency would be convertible into rubles, as into other currencies, and transactions between OS firms and ordinary Soviet enterprises would in that sense be feasible. But no plan targets, plan input allocations, or state orders would be permitted that impinged directly on OS firms. The logic of this requirement drove us to propose a high authority to guarantee the independence of the OS. At the same time, for the OS to be able to draw into itself 'normal' enterprises from the rest of the economy, it was necessary that ordinary enterprises have significant amounts of capacity not preempted by state orders. As with the need to control the ruble money supply (see below), our OS proposals, though apparently limited in initial scope, required policy measures of a difficult kind to be implemented for the economy as a whole.

The Soviet economist Nikolai Petrakov, one of the most sympathetic and constructive of our Soviet interlocutors, groaned most eloquently when the proposal of an 'OS Authority' was first made. "Not another ministry!" he said. He was, of course, quite right to be skeptical. But an administrative economy has a remorseless logic. If you don't abolish the whole structure, you need a kind of administration to defend the unadministered from the administered economy. Handing the OS over to a number of regional authorities was clearly not to be thought of. The regional authorities were, in late 1988, in the process of becoming more independent of Moscow (Helf 1994), but they were not in the process of becoming born-again free marke-teers. In any case, an important part of the OS would be real firms located outside any of the specially selected regions. In the course of the 1989 OS meetings, Bill Butler, together with a number of like-minded Soviet legal scholars, set about drafting a statute for the governance of the OS that would meet our objectives.

The OS plainly could not consist entirely of private firms. To begin with, the selected regions would have a social infrastructure, from law courts to roads (and, in practice, schools and hospitals, even though those might in time be privately operated) that entailed an OS public sector, supported by OS taxes. Moreover, whatever regions were selected, we would be starting with a population of state enterprises in them. These would not initially be real firms.

While aiming to secure rapid privatization within the OS, we hoped that state enterprises, when corporatized and subjected to a rigorous financial environment, would seek to minimize costs and find new markets and improved technologies because they would have to act like that to survive. Certainly, there would be no constraints in the OS on the founding of new, private firms.

The Soros team made the tactical mistake of referring to the OS currency early on as the *valiutnyi,* or hard-currency, ruble. Valuta rubles already existed as accounting units for expressing transactions denominated in deutschemarks or dollars in ruble terms, converting DM or $ magnitudes at the official exchange rate. The terminology was therefore misleading. There was discussion of a gold-backed ruble, with analogies with the chervonets of the 1920s, and rather franker discussions of the dollar as the OS currency. The dollarization of the Soviet economy was then in its early stages, but the emerging *de facto* dollar economy, which has performed some of the functions of our OS, was not something the Soviet government could be expected to endorse as part of a grand reform strategy.

A gold- or hard-currency-backed convertible OS currency was the gist of what we recommended, with an OS monetary authority. Conversion between the OS currency and the ruble had to be possible. We wanted a framework that would stimulate the OS to expand at the expense of the rest of the economy. A flexible, market-determined exchange rate was needed. The ruble was still not, in a centrally administered economy, freely convertible into goods and services or into foreign currencies. The OS currency, which would be, was therefore going to be more attractive to hold. Enterprises in the ordinary economy would be able to earn OS currency if they could produce output that would be marketable to OS firms that had the option to buy freely from abroad. The idea was that this lure would induce non-OS enterprises to raise their game; earn OS currency; and move, if they could, into the OS themselves. Real money would drive out rubles.

This would not work, however, if ruble cash and credit emission were unconstrained. If the quantity of rubles were constantly to increase, enabling ordinary Soviet entities to acquire OS currency at an ever-increasing exchange rate, the unreformed economy would siphon resources out of the Open Sector, undermining the whole project.[29] The conclusion was inescapable: for the OS to work in the way it was meant to, the Soviet authorities had to get their money supply under control.

This particular part of our proposal illustrates as well as any the paradoxes of the OS approach. To make the OS effective, the Soviet authorities would have had to do something that would have been of enormous benefit to the whole economy even if the OS had never been dreamt of.

Notoriously, they did not bring inflationary pressure under control, and that failure contributed to the Soviet economic disintegration.

Could the OS idea have worked? The question is, of course, in the strictest sense unanswerable. One cannot know what might have been. The outline just given will, I hope, explain how it was *meant* to work. Its success would have required, among other things, a macroeconomic stabilization of the ruble economy that did not, in the event, take place. That requirement aside, I think we were seeking a degree of political self-denial by the Soviet leadership that in retrospect looks implausible. By 'self-denial,' I mean that they would have had to take their hands off a chunk of the economy to enable the OS to develop properly. I suspect that neither the confidence nor the will to do this was present in the Soviet political establishment. In that sense, the fundamental difficulty was political. What is relevant here, though, is that the open-endedness of Gorbachev's whole approach had encouraged the thought that perhaps such self-denial was possible. The specific and proximate ways in which it proved not to be possible will be addressed in a moment.

There was a great deal more, in detail, in the OS proposals that were put forward, discussed, modified, and generally developed in the course of the discussions. I am aware that this exposition of the outline of the strategy makes the whole scheme appear still more utopian than it was. For the purposes of this chapter, however, it is the core idea that matters. It was the core idea that the Soviet side eventually declined to proceed with.

The Soviet Side

Our entry to the Soviet policy-making machine was through the GVK. It was one of the superministries whose heads had the status of deputy chairman of the CM (roughly, deputy prime minister). We were therefore in discussions with a part of one of the three main economic-policy-forming institutions of the period: the CC, Gosplan, and the CM. Nikolai Ryzhkov, as chairman of the CM (effectively, prime minister) was formally in charge of economic policy. And it was he who, at the end of our first, exploratory visit, gave the green light for discussions to continue. But CC officials were not included in the teams we met, neither in 1988 nor in 1989 (with one qualification, to be made in a moment). And Gosplan was not strongly and consistently represented.

Stepan Sitarian, then first deputy chairman of Gosplan and deputy chair of the Gosplan-led, interdepartmental Commission on the Improvement of Management, Planning and the Economic Mechanism, did take part in one meeting. As Gosplan's 'economic reform' man, he might have been an important participant. But he did not repeat his visit to the meetings (that, at least, is my memory). Whether he should be regarded as middle-of-the-road in his approach to reform, as Aslund (1987) suggests, or as an intelligent conservative (Ed Hewett's view) is for those who know his record well to decide. He was, however, on record as having said that the economy could not be divided into planned and market sectors (*Financial Times,* 8 June 1987, p. 3).

For most of the talks, Gosplan was represented by a middle-level official, Lev Vasiliev, who consistently referred to the proposal as being about an *osobiy* (special), rather than an *otkrytiy* (open) sector. Hewett and I constantly reminded him of the appropriate term, but the word *otkrytiy* seemed to stick in his throat. The Marxian-Freudian slip kept recurring. A jovial man of Party apparatus background, Vasiliev was a source of insights for the Russia watchers among us, but not of progress in the discussions. With hindsight, I conclude that Vasiliev himself was Gosplan's message to the Soros team.

At the time, the constellation of forces was less clear. It was, however, apparent that our main access was to a section of the government machine that was not necessarily the most influential, even if the CC apparatus could be left out of the picture which, of course, it could not.

Vladimir Kamentsev, the deputy prime minister and chairman of the GVK, was sixty at the time of our first visit. In his youth a specialist in trawler design, he had been deputy Minister of Fisheries from 1965 to 1979, and then Minister from 1979 until, in 1986, he was put in charge of the newly created GVK (*Izvestiia,* 3 September 1986, p. 1). He fell from grace before the Soros project was finally wound up. This may have contributed to the project's failure, though it is hard to believe it was a critical influence.

When parliamentary hearings were introduced to confirm members of the government in their offices, Kamentsev's reappointment was blocked, reportedly because of charges of nepotism raised against him by the mayor of Leningrad, Anatolii Sobchak (in the latter's capacity as a deputy of the USSR Supreme Soviet). Ryzhkov defended his deputy, saying the charges had been shown to be baseless, but Kamentsev was not renewed in his post (*Izvestiia,* 30 June 1989, pp. 1–2, and 5 July 1989, pp. 1–2). If this development did play a part in the outcome of the project, it would have been through diminishing Kamentsev's standing in mid-1989 and perhaps diverting Ivan Ivanov's energies to other matters (which is the reason Ivanov gave Soros for postponing, in May of that year, the final, wrap-up meetings on the project). My impression is, however, that he had never been a source of great influence anyway. From the extremely superficial acquaintance we had with him, I would say that he was business-like but not dynamic.

Ivan Ivanov, a deputy of Kamentsev and formerly an academic specialist in international economic relations, was both the ideas man and the main organizer on the Soviet side. Unlike most of the other Soviet participants, he spoke English well (the discussions were mostly conducted in Russian). Ivanov was clear that radical reform was needed but less clear how far it could and should go. It turned out, toward the end of the project, that even the generally sympathetic Ivanov had trouble seeing how any significant chunk of the economy could get by without at least some state orders.

The regular official participant who later attained the highest office was Valentin Pavlov, at that time chairman of the State Prices Committee. Whether Pavlov attended the meetings for anything other than amusement, I cannot say. The economist Nikolai Petrakov was, as I have already mentioned, another member of the Soviet team. He was also at that time a member of a committee linking academics and Goskomtsen officials, in which price reform ideas were being discussed (information from Petrakov at the time). The differences between Petrakov and Pavlov over possible changes in the price system were clear at our meetings. Petrakov considered the decontrol of prices (whatever reservations he may subsequently have expressed about decontrolled prices in a later period) to be in principle both desirable and feasible. Pavlov did not.

Other academic economists who took part included Igor Faminskii, a contemporary of Petrakov's, who headed the GVK's research institute; a more junior member of that institute, Vladimir Kuznetsov (who soon after became a deputy director of an Italian-Soviet joint venture); and two well-established and reformist colleagues of Petrakov's at TsEMI, Vilen Perlamutrov and Yevgenii Yasin. All these academic economists were open to radical reform ideas. They were not, however, so far as I could judge, close to the levers of power. Petrakov later became, for a time, an economic advisor to Gorbachev. But none of a succession of such kitchen-cabinet advisors to the Soviet leader had the clear official status of, say, the chair of the U.S. Council of Economic Advisors.

The head of the government, Nikolai Ryzhkov, facilitated discussion with the Soros team, but did not push hard for any particular outcome—at least not in any way that was visible to the Western participants. Our meeting in his Kremlin office on 31 October 1988, lasted four hours (to my eternal regret, I had to leave after an hour and a half to catch a plane, which was in the event delayed by an hour and a quarter).

While graciously encouraging the group to carry on talking, Ryzhkov does not seem to have ordered his subordinates to implement an OS strategy forthwith. In the absence of strong direction from the prime minister, other sources of initiative on the Soviet side might, just possibly, have made a difference. The role of Gosplan has already been discussed. Aware that we were being formally grouped with only a limited range of officials, we managed, outside the framework of the official discussions, to arrange a meeting with a senior CC official, Vladimir Mozhin. Mozhin was at that time first deputy head of the Economic Department of the CC. Originally an agricultural specialist, he had worked in Gosplan and was now deputy to the CC Secretary, Nikolai Sliunkov, responsible for the economy (*Izvestiia,* 30 July 1986, p. 3). Given the primacy of Party power (although it was already weakening), and the key role of CC secretaries, Mozhin's post made him potentially more of a powerful insider than Kamentsev or Ivanov.

The meeting was between, on our side, Soros, Hewett, Tardos, and myself, and on the Soviet side, Mozhin and (from memory) three assistants who declined to identify themselves. (We gave them our business cards—in return, they smiled.) Soros (1990, p. 30) recalls Mozhin engaging in 'automatic speaking' for about an hour. My memory of the meeting is not as dire as that, but certainly Mozhin gave little away. My memory agrees with Soros's further account, however: that one of the assistants asked some good questions, and that we were given no clear guidance in the course of the meeting. Like the prime minister, the CC Economics Department was polite, friendly, but non-committal.

At the January 1989 meeting we were joined by a young Estonian, Kalle Tenno, who was described as an advisor to the Estonian SSR Council of Ministers. The representation was otherwise entirely Moscow-based. The Soros team had refrained from suggesting that entire Soviet republics might be part of the OS. This was felt to be too politically sensitive, as the Baltic states, especially, were already pushing hard for greater autonomy. Tenno's presence, however, put the relationship between the republics and the federal center in the minds of the participants, if not explicitly on the agenda.

A group of Estonian writers and economists had already formulated a scheme of Estonian economic autonomy. Laws asserting the primacy of Estonian over Soviet legislation had been passed in the Estonian legislature (Hanson 1990). In the working group in which I was involved at the time, the Gosplan official, Vasiliev, tried to keep Tenno out of the discussion. I learned that he was also doing his best to exclude Tenno from subsequent meetings—a maneuver that Hewett and I did our best to thwart. Tenno's position was an awkward one for the Moscow officials involved in the meetings. He maintained that, while not at all opposed to the general idea of an OS, the Estonian leadership could not consign Estonia to the role of a guinea pig to be tested for the sake of Soviet economic reform. Estonia had its own laws and its own policies, and was not available as an instrument of Soviet policy. Whether Tenno really spoke for the Estonian leadership of that time, I rather doubt, but he certainly spoke for a strong current of nationalist feeling in Estonia, and his was not a voice that our Moscow colleagues wanted to hear.

Objections to Baltic autonomy were not confined to the officials. Siim Kallas, an Estonian economic journalist who in the post-Communist period was governor of the Estonian central bank, had proposed in September 1987 a kind of OS Estonia, without restrictions on private enterprise and with a convertible currency. At a subsequent Finnish-Soviet seminar in Tallinn, Nikolai Petrakov had poured cold water on this idea, saying that no Soviet republic was ready to pay its way in the world (*Financial Times,* 9 November 1987, p. 22). In Moscow even the good guys, in other words, were not enamored of the idea of republics taking off under the OS slogan and distancing themselves from Moscow.

It is worth considering whom we did not meet—at any rate officially. There were no high officials (to my knowledge) from the defense sector; Gosplan was underrepresented; we met high Party officials only outside the official talks and on our own initiative; and many of the leading reform intellectuals were not on Ivanov's invitation list.

Reformers who subsequently became prominent as policymakers were conspicuously absent. Of the authors of the '500 Days' program of 1990, only Petrakov and Yasin were involved in the OS discussions. Leonid Abalkin, then the director of the Institute of Economics, was a particularly interesting absentee from our meetings. He had already been invited by Ryzhkov, in the summer of 1988, to prepare an economic strategy document, and in the summer of 1989 he became, at Ryzhkov's invitation, a deputy prime minister with responsibility for chairing an economic reform commission.

If Ryzhkov had been seriously interested in the OS, if only as a possible strategy, he would surely have involved Abalkin, his new economic-policy mentor, in the discussions. The cast list suggests, on the contrary, that such initiative as there was on the Soviet side rested with the much lower-placed Ivanov. Interlocking membership of the GVK (itself a commission with membership from other government agencies) and the Gosplan-led Commission on the Improvement of Management, Planning and the Economic Mechanism, brought in representation at varying levels from Gosplan (mainly low level), from Goskomtsen (high level), and (at modest levels) from a few other departments.

Abalkin himself records (1991, p. 24) that he first met George Soros in late June 1989, on the eve of his assumption of the office of deputy prime minister. He gives no indication that he was aware of the OS project, though this secret exercise was by then common knowledge among the

Moscow intelligentsia, and Abalkin would at least have heard of it. The project's death had not yet been officially recorded, but Soros himself had already reached the conclusion that the idea was not viable (Soros 1990, p. 30). It looks as though, by that time, Abalkin, a wise man within the Soviet system, and Soros, a wise man outside that system, concurred in thinking the OS strategy utopian.[30]

The Reactions and Responses of the Soviet Side

As the discussions proceeded in plenary sessions and working groups, it became clear that only Petrakov, Yasin, and one or two others were thinking in terms that were close to ours. And they were skeptical. One of the more junior economists, Vladimir Kuznetsov of the GVK research institute, declared that the only way relative prices were ever going to make sense in his country was in the aftermath of a hyperinflation. He had no faith in reforms within the system, and his forecast has proved to be not far from the mark. The GVK officials, including the moderately reformist Ivanov, understandably saw the whole exercise through the prism of foreign economic relations. In the first place, this was their field, and they were the lead organization in the discussions. In the second place, they were under pressure from two sides: from Gosplan and production ministries who did not wish to lose any of their production assets to an uncontrolled OS, and from regional leaders who wanted their localities declared special economic zones. Ivanov told me in October 1988 that there were already twenty such proposals on his desk.

Small duty-free zones and tax havens can attract foreign investment and entrepot or assembly activities, either for exporting or, in the case of an otherwise closed economy, for sale to the wider domestic market. Whether such arrangements can normally be expected to contribute more, on balance, to a country's GDP than a more general liberalization will seem doubtful to most economists. An example of the role of a special economic zone in a closed economy is provided by Manaus, 3,000 kilometers from Rio de Janeiro in the Amazon jungle in Northwest Brazil. It was established in 1967 by the military regime of the time, as a location for foreign investment to produce for the otherwise closed Brazilian market, under exemptions from import duty and with subsidies provided to firms locating there. Sharp, Gillette, and Philips were among firms that found it worthwhile to locate there. Since the Brazilian economy began to be liberalized in 1991, employment in the Manaus free economic zone has fallen from 80,000 in 1990 to 50,000 in 1994. Sales almost halved from 1990 to 1992, and then began to recover as the firms located there began to adjust to a more competitive environment (*Financial Times,* 28 April 1995, p. 14).

Many of the people involved in special economic zone proposals in the USSR in 1988 and 1989, both in Moscow and in the regions, seem to have had something like the 1967 Manaus model in mind. The idea of the Soviet economy being open to foreign investment and imports in a general way probably seemed like the wildest fantasy. But to have foreign investment in your region was an obvious attraction to any local elite, and the political environment at that time had changed enough to make that, at least, seem possible. At the same time, just as the Brazilian authorities in 1967 had, according to the *Financial Times* report just cited, seen Manaus as a development hub for a remote region close to other countries' borders, so Moscow policymakers were inclined to favor undeveloped locations where development would serve some strategic advantage.

We found that ideas were circulating about special economic zones in regions such as the so-called BAM area. BAM is the acronym for Baikal-Amur Mainline, the additional rail link built, at enormous cost, parallel to a long section of the Trans-Siberian Railway, across eastern Siberia and into the Russian Far East. If there was any defensible reason for building the BAM, it would have been to do with security considerations relating to China. The territory around the BAM contains mineral resources, and there was much talk of developing them. But attracting foreign investment to this end would have been a forlorn hope. It is unreasonable to expect foreign firms to invest massively in the basic social infrastructure that the region needed. By the same token, however, BAM had the attraction for Moscow officials that existing production-branch ministries, apart from the Railways Ministry itself, had no real estate there that they would want to keep hold of.

The weakness of any central economic strategy was illustrated in another way, as well. Whatever the reformist misgivings about a special OS authority, it was clear to all the Western participants and to the few serious reformers on the Soviet side that leaving the administration of territories within an OS to the local authorities (i.e., the local Party) was completely incompatible with our aims. In practice, GVK and other Moscow officials seemed to find the idea of taking economic activity in a particular region out of the control of the local elite quite impracticable. Paradoxically, only a very strong central leadership could have done this.

The attractions of special zone status to local elites are indicated by an anecdote I was told at the time about the plans for a special economic zone in Novgorod. It was said that the scheme would go ahead provided a high fence could be built around the province of Novgorod. Why? To keep out the population from Pskov.

In this fashion, the Soros team's grand scheme for an OS got absorbed into a messy and shortsighted development of would-be special economic zones (SEZ), whose character was shaped by existing Soviet institutions and elites. A month after the scheduled date for the unveiling of an OS scheme, in June 1989, Ivan Ivanov, who had postponed further discussions with the Soros team, gave a press conference to announce the impending creation of three such zones, in Vyborg (on the Finnish border), Novgorod, and the Pacific port of Nakhodka (*Izvestiia,* 17 June 1989, p. 2). Reports of his press conference illustrated the gulf between the Soros plan and the GVK outcome.

Some of the things Ivanov said contained, it is true, echoes of our proposal. Soviet SEZs might, he said, be quite large territories. They would not be export-production enclaves but would be relatively strongly linked to the rest of the economy. There would be a variety of forms of ownership among the production units located in them. There would be the possibility of a special currency, perhaps common to all SEZs. But these were faint, distorted echoes. Characteristically, there was still only a 'draft conception' for SEZs in general. Meanwhile, he was clear that state orders would be used for production in SEZs, "probably for less than 50% of it"; and the highest authority would be the [existing] local authority, with a special SEZ administration subordinate to it.

In August *Izvestiia* reported (30 August, p. 1) that the Novgorod SEZ had been the subject of a local opinion survey. The scheme was described as a 'so-called open sector' arrangement for the province, the concept of which had been worked out by specialists at the Academy of the National Economy, at the Academy of Social Sciences of the CC, and in the province itself. The Soros team had had no contact, to my knowledge, with any of these three groups, except that in January of that year several of us had conducted a roundtable on Soviet economic issues in general in an auditorium at the Academy of the National Economy, with an audience of mid-career students of this Soviet management staff college. That meeting had nothing particularly to do with the OS.

On 19 September 1989, Ivanov announced at another press conference that a decision in principle had been taken to set up the three SEZs in 1990 (*Izvestiia,* 20 September 1990, p. 3). They were now called "zones of joint entrepreneurship." They would not be cut off from the rest of the economy, Ivanov said. Foreign currency would circulate in them alongside rubles. It was already beginning to circulate rather freely, albeit illegally, in Moscow.

In December 1989 it was reported that 'social forces' in Novgorod had forced the regional administration (*oblispolkom*) to abandon plans that would have allowed the region to keep 70% of foreign currency obtained from its planned SEZ specialization in tourism, VCRs, art videos, and holograms (*Izvestiia,* 27 December 1989, p. 2). The social forces were identified as Greens and a local United Workers' Front. They were said to have objected to an SEZ because it would bring in prostitutes and speculators, and would make the locals second-class citizens in comparison to foreigners. The *Izvestiia* report gently pointed out that the region had its defects already, and implied that talk of a flood of foreign tourists and businessmen might have been a little premature. The lighting in the St. Sofia Cathedral, the chief tourist attraction, was out of order for five days during the reporter's visit. He did not claim that the social forces involved might have been holograms, not real people. He did, however, make it clear that he thought their behavior was not in the best interests of the people of Novgorod.

It began to look as though even the limited notion of a Manaus-style SEZ was something that the Soviet administration was not able to implement. The center was not strong enough to override regional administrations and impose a uniform pattern on such zones. The regional administrations, in turn, could not cope with their local nationalists. One is tempted to say that the problem was democracy, but that may be too kind a view. In 1990 Larisa Piyasheva made fun of Ilya Zaslavskii's election promise to make the Oktyabrskii district of Moscow a 'free zone' by taxing some people more and others less (*Izvestiia,* 18 February 1990, p. 2). A month later (23 March) TASS reported that schemes for SEZs were being worked out in eight areas. By May, the newly elected governor of Sakhalin, Valentin Fedorov, was announcing that he would make that remote island a free-standing, free-market economy. It was given SEZ status in June 1991 by the Russian Republic (RSFSR) parliament (*Izvestiia,* 24 May 1990, p. 3, and 20 June 1991, p. 2).

The special economic zones were getting caught up in the jurisdictional battle between Russia and the USSR. Political games continued to be played with the words 'Special Economic Zone,' 'Free Economic Zone,' and 'Zone of Joint Entrepreneurship.' Very little, even of a modest, Manaus type seems to have happened on the ground. The OS proposal left almost no traces in Soviet policy.

Conclusion

The Soros mission was the forerunner of a whole series of Western attempts to advise Moscow about economic transformation. But it was a somewhat isolated forerunner. There is a continuum from the indigenous "500 Days" proposals, the Soviet-American plan (Allison and Yavlinsky 1991), the analyses and prescriptions of the international institutions (IMF et al. 1991), and of the European Commission, through the Western-funded Macroeconomics and Finance Unit advisors in Moscow in 1992–1994 to the legions of consultants and advisors now working on particular projects in the former Soviet Union.

The Soros team of 1988–1989 was different from most subsequent missions in several ways. Its activities were kept secret at the time, in deference to the Soviet authorities' wishes. It was not funded by Western public money. It was intended to influence top political leaders directly, rather than to work chiefly with officials operating under an acknowledged policy of transformation. It was intended to promote reform initially in only a small part of the economy. It had no aid to offer.

All these characteristics reflected the circumstances of the time. The Soviet leaders were uncertain how far they wanted to go with economic change (they never did make up their minds). It was not yet the case that the planning system had collapsed. The year 1989 was the last year of officially recorded growth in the Soviet economy. The acute urban food shortages of 1990–1991 and the open inflation of 1991 changed a great deal. In the late 1980s it was still possible for Moscow policymakers to believe that the old system could usefully be tinkered with, and did not have to be abandoned.

The simplest explanation of the failure of the OS proposal was that it was politically a nonstarter. Nobody in a position of influence really wanted to throw their weight behind a proposal that would have taken substantial resources away from existing institutions: USSR Gosplan, the CC CPSU, the industrial branch ministries. The implication of that view is that only the collapse of the Communist order allowed fundamental change in economic institutions to occur. In 1988, however, it was not self-evident that this had to be the case. Remarkable economic transformation was going on under a Communist one-party regime in China. A good deal had happened over twenty years in Kadar's Hungary. At times Mikhail Gorbachev seemed prepared to consider anything that would work, short of breaking up the USSR and disbanding the Soviet Communist Party.

George Soros's verdict, already described, was that the economic and social order was in an advanced state of decay, and there was no effective central decision-making power. Soros's judgment is not incompatible with the view that powerful vested interests blocked substantive change. It means that political leadership capable of overcoming those interests was lacking. It might be asked why, in that case, Soros had not focused on the very top: on Ryzhkov and Gorbachev. I believe that this was not an option. Soros's name did not have as much international political resonance in 1988–1989 as it acquired a little later. He already had high-level political access in the West, but I suspect (and this is only guesswork) that Gorbachev was out of reach.

Both these broad views are eminently defensible. But they are too broad to provide much insight into the process of Soviet disintegration. If one looks at more proximate influences, one can perhaps identify, from the story that has been narrated here, the following.

The machinery for economic decision making in Moscow in the late 1980s consisted of a number of institutional clusters—the CM, Gosplan, and the CC apparatus—that did not regularly act in a coordinated way. Of the highest-ranking politicos who might, just possibly, have knocked heads together for the sake of a grand strategy of reform, Gorbachev kept himself out of economic policy most of the time, and Nikolai Ryzhkov had no clear vision of what needed to be done. Those economists who were, in the late Soviet context, liberal reformers (Ivanov and Abalkin, for example) did not see the social order being fundamentally altered, or at least not quickly. Those who were rather more radical (Petrakov, for instance) were not really trusted by the powers that be. Those who were really radical (Gaidar, Yavlinskii, Yasin, Boris Fedorov, and Seliunin) were either too young, too discreet (Yasin), or too indiscreet (Seliunin) to be given a chance, at that time, to make policy.

The OS proposals were discussed only by a small part of the policy-making establishment. That part of the establishment had an occupational bias toward translating the OS idea into the much more limited and politically assimilable idea of SEZs. No high political figure showed the inclination or the drive to sponsor the idea and push for its implementation. The state administration was by that time so disorderly anyway that even the modest SEZ schemes that were endorsed at the top were not carried through on the ground.

Notes

1. Full understanding of this section and also of Chapter 9.2 by Nesterovich, requires a knowledge of how the planning of supply in the USSR worked. The standard work is Levine (1965). [Ed.]

2. Goskomstat data.

3. Data from a survey of engineering enterprises conducted by the Machine-Building Industry Research Institute of Gossnab in the summer of 1989.

4. This figure shows that the enterprises were handed plans stipulating the distribution of 86% of their output. Of course, the real share of independently sold output was much higher, since discipline was low. However, this nominal parameter is crucial as an indicator of the depth of the economic reforms as perceived by the administrative system itself.

5. Gossnab estimates, 1989.

6. Data of the Machine-Building Research Institute, 1990.

7. Gossnab data, 1990.

8. Gossnab data, 1989.

9. Strong sectors were not immune from supply disruptions. Thus, a deputy chairman of the VPK (in the transcript of the interview quoted from in Chapter 3.2): "Starting

around 1990, we began to experience shortages of lumber, which was critical because a lot of ammunition is packed in crates. We experienced the same problems as the civilian sector. It just took a little longer for the problem to catch up to us. The only way to solve these problems was to exercise all the leverage we had." [Ed.]

10. Goskomstat data.

11. Goskomstat statistics.

12. *Obshchesayuznyi prognoz pravitel'stva SSSR o funktsionirovanii ekonomiki strany v 1991 godu* (Moscow, 1990, pp. 40, 73).

13. For example, the financial crisis in the consumer sectors that forced the reform of retail prices led to a decline of the share of turnover tax in the GDP from 12% in 1990 to less than 6% in 1991.

14. The report (*'Radikal'naia . . .'* 1989) was described as "material for discussion" for the All-Union academic-practical conference on radical economic reform held on 30 October–1 November 1989 in Moscow. [Ed.]

15. The report was not the only product of the commission. Day-to-day work on reform-connected issues proceeded under the direction of P. Katsura, S. Assekritov, V. Pokrovskii, and A. Orlov. My department drafted a statute of the sectoral ministry (never actually completed), the Law on Property (subsequently passed by the USSR Supreme Soviet), and the decision on the creation of the country's first joint-stock company based on KAMAZ. The main work was done by the interdepartmental working groups and task forces. It was through the participation of its staff in these task forces that the commission influenced the content and direction of particular programs.

16. Ryzhkov 1989 and *'O merakh po ozdorovleniiu . . .'* 1989. [Ed.]

17. See Ellman and Kontorovich 1997, pp. 273–275. [Ed.]

18. Leszek Balcerowicz was deputy prime minister and Minister of Finance in the first Solidarity-led government of Poland (September 1989–December 1991). The 'Balcerowicz plan' was the well-known Polish 'shock therapy.' [Ed.]

19. The State Committee for Emergency Rule was the body that attempted the August 1991 coup. [Ed.]

20. Gosplan proposed that the price lists established by V. Pavlov back in 1988 should be announced to the enterprises. The latter should inform the superior body what they would produce under these prices, and Gosplan would use these data to decide which prices to set free and which to regulate. This complicated and clearly ineffective procedure was intended to ease the shock of the transition, but also served as a good target for critics.

21. The calculations were performed by Gosplan's Main Computer Center (director Ya. Urinson).

22. The idea that the reform would inevitably begin by making things worse had been argued since the late 1970s by the former Soviet economist Igor Birman. [Ed.]

23. Prices of fuel and energy, consumer necessities, basic medicines, schoolbooks, and transportation and utility rates were to remain controlled.

24. Free distribution of state property in the form of vouchers was not planned.

25. There were also objective reasons for their hindering it. It became clear that financial stabilization could not be achieved before the liberalization of prices, as the program envisioned. Starting in the summer, prices were already spinning out of control.

26. At the time we did not appreciate the extent to which the 1988 Law on Cooperation would lead to the creation of nominal cooperatives that were spun off from state enterprises to exploit loopholes in planning controls, and how many cooperatives would be symbiotically tied to state enterprises.

27. See the decree of the CM of 14 January 1987 in Golubov 1988, p. 325. [Ed.]

28. The Chinese territorial structure of input-output relations appears to be more conducive to such schemes than the Soviet one was, or the Russian one is.

29. This was close to the free rider problem identified later in the course of the breakup of the USSR. Why would any one successor state seek to stabilize a shared currency by acting with fiscal prudence (Havrylyshyn and Williamson 1991)?

30. In January 1989 Vladimir Treml brought to the Soros team's attention the fact that a home-grown variant of the OS scheme was being advocated by the veteran Soviet economist Viktor Belkin (e.g., Belkin 1989). In Belkin's scheme there would be two kinds of money in circulation: the ordinary, goods-inconvertible ruble and a heavy, or commodity-backed, convertible ruble. Enterprises of any ownership form that sold output to a real market (exports to the West or sales to Soviet households) would earn the convertible ruble, and their bank accounts would be denominated accordingly. If they chose to use those convertible rubles to buy from domestic input suppliers, those suppliers in turn would be earning convertible rubles. As in the OS proposal, there would be an incentive for producers initially outside the market sector to earn their way into it, and thus a mechanism by which it could grow. Like the OS scheme and for the same reason, Belkin's proposal was vulnerable to uncontrolled ruble emission.

9

Reforms on the Sectoral and Enterprise Levels

9.1 Conversion of Military Industry[1]
Sergei Belanovsky

XXXX (deputy chairman of VPK and previously head of the Defense Industry Department of Gosplan): "It was the spring of 1987. Masliukov [then chairman of VPK] came from a meeting with N.I. Ryzhkov and said: 'Gorbachev, Ryzhkov, you and I must devise a plan for drastically reducing our expenditures on weapons procurement. We have to figure out our options.' Our defense expenditures were about 13–14% of the GNP. It was proposed to cut them to 10% over the course of three years. I analyzed six alternative plans. I was the only one to make the actual calculations. I still remember all these calculations. I am not saying I did all the work. Other people worked on it after me. The order of magnitude of my estimated cuts in such areas as operational expenses, capital construction for the military, and the development of various weapon systems, was basically approved.

"When this work was finished, the actual conversion program had to be devised. Gosplan came up with a half-baked program which was approved sometime at the end of 1990 or the beginning of 1991. It was aimed primarily at dramatically increasing the output of consumer goods at the expense of the defense industry. Some funds were budgeted for this purpose. Everybody thinks that you can just stop producing automatic rifles and start producing sewing machines the next day. This is ridiculous. Anyway, some funding was promised for the conversion program, but in the event no funds actually arrived.

"At that time the country was already falling apart, and this doomed the conversion. From the end of 1990, Russia started to assert its independence, and so did all the other republics. A war around the profits tax was being waged at the time. The Union government set the rate at 45%; Russia, at 42%; the Union, at 38%; Russia, at 35%; and so on. I was present at a meeting where the Russian Finance Minister told Silaev [the Russian Prime Minister]: 'We cannot do this.' Silaev responded: 'Shut up. This is a political issue.'"

YYYY (deputy director of a research institute for military-industry machine building): "In 1989–1990, at all the meetings of VPK, 90% of the discussion and all the plans, were devoted to conversion. The USSR fell apart at exactly the moment when the Party was beginning to address the needs of the population."

I.S. Belousov (chairman of VPK and minister of the Ship-Building Industry): "At the peak of the arms race, 60% of defense industry capacities were devoted to the military and 40% was used for civilian needs. In 1985 we came to a decision on this issue and by 1988 we attained a ratio of 50/50. We were on our way to a 40/60 ratio between the defense-related output and civilian output at defense plants. The program which we formulated and began to implement in the period of so-called perestroika aimed to make us self-sufficient in many consumer goods—TV sets, cassette players, washing machines, bicycles, motorcycles—by 1995. The first years of implementing this program gave significant results, with double-digit growth rates of consumer goods production.

"When we announced the program of conversion to civilian production, everybody was captivated by it. However, the cumbersome coordination requirements paralyzed the entire process. The following episode is telling. In order to start production of hair dryers, twenty-six signatures had to be secured! Now, in order to get all these approvals one had to travel 10,000 kilometers. And this was just production of hair dryers!

"I don't think people thought of it that way—first we make drastic cuts in the defense budget and accumulate economic potential and then we renew the arms race and start catching up to the Americans.[2] Nobody entertained such an idea, neither Gorbachev, nor those before him. In terms of R&D, the things mentioned by our American colleague could have been accomplished at our own research institutes and training grounds. The real issue was mass production and the use of our production capacities. This was an economic question, a question of resource allocation. Here, we naturally lagged behind the United States. The trend toward arms reduction did not stem from our desire for a temporary breathing-space but represented an attempt to create preconditions for the economy to be more responsive to the consumer."

M.I. Gerasev (Institute for the USA and Canada): "Gorbachev began to cut down the size of the army and to reduce the defense budget. However, his relations with the military-industrial complex were not decisive in shaping the course of events. Gorbachev created new incentives—the newly gained opportunity to have access to foreign markets, greater openness within the country. There was no acute conflict between Gorbachev and the military-industrial complex. There was some displeasure on the part of the defense industry with Gorbachev's policies, particularly (I witnessed this myself) the irrational conversion program and the orders to the defense enterprises without regard for the nature of their output. People employed by the military-industrial complex are disciplined and therefore they tried to fulfill these orders, set up the production of new items, etc. In the end, all these efforts only ruined the enterprises."

9.2 Reform of the Supply System
Nikolai Nesterovich

The Stages of the Introduction of Wholesale Trade

The June 1987 Plenum of the CC decreed that the transition to wholesale trade was to be completed within four–five years.[3] Gossnab worked out a plan for the development of wholesale trade. Its maximum possible volume was calculated by excluding from the total volume of [gross output of producer goods] those products which, in Gossnab's opinion, could not be the object of wholesale trade: the output of the defense industry, fuel and power [*sic*], the value of repair work, intrafactory transactions, and some other products. It was estimated that 250 billion rubles (in 1987 prices and volumes) worth of producer goods could be transferred to wholesale trade.

To complete the transition by 1992, the following cumulative schedule was established:

Year	1987	1988	1989	1990	1991	1992
Wholesale trade, billion rubles	10	40	115	170	200	250

Gossnab started the preparations for transition to wholesale trade in producer goods in 1986. On 13 June 1986, Gossnab approved the 'Statute on wholesale trade in producer goods.' It stated that "wholesale trade in producer goods is the form of supply when resources are provided to the users without quotas and limits, according to their orders and based on the contracts with the territorial agencies of Gossnab." The users were to submit the orders as the need arose, and these were to be filled in a relatively short period.

This was the first, centralizing stage in the development of wholesale trade, characterized by the attempt to change the supply system without changing the existing system for managing the economy, and above all, production planning. The changes were limited to the link between the territorial organs of Gossnab and their clients.

One approach was to switch all the enterprises of a particular ministry to wholesale trade in all or most of their inputs. Alternatively, consumers located in one region, irrespective of their subordination, were transferred to wholesale trade, with the territorial organ of Gossnab acting as the only quota-holder, concentrating the region's resources and taking care of all the stages of supply, from the receipt of quotas to shipping the goods.[4] The enterprises would order and buy supplies from Gossnab's territorial organs, without submitting their estimated requirements (*zaiavki*) and obtaining quotas. They would no longer have to present voluminous documentation on their input requirements long before the needs actually emerged, and to haggle endlessly over the quantities actually allocated. Any additional needs could be provided for speedily.

The technology of working out plans remained unchanged. The territorial organs had to submit the same old estimated requirements for quotas of inputs to [the central apparatus of] Gossnab, which in turn had to present them to Gosplan. Instead of the enterprises and ministries, the determination of needs and defense of quotas was now the responsibility of the territorial organs and Soyuzglavoptorg, the newly created main administration of Gossnab.

This did not improve the quality of planning. Gossnab's territorial agencies, having taken on themselves the function of determining the needs of the enterprises they served without their estimated requirements, could do that only by the normative method or by forecasts. The normative method required information about the input norms and production plans, that is, practically the same information which the enterprises used to present in the calculations of their input needs. But in the new procedure the presentation of such documentation was abolished. And the method of forecasts at that time in the system of Gossnab meant an orientation to the previous year's figures.

The procedure of defending needs in Gosplan did not change at all, as estimated requirements and supporting calculations were still demanded. It did not matter that it was not a ministry appealing for resources on behalf of its enterprises, but Soyuzglavoptorg. In turn, Soyuzglavoptorg demanded estimated requirements and calculations of need from the territorial agencies, but there was no one for the latter to demand this documentation from, since under wholesale trade it had been forbidden to collect these documents from the enterprises.

The new procedure also exacerbated the problem of coordinating production plans with supply plans. Since most of the responsibility for supplying the enterprises was transferred from the ministries to Gossnab's organs, the ministries withdrew from coordinating the production tasks which they planned for the enterprises with the availability of inputs. The ministry, when determining production tasks, considered only capacity and in some cases labor constraints, as if intermediate inputs were plentiful. But Gosplan would allot Soyuzglavoptorg not as much as had been requested, but as much as the availability of the given resource would allow. This meant for most goods, last year's quantity at best.

Many enterprise officials perceived the transfer to wholesale trade as the supply agencies' obligation to provide unconditionally all their orders immediately, independently of the general level of (dis)equilibrium in the country. Therefore, they did not limit themselves at all in their orders. The overall volume of resources allotted for wholesale trade did not grow, and the enterprises' orders significantly exceeded it.

The enterprises of the Ministry of Construction and Roadbuilding Machinery were the first to switch to wholesale trade and got priority in the supply of inputs. They received more inputs, but their performance deteriorated. In 1987, more than 70% of enterprises of the Ministry did not fulfill their contractual obligations. [Moreover], the lifting of rationing limitations on the demand for material resources led to a growth in input inventories. In 1987, the Ministry's enterprises held 80 million rubles worth of above-norm inventories.

At the second stage of the transition to wholesale trade in producer goods, in 1988 and the first half of 1989, some types of products were completely removed from the centralized planning of production and distribution. The share of the state order [in production] was significantly reduced, leaving the enterprises in principle free to dispose of the remaining output. The volume of wholesale trade toward the end of this period exceeded 100 billion rubles.

The Reorganization of Gossnab

The Gossnab system had three levels: the central apparatus; the main supply administrations (*soyuzglavsnabsbyty*); and the territorial organs. The *soyuzglavsnabsbyty* were the core of the system, forming the economic ties for the products in which they specialized. It was precisely in this link that work on guaranteeing economy-wide balance for specific types of products was concentrated. *Soyuzglavsnabsbyty* determined disaggregated requirements of the users, negotiated with the suppliers on product mix plans, and then, by issuing schedule orders [*zanariadki*], attached users to suppliers.

The *soyuzglavsnabsbyty* were abolished, but their functions—the centralized determination of supply plans—were not. The central apparatus of Gossnab began to fulfill these functions, which led to an increase in its personnel from 1,500 to 4,000 people. The functions of forming economic ties underwent certain changes, but they were far from being improvements. The planning documents issued by the *soyuzglavsnabsbyty* for the delivery of production, in most cases, contained all the necessary parameters for the users to conclude contracts with suppliers without additional negotiations. However, after the *soyuzglavsnabsbyty* were abolished, it was simultaneously decided to give the enterprises more discretion in forming their economic ties. Now Gossnab, when issuing the planning framework for concluding contracts, indicated only the aggregated list of products which had to be delivered, and the users were supposed to independently agree with the suppliers on all the other parameters.

Problems arose for those producers who had many users (for example, metallurgy). Before, they had to agree on the product mix with a very limited number of intermediary organizations. Now, thousands of users simultaneously descended on the manufacturers during the strictly limited period of time scheduled for concluding delivery contracts. The task of reconciling the specific needs and other contract requirements of all the users while at the same time ensuring rational capacity utilization is a complex one. In all developed countries as a rule this is done by an intermediary. Here we took a certain step backward.

Gossnab should not have washed its hands of forming economic ties, but placed their realization on a *khozraschet* basis. After all, several suppliers at that time had agreed to establish discounts on their production, if an intermediary would form their orders portfolio. Many enterprises began to search for partners to replace Gossnab's liquidated units in working out delivery contracts. The *soyuzglavsnabsbyty* had uniquely detailed information about the production and requirements for particular (disaggregated) types of output. The production of many products was spread over various ministries, and it was precisely in the *soyuzglavsnabsbyty* that information about the general condition of production and demand in the country was available. However, it was simpler to change the status and functions of the *soyuzglavsnabsbyty* than to create a network of agencies to fulfill these functions from scratch.

The territorial administrations of Gossnab arose on the base of the *sovnarkhozy* disbanded in 1965 and therefore were interregional, which in practice gave them the status of national organizations. This was important for overcoming purely local interests, for the most part of regional Party officials. In order to get supply organizations closer to their clients, the interregional territorial administrations were broken up into single-region ones. The newly formed territorial organs were created on the base of the general-purpose administrations, which were previously part of the interregional territorial administrations.

The liquidation of the interregional territorial administrations led to the reduction in intermediary services for the enterprises. The interregional administrations created supply units specialized in particular products that served their whole area. The newly created single-regional administrations started setting up the full complement of specialized supply units, each in its own region.

Shipping also became more complicated. Interregional administrations had more opportunities for consolidating shipments into the minimum size accepted by the railroads than the large number of new regional territorial administrations. For example, previously Volgovyatglavsnab could consolidate shipments of the Gorky and Kirov regions, as well as the Chuvash, Mari, and Mordovian republics. Under the new conditions, however, each region began to handle shipments independently.

The creation of single-region territorial agencies significantly reshaped the system and gave rise to a mass of new problems, but did not contribute to the development of wholesale trade. The new organizations did almost all that the old organizations did, but frequently did it worse, since besides all the new problems mentioned above, there were no specialists ready to take up the newly created vacancies, and it was difficult to train them in a short time for such a specific area.

The Fruits of Reform

An investigation of the work of thirty enterprises from various sectors was carried out soon after the beginning of the transition to supply by unrationed orders. It found that routine questions of mutual relations between economic partners were now being solved much faster, thanks to the exclusion of all intermediate links. For example, the Gorky machine tool association could promptly switch to an alternative supplier of liquid glass after its usual supplier defaulted. The Mytishchi 'Stroiplastmass' concluded a direct agreement with the Mogilev silk fabrics producer for the delivery of the base for linoleum, having refused to deal with the enterprises of Soyuzglavvtorresursy because of irregular deliveries and low quality.

At that time, production cooperatives and leasing collectives began forming on the base of unprofitable and low-profit producer-goods enterprises. These new entities had much greater discretion in choosing their suppliers compared to the enterprises under state management.

The formation of an intermediary infrastructure adequate to the conditions of wholesale trade began. Gossnab created a network of information-commercial centers and increased the number of small-scale wholesalers and outlets where producer goods could be rented. There emerged cooperatives engaged in trade, and trade through factory outlets revived somewhat.

However, the overall results of the introduction of wholesale trade were unfavorable. Already in 1989 the quality of intermediary services in supply significantly deteriorated, in the opinion of most customers. Product mix was being changed to the detriment of the users. The producers curtailed the production of, or outright discontinued, products that were unprofitable, even if these enjoyed customer demand.

In 1988 the enterprises' own plans for industrial production turned out to be 3.3 billion rubles less than was foreseen by the control figures. In 1989 many enterprises took on lower plan obligations than in the previous year. This tendency continued in the development of the plan for 1990. Enterprises often reduced their output in physical terms, compensating with a growth of higher-priced products. For example, the association 'Energomash' (Leningrad) reduced production of AC generators with capacity higher than 100 kilowatts by 25%. Instead, it started to produce a more expensive product. The factory 'Gosmetr' (Leningrad) discontinued the production of inexpensive mechanical scales, which were in demand, and switched to expensive electronic scales. As a result, the enterprise's output increased by 24.4% in value terms in 1988–1990, but decreased by 19%, in physical terms.

An economic decline masked by a hidden growth of prices started in 1988. In spite of the general growth of production [up to and including 1989 according to official data], the volume of material resources going to final use declined 2% a year in 1988–1989, and 9% in 1990.[5]

The prime cause of the failures in the development of wholesale trade was the strategy of implementing radical economic reform based on the leading links principle.[6] In accordance with this strategy, one economic sphere would be chosen to fulfill the role of pioneer, dragging after itself the entire chain. The role of the leading link was placed on the system of supply. Wholesale trade was to be introduced as a constituent element of the market mechanism, in conditions where all the other elements of this mechanism were absent. The failures in the introduction of wholesale trade were intensified by a series of poorly thought-out organizational reforms of the system of Gossnab's agencies.

Gossnab's organs found themselves in a contradictory position. The resolution of the CC and the CM of 17 July 1987 'On the Perestroika of Supply and the Work of Gossnab in the New Conditions of Management' directed them to "make the decisive transition in the course of four–five years from the centralized rationing of material resources and attachment of the users to suppliers, to wholesale trade in producer goods" (*O korennoi* . . . 1987, p. 111). Yet the very same resolution placed on Gossnab's agencies, along with the Union ministries and agencies, and the Councils of Ministers of the Republics, a heightened responsibility "for the supply of the resources for the enterprises' plans and satisfying the economy's needs" (p. 113).

The methods of solving these two tasks were in many ways mutually exclusive. Wholesale trade was based on the enterprises independently planning their production. But this entailed the independent supplying of one's own plans with the essential resources. If, however, Gossnab was assigned this responsibility, then it was essential to give it the right to intervene both in production plans and in the distribution of output.

In the second half of 1990 political instability began to grow in the country, and the center's economic power began to shrink. Gossnab increasingly lost control of the process of forming economic ties. The President of Russia canceled mandatory state orders and the centralized establishment of economic ties by the decree 'On Economic Ties and Deliveries of Products in 1992' of 15 October 1991.

9.3 Perestroika in the Workplace
Rozalina Ryvkina

The Outcomes of Gorbachev's Economic Innovations[7]

Creation of Design and Construction Associations (PSOs)

Various organizations involved in construction projects—brick and concrete factories, construction firms, design institutes, and repair shops—though subordinated to the same trust or main administration, poorly coordinated their efforts. They broke production deadlines and worked 'on the side,' delaying the completion of projects. PSOs were meant to unite administratively all the technologically interrelated organizations.

In early 1989 we studied one PSO in Siberia that had been formed in 1987. We surveyed 640 managers and specialists and 380 workers. According to the managers and specialists (Table 9.1), the innovation only succeeded in increasing wages. The technological and economic goals were not attained. The worst results were in supply, the quality of construction, and introduction of new machinery, all areas where improvement was needed the most. The parties ordering the project and those who later used it did not gain anything from the creation of PSOs, according to two-thirds of managers and specialists (Ryvkina and Yadov 1989).

Table 9.1

Managers and Specialists Evaluate the Effectiveness of a PSO
(% of those surveyed)

	Reaching these goals		
Goals for which the PSO was created	Succeeded	Did not succeed	No answer
Increase workers' pay	41	46	13
Increase construction output	23	52	25
Shorten the period of construction	17	64	19
Coordinate the suppliers	12	63	25
Improve the quality of architectural and design solutions	12	63	25
Reduce costs	10	42	48
Improve the quality of management	8	74	17
Improve working conditions	8	83	9
Introduce new equipment	6	76	18
Improve the quality of construction	6	82	12
Improve the availability of supplies	5	81	14

Source: Own survey, 1989.

Regional Agro-Industrial Associations (RAPOs)[8]

These administrative bodies were created in the early 1980s to integrate farming and the food-processing industry at the level of the rural districts. In 1988 we surveyed fifty-eight RAPO chairmen of the Altai *krai* (representing 81% of the districts in the region). They indicated that the RAPO did not succeed in balancing the interests of the agro-industrial enterprises in the districts. The basic reason for this was the RAPO's limited independence in the key sphere of planning (see Table 9.2). As before, the plans were handed down from above and were often changed. In 1986–1988, additional obligations were imposed on 78% of RAPOs after the plan had been approved (Kalugina 1987, p. 30).

Collective Contracts in Agriculture

The organization of collective contracts in agriculture aimed at better motivating workers by paying the whole brigade for its output, rather than each worker individually for her or his input (e.g., hours worked or planned tasks fulfilled).[9] In 1984, we compared brigades working under collective contracts with those under the regular system (individual piecework). We found

Table 9.2

The Origin of Decisions Which RAPOs Communicated to the Enterprises
(% of those surveyed)

	More often communicated decisions		
Decisions in the area of:	Received from above	Made by RAPO	No answer
Planning	90	10	—
New forms of labor organization and compensation	36	60	4
Adoption of new technology	29	76	5

Source: Own survey, Altai *krai*, 1988.

Table 9.3

Worker Evaluation of the Working Conditions and Compensation System in Contract and Regular Collectives (% of those surveyed)

	Do you like?			
Payment systems:	Working conditions		Compensation	
	Yes	No	Yes	No
Contract	19	81	38	62
Regular	25	75	27	73

Source: Own survey, 1984.

no significant differences in the conditions and results of work, or in the workers' level of activity and initiative (see Table 9.3). The new system was different from the old one only in name and accounting procedures (Ryvkina and Yadov 1989, p. 247).

Introduction of Leasing in Agriculture

The introduction of leasing in agriculture seemed to have produced significant effects. Our 1989 investigation of thirty-two lease collectives found that labor productivity had nearly doubled. The majority of managers polled thought that people had begun to work better: observing technological rules and using equipment and materials more carefully. It seemed to many managers that workers' economic consciousness had changed and that their discipline had improved. They started taking into account the nonlabor elements in production costs. Under the conditions of leasing, the whole

Table 9.4

Leasing: Workers' Expectations and Their Realization (% of those surveyed)

	Categories of expectation			
	Increased compen-sation	Increased indepen-dence	Improved use of land, equipment	Collective will become harmonious
Held an expectation	68	57	41	45
Expectation was fulfilled	10	13	13	22

Source: Own survey, 1989.

amount of these costs saved should have been paid to the workers as a bonus.

In reality, savings were translated into extra compensation of the workers at the managers' discretion, rather than automatically. In 1986, units working under the lease had twice the labor productivity as the regular units, but paid the same wages (Ryvkina et al. 1990). Surprisingly high expectations tied to leasing were fulfilled only to a small extent (Table 9.4).

The Process Rolls On

These examples show that Gorbachev's economic innovations in 1985–1989 did not change the essence of the Soviet economy, which remained a state-run administrative system. It might have seemed that, as in previous reforms, everything would revert to the old Soviet economic models. But the process progressed further.

Lack of Interest in, and Understanding of, Market Organization

Our studies in 1987–1989 showed that the employees in industry, construction, and agriculture in Siberia were absolutely unprepared to work under any but the traditional Soviet system. Support for privatization was lacking. In a 1989 survey asking "Which forms of property seem to you most advantageous for your enterprise?" all the forms proposed in the questionnaire drew about equal approval (Table 9.5). Only one person said that "A PSO should become a private enterprise" (Ryvkina et al. 1990, p. 44). None of the nonstate forms offered as prompts received majority approval.

The workers' general knowledge of 'new forms of economic management'

Table 9.5

Forms of Ownership Regarded as the Best for PSOs (% of those polled)

Various forms of ownership	Considered the best among:	
	Managers and specialists	Workers
Remain state-owned	19	31
Become a lessee of fixed assets	14	—
Become a state-cooperative organization	24	23
Convert into an association of cooperatives	11	23
Become a joint-stock company	5	4
Needs to be disbanded	11	—
Other	4	5
Don't know	12	14

Source: Own survey, Novosibirsk 1989.

was quite low. For example, despite the workers' keen interest in cooperatives, they did not know what to expect from a job there, other than the higher pay. As to the other employment conditions, more than half of those polled could not answer the corresponding questions (Table 9.6). People were unable to make a well-informed choice between cooperatives and government enterprises (Ryvkina et al. 1990, p. 46). They vacillated between inefficient but tested state organization and incomprehensible (although attractive, according to word of mouth) nonstate organizations.

The respondents preferred those forms of ownership that increased their autonomy and at the same time did not require greater personal responsibility. A large majority of those surveyed wanted to end the status of the PSO as a state-owned enterprise (Table 9.5). Only 4–12% of those polled chose subordination to the city government, main administration, or the ministry. On the other hand, the majority of respondents favored aid from the authorities: the centralized allotment of machinery and equipment, allowing the PSO to keep a larger share of its profits. The subjects of our study wanted to have both independence and the security that comes with state ownership.

The tendency to rely on the favors of superiors rather than one's own efforts can also be seen in the managers' and specialists' opinions on technological innovation (Table 9.7) and ways of attaining autonomy from the state (Table 9.8). In choosing ways for a PSO to attain independence, the managers tended toward the more moderate options—direct ties with Gossnab outlets and leasing of state-owned plant. The options which demanded greater effort and those which were riskier (expansion to foreign

Table 9.6

Evaluations of Employment Conditions in Cooperatives Compared to State Enterprises (% of those polled)

Employment conditions	Better/higher		Worse/lower		The same		Do not know	
	Workers	Managers	Workers	Managers	Workers	Managers	Workers	Managers
Wages	78	80	1	1	2	1	19	18
Opportunity to be noticed	48	66	3	2	5	4	44	28
Labor organization and discipline	32	37	9	15	9	9	50	39
The type of work	25	29	3	9	10	13	62	49
Independence in work	50	68	1	2	8	6	41	24
Relationship with management	17	22	5	5	10	10	68	63
Availability of materials and equipment	34	—	10	—	5	—	51	—
Ability to improve housing	10	7	23	37	8	6	59	50
Relationship with collective	18	24	7	11	17	12	58	53

Source: Own survey, Novosibirsk 1989.

Table 9.7

Specialists' Views on the Most Effective Strategies for Adopting New Technology

Strategy	% of those surveyed
Leave a larger share of the profits with the enterprise	55
Centralized allocation of equipment	51
Reward innovators	33
Attract specialists willing and able to adopt new technology	25
Keep financing of projects to be commissioned at previous year's level	23
Import	14

Source: Own survey, Novosibirsk 1989.

Table 9.8

Managers' and Specialists' Preferred Methods of Attaining Enterprise Autonomy (%)

Direct ties with Gossnab outlets	40
Leasing the plant	33
Direct ties with suppliers	27
Getting the plant free from the state	23
Expansion to foreign markets	7
Buying out the plant	4

Source: Own survey, Novosibirsk 1989.

markets and the buying out of the plant) were chosen by no more than 7% of those polled.

Intentions and Outcomes

In 1985–1989 the participants in perestroika did not see the whole spectrum of possibilities for its development, just those within the bounds of socialism. G.Kh. Popov theorized about two possible types of perestroika: revolutionary-democratic and *apparat*-dominated. The former would take place with the participation of the masses and its costs would "rest on the shoulders of the bureaucratic *apparat*." In the latter, the *apparat* would drag out changes, preserving its leading role and placing the costs on the workers. While differing in speed and effectiveness, both represented change within the confines of the Soviet system. Popov did not even mention the possibility of systemic change. The moving force of his democratic variant was to

Table 9.9

USSR Foreign Trade Average Annual Rates of Growth (%)

Period	Constant prices		Current prices	
	Imports	Exports	Imports	Exports
1976–1980	5.8	4.8	10.8	15.6
1981–1985	6.0	1.9	9.3	7.9
1986–1990	1.0	0.3	0.4	–3.5

Source: Narodnoe khoziaistvo SSSR v 1990g (Moscow 1991) p. 644.

be "the best part of the workers and peasants, the best part of the economic officials, the best part of the intelligentsia" (Popov 1989, pp. 73–78). This illustrates the utopianism of the reform concept for which the Russian intelligentsia stood at that time.

At that time many authors mentioned the superficial and formal nature of the changes which were occurring. In polls taken in 1987–1988, up to 40–50% of those surveyed indicated that in their enterprises and in their regions perestroika was not occurring (Yadov 1990).

However, many social forces in the USSR had serious reasons to play the game called perestroika. The progressive press worried that if the chances were lost again, the disappointment of the masses would be even greater than it had been in the 1960s and 1970s. Having begun perestroika, Gorbachev had to lead it to some kind of completion. The active part of the intelligentsia thirsted for democracy. The predominant emotional state was terrible frustration with the old system. The opportunities and prospects for renewal of the Soviet system were not seriously analyzed.

9.4 Foreign Trade Liberalization
Viktor Kurierov

MVT Under Attack: 1983–1987

Foreign economic relations began to attract the Soviet leadership's attention in 1983–1985, due to the sudden decrease in the growth rate of exports in the 1980s (see Table 9.9).

The decrease could easily be explained as a result of the changed situation on the world market (especially for energy), as well as the Soviet economy's deterioration. But the Soviet leadership was accustomed to seek those personally responsible for economic problems and to demote, dismiss, or discipline them.

The foreign trade sector was an especially attractive and convenient target for a purge, having long aroused envy by its almost monopolistic access to foreign currency. This motive might seem trivial and too superficial, but at that time the ability to travel abroad and possession of convertible currency had profound impact on a person's well-being. That is why arguments about the 'unhealthy' monopoly of the Ministry of Foreign Trade (MVT), which occasionally could be heard at confidential meetings in the CM and the CC, soon became popular. The very thing that used to elevate MVT above other government departments became an additional vulnerable point. Yury Brezhnev, the son of the deceased general secretary, was MVT's first deputy minister.

A wide-ranging inspection of the foreign trade organizations' work conducted by the KGB took on the form of a political campaign, if not a purge, so typical in Soviet life. A number of quite sensational charges, both criminal and disciplinary, were brought. The most scandalous of these was the case of the deputy minister Sushkov who was charged with accepting bribes and given a lengthy prison term. A number of other high-ranking MVT officials were dismissed or expelled from the CPSU. The investigations were clearly slanted against the suspects.

Foreign trade was used by the Kremlin to bolster various regimes, to assist 'friendly firms' (i.e., linked with the local Communist parties), and 'friends' themselves (e.g., Armand Hammer). Occasionally, MVT had to conclude 'flashy' contracts timed to coincide with the visit of some Soviet dignitary to that country. MVT was constantly pressured from 'above' to meet the targets for hard-currency revenues and exports of finished goods, deemed politically prestigious. In all these cases, the leadership disregarded the disadvantageous terms of the contracts and even pushed foreign trade organizations to go ahead with the deal at any price. Instructions and 'recommendations' to this effect were not always properly documented, and sometimes were given orally. This made the officials carrying out such orders vulnerable. For instance, during the campaign against MVT the chairman of 'Nefteexport' Merkulov was accused of breaking the rules governing the signing of contracts, as well as other transgressions. He cited informal instructions given to him by his superiors, but his plea was ignored. Only his ripe old age and past accomplishments saved him from going to jail. He was, however, expelled both from the Party and from MVT.

These circumstances created a special nervous background for the development of the reform of foreign trade. MVT managed a special retail system ('Beryozka') selling goods for certificates, which were given to officials working abroad in exchange for the foreign currency they brought home. In 1987 this system was abolished, in an open tribute to social envy that was economically unjustified and violated the state's obligations. The removal of the customs service from MVT in 1988 (this was decided in 1987) can also be seen as the continuation of the same line. It was considered that the service's subordination to MVT made it too soft on Ministry officials crossing the border.

Reforms: 1986–1988

In August 1986 the CC and the CM adopted the decree 'On Measures to Improve the Management of Foreign Economic Ties'; and the next year, they adopted the decree 'On Additional Measures to Improve Foreign Economic Activity in the New Economic Conditions' and the Law on the State Enterprise. These documents gave ministries and enterprises greater rights and responsibilities in accessing foreign markets. The goal was to make the enterprises the main actor in the foreign economic complex.

At first, the right to carry out import-export operations directly was given to about 20 ministries and over 70 of the largest enterprises. By 1988, this privilege had been extended to 55 ministries and 140 organizations, associations, and enterprises. Sectoral ministries organized new commercial foreign-trade organizations on the basis of the foreign-trade associations transferred from the MVT system: Avtoeksport in the Ministry of Automobile Production, Soyuzkhimeksport in the Ministry of Chemical Production, and so on. Such large production associations as Uralmash, KAMAZ, ZIL, Moskvich, The Minsk Tractor Factory, and The First Moscow Watch Factory created their own foreign trade firms.

Contractual agreements started to replace bureaucratic commands in relations between the enterprises and the foreign trade associations. Enterprises were allowed to keep a certain portion of their foreign currency earnings (determined by a fixed norm), to be spent as they saw fit, and to obtain bank loans in foreign currency for the setting up and development of export production. It became considerably easier to establish direct ties with enterprises in CMEA countries. For the first time, cooperatives were allowed to participate in foreign trade, according to the Law on Cooperatives. In January 1987 the CM issued a decree allowing the establishment of joint ventures with firms from capitalist countries.

The enterprises that were allowed access to the foreign market were the gradually widening base of the new pyramid of management. The State Foreign Economic Commission (GVK), presided over by a deputy chairman of the CM, was at the top of this pyramid. The heads of the GKNT, Gosplan, Gossnab, the Ministry of Foreign Economic Relations, the Ministry of Foreign Affairs, and the permanent Soviet representative at the

CMEA became members of the GVK. The Ministry of Foreign Economic Relations (MVES) was established in January 1988 by combining the MVT and the State Committee for Economic Relations (which previously mainly managed aid programs). MVES, the Main Customs Administration (which had been taken out of MVT's jurisdiction), the State Committee for Foreign Tourism, and Vneshekonombank were directly subordinate to the GVK. The GVK also controlled the foreign economic activity of other organizations and managed the work of the Soviet sides of the intergovernmental commissions for economic, scientific, and technical collaboration with other countries.

The GVK was intended to formulate the national foreign economic strategy, carry out organizational reforms in its sector, and coordinate the activity of other organizations, as far as foreign trade was involved. Trade in commodities of national importance—fuel, raw materials, foodstuffs, and some machines and equipment—which taken together constituted the major share of Soviet foreign trade, remained the responsibility of the MVES. It was carried out by the Ministry's twenty-two foreign trade associations: Soiuznefteksport, Soiuzgazeksport, Soiuzpromeksport, Eksportkhleb, and others. The Ministry was to ensure that sectoral ministries and other actors in foreign trade observed state interests.

The rights of the republics and local authorities in the area of external economic activity were somewhat widened, especially concerning border and coastal trade. Republican external trade associations attached to the Councils of Ministers of the Union Republics began to be created. They were authorized to conduct border and coastal trade, to export goods produced above the state plan and also goods produced by enterprises under republic control. All the proceeds of exports within the framework of border and coastal trade remained at the disposal of the republican and regional authorities.

The next important step was granting all enterprises and production cooperatives whose products or services were competitive on the foreign market the right to carry out export-import activities as of 1 April 1989.[10] This concerned only the right to sell one's own output and to buy goods for one's own needs. Only specialized foreign trade associations had the right to engage in intermediary operations. Enterprises could trade independently or through these middlemen. In either case they had to cover their foreign currency outlays by their own foreign currency income, since the state was no longer responsible for their obligations.

Weaknesses of Reform Design

The concept of the foreign economic reform, as defined at the Twenty-Seventh Party Congress in 1986 and the June 1987 CC Plenum, for the first time recognized the objective, 'extra-systemic' nature of the internationalization of the economy. Foreign trade was beginning to be viewed as a powerful accelerator of technological and economic development. This reflected the leaders' illusions regarding the possibilities of the development of the foreign economic complex and its potential impact on the domestic economy, under the existing system. The unreasonable expectations were linked with the organizational reform, while the dependence of economic performance in the world markets on the state of domestic economy was underrated. One could trace this wave of foreign economic romanticism to an old misconception that the foreign economic sector is capable of successful development on its own, separately from the domestic sector—if, of course, the 'necessary measures' are taken.

The reform was conducted in a wasteful state-controlled economy with a rigid strict planning system, distorted relative prices, and an inconvertible currency. It was inspired not so much by the immediate economic needs of that system, as by abstract ideas, based on the experience of a fundamentally different economic system, of how foreign economic relations should be organized in a contemporary 'civilized' state. The reform design was also influenced by pressure from regional and sectoral authorities thirsting for independence in dealings abroad in the expectation of receiving advantages on the regional, departmental, or personal level.

The idea of joining the General Agreement on Tariffs and Trade (GATT), which arose in those years, exerted a certain stimulating influence on the path of reforms. Joining GATT was seen as an important step toward integrating the Soviet economy into the world economy, but other arguments had much greater weight. It was hoped that joining GATT would lift the discrimination against Soviet products on the world market (the significance and extent of which was unintentionally, or perhaps intentionally, exaggerated). Politically, joining GATT meant Western recognition and endorsement of the new economic course of the USSR, and an expansion of ties with the 'civilized' world. Supporters of the radical market reform thought that contacts with GATT and other international organizations would induce the country's rulers to implement their economic innovations more consistently and to heed international norms and requirements.[11] Departmental interests also played a role. It was hoped that contacts with the GATT would boost the prestige of the foreign trade and foreign policy departments, raise their status in the administrative hierarchy, create new high-level jobs abroad, and expand the possibilities for official trips abroad.

The reform was not preceded by any sober and calm study of its possible variants and consequences. Preventive measures to reduce the reform's possible destabilizing influence on the economic system were not worked out.

No thought was given to testing the reform on a small scale, say, in a single region. The necessary changes in the regulation of foreign trade were not worked out in advance so as to be introduced at the same time as the reform. These regulations were extraordinarily meager (it suffices to say that the country lived virtually without customs tariffs). The reform of foreign trade was extremely poorly coordinated with the sequence and the rate of the transformation of the entire economic system.

A quite important miscalculation was the lack of personnel essential for the organization of foreign economic work at the sectoral ministries, regions, and enterprises. The former MVT officials, who were now available because of the staff reductions, could not fill this personnel vacuum, even if they had been offered jobs at the enterprises newly active in the foreign market. However, they were not invited, as no one was inclined to share with 'outsiders' the expected material rewards. The behavior of the enterprises was determined by precisely these concrete rewards, and not by the abstract advantages of participation in the international division of labor. The personnel questions, although with great delay, gradually began to be resolved after the February 1988 decree of the CC and the CM on the training of specialists for foreign economic work.

A more serious issue was the economic system's lack of preparedness for the realization of the government's plans. The enterprises had no interest in raising the efficiency of foreign economic activity, not to speak of their quite limited ability to do so. Under the conditions of almost universal shortages and cost-plus prices, the enterprises were oriented toward obtaining foreign currency at any price, rather than raising the rate of profit or long-term gains. *Khozraschet* was only taking its first steps at that time, and even when fully implemented, turned out to be a palliative which did not change the type of economic behavior of the producers.

Why Was There No Professional Input into the Reform Decisions?

Sanctified by the decisions of the top Party leadership, reform aimed at the renewal of socialism and its new victories. It was considered intolerable for the reform to undergo any kind of serious discussions, reviews, or corrections which could slow down or change its path at all.

All important decisions, in particular those concerning foreign economic and political affairs, were as a rule worked out and adopted at the very top. If they were discussed, it was only at closed or semiclosed meetings in the CC and CM. The lower echelons of the hierarchy were permitted to discuss only the best way to implement the decisions which had, for all intents and purposes, already been taken. The liberalization of the political regime triggered by perestroika was rather superficial in this respect. And the foreign trade officials, worried about their career prospects, were less than enthusiastic about the impending reform. Moreover, for a while the content and orientation of the reform remained obscure. Gorbachev's concept of improving socialism gave little room for professional debate, and there was no question of transgressing the traditional framework of the socialist economic system at that time. In discussions people tried to avoid even mentioning the fate of the state monopoly of foreign trade, one of the sacred cows of socialist ideology.

There was no business-like discussion of the problems of the foreign economic sphere in the press either. Information about some criminal cases in this sector did appear in the press, but the criticism was mainly expressed in closed meetings.[12] As an organization dealing with external matters, including those of a sensitive character, MVT traditionally had its activities largely shrouded in secrecy and shielded from public debate. The foreign trade organizations' commercial secrets, cited as the official justification of this situation, were only a pretext. There were very close links between the Ministry and the security services. In addition to the 'first departments,' concerned with ensuring official secrecy and common in Soviet organizations, a system of open representatives of the KGB in every subdivision of the Ministry was introduced in approximately the early 1970s. (The presence of disguised KGB officers and informers goes without saying.) The Ministry's research institute (VNIKI) and the Academy of Foreign Trade were supervised by a lieutenant-colonel of the KGB who had a permanent office in the building of the Academy. The Engineering-Technical Administration of the Ministry was in charge of economic (and possibly not only economic) espionage. Foreign trade missions teemed with spies of all kinds and ranks.

The MVT was also distinguished by a heightened degree of ideological and political vigilance. The role of Party officials, working in close contact with the representatives of the KGB, was exceptionally important in this Ministry.[13] The slightest suspicion of political or ideological 'immaturity' might make one ineligible for foreign trips, the most feared punishment for a foreign trade official. Such an atmosphere prevailed in the first years of perestroika, as the waves of political change reached the conservative and very cautious MVT with a long lag.

For these reasons, no reform plans differing from the official ones were put forward. In private conversations and in working meetings specialists were highly skeptical about the reform's perspectives and its first steps. This was based in the first place on a disbelief in the reformist potential of the existing political system and the seriousness of the intentions of the Party leadership. The undecided and ambiguous position of the leadership on all the basic issues of reform was obvious.

[In 1988] the situation did change somewhat. A Scientific Council, headed by the well-known economist I. Ivanov, was set up at the GVK. The general orientation of the economic policy of the CPSU, which provided guidance for the reform of foreign trade, began to take shape. Discussions of the reform became more active and substantive, but as before they mostly took place *post factum*. At closed meetings, apprehensions were voiced about the behavior to be expected of the enterprises permitted access to the foreign market but still preserving their old character. These apprehensions later proved correct. Yet the only book on the foreign trade reform published at the height of all these changes did not contain the slightest doubt or critical reflection on the official innovations, just unreserved praise (Ivanov 1988).

From the purely economic standpoint, commercialization of the existing foreign trade organizations and the creation of new alternative commercial organizations, would have been a more efficient reform strategy. The foreign trade associations (Eksportkhleb, Mashinoimport, Prodintorg, etc.) were nominally autonomous, but remained subordinated to MVT (later MVES) or the branch ministries and worked under their strict control. They might have been given real operating discretion and turned into joint-stock companies responsible for their own profit or loss and for the receipt and repayment of loans, and allowed to expand the number of goods they traded in. Lifting restrictions on the commodities in which associations could trade would have introduced an element of competition. Unfortunately, the idea of commercialization was not implemented, despite being promoted by the Western experts whom the authorities respected so greatly. It was not a sufficiently radical idea, and was also too complicated to implement.

Commercialization could have been supplemented by decentralization through strengthening of republican or regional foreign trade complexes. Later, working through the regional organizations and with their help, independence could be extended to the enterprises. By the time this idea made the pages of the press (*BIKI*, 27 July 1991) it had already lost its relevance. Earlier, it could not be realized because of the center's reluctance to share its power with the republics.

The 'Emancipated' Agencies and Enterprises Start Trading

The newly formed export-import departments at the sectoral ministries and at the enterprises were not too much burdened by real work and became just an additional layer in the management system. It became much more difficult to keep track of foreign trade activity and to regulate it in the national interest. National authorities tried to control everything themselves, unwilling to delegate some of their functions to the republics and regions. (In fact, there was practically no one there to delegate them to.) The GVK was unable to carry out its strategic and coordinating role as the enterprises were getting more autonomy, and later the republics were gaining sovereignty. It often duplicated the already existing structures—the foreign trade section of the CM's apparatus, the MVES, and others.

In 1988 the balance of trade surplus fell by 72%, and in 1989–1990 the balance of trade was in deficit, the 1990 deficit being three times greater than that for 1989. The rate of growth of foreign trade continued to fall (see Table 9.9). The entities that first gained access to the world market in 1989 increased their trade turnover more than 3.4 times in 1990 and reached 10.2% of the USSR total. However, their trade deficit rose elevenfold, reaching 5.5 billion rubles (although their exports were only 4 billion rubles) (*BIKI,* 11 May 1991).

This deterioration in the foreign trade sector cannot be attributed only to the reform, all the more so because in such a short period its possible positive effect might not yet have shown up. However, the processes and tendencies which manifested themselves at that time in the foreign economic sector clearly contributed to the deteriorating performance just described. The level of professionalism in foreign trade fell sharply. Reports of trade representatives abroad to MVT and later to MVES contained quite a few stories of mass tours of representatives of the 'emancipated' Soviet enterprises to Western (especially) and developing countries. More often than not they would arrive without a clear goal, without the necessary preparation and knowledge of the language, and often without the money necessary for paying for these trips. Improbable and completely unprepared projects for the development of economic cooperation were put forward, and euphoric plans for attracting foreign capital and capturing Western markets were made. The epoch of 'protocols of intentions' had arrived. These documents meant nothing, but were signed by the hundreds with foreign firms with the sole objective of justifying the expenses for business trips.

The evaluations of the results of the foreign trade reform by the Soviet trade representatives abroad began to appear in the press only in 1990–1991. V. Pavlov, trade representative in Japan, wrote that there was taking place "the destruction of established contacts," and added, "many enterprises and associations which are now active on the foreign market, are often illiterate in questions of international business," which resulted in breaches of contract. G. Shcherbakov, trade representative in India, wrote that "confidence in the USSR as a reliable trade partner is falling." Soviet organizations were violating the conditions of the Soviet-Indian trade agreement, reexporting Indian goods for hard currency. The trade representative in France, R. Tarzimanov, cited the lack of professionalism shown by the new Soviet participants in foreign trade, the increased number of cases of breach of contract by them, and the growing payment arrears. The chairman of Amtorg (USA), Yu. Mashkin, wrote that the new Soviet traders failed to take account of the specifications and requirements of the American market. As a result of their incompetence they often agreed to unfavorable contract conditions, and cases of default had become more frequent.[14]

In the 'free' sector of foreign trade the trend to sell whatever possible at any price, just to obtain foreign currency, became ever more noticeable. The reduction of export prices and even dumping became a mass phenomenon, especially within the framework of barter operations. Government directives in April and May 1989 allowed enterprises to barter goods produced above the plan, scrap and other recycled materials, and difficult-to-dispose-of items, for materials and equipment for the production of consumer goods and for consumer goods, for their own employees. Increasing use of barter made transactions less transparent and allowed the exporters to hide below-market export prices (or above-market import prices). Reduced prices of exports became an ever more widely used means of hiding income and its illegal transfer abroad.

In the beginning of the 1990s, when for the first time Goskomstat and the Central Bank assessed the economy's losses from these practices, they were estimated at several billion dollars per year.[15] When barter trade was valued in 'foreign currency rubles,' barter exports in 1990 were 1.9 times barter imports. For trade with developed Western countries this ratio was 4. Dumping by 'free' traders depressed prices on some foreign markets, worsening the terms for the sale of the traditional Soviet exports and creating difficulties for the specialized foreign trade organizations.

Despite the reformers' expectations, the foreign currency earned was not invested in the expansion or modernization of production, but rather spent on luxuries, such as cars and consumer electronics. Reform encouraged entrepreneurial behavior by the enterprises, a more active inclusion of local resources in trade, and an expansion of direct contacts with foreign counterparts. Having shattered the state monopoly of foreign trade, the reform created a definite basis for further changes. But these modest positive results were accomplished at an excessive cost.

Managing the New Institutions

The regulatory mechanism to complement the new institutions was created late and in an *ad hoc* manner. Its first element, and perhaps the only one created in time, at any rate formally, was the registration of new participants of foreign trade activity.[16] Meant to enable the state to keep an eye on the quality of the new importers and exporters and the conformity of their activity with official goals, registration became an additional bureaucratic procedure. It was impossible and unnecessary to supervise from the 'center' thousands of economic actors. (By mid-1991, 30,000 exporters were registered, of which about 10,000 were active.) The GVK practically did not use its powers to deprive enterprises of foreign trade licenses for activity damaging to state interests.

Licensing of operations, introduced beginning 1 April 1989, was the main tool of the system of regulating foreign trade.[17] Licenses, issued for a limited period of time, were required for dealing in goods and services officially considered to be of national importance; for operations with goods or countries for which official limitations were in force (e.g., in order to balance trade with them); and as a preventive measure for enterprises practicing unfair competition and harming the state. (Licensing was practically never used for this last purpose.)

The licensing procedure was unwieldy, burdensome, and dependent on the arbitrary decisions of bureaucrats. It became one of the main sources of official corruption. When requesting an export license, for example, an organization was required to present information on who was the buyer, at what price and in what currency the goods were to be sold, by what means of transport they would be delivered, and where they would cross the border. Licenses for goods of national importance were issued by the Union ministries and by the Councils of Ministers of the republics in accordance with the lists of products for which they were responsible. These lists were compiled by the Union government. The organizations empowered to issue licenses sometimes delegated this function to their subordinates—all-Union industrial associations and republican agencies. The large number of agencies issuing licenses (fifty-eight by the beginning of 1991)[18] and the vagueness of their criteria sowed confusion, encouraged abuses, and contradicted GATT rules.

Licensed goods composed approximately 80% of exports and 5% of imports (*BIKI*, 11 May 1991). (The problem of protecting the domestic market from foreign competition did not exist then due to the shortages and the difference between domestic and world market prices.) The number of goods that could be freely exported was gradually reduced. At first primarily the exports of raw materials and semifinished goods were controlled. Subsequently almost all consumer goods fell under control, and quotas for their export were established.

The specialized foreign trade organizations of ministries and agencies got preferential treatment in licensing, which strengthened their monopoly position. It was practically impossible for 'outside' enterprises and coopera-tives to obtain a general license. They had to settle for one-off permission for a particular deal. The monopoly of the central authorities was also strengthened to some extent by the fact that the enterprises were obliged (although they did not always do this) to have their export prices approved by the principal exporters, that is, those same specialized organizations.

The excessive rigidity of the emerging regulatory system was clearly at variance with [the declared objective of] democratization of foreign trade. The reason for this 'counterreformation' lay in the unfavorable results of the changes carried out in the foreign trade sphere.[19] Another reason was the extremely weak development of economic methods of regulation, due to the lengthy period of complete state control of foreign trade, autarky, and the specific price structure which had formed on this basis. It was because of the lack of such methods that the government, a little less than a year after permitting barter by enterprises, began to limit it. Barter involving export of foodstuffs, petroleum products, coal, timber, and other products was forbidden as of 1 January 1990. In December of that year, barter operations were prohibited across the board, with the exception of the Min-istry of Trade, the Central Union of Cooperatives,[20] and Gossnab. (After a certain time the ban was lifted.)

Economic methods of regulating foreign trade required a radical change in the pricing of exports and imports, as well as the establishment of a realistic rate of exchange. Until 1987 internal prices of export goods and services were set equal to domestic industrial wholesale prices (with certain additions). Prices of imported goods were set both on the level of domestic wholesale and of foreign trade prices. Foreign trade prices had almost no direct effect on the revenues of enterprises. The foreign trade income of both enterprises and foreign trade organizations was almost completely con-fiscated by the state.

The reform made it imperative to find a method of converting foreign trade prices from foreign currency into rubles. The difficulty lay in the facts that internal relative prices differed sharply from those on the world market, and that the domestic system of price setting was on an individual cost plus basis. Beginning 1 January 1987, more than 3,000 currency coefficients differentiated by groups of goods and by five currency zones were intro-duced. Their value varied between 0.2 and 6.6. This cumbersome and in-flexible system of settlements with the state could not serve as a normal basis for commercial operations.

A quite 'civilized' Customs Code and a law on foreign currency regula-tion were also adopted in early 1991. The latter widened the possibilities of conducting foreign currency operations by legal and physical persons, creating a legal basis for determining the rate of exchange by supply and demand. (It is noteworthy that this only took place five years after the beginning of reforms.) These were all sensible if belated measures. The switch to convertible currency payments in trade with the CMEA countries from the beginning of 1991, by contrast, was based on abstract ideas about what was desirable rather than on a sober analysis of the actual situation. It reduced trade with these countries by 60%, while total exports in 1991 fell by 33%, and imports by 44%.

9.5 The Crisis and Collapse of CMEA
Boris Ladygin

CMEA in the Mid-1980s

The Council for Mutual Economic Assistance (CMEA), inaugurated in 1949 as a political response to the Marshall plan, came in the 1960s to be regarded as the socialist alternative to West European economic integration. Politically, CMEA came to be treated as synonymous with the 'socialist commonwealth,' uniting the majority of socialist countries around the USSR. CMEA as an organization was a slow-moving bureaucracy with an excess of rhetoric over action. Real economic cooperation was bilateral and based on five-year as well as annual agreements made by the national governments. They were *post factum* documented as multilateral agreements (for instance, multilateral protocols of coordination of the five-year plans) largely for propaganda purposes.

The USSR was CMEA's *de facto* leader, shaping its activity. Every Soviet leader left his mark on the CMEA. Under Stalin, it was a disciplined administrative body dealing with shipments of the most important commodities among the member countries. All transactions were shrouded in secrecy and based on clearing in U.S. dollars. Under Khrushchev an attempt was made to transform CMEA into a kind of international Gosplan with directive functions. 'Plan coordination' was instituted in 1956 in an attempt to develop a balanced five-year plan for all major products in CMEA. Against the backdrop of Khrushchev's liberalization, this initiative met with opposition on the part of several countries, led (in 1962) by Romania.

CMEA fell into a slumber in the beginning of the Brezhnev era, and came back to life following the events in Czechoslovakia [in 1968] under the banner of socialist economic integration. This was praised as being more extensive and modern than that of the European Economic Community. However, because of the resistance by Romania, Poland, and Hungary, this only led to verbal formulations and practical compromises. Formal 'fraternal unity' and praise for Brezhnev and the Soviet Union was valued more than the genuine efforts at integration.

It was in the 1970s that the USSR assumed the additional economic burden [of subsidizing its CMEA partners], to the great displeasure of Soviet economic officials. Their attitude was shared by the sectoral departments of the CC. CMEA and other joint economic institutions of the socialist countries were derogatorily called "plant management with no plants," "parasites," and "despoilers of the Soviet Union." Behind-the-scenes criticism of CMEA was allowed and even became fashionable.

The ministers, occasionally the CM, and the sectoral departments of the CC (perhaps with the exception of the military-industrial complex) could not object to the policies dictated by the political leadership. Instead, they would 'bury' these policies with perfunctory implementation. The favorite excuse to dodge additional spending on joint projects was to claim that all the available resources were fully allocated by the five-year plan. It was invoked in the case of the export of oil and petroleum products, lumber, nonferrous metals, construction of gas pipelines, and so on.

This, in turn, led to the attempt to incorporate integration projects into the national five-year plans. In the early 1970s there emerged 'Long Term Goal-oriented Programs of Cooperation' and the 'Coordinated Plan of Multilateral Integration.' However, these programs did not produce the desired results, since the resources needed to implement them were in short supply and Gosplan's primary objective was to finance domestic investment. The CMEA countries were invited to build [resource-extraction] projects inside the Soviet Union themselves, with their own machinery, labor, and materials. This rather crude approach was employed in building gas pipelines.

At the end of the 1970s, afflicted by constant requests for hard currency credits, the Politburo decided to set up a hard currency fund of the CMEA members, modeled on the International Monetary Fund (IMF). However, the idea was killed before it hatched. The Finance Ministry, supported by Gosplan and the Department of Financial and Planning Organs of the CC, failed to find the hard currency necessary to start the fund. It was said that "no hard currency—no fund." Actually, these organizations feared that pressured by the CMEA countries, the Soviet leadership would extend them subsidized hard currency loans.

This veiled struggle was the manifestation of a conflict between economic officials defending domestic interests and top politicians, together with the military-industrial complex, the KGB, and the Ministry of Foreign Affairs, making geopolitical considerations their top priority.

Recognizing these problems, Andropov planned a step-by-step reorganization of the CMEA to keep aid in line with the USSR's resources without sacrificing the political advantages of being the leader among the socialist countries. In January 1983 it was decided to hold, after careful preparations, a 'round table' of the leaders of the CMEA, to be chaired by Andropov. It was envisioned as a candid discussion aimed at obtaining a strategic consensus. Andropov himself had no clear-cut plan of action.

I took part in drafting the materials presented at the economic summit. The meeting, presided over by Chernenko, took place in June 1984. It failed to produce an informal and candid dialogue. The pompous atmosphere eclipsed Andropov's ideas that were actually incorporated into Chernenko's report. These ideas were perceived by other leaders of CMEA countries as policy-setting directives, which boded well for the future of socialism.

The economic summit adopted the proposal to conduct regular summit meetings every five years, prior to the coordination of the five-year plans. Chernenko's suggestion to double output of the CMEA economies by the year 2000 also encountered no opposition. The USSR vouched its support for the accelerated growth by a major increase in natural gas deliveries (with some reduction in oil exports), stepped up export of electric power, as well as assistance in building an extensive system of nuclear power plants in the CMEA countries. Bridging the gap with the West in electronics, automation, and biotechnology was made a special priority. Here, the USSR assumed the brunt of the burden. Finally, cooperation in the machine-building industry was to become much broader by reducing the barriers impeding direct ties between enterprises and the creation of joint ventures.

It is now apparent that the policy outlined at the economic summit was merely a declaration of intent, since it was not supported by adequate financing and management. However at the time the policy appeared quite feasible.

By the mid-1980s, the bilateral cooperation of most socialist countries with the USSR under the aegis of CMEA had created a truly integrated economic system. Trade among CMEA members (conducted mainly at world prices) was expanding at a rate comparable to that of world trade, and even faster prior to 1965. Soviet delivery of petroleum to CMEA countries increased from 1 million tons in 1950 to more than 100 million tons in 1985. In effect, the USSR was the sole supplier of oil, gas, metal, and nuclear equipment; all railroad sleeping cars used in the USSR were manufactured in East Germany; most buses were made in Hungary, and forklifts in Bulgaria.

Such narrow specialization created artificial monopolies with no competitive pressures or incentives to improve quality and productivity. However, this policy produced a true economic interdependence and a certain unity among the industrial sectors of CMEA members. The level of interdependence within CMEA was greater than within the European Economic Community. In some years trade among CMEA countries comprised 60% of their total volume of foreign trade.

1985–1986 Provided No Hint of the Change to Come

Early in his rule Gorbachev was optimistic about socialist economic integration and the prospects for the CMEA. After only five years and virtually without explanation, he acknowledged their failure and demise.

As a rule, drafts of the resolutions regarding CMEA were worked out by the government. However, all major decisions went through the Secretariat of the CC and the Politburo. Draft resolutions to be passed by the Secretariat of the CC and the Politburo were prepared by the staff of the CC. There was no unanimity within the staff on most issues. The disputes were settled by the secretaries of the CC and ultimately by the general secretary. His word was final and determined the nature of the CC's resolutions.

This put special responsibility on the shoulders of the leader of the Party and the country. Gorbachev had an opportunity to choose among a number of alternatives. The decision was in his hands, and he made his choice.

From the beginning of his rule Gorbachev paid much attention to CMEA. He enjoyed his status as the youngest and most dynamic and progressive leader of world socialism, a man both respected and feared by the Western leaders. Gorbachev would hold frequent meetings with the leaders of almost every socialist country.

Gorbachev took part in the 1984 economic summit and initially stuck to its line when he became general secretary, sometimes even overstressing central planning. In May 1985, Gorbachev spoke at the conference held by the CC secretaries for economic affairs of CMEA states. His speech, focusing on past and future accomplishments, was traditionally optimistic. But he also made a statement that was not in the written draft to the following effect: "Some people want to clutch at the market as if it were a life raft. Meanwhile, a well-equipped ship—a system of socialist planning—is standing nearby."

Many people in the CC, the CM, and the CMEA countries were confused, thinking that Gorbachev was antimarket. Khrushchev-like schemes for setting up an international Gosplan and the corresponding pressure on the socialist countries was feared. There was talk of poor planning and lax discipline in the socialist camp, as well as talk to the effect that the Soviet Union ought to "put the house in order" or risk defeat in the economic race with the West.

Gorbachev's next major initiative was completing the CMEA Comprehensive Program for Technological Progress through the year 2000.[21] The idea for such a program arose in the process of preparation for the 1984 economic summit and was endorsed by Andropov. Other members did not object. Most innovations were generated in the Soviet Union, and according to CMEA rules had to be made available free of charge to its partners. The program seemed to allow the CMEA countries to tap into the immense R&D potential of the Soviet Union. At the end of 1985, when Ryzhkov became the chairman of the CM, he was charged with completing the Comprehensive Program and urgently coordinating it with the official CMEA bodies. Various departments of the CC were put to work on this task. I was directly involved in this assignment.

In collaboration with the AN, five high-priority areas of technological change, ranging from computerization to biotechnology, were outlined. Each of the five areas was further divided into specific innovation projects (e.g., the supercomputer project and design of a high-efficiency low emissions automobile engine). The mechanism for managing the program was modeled after that of the Soviet nuclear and missile-space projects. High government officials and prominent members of the AN were put in charge of specific high priority areas of the program.

The main flaw of the Comprehensive Program, as well as other CMEA policies, was the uncertainty concerning the volume and sources of financing and the lack of an implementation mechanism. The Comprehensive Program had no budget of its own. There was just a list of national organizations assigned to work on the specific projects in the program. The work on the program was actually performed by each country's domestic organizations with rather weak international coordination. Business trips, correspondence, meetings, paperwork, and protocols occupied the whole of 1986, with few substantive results.

Perestroika at CMEA

The onset of perestroika in the USSR gave rise to attempts to restructure CMEA. The shift "from coordinated planning to coordinated economic policy" was announced, although nobody understood what this was supposed to signify. In practice it meant that at the meetings of the CMEA Executive Committee, the head of each delegation would say something about his country's economic policy, make demands and requests. These "joint consultations on economic policy" did not result in any actual decisions being taken.

The rhetoric of perestroika caused havoc among CMEA officials. The Soviet contingent in a disciplined fashion started to invent all kinds of projects for radical change and improvement. The main, albeit well concealed, principle was 'shove it aside.' Few officials believed that perestroika would endure for any length of time or be effective.

The grand initiative of that period was the promotion of international cooperation through direct ties among enterprises and the setting up of joint ventures. Cooperation in design, production, and distribution was one of the weakest links in the economic integration of CMEA countries.[22] To address this problem, enterprises were to be allowed to contact their CMEA counterparts and negotiate contracts with them. Indeed, incentives were to be provided for such activity. It was assumed that thousands of enterprises would spring into action within a few years forming an interdependent network of cooperation in research, manufacturing, and joint ventures.

Gorbachev was an active proponent of this plan, adopted on the advice of dilettantes from his milieu (the likes of Shakhnazarov) with initial support by academics. They failed to comprehend that state enterprises that are not legally and actually free to trade at home cannot independently engage in efficient international exchange.

Some enterprise directors did become enthused about gaining access to foreign markets or improving their situation with foreign assistance. A few even achieved visible results. Kabaidze from Ivanovo, who established true cooperation with Bulgarian enterprises to produce advanced automated machine tools, received official praise and much publicity.

Overall, the hopes pinned on direct ties and joint enterprises were disappointed. One reason for that was the difficulty of pricing the goods. In principle, world prices in convertible currency should have been used. However, no one knew what these were. Pricing turned into a nightmare for the enterprises' economists. Many enterprises used domestic wholesale prices, but this drew objections by the central authorities as well as the trading partners.

A [Soviet domestic] directive specified that enterprises should not be given any hard currency, and instead precisely balance their cooperation with CMEA partners. Such barter cooperation was impossible at the level of individual enterprises. (A number of Bulgarian enterprises offered their Soviet partners tomatoes and brandy to cover their imbalances.)

The transferable ruble was confusing for enterprise managers. They erroneously believed that it was equivalent to the domestic ruble in terms of buying power. Enterprise directors did not know how to legally establish direct contacts and joint ventures. Official guidelines were lacking as was a legal framework for these operations. In fact, enterprise directors had no legal right to make trade agreements or negotiate prices with foreign partners. Long distances between partner enterprises, breakdowns in domestic production schedules, poor transportation, and a lack of penalties for late deliveries made supplies under CMEA cooperation unreliable.

Most directors were ill-prepared psychologically to make independent decisions that had previously fallen outside their jurisdiction. Rather than provide assistance, the sectoral ministries sowed fear and confusion. Gosplan, the Ministry of Foreign Trade, the Finance Ministry, and the Chief Prosecutor's Office were all antagonistic toward the idea of direct foreign economic ties. Enterprise directors were only too happy to visit each other abroad, agree on future meetings, sign meaningless agreements, and demand hard currency and multiuse visas from the central authorities.

This story illustrates the economic policy environment of the time. The idea of direct cooperation was adopted despite the opposition of most major government bodies. The decision was made behind the scenes with the assistance of consultants[23] and experts. The government agencies loyally accepted the new policy, at least formally. However, since control over policy execution was lax, and there were no sanctions for failure to implement the policy, actual performance deviated far from the superficial acceptance. Top decision makers either pretended not to notice this or else were told that their decisions were being carried out. The political leadership had relinquished control and lost its political willpower.

The failure of CMEA to establish viable direct ties and joint enterprises was never formally acknowledged. Reports on the hundreds and thousands of contracts signed by 'related enterprises from the sister nations' were intentionally falsified. During his trips to Bulgaria or Czechoslovakia, Gorbachev would visit these enterprises, talk to the workers, sign the honorary guest book, make speeches, and extend praise for "achievements in the area of integration."[24]

Controversies Within CMEA

Foreign economic ties and the prospects for their reform became a subject of sharp controversy within the Party and the government. While the contested issues were often quite specific, the debate was actually about the nature of the country's social and economic system and the fate of the socialist camp.

Whenever a scholar or a government official said anything controversial about CMEA, it was perceived to be the position of his country, with an easily decipherable hidden meaning. For example, a Romanian arguing for complete equality and national sovereignty was implicitly criticizing the USSR. A Hungarian or a Pole advocating the broad use of EEC experience implied dissatisfaction with planned socialist methods of cooperation within CMEA.

What follows is an overview of the main controversies of the late 1980s.

i. Should CMEA retain its socialist nature with economic planning and the state monopoly over foreign trade? Or should foreign trade be depoliticized and decentralized, that is, governed by commercial considerations? This debate heated up in 1989 and ended with a compromise. It was agreed that CMEA should be a voluntary organization with a mixed planned-market system which should use the best of both capitalist and socialist integration. CMEA should also open its doors to any country (for instance, Finland or India).

ii. Should CMEA assume supranational functions (at least to the same extent as the EEC), or be an association of fully sovereign states with all decisions based on bilateral or multilateral agreements? CMEA's supranational powers were supported by those Soviet officials and scholars for whom running an economy meant issuing commands, which in turn required a single planning center. Some pro-market Soviet economists supported supranational powers for CMEA because the West European model of integration also had them. CMEA's supranational authority was vehemently opposed by the representatives of *all* other CMEA countries as well as many Soviet officials and academics. It was decided to keep the supranationality issue on hold. CMEA was to be modeled on a free trade zone or an information and coordinating body with consultative functions where all interested parties could meet to strike agreements.

iii. Should intra-CMEA trade be conducted at its own special prices, or should prices be set in the process of exchange, tending toward world market levels? This question was always the most complex. There was no agreement on the basic notions: what are 'CMEA prices' and what are 'world prices' (particularly of goods not traded on world markets). The proponents of adopting world prices eventually gained the upper hand, but the principle was never followed consistently even during the last months of CMEA's existence.

iv. Should the U.S. dollar become the means of exchange instead of the transferable ruble? The USSR was sensitive about the prestige of the transferable ruble. Because of that, advocates of payments in hard currency pushed for complete convertibility of the ruble, that is, for turning it into a hard currency. Even Kosygin fell for this scheme. Having no understanding of the issue, all the political leaders of the CMEA countries voiced their support for making the ruble convertible. Gierek (prompted by his 'academic' aides) asked Brezhnev practically to declare the transferable ruble to be a hard currency. It was extremely nerve-racking for the experts to [have to] explain to every new leader that no currency can simply be declared convertible. The only feasible alternative was to switch back to the dollar (as at the beginning of the CMEA), but this would have undermined the prestige of the Soviet Union.

For many years all CMEA countries were critical of the transferable (clearing) ruble. However, when the USSR proposed switching to dollars, this proposal met with a stiff resistance from its partners. Behind the scenes, representatives from a number of countries tried to convince us that the switch to hard currency and free prices would inevitably destroy CMEA. These people were quite right, while those who advised the Soviet leadership to push for these changes either failed to recognize the real foundations of CMEA or consciously wanted to destroy it.

Curiously, both Soviet 'Westernizers' and 'patriots' applauded the use of world market dollar prices. The former argued that USSR should live by the rules of the world market, rejecting inefficient self-isolation imposed by the CMEA. The latter argued that it was time to stop 'plundering' Russia, that its natural resources ought to command their true worth in hard currency rather than being exchanged for 'junk.'

v. The export of [Soviet] raw materials, particularly oil, was the primary force cementing CMEA members together. The situation started to change in the mid-1970s, as world oil prices skyrocketed and CMEA prices followed suit. The CMEA price of a ton of oil increased more than tenfold within a few years after 1973. Oil production reached a plateau, the cost of extraction kept climbing, and Soviet domestic demand grew. Higher exports to the West were vital as a source of hard currency. At the beginning of the 1980s the USSR attempted to curtail oil exports to CMEA countries. These attempts met stiff opposition from the leadership of the other socialist countries, which forced the Kremlin to cave in.

To an extent the 'subsistence ration' of oil was compensated for by higher production and export of gas and a newly constructed network of nuclear power plants. Nonetheless, the controversy among the socialist countries surrounding the export of Soviet oil and other raw materials intensified. It was mirrored by a dispute within the Soviet Party and economic leadership. The latter got so severe that by the end of 1980s many complex and pressing problems of cooperation within the CMEA were simply ignored. Gorbachev delegated all these problems to the government, which did no better than the Party.

vi. One issue was aid to developing countries, including Cuba, Vietnam, and Mongolia. The foreign aid 'engine' went into high gear in the early 1970s, fueled by poorly coordinated decisions which failed to take into account the economic resources of the Soviet Union. Foreign aid climbed as the USSR made concessions on the prices of exports and imports and provided subsidized loans, free professional training, and technical assistance. When at the beginning of the 1980s the amount of foreign aid was calculated according to the UN methodology, it came out at about 2% of Soviet NMP. The Party and the economic officials were shocked at this figure and decided not to publish this statistic at home. At the same time, the Ministry of Foreign Affairs and the international departments of the CC proposed that this information be presented to the UN to fend off accusations that USSR was not doing enough to assist developing countries.

At the end of the 1980s genuine attempts were made to introduce order into the procedures and to cut foreign aid. In late 1989–early 1990 the Politburo and the CM adopted a number of stern directives calling for complete observance of the principle of mutual profitability in dealing with all countries. However, Mongolia, Cuba, North Korea, and Vietnam enjoyed certain privileges until the very collapse of the Soviet Union. Still, the top priority of domestic interests was firmly established from the beginning of 1990.

The Agony

The year 1989 marked the last genuine attempts to overhaul the CMEA, all of them unsuccessful. The political structure and economic policy of Poland and Hungary changed, followed toward the end of 1989 by East Germany and Czechoslovakia. Other European CMEA members and subsequently the USSR and Mongolia followed suit.

The conflicts that ultimately tore the socialist camp apart were rooted in the problems experienced by the individual countries. The leadership and particularly the opposition in most countries was becoming increasingly antagonistic toward CMEA. Acute conflicts arose between the 'superpower' and the 'satellite' states, between the 'haves' and the 'have nots,' and between domestic considerations and international obligations. Most CMEA countries thought they were economically exploited [by CMEA] and regarded their international obligations [within CMEA] as burdensome. This discontent came to the fore in the 1980s when the exchange of previously cheap raw materials for noncompetitive finished products began to decline. Almost all European CMEA members including the Soviet Union began to gravitate toward the West, realizing its technological leadership. CMEA, as an institution dominated by the USSR and a symbol of Soviet power, was losing its political and ideological appeal.

Gorbachev's personality and actions contributed to this process. In mid-1985, prompted by the anti-alcohol campaign, the USSR violated its contractual obligations to import alcoholic beverages from CMEA countries.

Bulgaria, Hungary, and Romania were particularly hurt by this move. Even more blatant violations of export-import contracts as well as agreements on various pilot projects and investment ventures followed.

There was also an about-face in the Soviet official views regarding economic reform. Prior to 1987–1988, the Soviet leadership was apprehensive and suspicious of the national models of market socialism (Yugoslavia, Hungary, and Poland). Then market mechanisms came into favor, and administrative methods of management came under fire. This served to undermine the clout enjoyed by the leadership of the GDR and Czechoslovakia, which were the USSR's main trading partners.

Gorbachev had promised Erich Honecker and Miloš Jakeš to call a working summit on economic issues in Prague in 1989. A request was filed that the drafting of the documents for the summit be supervised by the Czechs and the Germans. The main documents, outlining CMEA reform, implementation of the Comprehensive Program, expansion of trade, coordination of trade with the West, and ties with Western economic organizations, were drafted and got preliminary approval of the member countries. The summit was also to focus on the exchange of know-how on economic reform and domestic economic policy.

It seemed at the time that the jointly elaborated measures were progressive and geared toward long-term development. However they were destined to remain on paper. Around the time the preparations for the economic summit (October–November 1989) were nearly complete, East Germany and Czechoslovakia underwent major political upheaval. The individuals involved in the preparations sensed that a major change was coming. Unlike most previous high-level meetings, this one was almost devoid of acrid arguments and controversies. The proposals jointly advanced by the Communist Parties of Czechoslovakia, the GDR, and the USSR had an easy time being adopted. The experts themselves appeared depressed and dazed. Their concern lay not so much with the future of CMEA as with the fate of their Parties and their countries.

During late 1989–early 1990, inter-Party communication on economic cooperation seized up completely and most of those involved in this work simply retired. The final dismantling of CMEA (through 1991) proceeded at the government level and occasionally events simply unfolded without any prior arrangement.

Notes

1. This section is drawn from the interviews excerpted in Chapter 3.2. [Ed.]
2. This remark was prompted by a text shown by the interviewer. [Ed.]

3. In the USSR wholesale trade was understood as the opposite of distribution via quotas and rationing. It included "free buying and selling through direct contracts between users and producers, through contracts with intermediaries, in particular with territorial supply organs, and through factory outlets" (*Materialy . . . 1987*, p. 96).

4. This means that instead of all the enterprises applying for quotas of the rationed goods, only the territorial organ of Gossnab would do so, and the intention was that all the users would be able to buy supplies of the goods when needed, and get them delivered quickly, from the territorial organ of Gossnab. [Ed.]

5. According to Soviet official statistics, GNP rose by 5.5% in 1988, rose by 3% in 1989, and only fell (by 2.3%) in 1990. [Ed.]

6. The 'leading links principle,' that is, to concentrate efforts on one or a small number of key sectors or 'leading links,' was a basic principle of traditional Soviet planning. See, for example, Ellman 1979, p. 18. [Ed.]

7. The case studies in Chapter 9.3 are based on the information collected in our field research in the late 1980s.

8. RAPOs appeared before Gorbachev became general secretary, but were still actively touted in his first years in that position. They originated when he was still the CC secretary in charge of agriculture. [Ed.]

9. This development received a boost in 1983 when Andropov was general secretary and Gorbachev was responsible for agriculture. For a Western discussion, see Ellman (1988). [Ed.]

10. CM decree no. 1405, December 1988.

11. Subsequently, when work began on a customs code and a customs tariff, GATT documents were indeed used extensively.

12. The serious dissatisfaction of the leadership with the work of the foreign economic agencies did emerge in the report of the chairman of the CM, N.I. Ryzhkov, at the Twenty-Seventh Party Congress. There he stated that "There are still serious inadequacies and omissions in the work of the Ministry of Foreign Trade and the State Committee for Economic Relations, which are only slowly being overcome" (*Materialy XXVII S''ezda . . . 1986*, p. 258). For those familiar with the complicated and specific norms of Party-bureaucratic relations of that period, these were very significant words.

13. For example, the contacts of Party secretaries from the various sections of the Ministry with the KGB officials who supervised these sections were so regular that they were even mentioned at Party meetings.

14. *BIKI,* 11 May 1991. See also *Mirovoe . . . 1990*, p. 184.

15. These estimates were contained in the statistics of the Russian balance of payments published in 1992–1993 in the weekly *Ekonomika i zhizn'*.

16. Introduced by CM decree no. 203 of 7 March 1989.

17. Other elements, introduced mostly by CM decree no. 203 of 7 March 1989, were the declaration of goods being moved across borders, fixing of quotas, and a temporary suspension of the operations of participants in foreign trade.

18. According to a speech by I. Ivanov, the chairman of the Scientific Council of the GVK. *BIKI* for 11 May 1991 gives a different figure: fifty.

19. This is impossible to prove, but to me, on the basis of the facts and arguments presented in the main body of the text, it seems clear enough. A similar interpretation of the return to administrative methods is given by Kuznetsov (1990). Another explanation of these phenomena (and not just in foreign trade) relies on the plots of the antireform forces, but I do not support it.

20. These are not the cooperatives legalized by the 1988 law (*de facto* private firms), but rather a *de facto* state organization which was part of the old state-run system of retail trade. [Ed.]

21. News of the impending completion of the West European R&D program 'Eureka' served as the impetus to speed up work on the Comprehensive Program.

22. The author speaks of *proizvodstvenno-tekhnologicheskaia* specialization and cooperation. While CMEA established country specialization by finished product, there was very little specialization in parts, components, assemblies, etc. See Pécsi 1981, p. 13. [Ed.]

23. 'Consultant' was the title of some officials on the CC staff. [Ed.]

24. Cooked data on direct ties and joint ventures did not invalidate reported statistics on imports and exports. The point is that the volume of intra-CMEA trade continued to be determined almost wholly in a centralized fashion, rather than by the enterprises themselves, as the propaganda claimed.

10

From Reform to the Eve
of Revolution

10.1 The End of Economic Reform
Yevgenii Yasin

With the failure of the '500 Days' program, Gorbachev the reformer missed his last chance. He lost the strategic initiative, which could now end up either with the Communist center, which had quashed Gorbachev as a real leader, or with Yeltsin. The struggle for power between them became the key event of 1991. The economy was put on the back burner, and at best was only used for political purposes, which made things even worse. Reform was not even discussed.

Economic performance in 1990 turned out to be highly discouraging. For the first time since the war, official statistics showed a decline in GDP (by 2.3%) and in industrial and agricultural production. Petroleum production went down from 607 to 571 million tons, and petroleum export, from 127 to 109 million tons. Even though international prices had sharply increased in the previous two years, 32 million tons of grain had to be imported. The foreign debt increased sharply, having doubled since 1985. The domestic national debt grew from 141.6 billion rubles in 1985 to 940 billion rubles in 1990. The amount of cash in circulation in 1990 grew by 24.3%.

In 1994 [the year this text was written], when industrial production had shrunk by half from the 1991 level, all these numbers do not seem to suggest an impending catastrophe. Yet what matters is the internal dynamics, the forces deepening the crisis compared with those resisting it. Back then, one could see no reason for getting out of the crisis, unless entertaining groundless hopes. Out of at least three programs that were elaborated, not one was realized. For a year, practically nothing was done to advance economic reforms or stave off the impending crisis. The paralysis of the government was coupled with the paralysis of economic incentives, which, in the context of the monetary collapse, pervasive shortages, and irrational control mechanisms, served to aggravate the crisis. The unwillingness of Ryzhkov's government to institute a strict fiscal policy and to remove price controls led to the demise of the monetary system that united the country, and produced shortages of goods that provoked all the republics and regions to think only of themselves. The republics and regions would not give their resources to the center or to other republics or regions, and were willing to engage in barter at best. This was conducive to separatism and nationalism.

In 1991, all these trends intensified as a result of the more acute political struggle. Yeltsin went on the offensive during the review of the Union budget in the USSR Supreme Soviet. He declared that Russia would contribute only 23 billion rubles to the budget, about three times less than in 1990, and would double its own budget outlays. The Union budget, which financed, among other things, the armed forces, lost a large part of its revenues and was forced to cover its spending through monetary expansion. Negotiations failed to yield an agreement. Other republics started following Russia's example, although warily. From the beginning of the year it was already clear that the deficit of the consolidated USSR budget would be at least double that of 1990, even assuming there would be no large drop in production.

V. Pavlov replaced N. Ryzhkov as prime minister at the end of 1990 and made attempts at financial stabilization. On 1 January 1991 roughly 40% of wholesale prices were freed, as decreed by Gorbachev on 4 October 1990. A 5% sales tax along the lines of a value added tax was imposed. In January, large denomination bills were exchanged and people's deposits in the Savings Bank were temporarily frozen in a mini–monetary reform. The Union government held negotiations with the republics on raising retail prices and compensating the population for the resulting losses. The negotiations dragged on because no one wanted to assume responsibility for this move and everyone tried to dump it on Pavlov. In the end, retail prices were increased only on 1 April.

Had they been coordinated in time and better implemented, these policies could have produced a certain effect. But the way it was actually done, each step was a new blow to the Soviet government. The sales tax was immediately christened 'presidential' and became the target of popular discontent. The monetary reform without price liberalization looked like a humiliation without any reason. The retail price hikes in April improved the consumer market situation for no more than two months, and not by much. Yet they annoyed the people a great deal. Everything the Soviet government did worked against it. It became clear that Communists, whether reformers or not, could not accomplish anything.

The shooting and deaths on the streets of Baltic cities in January signaled the coming of the showdown and indicated that Gorbachev did not control the actions of his team. Shevardnadze and other proponents of liberal reform abandoned Gorbachev, who practically lost his democratic and reformist image and was left alone to deal with the future State Committee for Emergency Rule. By initiating the process of formulating a new Union treaty at Novoogarevo, he tried once again to regain this aura and to become independent from those who had elected him general secretary. But it was too late.

There were practically no attempts to bring back elements of the old system prior to August 1991.[1] The struggle within the leadership was between the radical and moderate proponents of reform. Its real opponents were demoralized if only because they were used to following the Party leadership and Gorbachev was the head of the Party. They had no real impact on political decision making. Only in December 1990, Tiziakov and his followers among the enterprise directors and the Military Industrial Complex bared their teeth by openly criticizing Gorbachev and Ryzhkov at their conference. A conservative group under the name 'Union' was formed in the Supreme Soviet. One can speak of the inconsistency and ineffectiveness of Gorbachev's policies, but prior to that time and then till August 1991 he had not really been confronted by any organized opposition. When the opposition did band together, it was not so much in response to his economic reform as to the threat of disintegration of the Union.

In the first nine months of 1991, industrial output fell by another 6.4%, compared to the same period in 1990; food production fell by 8.3%; and the commissioning of new production capacity declined by 15%. Retail prices grew by 70%. Bank loans grew by 58%. The Union budget collected only 40% of planned revenue. Deposits in the Savings Bank grew by 25%, while the amount of cash held by households went up from 132 to 199 billion rubles. Store shelves were practically empty. It was unclear what could change the direction of events, or what it was possible to hope for.

10.2 The Republics Take Over
Viktor Kurierov

From the end of 1989 the Soviet republics one after another began to adopt declarations of sovereignty or independence, as well as amendments to their constitutions stating the priority of republican laws over all-Union ones. But the real threat to the existence of the Union emerged when the leadership of the Russian Federation joined this process. In June 1990 the Supreme Soviet of Russia passed a declaration about the sovereignty of the republic.

There followed laws giving Russia exclusive authority over all the foreign economic issues touching on its interests: the appointment of the head of the customs service, determining the foreign trade and foreign currency systems, licensing, the registration of the participants of foreign economic activity, and authority over natural resources. The question of dividing up the Soviet gold, diamond, and foreign currency reserves among the republics was raised. In July 1990 the Russian Ministry of Foreign Economic Relations was created.

The 'war of laws' flared up after that. Russian authorities started grabbing the powers belonging to the Union and attempted to block Union decisions that did not suit them. All foreign trade deals involving the sale of natural resources located on Russian territory, as well as international loans negotiated without the agreement of the Russian government were declared void. The conflict between the 'center' and the republics, especially Russia, harmed business, confusing the system of foreign economic regulation and substantially complicating the government's commercial contacts with other countries and international organizations. But priority was unconditionally given to the interests of the power struggle, and all other considerations played a very minor role.

The center of gravity of foreign economic reform gradually moved to the republic level. By the middle of 1991 the Russian Federation obtained the right to issue licenses and fix quotas for foreign trade, excluding transactions in basic raw materials and weapons, to conduct barter deals independently, to register participants in foreign economic transactions, and to negotiate foreign loans. Lacking their own legal norms, the Russian authorities continued to use Union laws and decrees in many foreign economic questions, but it was clear that their replacement by republican laws was only a matter of time.

In the foreign economic area, as elsewhere, the Russian leadership set a course for breaking up the single economic space [of the Union]. Yeltsin's decree of 15 November 1991 on the liberalization of foreign economic activity provided for further steps toward a sharp limitation of the rights and powers of the Union authorities in regulating trade and currency matters. Rather inconsistently, it was based on the idea of preserving the unified customs space within the borders of the USSR. This cost the Russian state dearly after the collapse of the Soviet Union, as it suffered huge losses because of its inability to organize effective control over the flow of foreign trade and foreign currency [within the former Soviet Union].

10.3 Disappointment in the CC Apparatus
Yurii Belik

The great enthusiasm accompanying Gorbachev's ascent to the Party Olympus was slowly displaced by an ever-growing discontent. The idea of per-

estroika and its initial stages were fine. However, the course of its implementation proved that specific goals and programs of action, as well as
the essential coordination of policies, were all lacking. Events unfolded in a
chaotic fashion, without aim or direction, perplexing and confusing the
Department's staff.

Initially, perestroika stood for the improvement of socialism on the basis of
technological progress and democratization. It was well received by the Party
and the population. Yet the noble mission of modernization of our society and
the Party itself fell into the hands of politicians (Gorbachev, Yakovlev,
Shevardnadze, and Medvedev) who senselessly ruined everything.

The deepening crisis facing the country was much debated by the CC apparatus. The events of 19 August 1991 were hailed by the great majority of the
CC apparatus as a necessary and even an overdue step. "Finally, they are
getting down to business," said my friends and colleagues after the documents
prepared by the State Committee for Emergency Rule were published. During
those days everyone was waiting for a plenum of the CC and Gorbachev's
removal at it from his post as general secretary of the Party.

10.4 The Real Achievements of Reform
Lev Freinkman

In spite of the inconsistency and vacillations in government policy, during
1988–1990 the autonomy bestowed upon the enterprises expanded considerably. The actual volume of decentralized transactions did not grow as
much as is generally thought. Prior to the reform, the semilegal trade in
goods when the real recipients of the goods and the terms of exchange were
actually set by the producers themselves rather than by the administrative
organs, was much more developed than official estimates would have us
believe (Medvedev, Nit, and Freinkman 1989a; Aven and Shironin 1987).[2]
On the other hand, at the end of the 1980s the real volume of output
independently exchanged by the enterprises was considerably less than the
volume of wholesale trade for which the leaders of Gossnab were responsible (see Chapter 8.1).

The volume of decentralized transactions expanded thanks to the addition of the output over and above the state order, accumulated reserves,
by-products, second-hand machinery, samples produced in testing pilot projects, and so on. The basic changes that took place were qualitative rather
than quantitative in nature: the market for producer goods assumed legal
forms, and owing to advertising in the media and the emergence of special
commercial publications, it became part of public life. The legislative affir-
mation of the enterprises' right to the independent use of the fruits of their

labor coupled with the profound political discrediting of the centralized planning system were very important from a political point of view. An attitude toward administrative intervention as being inherently illegitimate was emerging. At the same time expectations of further reduction of such interference were raised.

The Law on the State Enterprise allowed the labor collectives to transfer to their partners a part of any asset belonging to the enterprise, including the legalization of free (i.e., without the involvement of government bodies) exchange of resources among the enterprises and mutual financing. At the same time, enterprises gained new freedoms in using freely agreed-upon prices, especially when it came to new products. Beginning in the summer of 1989 the various agencies of Gossnab were granted the right to set commercial prices for scarce and unprofitable items produced in excess of the volume specified in the state order. As a result, the monopoly of the State Price Committee in setting wholesale prices was undermined, which helped to resolve some differences in the profitability of different products produced by manufacturers.

On the whole, however, in 1988–1989 the role of commercial and contract prices was still very limited. For instance, in 1988 Gossnab procured only 130 million rubles worth of commercially priced goods (0.014% of total industrial output). Relatively more effective was the reform of supply in the small-scale nonindustrial sector, as well as in most research institutes and design bureaus. These organizations no longer had to submit requests for resources a year in advance to some department of Gossnab. Since these organizations operated under more volatile and uncertain demand for their product, the reform generally cut down on the time spent waiting for the materials to come in. In the summer of 1990 several decrees of the CM allowed the use of hard currency for domestic operations. This legalized hard-currency payments for producer goods.

There emerged a system of new supply organizations—self-financing commercial centers aiming to provide a service to the enterprises, particularly in the areas of economic ties, marketing, advertising, the sale of surplus resources, and so on. These organizations lacked any kind of administrative control over the buyers of their services. The commercial centers were active in setting up local and regional commercial data banks, and in conducting fairs and auctions.

The central subdivisions of Gossnab responsible for distribution underwent major transformation. Nineteen self-financing firms specializing in wholesale trade in specific product groups were formed from the purely administrative departments of Gossnab. The firms were intended to combine administrative-distribution functions (primarily ensuring the supply of goods to certain industries and regions that were unable to adequately compete in the free market) and indirect regulatory functions concerning market processes during the emergence of the market.

The newly formed association Vneshtekhobmen became a new powerful intermediary competing with its counterparts in the Ministry of Foreign Trade in imports. Vneshtekhobmen provided comprehensive services for nearly 110,000 buyers (including handling orders, making financial calculations, and arranging deliveries) and was the sole payer for foreign suppliers. This association organized fairs for Soviet enterprises that kept hard currency accounts. Through these channels enterprises producing goods for export gained additional opportunities to spend their income.

During 1990, as barter trade expanded, there appeared various commodity exchanges, originally geared primarily toward facilitating barter operations and the effective organization of multilateral barter deals (*Birzhi v SSSR* 1991). As new forms of industrial organizations (see below) emerged, many of them began to set up their own self-financing supply firms, creating a rudimentary competition among the suppliers.

Auctions emerged as a method for marketing specific and unique items, better-quality products, and products (in excess of the state order) that were in extremely short supply. At the first auctions, conducted in early 1989, the average level of sale prices exceeded the standard list prices by 80%, and this gap subsequently increased (*Ekonomicheskaia gazeta,* 1989, no. 39, p. 16). At the end of 1989, the regulations governing auction sales were completely changed: 70% of the difference between the original and auction prices had to be paid to the state budget and only 30% was available for the producers of the goods and the auction organizers. Such conditions rendered the auctions unattractive for the manufacturers.

Another such regulation obviously contradicting the officially proclaimed goals of the reform was the reduction of the penalty for breaching a contract from 12% to 8% of the cost of the undelivered portion of the order (*Ekonomicheskaia gazeta,* 1989, no. 39, p. 6). In spite of criticism, the system of compulsory discounts on obsolete engineering output that was paid for out of the enterprise's incentives funds was preserved. This forced the enterprises to convert to the production of new, more expensive items with features in excess of those demanded by consumers and to shun the production of goods truly in demand. Moreover, until 1991 enterprises enjoyed a privileged system for distributing above-plan profit as well as additional incentives if they fulfilled 100% of their contract obligations. This kept the expansion of output in check by inducing the producers to undervalue their real production capacities and turn down new orders.

The Law on the State Enterprise allowed enterprises to invest in each other, particularly in their suppliers. The Minsk Tractor Factory, one of the first enterprises to take advantage of this ruling, invested the foreign exchange equivalent of 4.5 million rubles to expand the production of universal joint shafts manufactured by one of its suppliers. This allowed the tractor manufacturer to terminate their unreliable suppliers in Kazakhstan (*Izvestiia,* 26 January 1988). Given the growing barterization of the economy, investors counted not so much on the dividends from their investments as on additional supplies. Financially secure collective farms provided very favorable financing to the biggest manufacturers of agricultural machinery, who were experiencing financial difficulties. The most important stipulation in disbursing these loans was giving the creditors top priority in the distribution of spare parts.

New organizational structures, largely independent of the old administrative system, began to appear. At first, decisions regarding the founding of concerns, consortia, and large joint-stock companies were made on an individual basis. 'As an exception,' new entities received additional rights in marketing their output and disposing of their income, including foreign currency (e.g., the concern Kvantemp in 1989). The process gained momentum as new regulations governing the setup of these organizations were passed. The formation of such organizations reduced the center's ability to intervene in daily economic activities, increased the pressure of most enterprises to expand their autonomy, and formed a general expectation of a weakening of plan discipline.

10.5 A Missed Chance?
Sergei Belanovsky

The Pro-Market Explanation of the Crisis

Adherents of the market economy saw the main flaw of the Soviet economy in its low efficiency, which caused waste of resources, a technological lag behind the West, and low living standards.[3]

At its birth the planning system embraced only a narrow sector of the economy, including ferrous metals, power generation, and machine building. The peasants, making up about 70% of the population, lived in relative autarky.[4] The urban standard of living declined significantly from its pre-Revolutionary level, not only due to the decline in the quantity of goods and services, but also—crucially for this explanation—due to the decline in the variety of goods. Therefore, the planners had to concern themselves with balancing a relatively short list of products, which made their task simpler.

The situation changed in the 1950s. Industry had grown in size and had become more complex. Urbanization, an increase in the urban standard of living, and attempts to improve the rural standard of living forced the state to assume direction of the consumer-goods sector, which was growing rapidly in size and complexity, making it also the object of planning. Finally, technology had changed. In the nineteenth and the first half of the twentieth centuries, industrialization was directly correlated with the growing production of ferrous metals. In the mid-twentieth century, the most dynamic sectors of the economy became the multiproduct ones—machine-building, nonferrous metals, and electronics. Ferrous metallurgy itself became a multiproduct sector, as the number of types of steel and rolled metal increased many times.

All this led to an increase in complexity of the economic system subject to planning. The subsistence sector, which previously served as both a buffer and a supplier of resources, had almost disappeared by the early 1970s.[5] This increase in complexity of the object of planning is seen in the pro-market explanation as the main and irremediable cause of the decline in economic efficiency. This conclusion has been bolstered by citing a significant (about fivefold, according to some estimates) increase in the number of product balances compiled by Gosplan in 1950–1980. The evident increase in shortages of both consumer and producer goods was seen as another piece of corroborating evidence.

It was conjectured that the growth in the number of balances—the main tool of planning—lagged behind the growth of the number of products, itself a manifestation of the growing complexity of the economy. The increase in the number of product balances was limited not so much by the resources required for building up the planning apparatus, as by the increasing complexity of ensuring consistency across the balances. For this reason, the increase in the number of balances yielded diminishing returns in terms of balancing the real flows in the economy. The increasing imbalance was the main factor impairing economic performance.

This explanation is logically consistent, but has poor empirical support. The data on the growth in the number of balances and actual products are highly arbitrary. The number of balances, even if correct, related only to those compiled by Gosplan and sometimes Gossnab. Balances compiled by the Gosplans of the republics; Union and republic ministries and agencies; planning administrations of regions, districts, and cities; and territorial administrations of Gossnab were not taken into account. Also omitted from the pro-market theory were large-scale barter and informal coordination among the economic actors, which served as a strong buffer against the flaws of central planning. The number of products in the economy is altogether an elusive concept. It is difficult to operationalize and account for.

The official statistics did not try to count all the variety of products in the economy, and had no capability to do so.

It is possible (though not proven) that the declining efficiency of the Soviet economy was to some degree due to the lagging ability of central planning to coordinate the growing economy. However, this was not the only, and most likely not the main, cause. The next section suggests that the disintegration of the state was a more powerful cause.

An Alternative Explanation

The search for alternative explanations led us to interview a number of former Soviet *apparatchiks* [from the military-industrial complex], who were asked the same basic question (with only minor variations): "What was the cause of the crisis of the Soviet political and economic system?"[6]

The erosion or disintegration of the central authority was unanimously cited as the primary reason for the crisis. In the words of General M.A. Gareev, "In the 1970s we (i.e., the USSR) had lost our ability to set priorities that reflected the interests of the country as a whole and to allocate resources accordingly. As a result, the truly pressing problems remained unresolved while tremendous resources were thrown at problems of secondary importance."

The primary goals of the Soviet leadership in the immediate post–World War II period were the development of nuclear and rocket weapons and the recovery from the colossal destruction inflicted by the war. These goals were achieved in a relatively short time due to the concentration of all the nation's resources on the task. Around the time of Stalin's death, new long-term priorities for the country had to be determined.

The postwar evolution of the Soviet state brings to mind Toynbee's idea that a society that has successfully responded to a major historical challenge instinctively gears up for a repeat, which makes it ill prepared to face other kinds of challenges.[7] Interviews with former high-ranking Soviet officials shed some light on the specific mechanism underlying this historical pattern. The institutions set up to respond to the historical challenge are given top priority. They refuse to surrender this priority to other institutions responsible for dealing with other potential challenges. Paradoxically, in a centralized state this change of priorities can be carried out only by a powerful dictator who clearly sees new goals and can dictate to the government agencies. In the 1930s, Stalin succeeded in suppressing departmental and territorial disintegration of the country by force. However, a replay of this scenario with a different set of objectives in the 1950s and 1960s, even by a powerful dictator, would have been problematic. Khrushchev certainly made such an attempt, but even his half-hearted initiatives ultimately resulted in his own dismissal.

In the next twenty years (1965–1985) the weakened central authority abandoned the attempt to exert coercive pressure on the ministries, basically letting things take their course. On the other hand, tough new problems that had lurked in the background in the 1950s emerged with full force in the 1970s. According to our interviewees, Soviet leaders were aware of at least two such 'superproblems': making good on the social debt and catching up with the new technology.

'Social debt' refers to bringing actual consumption in line with the new consumer aspirations. In the 1950s and 1960s the level of consumption in the USSR grew rather fast, presenting a sharp contrast to the hardships of the preceding decades. But in the 1970s the standard of living virtually stopped growing, and in the early 1980s began to slip. At the same time, people's expectations continued to rise, due, among other reasons, to the 'penetration' of information about Western and East European living standards through the iron curtain. Stagnation followed by a decline in the living standard, coupled with growing expectations, bred increasing disappointment in all strata of Soviet society.[8]

The second major task recognized by the Soviet political elite was to push the country to a new level of technological development. General Gareev, quoted above, also commented on this: "At one point we developed a nuclear industry by focusing all of the country's resources on this one goal. In the 1970s we should have concentrated on developing our own microelectronics industry and other related high-tech sectors (lasers, etc.) which would have improved the country's defense capability. Instead resources were squandered upon numerous programs aimed at expanding and modernizing obsolete weapon systems (armored vehicles, aircraft carriers, etc.) which were overproduced anyway." He followed this statement with a rather trivial remark to the effect that if one wants to achieve something, one must limit the less vital needs.

The third problem facing the country was low productivity and inefficiency. Members of the ruling elite recognized it, even if they did not speak often on the issue. The degradation of the civilian sector of the economy, which became manifest as early as the mid-1970s, was no secret, but opinions on its causes varied. The 'pro-market' view (outlined at the beginning of this section) boiled down to the immanent inefficiency of the planned economy. 'Conservatives,' on the other hand, cited the heavy defense burden, complemented by psychological factors including drunkenness, lack of discipline, theft, and other irremediable negative characteristics of the people.[9]

The surveyed 'conservatives' acknowledged that the three key problems—rising social discontent, the technological gap with the West, and the deterioration of the nondefense sector of the economy—were largely the result of the arms race, or to be more precise, its grotesque forms. The very structure of the defense industry which was shaped during and right after the war was becoming obsolete. Soviet defense industry, pressured by industrial lobby groups, continued to pursue the 'steel' card while the rest of the world was making a switch to 'electronics.' The unrestrained resource appetite of military industry was squeezing the civilian sector.

The 'conservative' explanations for the crisis is more realistic in the sense that in the 1970s and 1980s the phenomena it describes predominated over those described by the 'pro-market' theory (though the latter may have also be present and should not be discounted a priori).

Both theories analyze the deterioration of the Soviet economy leading toward the crisis, rather than the crisis itself and the subsequent collapse of the Soviet state, which occurred in a specific historical moment.

Was the Crisis Avoidable?

The 'marketeers' contend that the planned economy was doomed and the only real issue was how long it could hold out by eating away (ever less efficiently) at the available resources.

The 'conservative' view is predicated on geopolitics rather than on pure economics. According to the reform-minded 'conservatives,' the first step in any reform was to acknowledge that neither the United States, nor NATO, nor even China was about to attack the Soviet Union, not to speak of unleashing a nuclear war. Soviet stockpiles of nuclear weapons ensured strategic defense for decades to come, even if other countries were to develop new weapons and the USSR was to maintain the existing ones. This is not to say that the 'conservatives' advocated abandoning the development of new weapon systems. They merely maintained that military programs ought to have focused on R&D potential and on specific weapon systems based on cutting-edge technologies and produced in minimal quantities.

The key concept advanced by the 'conservatives' was the 'economic power of the country.' In the words of a former military intelligence officer, Colonel V.V. Shlykov, "Our main goal ought to have been economic power, since military power is contingent upon economic power." This objective could have been achieved within the framework of a planned economy, which allowed for an effective large-scale restructuring of the economy.

The military-industrial complex would have been the primary source of the resources needed for implementing the planned restructuring of the

Soviet economy. Other possible sources included Western investment and the sale of a large proportion of the strategic reserves (mainly nonferrous metals). Arms production would have been drastically curtailed, and the freed raw materials could have been exported. The manufacturing plants would have been retooled under a large-scale conversion program, with most production lines geared toward weapons production dismantled.

Planned restructuring of the Soviet economy would have unfolded along three main directions:

- Development of the high-tech sectors, primarily electronics, including mass production of personal computers, videocassette recorders, and electronics-laden appliances.
- Settling social debts, first and foremost by increasing the output of consumer durables. According to experts, even a limited conversion of military-industrial capacities would have allowed this program to be implemented within a five-year period. The long-range objectives would have included mass production of autos, highway and residential construction, an expanded retail network, and major improvements in the standard of living in the rural areas.
- Rehabilitation of the efficiency of the civilian sector of the economy. This could have been achieved by raising investment 'quality,' that is, by introducing modern, highly efficient machinery as part of the program of conversion of the defense industry. The other facet of this problem was improving discipline and adherence to technological guidelines and, more generally, reversing the process of social decay (at many enterprises, one-third or even more of the workforce were chronic alcoholics). Part of the solution was to make more consumer goods available to the public. As one of the respondents put it: "with [repressed] inflation, the vacuum on the consumer goods market is getting filled with alcohol." The other part was to restore labor discipline and improve labor organization. The most insightful interviewees went beyond proposing disciplinary measures. Rather, they called for easing the tautness of enterprise plans, thus making it possible to eliminate overreporting and false accounting which was the practice at practically every nondefense plant.

Except for the rather utopian idea of reversing social decay, all the facets of the program seem quite feasible. As proposed by those surveyed (and we tend to agree), even a partial implementation of such a reform would have produced major results. So, why wasn't there any attempt to implement this program?[10] The response given by those surveyed was uniform: the loss of unity of the state, inability to make difficult decisions, and stalling by powerful self-interested ministries.

The picture would not be complete without a stagnation scenario [in addition to the 'pro-market' and 'conservative' scenarios]. In the words of an analyst from one of the high-security academic institutes, the key prerequisite for such a scenario was that "the arms race, as pursued by both sides, had a strong element of bluff since neither side was planning to start a war. This meant that the USSR could imitate a military-industrial and ideological confrontation indefinitely, while inflating its fictitious component." This course of events did not materialize for reasons that probably are psychological and outside the economic or geopolitical realm. Neither an individual nor society as a whole can carry out a meaningless scenario. If Gorbachev and other top Soviet leaders had aimed at extending the Brezhnev-type period and dying in their posts, it is quite possible that they would have succeeded in this. There were no signs of social instability in the USSR in 1985 and even the most outspoken critics of the regime thought the crisis of the Soviet system would come about no earlier than the third millennium.

The Soviet state and its economy of the 1920s and particularly the 1930s were geared to war.[11] The outcome of World War II imposed certain objective limits on possible Soviet expansionist plans and turned the arms race from a legitimate endeavor into a senseless one. This deprived the Soviet political and economic system of its *raison d'etre* and caused its disintegration along departmental lines. Was it possible for this already molded and in a way effective system to switch tracks and pursue other objectives? This is equivalent to asking whether it was possible for a strong dictator to come to power in the USSR, cut weapons production down to a reasonable or even minimum level, make his main objective reaching parity with the United States in the output of consumer goods, and for that purpose dismantle his own military-industrial ministries. I believe such a dictator could have achieved tremendous results. However, the emergence of such a historical figure is a utopian dream. Furthermore, the long-term survival of the Soviet civilization, even in this utopian scenario, is problematic.

Conclusion

The arms race was not the primary cause but an intermediate link in the chain of cause and effect that spelled the ultimate demise of the Soviet system. The arms buildup imposed a burden on the economy that was unsustainable in the long run. The arms race itself was due to the inability of the Soviet state to alter its priorities which were molded essentially during the Civil War and became obsolete by the end of World War II. The arms race dampened the growth in the standard of living and by the early 1980s actually led to its decline. It was indirectly responsible for the decay of the economy's civilian sector and the demoralization of its workers, itself an important component of the society-wide demoralization. Still, the buildup of negative phenomena could have continued for a long time. The immediate factor which precipitated perestroika was the loss of a historical perspective which enveloped the entire society including the ruling elite.

The negative trends in the economy and society stimulated a search for a solution. The plan-based reform program, which was a viable alternative to the market program, was lurking in the minds of the Soviet leaders. However the system's inertia precluded this alternative from being formulated. Even today, when the collapse of the USSR is history, this program can only be extracted from the *apparatchiks'* minds in the course of in-depth sociological interviews.[12]

Notes

1. Amending the Law on the State Enterprise to repeal the election of directors was not an attempt to roll back the reforms but a case of common sense prevailing.

2. The true scale of such independent trade is illustrated by the following example: By the end of 1986 just the officially accounted spare metal owned by the enterprises located in the jurisdiction of the Tula regional agro-industrial directorate was more than four times greater than the entire annual quota allocated to this concern for the purchase of metal (*Izvestiia*, 19 November 1986).

3. The exposition below relates to declining, rather than low efficiency. [Ed.]

4. This is a significant overstatement. The flow of goods between agriculture and industry was one of the central issues of the Soviet economy in the 1920s. See Nove 1992, chapters 4–6. [Ed.]

5. But the household plots of the collective farmers, and the gardens of state farmers and urban dwellers, remained an important source of food for the population. [Ed.]

6. Excerpts from these interviews appear in Chapter 3.2. [Ed.]

7. See, for example, Toynbee 1947, pp. 317–326. [Ed.]

8. Shlapentokh in Chapter 3.1 disagrees with this conclusion. [Ed.]

9. For an analysis of the opportunity costs of military programs for civilian investment in OECD countries, see R. Smith 1980. For a classical discussion of the situation in the USSR by Western economists, see Green and Higgins 1977, pp. 71–73. [Ed.]

10. For a description of the conversion program actually implemented, see Chapter 9.1. [Ed.]

11. For a well-informed history of the Soviet military-industrial complex in the Stalin-Khrushchev period, which tends to support this statement, see Simonov 1996a. [Ed.]

12. An alternative is to study the writings of well-informed Russian economists. For example, Yu. Yaremenko wrote about the possibility of a planned restructuring of the economy in the 1980s making extensive use of the resources of the military-industrial complex. [Ed.]

Bibliography

Abalkin, L.I., *Neispol'zovannyi shans*. Moscow: Politizdat, 1991.

Akhromeev, S., and Kornienko, G., *Glazami marshala i diplomata*. Moscow: Mezhdunarodnye otnosheniia, 1992.

Alekseev, Valery, "Tshchetnye usiliia," *Nezavisimaia gazeta,* 2 March 1995.

Alexeieva, Ludmilla, *Istoriia inakomyslia v SSSR. Noveishii period*. Benson, VA: Khronika Press, 1984.

Albats, Evgeniia, *The State Within the State*. New York: Farrar, Strauss, and Giroux, 1994.

Allard, E., *A Frame of Reference for Selecting Social Indicators*. Helsinki: Comentationes Scientarum Socialium, 1972.

Allison, Graham, and Gregory Yavlinsky, *Window of Opportunity*. Cambridge, MA: Pantheon, 1991.

Andrews, Frank, ed., *Research on the Quality of Life*. Ann Arbor: The University of Michigan Press, 1986.

Anisimov, S.V., paper presented at the conference 'The Market in the USSR: Mechanisms of Formation and Stages of Development,' Sverdlovsk, 12–14 June 1990.

Arbatov, G.A., *The System: An Insider's Life in Soviet Politics*. New York: Times Books, 1992.

Arnol'dov, A., et al., eds., *Obraz zhizni v usloviiakh sotsializma*. Moscow: Nauka, 1984.

Aslund, Anders, "Gorbachev's Economic Advisors," *Soviet Economy,* vol. 3, no. 3, pp. 246–269, 1987.

————. *Post-Communist Economic Revolutions*. Washington, DC: Center for Strategic and International Studies, 1992.

Aven, P.O., and V.M. Shironin, "Reforma khoziaistvennogo mekhanizma: Real'nost' namechaemykh preobrazovanii," *Izvestiia Sibirskogo otdeleniia AN SSSR: Seriia ekonomika i prikladnaia sotsiologiia* no. 13, vyp. 3 1987. (English translation in *Problems of Economics,* vol. 31, no. 2, June 1988.)

Baibakov, N.K., *Sorok let v pravitel'stve*. Moscow: Respublika, 1993.

Bekker, A., "Yegor Gaidar: Programma akademikov—'ochen' interesnyi dokument,' " *Segodnia,* 26 November 1994.

Belanovsky, Sergei, ed., *Proizvodstvennye interv'iu.* vyp. 3. Moscow: Institut narodnokhoziaistvennogo prognozirovaniia, 1991.

————. *Metodika i tekhnika fokusirovannogo interv'iu*. Moscow: Nauka, 1993.

————. "Voenno-tekhnicheskaia politika: Retrospektivnyi analiz," *Problemy prognozirovaniia,* no. 2, 1996a.

————. "Voenno-tekhnicheskaia politika: Retrospektivnyi analiz," *Problemy prognozirovaniia,* no. 3, 1996b.

————. "Ugrozy real'nye i mnimye," *Problemy prognozirovaniia,* no. 4, 1996c.

Belkin, Viktor, "Kontseptsiia rynka i pozitsiia banka," *Izvestiia,* 30 January 1989, p. 2.

Bell, J., and J. Rostowski, "A Note on the Confirmation of Podkaminer's Hypothesis in Post-Liberalisation Poland," *Europe-Asia Studies,* vol. 47, no. 3, May 1995.

Berman, H.G., *Law and Revolution: The Formation of the Western Legal Tradition.* Cambridge, MA: Harvard University Press, 1983.

BIKI (Biulleten' innostrannoi kommercheskoi informatsii), various issues.

Birman, Igor, *Ekonomika nedostach.* New York: Chalidze, 1983.

———. *Personal Consumption in the USSR and the USA.* London: Macmillan, 1989.

Birzhi v SSSR. Moscow: Institut issledovaniia organizovannykh rynkov (INIOR), 1991.

Blumer, H., *Symbolic Interactionism: Perspective and Method.* Englewood Cliffs, NJ: Prentice-Hall, 1969.

Boettke, P.J., *Why Perestroika Failed.* London and New York: Routledge, 1993.

Bond, Daniel L., and Herbert S. Levine, "An Overview," in Abram Bergson and Herbert S. Levine, eds., *The Soviet Economy: Toward the Year 2000.* London: George Allen and Unwin, 1983.

Borodkin, F., ed., *Blagosostoianie gorodskogo naseleniia Sibiri.* Novosibirsk: Nauka, 1990.

Breslauer, George, ed., *Can Gorbachev's Reforms Succeed?* Berkeley: University of California Press, 1990.

Brus, W., "Marketisation and Democratisation: The Sino-Soviet Divergence," *Cambridge Journal of Economics,* vol. 17, no. 4, December 1993.

Campbell, A., *The Sense of Well Being in America.* New York: McGraw-Hill, 1971.

Campbell, A., P. Converse, and W. Rogers, *The Quality of American Life: Perceptions, Evaluations, and Satisfactions.* New York: Russell Sage Foundation, 1976.

Central Intelligence Agency (CIA), *Handbook of Economic Statistics, 1985.* September 1985.

Chekalin, A., "Na kofeinoi gushche. . . ," *Pravda,* 18 February 1989.

Cherniaev, A.S., *1991 god: Dnevnik pomoshchnika Prezidenta SSSR.* Moscow: Respublika, 1997.

Chuev, F., *Sto sorok besed s Molotovym.* Moscow: Terra, 1991.

———. *Tak govoril Kaganovich.* Moscow: Otechestvo, 1992.

Churbanov, Yu., *Ia rasskazhu vse, kak bylo. . . .* Moscow: Nezavisimaia gazeta, 1992.

Cook, E.C., "Agriculture's Role in the Soviet Economic Crisis," in Ellman and Kontorovich 1992b.

Crosby, F., *Relative Deprivation and Working Women.* New York: Oxford University Press, 1982.

Crouch, C., "Sharing Public Space: States and Organized Interests in Western Europe," in J.A. Hall, ed., *States in History.* Oxford: Blackwell, 1986.

Dallin, Alexander, and Gail Lapidus, eds., *The Soviet System from Crisis to Collapse.* Boulder, CO: Westview Press, 1995.

Danilov-Danilian, A., and L. Freinkman, "Unbalance of the Wholesale Industrial Market in the USSR in the 1980s," paper presented at the Eighth Summer Workshop of Soviet and Eastern European Economies in Pittsburg, July 1992.

Dobrynin, A., *In Confidence.* New York: Random House, 1995.

Ellman, M., *Socialist Planning,* 1st ed. Cambridge: Cambridge University Press, 1979.

———. "Contract Brigades and Normless Teams in Soviet Agriculture," in J. Brada and K.-E. Wädekin, eds., *Socialist Agriculture in Transition.* Boulder, CO: Westview, 1988.

———. *Socialist Planning,* 2d ed. Cambridge: Cambridge University Press, 1989.

———. "The Many Causes of the Collapse," *RFE/RL Research Report,* vol. 2, no. 23, 4 June 1993.

————. "*Perestroika* Economics from the Inside," in E. Maskin and A. Simonovits, eds., *Planning, Shortage and Transformation*. Cambridge, MA: MIT Press, 1998.

Ellman, M., and V. Kontorovich, "Overview," in M. Ellman and V. Kontorovich, eds., *The Disintegration of the Soviet Economic System*. London: Routledge, 1992a.

————. *The Disintegration of the Soviet Economic System*. London: Routledge, 1992b.

————. "The Collapse of the Soviet System and the Memoir Literature," *Europe-Asia Studies*, vol. 49, no. 2, March 1997.

"Eshchë raz ob itogakh 'shokovoi terapii,' " *Nezavisimaia gazeta*, 4 March 1994.

Eydelman, M., "Peresmotr dinamicheskikh riadov osnovnykh makroekonomicheskikh pokazatelei," *Vestnik statistiki*, no. 4, 1992.

————. "Pereschet dinamicheskikh riadov produktsii stroitel'stva na 1961–1990 gg.," *Vestnik statistiki*, no. 7, 1993.

Fairbanks, Charles H., Jr., "Introduction," *The National Interest*, no. 31, Spring 1993.

Ferge, Z., and S. Miller, *Dynamics of Deprivation*. Aldershot, England: Gower, 1987.

Festinger, L., "A Theory of Social Comparison Process," *Human Relations*, 7, 1954.

Fetisov, T.I., comp., *Prem'er izvestnyi i neizvestnyi: Vospominaniia o A.N. Kosygine*. Moscow: Respublika, 1997.

Field, Mark, "Medical Care in the Soviet Union: Promises and Realities," in Herlemann 1987.

Firsov, Boris, *Puti razvitiia sredstv massovoi kommunikatsii*. Leningrad: Nauka, 1977.

Fukuyama, Francis, "The Modernizing Imperative," *The National Interest*, no. 31, Spring 1993.

Gaidar, Yegor, "Vystuplenie Ye.T. Gaidara," *Rossiiskaia gazeta*, 4 December 1992.

————. "Kak nomenklatura privatizirovala svoiu vlast'," *Literaturnaia gazeta*, no. 45, p. 10, 9 November 1994.

Glezerman, G., M. Rutkevich, and S. Vishnevskii, *Sotsialisticheskii obraz zhizni*. Moscow: Izdatel'stvo politicheskoi literatury, 1980.

Goffman, E., *The Presentation of Self in Everyday Life*. Garden City, NY: Doubleday, 1959.

Golubov, G.D., ed., *Sovmestnye predpriiatiia, mezhdunarodnye ob''edineniia i organizatsii na territorii SSSR*. Moscow: Iuridicheskaia literatura, 1988.

Gorbachev, M., *Perestroika i novoe myshlenie dlia nashei strany i vsego mira*. Moscow: Politizdat, 1987.

————. closing speech at the Plenum of CC CPSU, April 1989.

————. "Andropov: Novyi general'nyi secretar' deistvuet," *Svobodnaia mysl'*, no. 11, 1995a.

————. *Zhizn' i reformy*, vol. 1. Moscow: Novosti, 1995b.

————. *Zhizn' i reformy*, vol. 2. Moscow: Novosti, 1995c.

Gordon, L., and E. Klopov, *Chelovek posle raboty*. Moscow: Nauka, 1972.

Goskomstat SSSR, *Narodnoe khoziaistvo SSSR v 1987 g*. Moscow: Finansy i statistika, 1988.

————. *Narodnoe khoziaistvo SSSR v 1988 g*. Moscow: Finansy i statistika, 1989.

————. *Narodnoe khoziastvo SSSR v 1990 g*. Moscow: Goskomstat SSSR, 1991a.

————. *Mneniia naseleniia o tsenakh na tovary i uslugi*. Moscow: Goskomstat, 1991b.

Green, D.W., and C.I. Higgins, *SOVMOD 1: A Macroeconometric Model of the Soviet Union*. New York: Academic Press, 1977.

Greenfield, S., ed., *The Quality of Life Concept*. Washington, DC: Environmental Protection Agency, 1973.

Grigorenko, P., *Memoirs*. New York: Norton, 1982.

Grushin, B., "Rossia-93: Novye mify—novaia real'nost'," *Nezavisimaia gazeta*, 17 April 1993.

Grushin, Boris, and Lev Onikov, eds., *Massovaia informatsiia v Sovetskom promyshlennom gorode.* Moscow: Politizdat, 1980.

Gudkov, L., "Mnogie gorozhane toskuiut o proshlom," *Segodnia,* 25 June 1994.

Hanson, Philip, *The Baltic States. The Economic and Political Implications of the Secession of Estonia, Latvia and Lithuania from the USSR.* London: Economist Intelligence Unit Special Report no. 2033, March 1990.

———. *From Stagnation to Catastroika.* The Washington Papers. no. 155. New York: Praeger, 1992.

Harmstone, R.C., and J.F. Patackas, Jr., "Unearthing a Root Cause of Soviet Economic Disintegration," *Europe-Asia Studies,* vol. 49, no. 4, 1997.

Harrison, Mark, "Soviet Economic Growth Since 1928: The Alternative Statistics of G.I. Khanin," *Europe-Asia Studies,* vol. 45, no. 1, 1993.

Havrylyshyn, O., and J. Williamson, *From Soviet DisUnion to Eastern European Economic Community?* Washington, DC: Institute for International Economics, 1991.

Helf, Gavin, *All the Russias: Center, Core and Periphery in Soviet and Post-Soviet Russia.* Ph.D. dissertation in Political Science, University of California at Berkeley, 1994.

Herlemann, Horst, ed., *Quality of Life in the Soviet Union.* Boulder, CO: Westview Press, 1987.

Holman, Paul, et al., *The Soviet Union After Perestroika: Change and Continuity.* Cambridge: Institute for Foreign Policy Analysis, 1991.

Holzman, Franklyn D., "Inefficient Soviet Economy Halted Cold War," Letters, the *New York Times,* 22 November 1992.

Hough, Jerry F., "Pluralism," in Susan Gross Solomon, ed., *Pluralism in the Soviet Union.* New York: St. Martin's Press, 1983.

———. "Consolidating Power," *Problems of Communism,* July–August 1987.

———. *Democratization and Revolution in the USSR, 1985–1991.* Washington, DC: Brookings Institution Press, 1997.

Hough, Jerry F., and Merle Fainsod, *How the Soviet Union Is Governed.* Cambridge, MA: Harvard University Press, 1979.

Houslohner, Peter, "Politics Before Gorbachev: De-Stalinization and the Roots of Gorbachev's Reforms," in Dallin and Lapidus, 1995.

Inkeles, Alex, and Raymond Bauer, *The Soviet Citizen.* New York: Atheneum, 1968.

International Monetary Fund (IMF) et al., *A Survey of the Soviet Economy.* Washington, DC, 1991.

Istoricheskie . . . Istoricheskie sud'by radikal'noi ekonomicheskoi reformy. Prague: Laguna, 1995.

Ivanov, Ivan D., "Restructuring the Mechanism of Foreign Economic Relations in the USSR," *Soviet Economy,* vol. 3, no. 3, pp. 192–219, 1987.

Ivanov, I.D., ed., *Novyi mekhanizm vneshneekonomicheskoi deiatel'nosti i mezhdunarodnogo sotrudnichestva.* Moscow: Mezhdunarodnye otnosheniia, 1988.

Kalugina, Z.I., *Sotsial'nye kachestva rabotnikov: Otsenka i puti uluchsheniia.* Preprint. Novosibirsk: Institut ekonomiki i organizatsii promyshlennogo proizvodstva SO AN SSSR, 1987.

Kapustin, E., et al., eds., *Problemy sotsialisticheskogo obraza zhizni.* Moscow: Nauka 1982.

Khanin, G.I., "Al'ternativnye otsenki rezul'tatov khoziaistvennoi deiatel'nosti proizvodstvennykh iacheek promyshlennosti," *Izvestiia Akademii Nauk SSSR. Seriia ekonomicheskaia,* no. 6, 1981.

———. "Puti sovershenstvovaniia informatsionnogo obespecheniia svodnykh planovykh narodnokhoziaistvennykh raschetov," *Izvestiia Akademii Nauk SSSR. Seriia ekonomicheskaia,* no. 3, 1984.

————. *Dinamika ekonomicheskogo razvitiia SSSR.* Novosibirsk: Nauka, 1991.
————. "Otsenka dinamiki valovogo vnutrennego produkta Rossii za period 70–kh-90–kh godov," Novosibirsk, mimeo, 1996.
Kiesler, A., and S. Kiesler, *Conformity.* Reading, MA: Addison-Wesley, 1969.
Kim, M., *Problemy teorii i istorii real'nogo sotsializma.* Moscow: Nauka, 1983.
Kochergin, Albert, and Vladimir Kogan, *Problemy informatsionnogo vzaimodeistviia v obshchestve. Filosofsko-sotsiologicheskii analiz.* Novosibirsk: Nauka, 1980.
Kolositsyn, I., A. Krasnosel'ski, S. Sinel'nikov, and L. Freinkman, "Reforma roznichnykh tsen," *Kommunist,* no. 8, 1991.
Konovalov, B.P., *Pervye shagi perestroiki.* Moscow: Mashinostroenie, 1987.
Kontorovich, V., "The Economic Fallacy," *The National Interest,* Spring 1993.
Kopelev, L., *Khranit' vechno.* Ann Arbor: Ardis, 1975.
————. *I sotvoril sebe kumira.* Ann Arbor: Ardis, 1978.
Kordonsky, S., "Stsenarii igrek," *Vek XX i mir,* no. 2, 1990.
————. "Listki bukvaria," *Vek XX i mir,* no. 2, 1992.
Kornai, J., "The Dilemmas of a Socialist Economy," *Cambridge Journal of Economics,* vol. 4, no. 2, June 1980.
————. *The Socialist System.* Princeton: Princeton University Press, 1992.
Kornienko, Georgy, "Zakonchilas' li 'kholodnaia voina,'" *Nezavisimaia gazeta,* 16 August 1994.
Kort, Michael, *The Soviet Colossus: The Rise and Fall of the USSR,* 3d ed. Armonk, NY: M.E. Sharpe, 1993.
Kotz, David, with Fred Weir, *Revolution from Above.* London and New York: Routledge, 1997.
Kurtzweg, Laurie, "Trends in Soviet Gross National Product," in U.S. Congress, Joint Economic Committee, *Gorbachev's Economic Plans,* vol. 1. Washington, DC: Government Printing Office, 1987.
Kuznetsov, V.V., chapter in *Mirovoe* 1990.
Lane, D., "The Gorbachev Revolution: The Role of the Political Elite in Regime Disintegration," *Political Studies,* vol. 44, no. 1, 1996a.
————. "The Transformation of Russia: The Role of the Political Elite," *Europe-Asia Studies,* vol. 48, no. 4, 1996b.
————. *The Rise and Fall of State Socialism.* Cambridge: Polity, 1996c.
Latsis, Otto, "The Deep Roots of Our Problems," in Abraham Brumberg, ed., *Chronicle of a Revolution.* New York: Pantheon Books, 1990.
Levada, Yu., ed., *Est' mnenie.* Moscow: Progress, 1990.
————. *Sovetskii prostoi chelovek.* Moscow: Mirovoi okean, 1993.
Levine, Herbert S., "The Centralized Planning of Supply in Soviet Industry," in Morris Bornstein, ed., *Comparative Economic Systems: Models and Cases.* Homewood, IL: Irwin, 1965.
Levykin, I., "K voprosu ob integral'nykh pokazateliakh sotsialisticheskogo obraza zhizni," *Sotsiologicheskie issledovania,* vol. 2, 1984.
————. *Obshchee i osobennoe v obraze zhizni sotsial'nykh grupp sovetskogo obshchestva.* Moscow: Nauka, 1987.
Liberman, L., and L. Freinkman, "Usilenie nesbalansirovannosti v sovetskoi ekonomike (1988–1990): Prichiny i puti preodeleniia," *Material'no-tekhnicheskoe snabzhenie,* no. 1, 1991.
Ligachev, E., "Rastit' aktivnykh bortsov perestroiki," *Uchitel'skaia gazeta,* 27 August 1987.
Lindzey, Gardney, and Elliot Aronson, eds., *Handbook of Social Psychology,* vol. 2. New York: Random House, 1985.

Liuboshits, Yefim, and Vitaly Tsymbal, "Kak sformirovat' oboronnyi biudzhet Rossii," *Nezavisimaia gazeta,* 9 July 1992.
Loginov, V., "Prichiny krizisa Sovetskoi ekonomiki: Vosproizvodstvennyi aspekt," *Voprosy ekonomiki,* no. 4–6, 1992.
Luckman, T., and P. Berger, *The Social Construction of Reality.* Garden City, NY: Doubleday, 1966.
McClelland, David, *The Achieving Society.* Princeton: Van Nostrand, 1961.
Materialy XXVII s''ezda kommunisticheskoi partii Sovetskogo Soiuza. Moscow: Politizdat, 1986.
Materialy plenuma TsK KPSS 25–26 iunia 1987 g. Moscow: Politizdat, 1987.
Matthews, Mervyn, "Aspects of Poverty in the Soviet Union," in Herlemann 1987.
Medvedev, P.A., and I.V. Nit, "Nominal'nye tseli i real'naia effektivnost' administrativnogo upravleniia," *Voprosy ekonomiki,* no. 12, 1988.
Medvedev, P.A., I.V. Nit, and L.M. Freinkman, "Vneshnii razdrazhitel' delovoi aktivnosti," *Material'no-tekhnicheskoe snabzhenie,* no. 12, 1989a.
———. "Radikal'nye reformy v vedomstvennoi kolee," *Sotsialisticheskoe sorevnovanie,* no. 1, 1989b.
Millar, James, ed., *Politics, Work and Daily Life in the USSR: A Survey of Former Soviet Citizens.* Cambridge: Cambridge University Press, 1987.
Mirovoe khoziaistvo i sovetskaia ekonomika. Shansy i illuzii. Moscow: Mezhdunarodnye otnosheniia, 1990.
Mises, Ludwig von, *Socialism.* Indianapolis: Liberty Press, 1981 (1922).
Morton, Henry, "Housing Quality and Housing Classes in the Soviet Union," in Herlemann 1987.
Naishul, V., *The Supreme and Last Stage of Socialism.* London: Centre for Research into Communist Economies, 1991. (Russian original, "Vysshaia i posledniaia stadiia sotsializma," in T.A. Notkina, ed., *Pogruzhenie v triasinu.* Moscow: Progress, 1991.)
———. "Liberalizm i ekonomicheskie reformy," *Mirovaia ekonomika i mezhdunarodnye otnosheniia,* 1992, no. 8. (English translation, "Liberalism, Customary Rights and Economic Reforms," *Communist Economies and Economic Transformation,* vol. 5, no. 1, 1993.)
———. "Obychnoe pravo i sudebnaia liberalizatsiia" ("Customary Law and Legal Liberalization"), paper presented at the conference 'Chernyi rynok kak politicheskaia sistema' ('The Black Market as a Political System'), RGGU (Russian State Humanities University), 26 February 1994.
Nelson, Richard R., and Sidney G. Winter, *An Evolutionary Theory of Economic Change.* Cambridge, MA: Harvard University Press, 1982.
Nove, A., "Has Soviet Growth Ceased?" paper presented to the Manchester Statistical Society, 15 November 1983.
Nove, Alec, *An Economic History of the USSR 1917–1991,* 3d ed. London: Penguin Books, 1992.
O korennoi perestroike upravleniia ekonomikoi. Sbornik dokumentov. Moscow: Politizdat, 1987.
"O merakh po obespecheniiu bor'by s ekonomicheskim sabotazhem i drugimi prestupleniiami v sfere ekonomiki," *Pravda,* 28 January 1991.
"O merakh po ozdorovleniiu ekonomiki, etapakh ekonomicheskoi reformy i printsipial'nykh podkhodakh k razrabotke trinadtsatogo piatiletnego plana," *Pravda,* 22 December 1989.
"O neotlozhnykh merakh po stabilizatsii khoziaistvennykh sviazei v chetvertom kvartale 1990 goda i v techenie 1991 goda," *Pravda,* 28 September 1990.

"O pervoocherednykh merakh po perekhodu k rynochnym otnosheniiam. Ukaz prezidenta SSSR," *Izvestiia,* 5 October 1990.

"Ob uluchshenii planirovaniia i usilenii vozdeistviia khoziaistvennogo mekhanizma na
povyshenie effektivnosti proizvodstva i kachestva raboty," in *Sovershenstvovanie
khoziaistvennogo mekhanizma. Sbornik dokumentov.* Moscow: Pravda, 1982.

OECD Social Indicator Development Program, *Measuring Social Well-Being.* Paris,
1976.

Orlova, R., *Memoirs.* New York: Random House, 1983.

Panin, V. and V. Lapkin, "Chto ostanovilos' v epokhu zastoia?" in T.A. Notkina, ed.,
Pogruzhenie v triasinu. Moscow: Progress, 1991.

Pavlov, Valentin, *Avgust iznutri.* Moscow: Delovoi mir, 1993.

———. "V povestke dnia stoiala burzhuazno-demokraticheskaia revoliutsiia,"
Segodnia, 29 November 1994.

———. *Upushchen li shans?* Moscow: Terra, 1995.

Pechenev, V., *Gorbachev: K vershinam vlasti.* Moscow: Gospodin narod, 1991.

———. *Vzlet i padenie Gorbacheva.* Moscow: Republika, 1996.

Pécsi, Kalman, *The Future of Socialist Economic Integration.* Armonk, NY: M.E.
Sharpe, 1981.

Perekhod k rynku. Kontseptsiia i programma. Moscow: 'Arkhangel'skoe,' August 1990.

Popov, G.Kh., *Koren' problem: O kontseptsii ekonomicheskoi perestroiki.* Moscow:
Politizdat, 1989.

Popov, V.V., and N.A. Shmelev, eds., *Sovetskaia ekonomika: Ot plana k rynku.* Moscow: Progress, 1991.

"Postanovleniia Politburo TsK KPSS," *Izvestiia TsK KPSS,* no. 6, 1990, pp. 6–8.

Prokhanov, A., "U vlasti stoyal predatel'," *Zavtra,* no. 30, 1995.

Pryce-Jones, David, *The War That Never Was. The Fall of the Soviet Empire 1985–
1991.* London: Weidenfeld and Nicholson, 1995.

Racket, "Reket: Vzgliad s blizkogo rasstoianiia," *Problemy prognozirovaniia,* no. 5,
1994.

"Radikal'naia ekonomicheskaia reforma: Pervoocherednye i dolgovremennye mery,"
Ekonomicheskaia gazeta, no. 43, October 1989.

Remnick, David, *Lenin's Tomb.* New York: Random House, 1993.

Resheniia partii i pravitel'stva po khoziastvennym voprosam, vol. 15, part 1. Moscow:
Izdatel'stvo politicheskoi literatury, 1985.

Rigby, T.H., *The Changing Soviet System.* Aldershot, England: Edward Elgar, 1990.

Robinson, John, Vladimir Andreyenkov, and Vasily Patrushev, *The Rhythm of Everyday
Life.* Boulder, CO: Westview Press, 1989.

Rowen, Henry, "Central Intelligence Briefing on the Soviet Economy," statement of the
Honorable Henry Rowen, Chairman, National Intelligence Council, Central Intelligence Agency, before the Joint Economic Committee, Subcommittee on International Trade, Finance, and Security Economics, 1 December 1982.

Runciman, W., *Relative Deprivation and Social Justice.* Berkeley: University of California Press, 1966.

Rush, Myron, "Fortune and Fate," *The National Interest,* Spring 1993.

Rutland, P., *The Politics of Economic Stagnation in the Soviet Union.* Cambridge:
Cambridge University Press, 1993.

Ryvkina, R.V., E.V. Kosals, L.Ia. Kosals, and O.V. Sharnina, *Sotsial'nyi mekhanizm
ekonomicheskoi reformy.* Novosibirsk: Izdatel'stvo Sibirskogo otdeleniia AN SSSR,
1990.

Ryvkina, R.V., and V.A. Yadov, eds., *Sotsial'no-upravlencheskii mekhanizm razvitiia
proizvodstva.* Novosibirsk: Nauka, 1989.

Ryzhkov, N.I., "Ob osnovnykh napravleniiakh ekonomicheskogo i sotsial'nogo razvitiia SSSR na 1986–1990 gody i na period do 2000 goda," *Pravda,* 4 March 1986.

———. "Effektivnost', konsolidatsiia, reforma—put' k zdorovoi ekonomike," *Pravda,* 14 December 1989.

Salutskii, Anatolii, *Proroki i poroki.* Moscow: Molodaia gvardiia, 1990.

Samarina, T.P., "Problemy razvitiia deistvuiushchei formy optovoi torgovli," in *Ot fondirovaniia k optovoi torgovle.* Moscow: Ekonomika, 1990, pp. 37–54.

Schlesinger, Arthur, Jr., "Who Really Won the Cold War," *The Wall Street Journal,* 14 September 1992.

Schroeder, Gertrude E., "The Soviet Economy on a Treadmill of 'Reforms,' " in U.S. Congress, Joint Economic Committee, *Soviet Economy in a Time of Change,* vol. I. Washington, DC: Government Printing Office, 1979.

———. "Soviet Living Standard in Comparative Perspective," in Herlemann 1987.

Schutz, A., *Collected Papers.* The Hague: Martinus Nijhoff, 1976.

Seliunin, Vasilii, and Grigorii Khanin, "Lukavaia tsyfra," *Novyi mir,* no. 2, 1987.

Sen, A., *Standard of Living.* Cambridge: Cambridge University Press, 1987.

Shakhnazarov, G., *Tsena svobody.* Moscow: Rossika, 1993.

Shatalin, S., "Ne gadaem 'na kofeinoi gushche,' " *Pravda,* 4 May 1989.

Shcherbakov, Vladimir, "Dazhe martyshka ne stanet glotat' neznakomye plody," *Izvestiia,* 15 December 1995.

Shironin, V., *Pod kolpakom kontrrazvedki.* Moscow: Paleia, 1996.

Shlapentokh, V., *Chitatel' i gazeta: Chitateli truda.* Moscow: Institut konkretnykh sotsial'nykh issledovanii, 1969.

———. *Sotsiologiia dlia vsekh.* Moscow: Sovetskaia Rossia, 1970.

———. *Kak segodnia izuchaiut zavtra.* Moscow: Sovetskaia Rossia, 1975.

———. *Problemy reprezentativnosti sostiologicheskoi informatsii.* Moscow: Statistika, 1976.

———. "Moscow's War Propaganda and Soviet Public Opinion," *Problems of Communism,* September–October 1984.

———. "Two Levels of Public Opinion: The Soviet Case," *Public Opinion Quarterly,* Winter 1985.

———. *Soviet Public Opinion and Ideology.* New York: Praeger, 1986.

———. *Public and Private Life of the Soviet People.* Oxford: Oxford University Press, 1989.

———. *Soviet Intellectuals and Political Power.* Princeton, NJ: Princeton University Press, 1990.

———. "Early Feudalism—The Best Parallel for Contemporary Russia," *Europe-Asia Studies,* 1996, no. 3, May.

Shlapentokh, D., and V. Shlapentokh, "Letters to the Editor on the Ideologies in the USSR during the 1980s" in Anthony Jones, ed., *Research on the Soviet Union and Eastern Europe.* Greenwich: JAI Press, 1990.

———. *Soviet Cinematography 1918–1991.* New York: Aldine De Gruyter, 1993.

Shmelev, Nikolai, "Avansy i dolgi," *Novyi mir,* no. 6, 1987. (English translation in *Problems of Economics*, vol. 30, no. 10, February 1988.)

Shmelev, V., and Popov, N., *Na perelome: Ekonomicheskaia perestroika v SSSR.* Moscow: Novosti, 1989.

Shpagin, Alexander, "Rekviem v stile roka," *Literaturnaia gazeta,* 31 August 1994.

Shtromas, A., *Political Change and Social Development: The Case of the Soviet Union.* Frankfurt: Verlag Peter Lang, 1981.

Simonov, N., *Voenno-promyshlennyi kompleks SSSR v 1920–1950-e gody.* Moscow: ROSSPEN, 1996a.

————. " 'Strengthen the Defence of the Land of the Soviets': The 1927 'War Alarm' and Its Consequences," *Europe-Asia Studies,* vol. 48, no. 8, 1996b.

Sitnin, V.K., "Iz opyta finansovo-kreditnykh reform v SSSR," *Problemy prognozirovaniia,* no. 6, 1994.

Smith, Hedrick, *The New Russians.* New York: Avon Books, 1991.

Smith, R., "Military Expenditures and Investment in OECD Countries, 1954–1973," *Journal of Comparative Economics,* vol. 4, no. 1, March 1980.

Soros, George, *Opening the Soviet Economy.* London: Weidenfeld and Nicholson, 1990.

Sovershenstvovanie khoziaistvennogo mekhanizma. Sbornik dokumentov. 2d ed. Moscow: Pravda, 1982.

Starikov, E., "Marginaly," in Vishnevskii 1989.

Steury, D.P., ed., *Intentions and Capabilities: Estimates on Soviet Strategic Forces, 1950–1983.* Washington, DC: Center for the Study of Intelligence, 1996.

Strelianyi, Anatolii, "Skif," *Literaturnaia gazeta,* 8 January 1992.

Stone, L., *The Causes of the English Revolution.* London: Routledge and Kegan Paul, 1972.

Teckenberg, Wolfgang, "Consumer Goods and Services: Contemporary Problems and Their Impact on the Quality of Life in the Soviet Union," in Herlemann 1987.

Thibault, J., and H. Kelly, *The Social Psychology of Groups.* New York: Wiley, 1959.

Timofeev, L.P., *Tekhnologiia chernogo rynka, ili krestianskoe iskusstvo golodat'.* Bayonne, NJ: Tovarishchestvo Zarubezhnykh Pisatelei, 1982.

Tocqueville, A. de, *The Old Regime and the French Revolution.* Garden City, NY: Doubleday Anchor, 1955.

Townsend, P., *The Concept of Poverty.* New York: American Elsevier, 1970.

————. *Poverty in the United Kingdom.* Harmondsworth: Penguin, 1979.

Toynbee, Arnold J., *A Study of History.* New York: Oxford University Press, 1947.

Treml, Vladimir G., "Two Schools of Thought," *RFE/RL Research Report,* vol. 2, no. 23, 4 June 1993.

Trotsky, L., *The Revolution Betrayed.* Garden City, NY: Doubleday, 1937.

Tsentral'noe statisticheskoe upravlenie pri Sovete ministrov SSSR, *Chislennost', razmeshchenie, vozrastnaia struktura, uroven' obrazovaniia, natsional'nyi sostav, iazyki i istochniki sredstv sushchestvovaniia naseleniia SSSR.* Moscow: Statistika, 1971.

Tsipko, Alexander, "Vozmozhnosti i rezervy kooperatsii," *Sotsiologicheskie issledovaniia,* no. 2, 1986a.

————. "Kontseptsiia 'edinoobraziia' v usloviiakh perestroiki," *Sotsiologicheskie issledovaniia,* no. 4, 1986b.

————. "Istoki stalinizma," *Nauka i zhizn',* nos. 11–12, 1988, and nos. 1–2, 1989. (English translation, *Soviet Law and Government,* vol. 29, nos. 1–2, 1990.)

————. "O Gorbacheve, 'predateliakh' i russkoi dushe," *Nezavisimaia gazeta,* 6 April 1995.

Ulanovskaia, M., and N. Ulanovskaia, *Istoriia odnoi sem'i.* New York: Chalidze Publishers, 1982.

Valovoi, D., *Ot zastoia k razvalu.* Moscow: Nauka, 1991.

————. *Kremlevskii tupik i Nazarbaev.* Moscow: Molodaia gvardiia, 1993.

Vernadsky, V., "Ia ochen' redko vizhu ideinykh kommunistov," *Nezavisimaia gazeta,* 9 June 1992.

Vishnevskii, A., *V chelovecheskom izmerenii.* Moscow: Progress, 1989.

White, S., et al., "Interviewing the Soviet Elite," *The Russian Review,* vol. 55, no. 2, April 1996.

Winden, F. van, and G. de Wit, "Nomenklatura, State Monopoly, and Private Enterprise," *Public Choice,* vol. 77, 1993.

Yadov, V., ed., *Chelovek i ego rabota*. Moscow: Mysl', 1967.

————. *Sotsial'no-psikhologicheskii portret inzhenera*, Moscow: Mysl', 1977.

————. *Samoreguliatsiia i prognozirovanie povedenia lichnosti*. Leningrad: Nauka, 1979.

————. *Sotsiologiia perestroiki*. Moscow: Nauka, 1990.

Yakovlev, A.N., "Dostizhenie kachestvenno novogo sostoianiia sovetskogo obshchestva i obshchestvennye nauki," *Vestnik AN SSSR*, no. 6, 1987.

————. *Realizm—zemlia perestroiki*. Moscow: Politizdat, 1990.

————. *Gor'kaia chasha*. Yasoslavl': Verkhne-Volzhskoe knizhnoe izdatel'stvo, 1994.

Yashin, Alexander, "Rychagi," in *Literaturnaia Moskva*, vol. 2, Moscow: Sovetskii Pisatel', 1954.

Yasin, Ye., "Izmenit' 'sostoianie umov,' " *Ekonomika i organizatsiia promyshlennogo proizvodstva (EKO)*, no. 8, 1994.

Yeltsin, B., *Ispoved' na zadannuiu temu*. Sverdlovsk: Sredne-Ural'skoe knizhnoe izdatel'stvo, 1990.

Yun', O.M., *Intensifikatsiia ekonomiki: Teoriia i praktika planirovaniia*. Moscow: Ekonomika, 1986.

Index

Abalkin, Leonid, 18, 92, 95, 114, 119, 133*n.15,* 137, 142, 143, 158, 161*n.2,* 228, 232–233, 248–249, 254
Abalkin commission, 10, 228–230
'Abalkin' tax, 188, 210*n.30,* 213, 218
'Abalkinization', 230
Acceleration, 40, 110–112, 123, 126, 127–129, 132*n.5,* 143, 212
Afghanistan, xix, 33, 52, 61, 86
Aganbegian, Abel, 82, 92, 94, 95, 99*n.21,* 112, 114, 118, 133*n.15,* 137, 141, 142, 143, 159, 161*n.2*
Agroprom, xvi, xix, 133*n.12*
Akhromeev, Sergei, 42, 69*n.45*
Anchishkin, Alexander, 82, 83, 85–86, 90, 137, 143, 161*n.2,* 179
Andropov, Yuri, 13, 66, 81
  becomes general secretary, xv
  and CMEA, 285–286
  death of, 101
  and economy, 92, 95, 127
Anti-alcohol campaign
  announced, xvi
  and CMEA, 293–294
  and economy, 74, 107–108, 125, 131
  role of Ligachev and Solomentsov in, 128

Arms race, 47, 52, 60, 61–66, 308, 310–311
Aslund, Anders, 30, 240, 245
Austro-Hungarian Empire, 5

Baibakov, Nikolai, 79, 86, 88, 89, 91, 92, 94, 99*n.22,* 141
Balcerowicz, Leszek, 231, 255*n.18*
Barter, 203–206, 222–225, 281
Belkin, Viktor, 256*n.30*
Birman, Igor, 66*n.3,* 255*n.22*
Brezhnev, Leonid, 41, 273, 285
  death of, xv, 85
  and economy, 79, 94, 179, 291
  and fear of China, 41
Budget deficit, xvi, 18, 120, 128–129, 153, 298

Centralized allocation of resources, 216, 221
Chernenko, Konstantin
  becomes general secretary, xv, 101, 122
  and CMEA, 286
  death of, xvi, 177
  and economy, 6, 14, 90, 93, 97, 100–105, 122–123
China, 80
  and economic reform, 22, 162*n.16,* 168–169, 176, 253, 256*n.28*
  as military enemy, 41, 68*n.34,* 308

About the Editors

Michael Ellman is professor of economic systems, with special reference to transition economics, at Amsterdam University. He has published extensively on economic systems, the Soviet and Russian economies, and transformation questions. He is a foreign member (an Academician) of the Russian Academy of Economic Sciences and Entrepreneurship, a Fellow of the Tinbergen Institute and of the Netherlands Network of Economics (NAKE), and a member of the Economic Program Group of the European Forum for Democracy and Solidarity. He has worked as a consultant for agencies of the UN, the European Union, and the Dutch government. Professor Ellman was awarded the 1998 Kondratieff gold medal for his contribution to the development of the social sciences.

Vladimir Kontorovich is an associate professor of economics at Haverford College. He has published articles on Soviet growth, inflation, research and development, and economic reform. Together with Michael Ellman, he edited the first Western book on the economics of the Soviet collapse, *The Disintegration of the Soviet Economic System* (London: Routledge, 1992). His current work focuses on the burden imposed on Russian economic transformation by the legacies of the Soviet system.

38 113000